MW01626098

Dreamscapes THE ART OF JUAN GONZÁLEZ

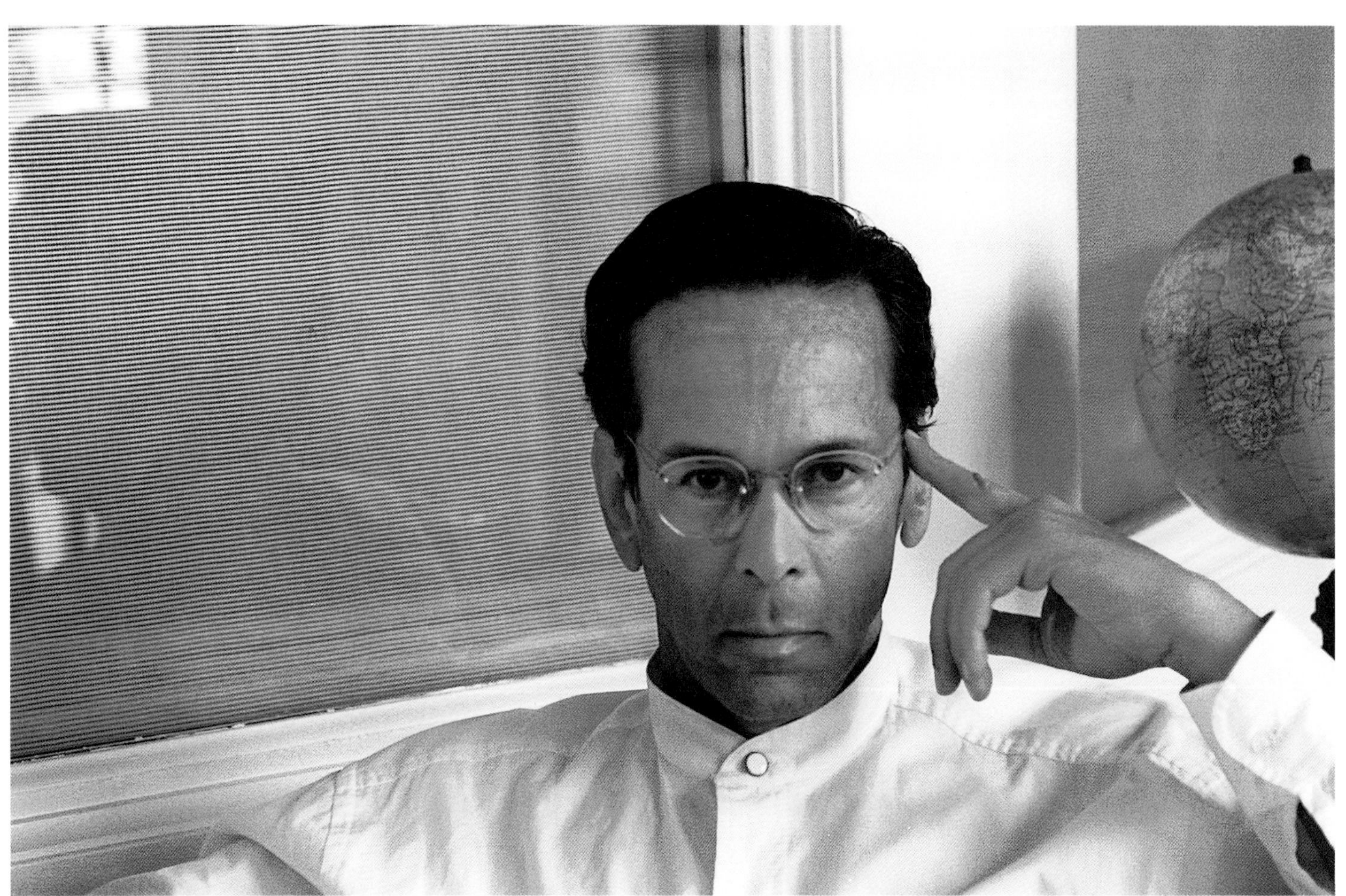

DREAMSCAPES

The Art of Juan González

by Irene McManus

Hudson Hills Press, New York

First Edition

Published in the United States by Hudson Hills Press, Inc., Suite 1308, 230 Fifth Avenue, New York, NY 10001-7704.

Distributed in the United States, its territories and possessions, Canada, Mexico, and Central and South America by National Book Network.
Distributed in the United Kingdom and Eire by Art Books International Ltd.
Exclusive representation in Asia, Australia, and New Zealand by EM International.

Editor and Publisher: Paul Anbinder

Copy Editor: Fronia W. Simpson

Proofreader: Lydia Edwards

Indexer: Karla J. Knight

Designer: Sisco & Evans LTD., New York

Composition: Trufont Typographers

Manufactured in Japan by Dai Nippon Printing Company

Library of Congress Cataloguing-in-Publication Data
McManus, Irene, 1951–
Dreamscapes : the art of Juan González / Irene McManus. — 1st ed.
p. cm.
Includes bibliographical references and index.
ISBN 1-55595-082-5
1. González, Juan, 1942–1993—Themes, motives. I. González, Juan, 1942–1993.
N6537.G627M38 1994
759.13—dc20 94-13849
CIP

Frontispiece: Juan González, 1993

Contents

Preface and Acknowledgments

Juan González knew in 1984, when he was finishing *After Philadelphia*, that he was HIV-positive. Every work he made after that year was touched in some way by that knowledge. Surrounded by friends and family, he died of AIDS on Christmas Eve, 1993, around 5.30 P.M. The publication of this book, in which he was involved at every step of the way, was one of his last great projects.

Writing this book has been for me a painful but profound experience. It was harrowing to work with an artist succumbing by degrees to AIDS, a gentle man whose entire life seemed to have entailed heroic struggle on every level. I was impressed by the energy and enthusiasm he always found to discuss his work with me, and by his intense, almost primitive, religious faith. He realized most of his own early dreams before he died and changed the lives of many as teacher, mentor, and friend. A rare human being for all who knew him, he will be fondly remembered, while his art lives on.

Thanks, then, first and foremost to Juan for his courage and tenacity in seeing the project through. I would also like to express warm appreciation for the efforts of the many other individuals who have contributed to the long making of this book. The artist's daughter Maria González Schleifman and her husband Daniel Schleifman have been particularly generous and deserve very special recognition. Heartfelt thanks, too, to Nancy Hoffman (who has been for Juan a true artist's "angel") and her lively staff, Katherine Naylor, Christopher Watson, Judith Nichols, and Sique Spence; to Anne Minich for her valuable insights into her friend's work; to Joan Tripp, Deborah Dalton, and the rest of the gang at the Village Library, Cooperstown; to Paul Anbinder and Fronia Simpson of Hudson Hills Press, for their patient, sympathetic, and hawk-eyed editing.

Last, but definitely not least, I wish to thank my forbearing family, my wonderful husband, Walter Dusenbery, and splendid son, Finn, for their cheerful support and understanding over the last three years.

Irene McManus
Fly Creek, New York, 1994

Dreamscapes THE ART OF JUAN GONZÁLEZ

The Art of Juan González

Though Juan González is a contemporary artist, working and being viewed in a contemporary context, his work touches continuously on themes that connect it with other times and places—with ancient dreams of infinite skies and deep oceans, with a mystical vision of ascension toward the light, or a baptismal immersion in dark, primeval waters. His works are imbued with poetry and mystery; his goal a beauty that stirs the soul; his method the magic of a grand illusionist.

Born in Cuba in 1942, exiled to America at the age of eighteen, he is in many ways a quintessentially Latin American artist, fitting the profile outlined in *Art of the Fantastic: Latin America, 1920–1987,* the ground-breaking study of Latin American art by Holliday T. Day and Hollister Sturges. "Poetry, mystery, dramatic impact, metaphor, and spiritual ambience" form the highest values of the Latin American aesthetic, observe Day and Sturges,[1] with fantasy being a hallmark of both art and literature—a fantasy not programmatically surrealist but rather directly rooted in the reality of the cultural forces enmeshing the Latin American artist today.

First among these forces, the Catholic church was certainly González's earliest theater of mystery, drama, and magic. The Annunciation, Christ's baptism at the hands of Saint John, the Passion of the Crucifixion marked out in the Stations of the Cross, the mystery of the Resurrection, and finally the Ascension of Christ into heaven, are everywhere an inspiration in the work of this essentially spiritual artist—often presented in an ornately theatrical baroque context, blending realism and illusionism to achieve a seductive immediacy for the viewer.

González's first self-portrait, *Untitled (Self-Portrait)* (Plate 4), for example, depicts a trompe-l'oeil image-within-an-image, the artist's gauze-masked, possibly mirrored head, crowned not in thorns but in gold ribbon. *Miércoles de Ceniza* (Ash Wednesday) (Plate 34), the artist's earliest undisguised self-portrait, features González's mirrored face and chest emerging from a filmy, almost fluid purple fabric draped over a ledge, transforming the artist into a living religious sculpture—the artist thinking in particular of the way Cubans drape sculptures of saints with purple cloth on Ash Wednesday.

Portraits of family and friends are similarly cast in traditional iconic roles. In *La Educación de Maria* (The Education of Maria) (Plate 41), the artist's older daughter Maria, hopeful novice architect, is tenderly viewed as a youthful, curtain-alcoved Virgin of the Annunciation, contemplating the trials and glories ahead of her, as the child Mary views her future with mingled emotions in Francisco de Zurbarán's *Young Virgin Praying* of 1632–33. In *A la Cabeza del Bautista en Sevilla/To the Head of John the Baptist in Seville* (Plate 35), the artist's friend Patrick, the recent recipient of a severe haircut, is portrayed as a Spanish baroque head of John the Baptist from about 1625 at Seville cathedral: decapitated—but alive, bespectacled, and laughing. Even a relatively simple and austere still life of lilies against a modernist grid of bathroom tiles becomes exalted as a crucifixion scene housed in a white-washed cabinet in *El Lirio Cuadral* (The Square and the Lily) (Plate 24).

Staging the portrait or still life is a vital part of visualizing the image for González. Very often, the work presents itself as a miniature stage set—the stage curtain sinking the image back into the realm of theatrical illusion and sparkling fantasy, a scenographic space announcing layers of artifice, even while the raised or drawn curtain also implies dramatic revelation, a "lifting of the veil" of the hidden self.

The artist's works are obsessively constructed, often incorporating a ledge like the foreground ledge of a theater stage, or the uppermost step or platform of an altar. In works like *Double Portrait of Jimmy, N.Y.C.* (Plate 45) or *In His Silence* (Plate 57), the panels surrounding the interior image resemble the "puppet booth" of the Spanish baroque painter Zurbarán, the curtained arena of gorgeously painted still lifes into which frozen saints have been somewhat artificially installed. But González's theatrical space is also the highly personal, psychological, interior space of deep introspection. His toy theaters imply not only revelation but also its formal antithesis, concealment. González has an abiding fascination with the hidden art work, beginning with his own masked self-portrait, progressing through the radiant headless (therefore faceless) brides of *The Sparrow and the Maiden* (Plate 12), *Mar y Espejo* (Sea and Mirror) (Plate 19), and *Así que Pasen Cinco Años/When Five Years Pass* (Plates 71–76), to end with the *Bride for Lorca* (Plate 77), in which the apparitional bride is finally veiled in pure white light against a starlit night sky.

This mystical white bride, the personification of a "sacred marriage" integrating the spiritual and the physical aspects of the self—veiled in dazzling light rather than in shadow, like Odilon Redon's *Luminous Profile* of 1886 (Musée du Petit Palais, Paris)—has been in evidence throughout González's work in one way or another, from the first faceless *Untitled* self-portrait, appearing like a veiled nun or bride, and the white bird trapped in the white room (creature-emblem of Blanche, whose name, of course, means "white") of *Hot White Tennessee Williams* (Plate 6). In 1974 the artist created *La Misa Blanca* (The White Mass) (Plate 14), his white ocean veil deriving from Raphaelle Peale's trompe-l'oeil veil, concealing the naked *Venus Rising from the Sea* (Nelson-Atkins Museum of Art, Kansas City, Missouri)—a veil, in other words, cloaking a pagan goddess forerunner of the Virgin. The three white bull terriers prowling the shore below the veil, like the white bull terrier in *Good Friday* (Plate 10), subtly imply another concealed feminine presence, since they derive from Lucian Freud's *Girl with a White Dog,* 1951–52 (Tate Gallery, London).

In 1976 the artist transformed the three light-transmitting white scenes on the shore of *Mar y Espejo* into a white, mirror-floored cradle for a girl cousin, in whom he saw the reflection of his own conflict with familial and cultural pressure to conform to conventional Cuban social expectations. With the mystical conjunction of his male self and his female cousin in the white screens of *La Cuna/The Cradle* (Plate 20), González achieved one of his most memorable redeeming motifs—a magical, white, androgyne "birth" implied in the union of opposites and in the white-veiled pink candle at the head of the silken "cradle."

With *Nacimiento/Nativity* (Plate 30), he further developed the theme of sacrifice and death to the old life, embrace of the new, in the white trinity formed between his own two mirrored selves and the white-robed angel who kneels before the baby Christ—Jung's ideal androgyne. In 1980, in *Songs for My Father* (Plate 32), he became the white-clothed child held lovingly in his father's arms—his haloed, saintly father here enfolding him in all the tenderness usually associated with the Virgin or a mother, in complete contrast to the indifference he had displayed in *Nacimiento/Nativity*. In the 1983 self-portrait, *Letter to Veronica* (Plate 42), in which González integrated his face and body with the veil of Saint Veronica, he literally and repeatedly "veiled" his face in layers of whitewash, to attain a ghostly effect of life-in-death, a sacred marriage of female veil and male portrait.

Finally, Lorca's white-faced androgyne Moon in the 1988 *Blood Wedding* collage series (Plates 59–62), his androgyne Second Friend dressed in white, and the Mannequin bride in the ocean of *Así que Pasen Cinco Años/When Five Years Pass* in 1991, coalesce in González's shimmering mystery of a Virgin *Bride for Lorca,* radiant in her aura of white light. Whiteness itself is associated with mystic veiling in González, as the expanding noncolor of spiritual illumination in works like *Cultivo una Rosa Blanca* (I Grow a White Rose) (Plate 58), where the artist moves from the rich color in darkness of his night theaters, *Cycle* (Plate 55) and *In His Silence,* to a dazzling white light. The image blazes with a spectral whiteness—the artist imagining a distant gray world relinquished at the low edge of the drawing for the Dantesque paradise of a heavenly theater conceived by the Italian poet as a vast white rose in the sky. The pure whiteness of the paper assumes mystical, almost alchemical significance as the symbol of sanctity and redemption, of the transcendence of the spirit over the flesh, and the sublimation of the self in art. It also reflects the artist's ritualistic approach to his art—his rare reverence for surface and medium.

The artist's attraction to the hidden artwork—"a veiled beauty and mystery, a miracle"[2]—has personal roots in his boyhood habit of drawing in secret beneath his aunt's bed, after his mother, worried about his obsession with drawing beautiful female faces, had forbidden him ever to draw again. It may also have something to do with cherished childhood memories of belonging to the Society of the Little Jesus of Prague, and receiving every other month or so a small antique mahogany shrine "with doors which opened and closed," housing a doll-like infant Jesus in sumptuous costume—a devotional object that the young González found utterly captivating and that, years later, inspired the central presence of the sacred infant in the important paintings *El Niño* (The Child) (Plate 44) and *Memory Piece* (Plate 66). Even the artist's preoccupation with miniature theaters seems to have had its inception in childhood, relating to a time when González and his father transformed shoe boxes into shadow-box theaters, cutting out cartoon characters and lighting them from behind with candles.

Throughout this artist's work there is a fixation on framing, and on transforming the beautiful image into an object of devotion, enshrined within an architectural context. González attempts with each fresh image to reach beyond drawing, painting, and sculpture, to create an icon, a powerful and mysterious image dictating its own style and medium, almost independently of its creator. He is as committed as Ezra Pound, founding father of the imagist poets, to the paramount importance of the "Image": "that which presents an intellectual and emotional complex in an instant of time."[3] For González, this is the "flash"—the split second of visionary revelation opening up the true nature of reality to the eye of the artist. Most of González's images have come into being through this initial flash, followed by months, if not years, of working and reworking the image (he would certainly concur with Pound that "it is better to present one image in a lifetime than to produce voluminous works").[4]

This is surely the reason why no consistent technique can be identified from one González work to another, and why sometimes, within the bounds of a single art work like *Bathers of Blenheim* (Plate 40), it seems almost as if two separate hands had been at work. González ranges from the relative simplicity of his colored-pencil-on-paper drawings (which by the time of *Summer Flies* [Plate 7] have begun to look like old-master drawings), to pastel in *July 11, 1974* (Plate 15). In remarkably restrained and understated ways he mingles watercolor, pencil, and pastel for *Mar y Espejo, The Warning* (Plate 21), and *P. M. Times* (Plate 22), before moving on, via the minimalist grid of *P. M. Times,* to the constructed cabinets of *Prisma y Prisión/Prism and Prison* (Plate 27) and *El Cuarto en el Fondo del Pozo* (The Room at the Bottom of the Well) (Plate 28). After visiting the great museums of Europe in 1978, he turned to bright color, experimenting with a combination of tempera and gold leaf for his *Untitled* landscape (Plate 29), and lively watercolor for *Nacimiento/Nativity*. Influenced by his studies of Seurat's drawings in Conté crayon, González then produced largely monochrome works such as *Songs for My Father* and *A la Cabeza del Bautista en Sevilla/To the Head of John the Baptist in Seville,* adding to the former the complication of a passage of Mantegna-inspired yellow gold, to the latter some careful touches of color typical of the manipulations of Fernand Khnopff in his charcoal drawing enlivened with blue pastel, *Weihrauch/Incense,* ca. 1898 (Gallery Georges Giroux, Brussels). Meanwhile the restless González was also studying Flemish and Venetian painters, along with a personal favorite, Vermeer. Newly fascinated by oils, he embarked on *Portrait of Mari* (Plate 36), *Whistler* (Plate 37), and *El Soñador/The Dreamer* (Plate 39), feeling inclined, however, to rework *Whistler* in a different medium and context during the same period. The viewer intuits a personality much like the dual and fragmenting Jean Genet's in the multiple influences, techniques, and media deployed in these works, the irresistible shifting within opposite poles. After this point, González switches at whim from monochrome to color, from oil to pencil, watercolor, tempera, and acrylic (sometimes mixing them together), before finally coming to the total freedom of the mixed-media stage sets for *Blood Wedding,* where he photocopies, cuts, paints, and varnishes the assembled elements, and *Así que Pasen Cinco Años/When Five Years Pass,* where he uninhibitedly glues to his Gator board support ribbons of lace, panels of metallic glitter paper, cutouts of family, friends, and art-historical characters, under plush Zurbarán-styled drapes. González coats these elements so heavily with paint and varnish they can scarcely be called collaged. He aims for a fluent perfection of surface, as mystifying as his realism of detail, in which the image—the vision—is all.

Without knowing the medium, it would be hard to tell if *Roma* was drawn or painted. Brushstrokes are virtually impossible to detect in works like *El Soñador/The Dreamer, Double Portrait of Jimmy, N.Y.C.* (Plate 45), or *Jardín de un Sueño* (Garden of a Dream) (Plate 53). The artist himself, looking back on his work, wonders at the lifelike strands of hair in *Miércoles de Ceniza,* the soft varicolored sheen of the monochrome tulips in *Still Life in Red for Manuel* (Plate 51). Mystification, too, is the key to this artist's strange miniaturism: the minuscule portrait of his mother in *Nacimiento/Nativity* was done with the aid of a jeweler's magnifying glass, and the viewer must strain to see it. Often confounded, the viewer speculates how this image was made, or what might be hidden there, though all is rooted in reality. González's intention is like the intention of the great trompe-l'oeil artists he has long admired: to mirror and transcend reality, as dreams mirror and transcend reality. He wants, as he repeatedly puts it, "to invent a new reality"—a reality that reflects the intimate preoccupations of the hidden hand that created these obsessive images. He wants these images to reveal himself.

Among contemporary artists, González is one of the great illusionists, having a deep love and knowledge of the devices and conventions of trompe l'oeil, which he uses in unique ways. His art looks back to the illusionistic frescoed walls of ancient Pompeii, the Renaissance window and parapet, the Flemish mirror relaying space beyond the art work, and the velvet-curtained niche of Spanish baroque art. He is conscious of the origin of the picture frame as reliquary—the architectural ornament of the altarpiece. And trompe l'oeil is for him no outmoded or mechanical demonstration of technical skills, but rather an exercise in transcendence. In *In His Silence,* for instance, González combines the *cartellino,* or scrap of inscribed paper beloved of the illusionist artist of earlier centuries, with panels of grained wood—a classic trompe-l'oeil background redefined by González as representing the wood of the Redeemer's cross. Finished with borders of glittering Ravenna-inspired trompe l'oeil, the image presents an array of textures painted with breathtaking realism, while the ascending ovals of the modest plywood panels contribute a quiet rhythm of ascension in vertical counterpoint to the fiery oval of the displaced halo at the side of the saint's head. The white saint is one of González's many metamorphosing sculptures, an idealized being of pristine carved marble on the miraculous point of becoming living, breathing flesh and blood, as he attains immortality.

Two years later, González was still mesmerized by the trompe-l'oeil texture of painted wood—combining it with the reflective glass of a mirrored landscape for his remarkable *Memory Piece.* This spectacular image incorporates its own subtly integrated wooden frame—an architectural ornament featuring stylized palms relating to the fractured "mirrored" palms of the interior landscape—while also poetically evoking the trompe-l'oeil tradition of hunting still lifes, images of slain fowl hanging with ruffled feathers from nails driven into panels of grained wood. The palms of *Memory Piece,* like the palms of the mirrored landscape in *Il Giardino delle Sorelle* (The Garden of the Sisters) (Plate 52), remind González of the flying feathers of his father's Cuban fighting cocks. In *Memory Piece* González produces a painting where frame and interior image are perfectly in harmony, a poetic unity triumphantly acceding to the level of the devotional object housed in a wooden reliquary.

It might be argued that the body of González's work forms a glittering treasury, or "healdom," of spiritual marvels, relics of the Redeemer's Passion imaginatively coexisting with symbols of beauty, joy, and celebration—pearls, gold leaf, and sparkling gems lighting the way to a celestial glory, a golden glimpse of heaven here on earth. Crowns and haloes are scattered through the images, signifying ascension and divinity. In his earliest works, the massive acrylic wall paintings with which he began his career, González had already nursed a notion of setting jewels of beauty in unlikely quarters, impressed by Genet's insight in *Our Lady of the Flowers:* "But what is to be said of one of the strangest of poetic phenomena: that the whole world—and the most terribly dismal part of it, the blackest, most charred, dry to the point of Jansenism, the severe, naked world of factory workers—is entwined with marvels?"[5] Studying for his M.F.A. degree at Miami from 1970 to 1972, approaching the age of thirty and having recently left his wife and family, González had discovered Jean Genet in the university library—the first vital poetic influence over his art. Genet's lyrical and baroque dreams of sin, sacrifice, redemption, and ascension, his unconventional but authentic preoccupation with God, his homoerotic fantasies and rituals, all had a profoundly awakening effect on González. The glass and window imagery reflecting inner mental states in *Our Lady of the Flowers,* the ledge conveying the terror of annihilation in *The Balcony,* the garlands of white roses that are Genet's *Miracle of the Rose,* the barriers between life and death, conscious and unconscious, reality and illusion, that are *The Screens*—parallels to all these motifs may be traced throughout González's art, together with a Genet-like compassion for all things. Genet-like, too, is the celebration of the androgyne, the magical dual creature, the female being caged in a male body. González's one overt reference in his art to Genet occurs with *Untitled (Divine Takes Off Her Dress)* (Plate 5), in which González pictures himself as Genet's scarred feminine alter ego Divine in *Our Lady of the Flowers.* González clearly never forgot the visions of Genet.

The Spanish poet Federico García Lorca (a great favorite with the family of González, so that he grew up listening to Lorca's poems, though he did not intensively study them until he went to university in Miami) would eventually follow Genet as a major poetic influence in González's work. Other writers, like Tennessee Williams and Truman Capote, have touched him in demonstrable ways. But the "stuff," the rich heart's blood of González's art, the essential medium of his art, comes from the centuries upon centuries of other art that has bewitched him, from the ancient Greeks to pop art, from Michelangelo to Fernand Khnopff. In these wildly various artists González has searched for reflections of his own feelings and passions, for qualities of mystery and beauty.

Haunted in particular by the need to make portraits of beauty, to draw "the perfect female face" since he was a young child, his adult portraits and self-portraits have virtually all been conceived as objects of spiritual contemplation, set within actual or trompe-l'oeil shrines and reliquaries of increasingly fantastic devising. His first colored-pencil portrait, *Teresa* (Plate 17), depicts his younger daughter in a Joseph Cornell–style box, framed and "mirrored" in trompe-l'oeil beneath a raised window blind—a blind-pulling device to one side implying that the blind may be pulled protectively down at any moment, concealing the subject of the portrait. In *Teresa en Verde* (Teresa in Green) (Plate 48), Teresa is enshrined in a large white columned niche constructed by the artist—literally an object, almost a sculpture, half ancient Greek tomb and half Giacometti woman-cage, its three-inch-deep interior ledge mirror lined, while a finely drawn green line bordering the interior image implies that the center of the shrine may be a mirrored mirage, a reflected vision existing beyond the elaborate white frame, an elusive mystery that will never quite be apprehended.

Many recurring themes inform the artist's work, which is truly a model of circular consistency, a hermetic system or code of accumulative meaning—though all elements tend, in the end, to work toward the grand themes of the question of salvation and the mystery of the self. One vital issue is the light-dark continuum expressed in subtle ways in works as diverse as *After Philadelphia* (Plate 43) and *El Niño* (The Child) (Plate 44). The entire surface of the drawing in *After Philadelphia* presents a dusky, Seurat-inspired monochrome, though watercolor washes are paradoxically concealed within the drawing. The atmospheric muzziness of this image of a flooded town, derived from an obscure newspaper photograph, correlates with the apparitional quality of Seurat's drawings, evoking the tenuous nature of existence—a medium appropriate for portraying the plight of a town in flood. In *El Niño* the composition is split into two halves—the dark mirrored half reflecting a vase of flowers, the light open half radiant with the glow of a blazing oil lamp. The disparate halves of this still life with a divine theme meet in the pivotal figure of a tiny Saint John the Baptist, poised between the light and the dark, the real and the reflected. The painting deals with a release from darkness and illusion and with an ascent to open space and light. The style in which González elected to paint the work, evident in the modeling of the tulips and the baby saint, derives from the artist's close study of Vermeer. There is no blending here; the colors are broken down into clearly differentiated separate values, expertly applied transitional tones. In a work about ascending from darkness to light, every brushstroke is a carefully considered gradation of steps, matching form to the spiritual content of the image.

But González's work is replete with dualities, with opposite principles in formal antithesis, with magical conjunctions: revelation and concealment; the real and the reflected; night and day; moon and sun; male and female; rose and thorn; monochrome and polychrome; horizontal and vertical; large and small; ascent and descent; and so on, ad infinitum. The power and mystique of a spiritual union of opposites is present in almost all of these objects of contemplation—the restless movement between polar extremes like light and darkness an aesthetic strategy arising from the deepest recesses of the artist's psyche.

By far the most powerful recurring theme in González's work is the myth of Narcissus, the beautiful boy who falls fatally in love with his own mirror image in the water—the personification of a profound duality. Narcissus, water, mirror: these elements, often split or doubled, combine and surface again and again, as a means to ponder the complex issue of the representation of the self in art; the motif of self-reflection and self-absorption; the mystery of the interior, perhaps unconscious self, only to be reached through dreams or death. Water is for González, as it was for Poussin, an ambivalent element—baptismal life giver and treacherous destroyer. An ominous presence on the floor in *A.M.* (Plate 3) or *Occupant, Port Authority N.Y.C.* (Plate 9), water becomes a major component of works like *Mar y Espejo* and *Mar de Lágrimas/Sea of Tears* (Plate 54), where ocean expanses seem to evoke the depths of the unconscious mind, even while the artworks function as magical-realist mirrors.

"In the presence of water," observes Gaston Bachelard in *Water and Dreams,* "Narcissus receives the revelation of his identity and of his duality; of his double powers, virile and feminine; and, above all, the revelation of his reality and his ideality."[6] González was already fascinated by the duality of Narcissus in 1974—in the mirror-imaged pair of headless men (their very headlessness addressing the notion of a split self) playfully confronting one another in *Untitled* (Plate 11), both figures deriving from the figure of the artist himself in *Good Friday,* made earlier that year. This doubling recurs in later images: *Double Portrait of Jimmy, N.Y.C.* and *Untitled* (Plate 56). Many key works are split in the center, for instance *El Cuarto en el Fondo del Pozo/The Room at the Bottom of the Well, Letter to Veronica,* and *El Niño; Il Giardino delle Sorelle,* in which both reflecting halves of a mirrored landscape reflect again in a stretch of water at the bottom of the image; *Memory Piece,* in which the central spine that runs through the image is camouflaged by the glittering prismatic surface of the whole painting, a fragmented mirrored landscape of early memories; and *Vermeer's Frame* (Plate 67), discreetly dissecting the artist's own figure, as his face was dissected in *Letter to Veronica.* González's concept of the art work as a "split mirror" is a particularly effective reinvention of the Narcissus myth—incorporating reflection and symmetry on the one hand, with change, distortion, and asymmetry on the other. Narcissus, after falling in love with the impossible opposite of his own reflection, changed or metamorphosed into a yellow flower (hence his place in the *Metamorphoses* of Ovid). Deceptive or disrupted symmetry is as fascinating to González as true symmetry. The artist's adopted muse, Lorca, wrote a line that González has always taken to be a reference to Narcissus: "Why was I born among mirrors?"[7] It is a line that rings through this artist's work, the mirror his isolating instrument of self-scrutiny and self-revelation.

The scintillating stage-set designs for *Así que Pasen Cinco Años/When Five Years Pass,* featuring González, his daughter Maria, and his friends, literally playing the characters of Lorca's surrealist drama (the characters all phantoms within the central protagonist's fearful mind), become González's ultimate curtained and niched mirror on a fantasy dream world rooted in the reality of his own life. Lorca's play is truly González's mirror—recording the slow dance of the loss of the self to love and time. As Lorca's doomed Young Man, González himself becomes the sleeping Narcissus, mythic and poetic embodiment of the issue of the self and its reflection in art—and the Christ of countless pietàs as he stretches out on the pink sofa of his early baroque stage set, *Cuatro Pilares* (Four Pillars) (Plate 16), succumbing at last to the twin forces of Eros and Thanatos, the "mirror" of the *Así que Pasen Cinco Años/When Five Years Pass* stage-set collages reflecting the truth of the dying artist's own heart.

The realities of González's curious life as an exile on many levels are charted in these superficially fantastic works. They are his true memoir—his art being bound up with and colored by his experiences as first a son, a husband, and a father in the Cuban community of Miami; then, after the personal transformation and liberation of his coming-out, as a homosexual artist in New York. His art is not political (except in the broad sense that for the gay man or woman, the personal is always political). González treats the dread theme of AIDS in a subjective, spiritual, elegiac, and intimate way in works like *After Philadelphia, New York, Year 1986* (Plate 50), the Paestum *Diver's Journey* (Plate 63), *Mar de Lágrimas/Sea of Tears,* and *Il Giardino delle Sorelle,* seeking to transcend earthly pain and suffering, to communicate, beyond terror, its antidotes—a celebratory joy, an openness dispelling fear and darkness, a sense of forgiveness of self and others, of love and reconciliation. In the ecstatic, visionary work *Rembrandt's Hands, Vermeer's Frame and the Passing of the Moth* (Plate 68), death itself is accepted as pure illumination.

A week or so before he died, as the galleys for this book neared completion, Juan González finished *Free Fall,* like most of his other images a type of self-portrait.

Free Fall reworks favorite themes. The "split mirror" composition is filled with Muybridge figures in ghostly repetition, a spiraling "sacred seven" divers dissected by or trapped in fragmented beams of light or glass shafts, cyclically ascending and descending. The angelic sleeping Amor of *To the Dream of the Apples* radiates golden light as he rests in a black void at the bottom of the ocean, González for the last time deploying the gold and black color combination that had come to symbolize his innermost gay selfhood.

The artist's bird-man, or angel, at the center of *Free Fall* moves his arms in flight above a deathly trinity of moths, contained within a circle of life, fulfillment, and perfection. Death has liberated him. As he soars free he looks back down upon the Amor, sleeping peacefully under the rolling waves, sunk like the golden ring of *Mar y Espejo* beneath "the mirror's sand." With *Free Fall,* González embraces death as release and metamorphosis, a longed-for ascension to the realm of the spirit.

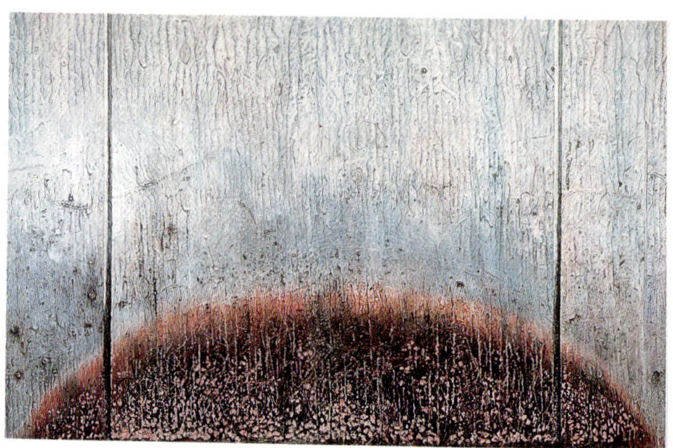

Pearls for J., about 1970
Acrylic on canvas, 84 × 132 inches
Collection of Mr. and Mrs. Marcos Pineda

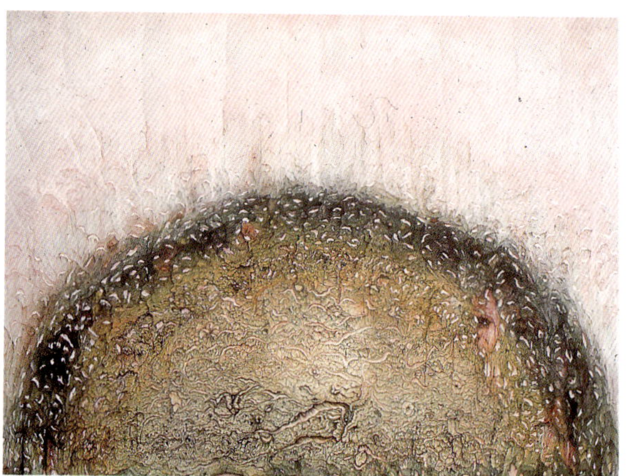

Pink Wall, about 1970
Acrylic on canvas, 97¼ × 97½ inches
Collection of Teresa and Larry Katz

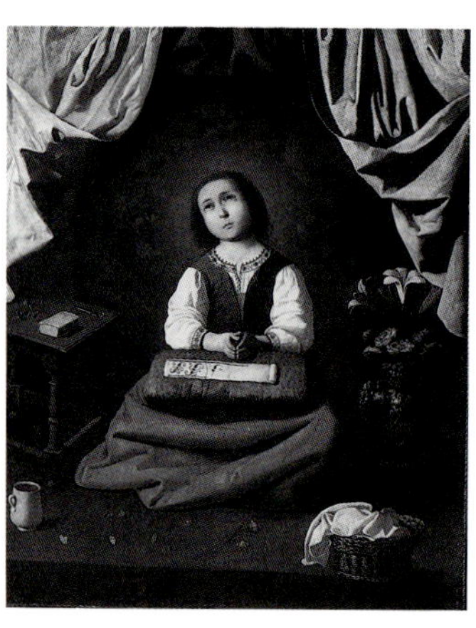

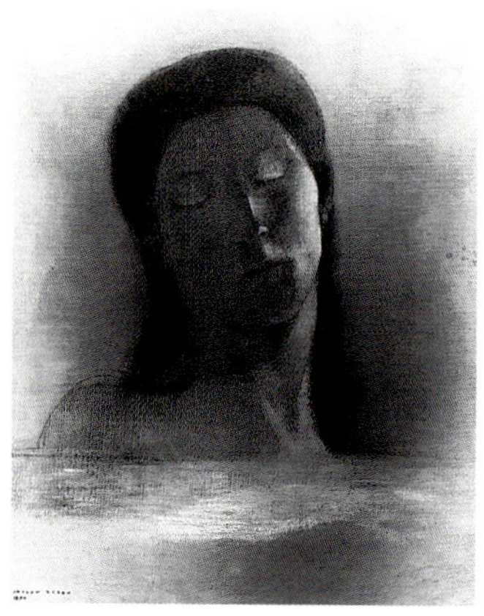

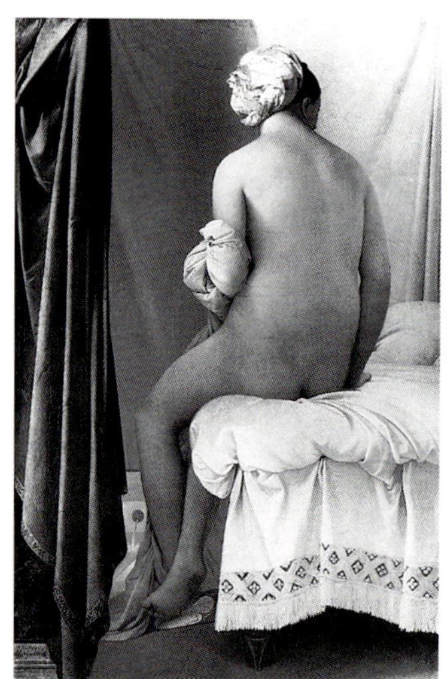

From the left

Francisco de Zurbarán
The Young Virgin Praying, about 1632–33
Oil on canvas, 46 × 37 inches
The Metropolitan Museum of Art, New York, Fletcher Fund, 1927.(27.137)

Odilon Redon
The Closed Eyes, 1890
Oil on cardboard, 17 5/16 × 14 3/16 inches
Musée d'Orsay, Paris

Jean-Auguste-Dominique Ingres
The Bather of Valpinçon, 1808
Oil on canvas, 57½ × 38⅜ inches
Musée du Louvre, Paris

Free Fall, 1993
Mixed media, 38¾ × 29½ inches
Collection of Teresa Katz
and Maria Schleifman

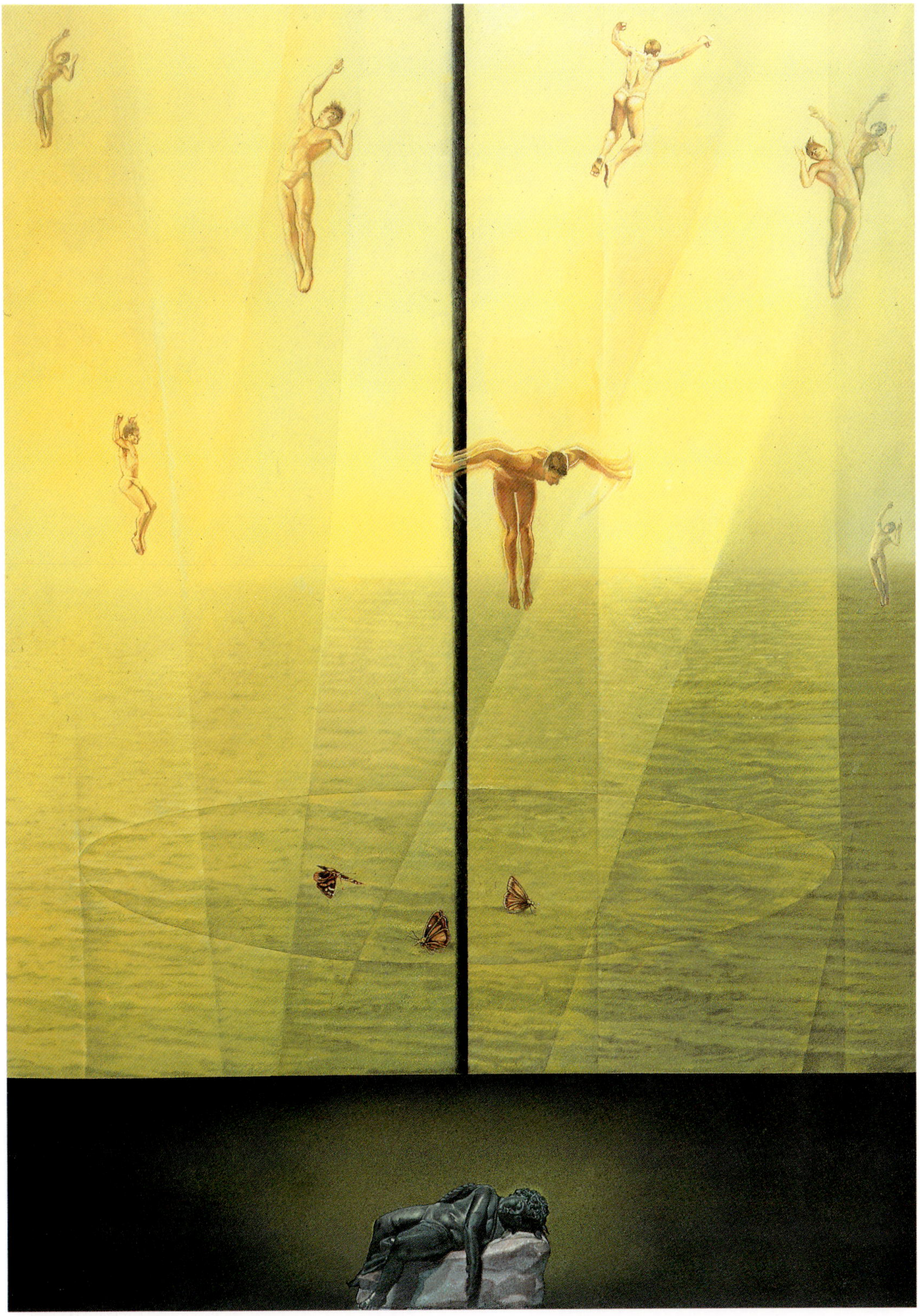

I *Ascension* 1972

Colored pencil on paper, 28 × 20 inches
Charles Cowles, New York

In 1972 the life and work of González changed dramatically. He abandoned the huge mural paintings for which he had already gained substantial recognition, and he left his family home, his wife, and two daughters, to move into the cramped quarters of a Miami rooming house, where he embarked on a series of comparatively small colored-pencil drawings, beginning with *Ascension*. González looks back to his early acrylic wall paintings in one obvious way here, however, treating the flat white surface of the paper as a magical wall, flush with the paper yet giving way to the radiant vertical recess or niche of the closet—an alluring, evasive door into the beyond, filled with golden light.

The space in the artist's rented room was minimal. He had a bed, a mirrored dressing table, a closet—and nothing more. He had to draw sitting on the bed. This tiny room happened to be a suitably claustrophobic space in which to begin exploring his inward-looking art. The space reminded him, too, of childhood, when he would hide under a bed in his aunt's house to draw in secret—after his mother, disturbed by his obsessive quest to draw the perfect female face (a composite of movie-star faces remembered from films and posters), sternly forbade him ever to draw anything again.

Ascension is a drawing rich in symbolist and Catholic significance: a vision of the rooming-house closet in which the artist's T-shirt hung—both shirt and closet suffused with a supernatural light. The shirt is full of flowing lines, suggesting movement, flight, the presence of something living yet invisible. The artist will associate the pink color of the shirt with the androgyne in later works like *La Cuna/The Cradle,* 1976, and *Así que Pasen Cinco Años/When Five Years Pass: Act 2, Scene 2,* 1991. The title of the drawing refers specifically to the Catholic feast of Ascension Day, occurring forty days after Easter and celebrating the final appearance of Christ on earth and his mystical ascent into heaven. The glowing shirt and golden light suggest that González has experienced some momentous release into a newly elevated or transcendent state.

The potent dream of flying, or ascension—of defying gravity and floating upward—is constantly evoked in the work of this artist, always signifying freedom. His work is full of hanging elements or spiraling forces moving up and down; layers of crystalline transparencies like moving veils; elements of aerial architecture; cosmic clouds and stars, spirit-messenger birds and Annunciation angels—expressing a lightness of being, the uplifting discovery of a spiritual light and transforming serenity within the self, a liberation from the gross weight and solidity of the flesh, and a metamorphosis from the human to the celestial or angelic state.

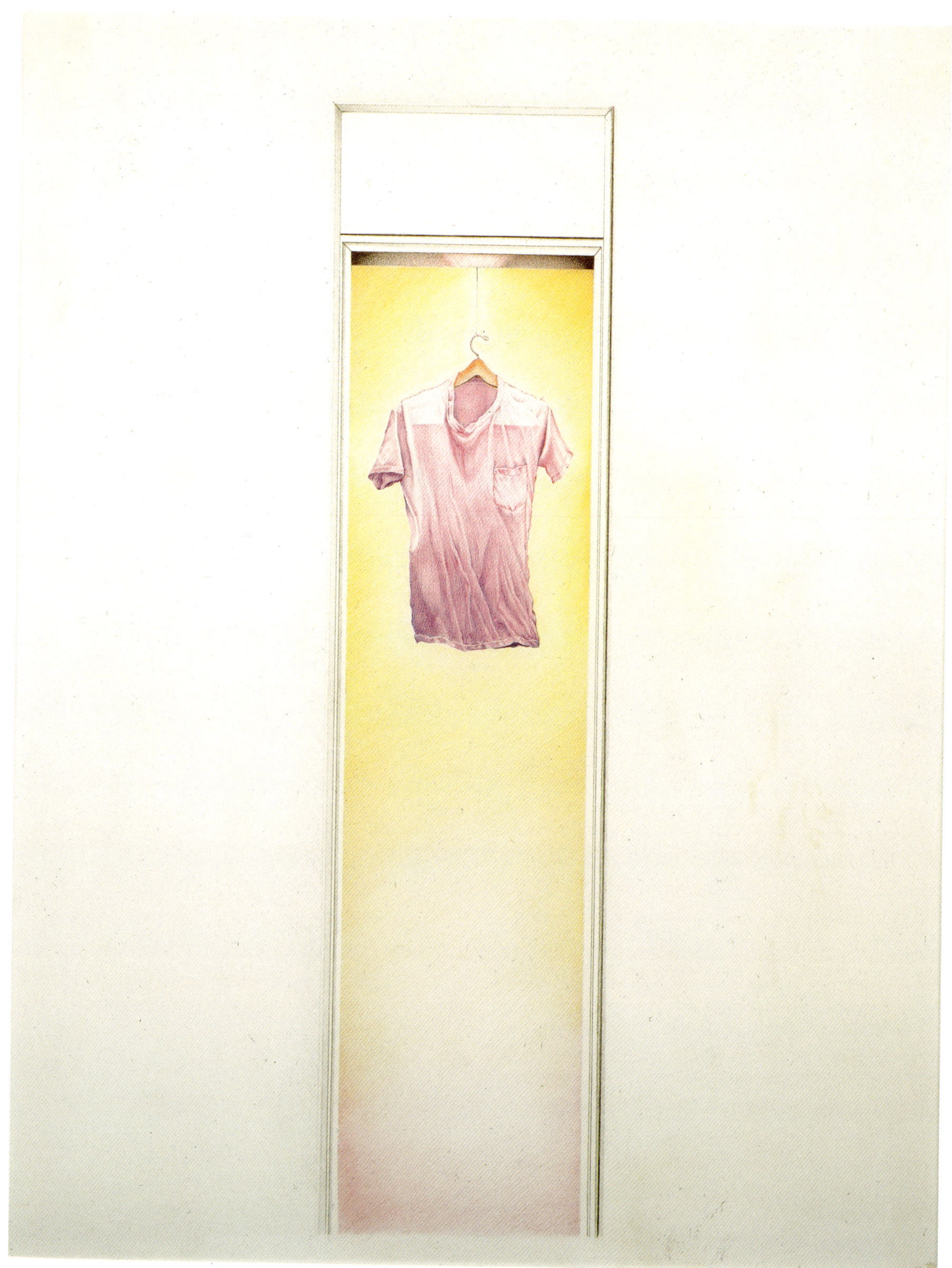

2 *Morning Ride* 1973

Colored pencil on paper, 26½ × 21 inches
Maria and Daniel Schleifman

Is *Morning Ride* a landscape, seascape, or some kind of mystical garden? Perhaps it is pure, abstract sensation. It relates to the final three large acrylic paintings González executed about 1970: *Pearls for J.* (a gesture of farewell to his wife, who loves pearls), *Pink Wall* (see page 14), and the strange *Self-Portrait in Black Wrapping,* with its startling view from just above the lightly furred chest down the foreshortened length of the artist's naked torso lying in the grass—the grass having a marked textural affinity with González's body hairs. Hair is famously symbolic of life force and virility. González shows individual bejeweled hairs rising upward in *Morning Ride,* symbolic of magical powers and divine possession. The idea of riding also has erotic associations, of course.

A year or so after he made this picture, González came across a short story by Tennessee Williams that he realized with a shock corresponded with the sense of indefinable yearning he was struggling to convey in *Morning Ride:*

> Called *Two on a Party,* it's about this man who's getting older, and his girlfriend, who's also getting older, and they go out to bars every night, and pick up sailors. It's a fantastic story, because Williams gives you all this very earthy, real foundation; and then, in between the lines, these mystical suggestions of things. He talks about how they go on these binges, and then he describes how they feel in the morning. The emptiness, the loneliness.[1]

González was struck by the marine metaphor Williams chose to evoke Billy and Cora's feelings after their nightly adventures: "The nights were like waves rolling in and breaking and retreating again and leaving you washed up on the wet sands of morning," wrote Williams. This sense of longing for something inexpressible and ungraspable speaks directly to the work of González, who believes with Teilhard de Chardin that aesthetic beauty fills us with a nostalgia and sadness, "created by God, the presence of the *Otherness* that is contained in art."

Yet *Morning Ride* also has a literal and mundane dimension. Every morning, driving in to the School of Fine Arts in Miami, González would pass grass-covered sand dunes:

> I would drive on the expressway and there would be this hill with grass growing on it, and I thought of hills and grass as a reflection of the human body, with the grass being hair, and the curves of the earth being curves of the body. I made an abstraction of that hill. The top part looks like lace—but it's actually based on an aerial photograph of waves rolling back into the ocean, after the sea has ridged the sand of the shore.

Morning Ride is an unusually abstract expression (for González at least) of a sparkling creative vision, charged with a conviction of the power of art to transport. Normal boundaries are here dissolving into a mystically perceived, all-enveloping, pansexual universe, reflecting the "oceanic" state identified by Sigmund Freud. The pictorial space is ambiguous, with pink-purple cloud shapes over the hill/torso giving way to the aerial abstraction of ocean waves encroaching on the thin dark strand of wet sand at the top of the picture. The ocean will turn out to be of central importance in the future work of González. The sea, and water in general, has been significant in symbolist art. G. K. Chesterton complained that in all of George Frederick Watts's paintings, "There is nothing there but the eternal things, day and fire and the sea, and motherhood and the dead." As Edward Lucie-Smith notes in his book *Symbolist Art,* this is "an excellent list of typically Symbolist subject-matter."[2]

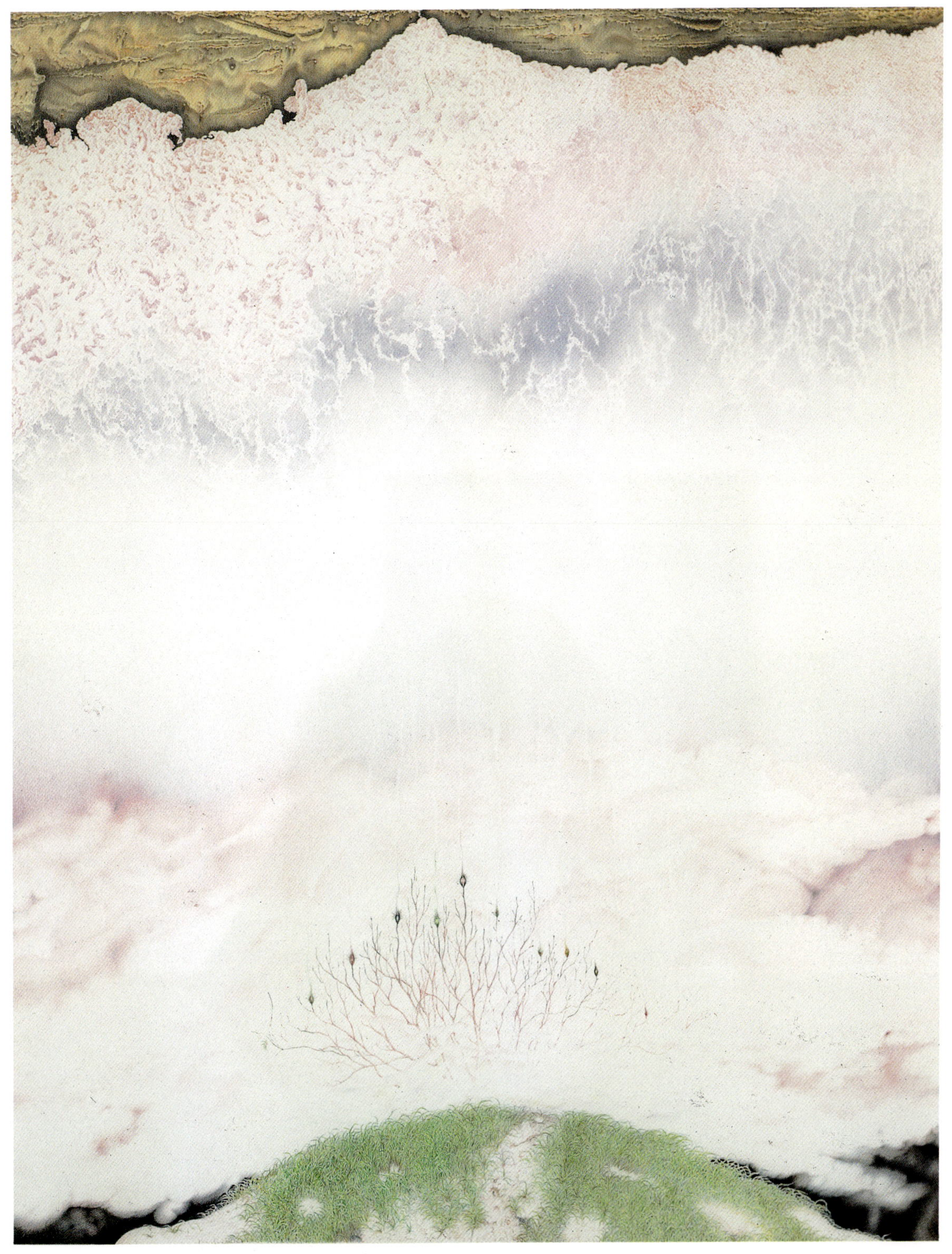

3 *A. M.* 1973

Colored pencil on paper, 26½ × 21 inches
Private collection

A. M., besides involving a reference to time, always a thematic preoccupation with González, is a tribute to a woman friend of long standing, whose initials these are. Anne Minich is an artist herself, and in 1973 González believed that she was the only person who saw his art with clear eyes, who understood the inner tensions fueling his work. This drawing is a dream portrait of González and his friend Anne. "She was really like a spiritual guide for my work," says González. "So I see myself as the door, which is blank, and she's represented by the piece of striped blanket (which actually belonged to her) resting on the door and giving color and light to the drawing."

Black water rippling under the door adds an element of mystery. In symbolist terms water is often the grave of unhappy love, the last resort of suicidal lovers like Ophelia. In religious symbolism water or blood signifies baptism, initiation, the old life washed away in the sanctification of the new life. Like the door, a symbol of passing over a threshold and entering a new state of consciousness, water is, as Gaston Bachelard points out in *Water and Dreams,*

> truly the transitory element. It is the essential, ontological metamorphosis between fire and earth. A being dedicated to water is a being in flux. He dies every minute; something of his substance is constantly falling away. Daily death is not fire's exuberant form of death, piercing heaven with its arrows; daily death is the death of water. Water always flows, always falls, always ends in horizontal death. In innumerable examples, we shall see that for the materializing imagination, death associated with water is more dream-like than death associated with earth: the pain of water is infinite.[1]

González dreams of both water and air, of floating up to the light and plummeting down to the submerged ocean depths. But the black water of this drawing also suggests the very early influence on this artist of a favorite painter, Francis Bacon, whose *Three Portraits* (private collection), depicting himself, his recently deceased companion George Dyer, and Lucian Freud, their lower bodies all liquefying into a black meltdown of mortality, was finished in 1973, the year González made *A. M.*

Structurally, the drawing functions on two levels simultaneously. It is both a flat frame-within-a-frame, enhanced and defined by the striped blanket and corner of black water, and an illusionistic door, opening off the surface of the paper toward the viewer. With the striped blanket we see for the first time the emergence of a device that González will return to repeatedly: the baroque curtain of a toy theater pulled to one side, creating an expectation that sacred mysteries within will be revealed. The striped spill of the curtain is balanced in the lower right-hand corner of the door by a thin vertical spectrum of color, the tantalizing suggestion of a miraculous rainbow hidden beyond the teasing void of the door.

In studying the work of González, Odilon Redon's famous statement about the necessity of injecting art with mystery springs to mind: "Mystery means keeping continually to the dual and triple aspects of things, the faintest shades of an aspect (pictures within pictures), forms which are about to be or will be according to the viewer's state of mind. All things more than suggestive, since they appear to the eye."[2]

González credits Anne Minich with teaching him the necessity of the sacred in art, of mystery. In *A. M.* he creates for the first time a conjunction between the opposite principles of male and female, himself and Minich, to realize the redemption of a new life, a new beginning, in the mystery of the blank white interior contained within the door frame.

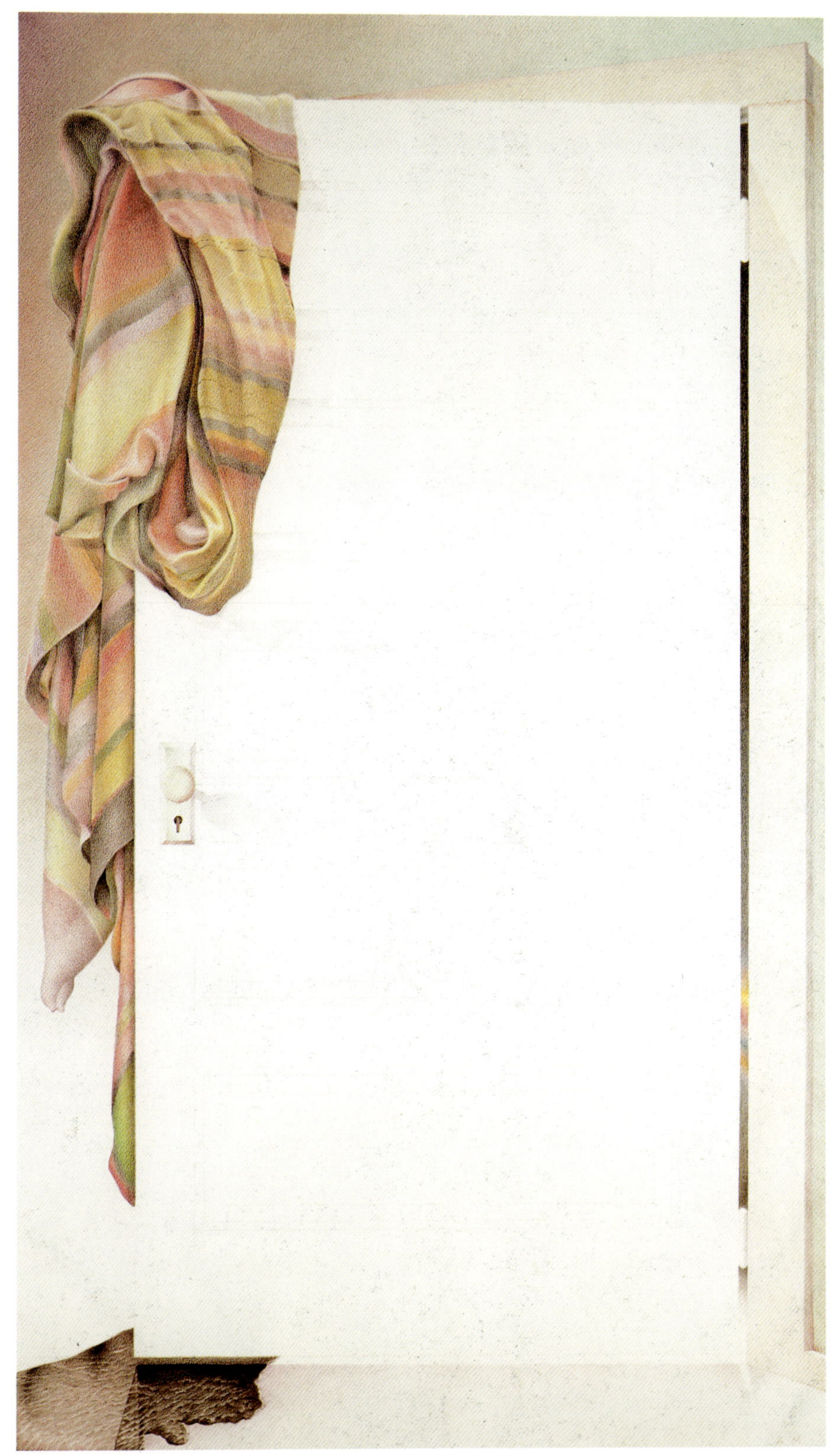

4 *Untitled (Self-Portrait)* 1973

Colored pencil on paper, 26½ × 21 inches
Private collection, Miami

The trompe-l'oeil effect of a picture-within-a-picture is carried to new heights in this drawing. González presents us with an ultrarealist drawing full of superfine textures. We can make out the weave of threads in the gauze or muslin mask; we can see the minute stitches that border the gold ribbon, which is a kind of crown. The artist illusionistically hangs the drawing on a "wall," skillfully contrasting the taut thread on which the solidly framed drawing is hung with the loose thread that flares out lightly below the nail and its convincing shadow. There is striking play, too, between the vibrantly splashed scarlet of the carnation heads, emblematic of passionate love and the blood of martyrdom, and their elusive shadows.

Considering dual aspects reminds us of Jean Genet's *Our Lady of the Flowers,* which opens with the curious line: "Weidmann appeared before you in a five o'clock edition, his head swathed in white bands, a nun and yet a wounded pilot fallen into the rye one September day like the day when the world came to know the name of Our Lady of the Flowers."[1] There is something of Genet's nun/aviator about González's masked self-portrait, though the portrait most strongly evokes a veiled self, and perhaps an inward searching of the soul.

The nail and the long, straight line of the taut thread in the center of the drawing have a religious significance that only a singularly devout Spanish Catholic might guess at. For González they represent the instruments of Christ's Passion, when he was nailed to the cross—though the nail may also refer to a work by the Anglo-Irish Catholic painter Francis Bacon, whose *Portrait of George Dyer Staring at a Blind Cord* of 1966 (Collection Maestri, Parma) isolates Dyer's face in a rectangular frame fixed illusionistically to the wall with a long, wounding nail just over the sitter's head. The taut thread that holds up González's masked self-portrait is intended, according to the artist, as a reference "to the spear with which Christ's side was lanced at the Crucifixion," a moment graphically recorded in the broken, bleeding bodies of Christ that are the glory of the Spanish baroque altar. González is a connoisseur of crucifixions, keeping a collection of them hung round his New York studio.

In this self-portrait he depicts himself as crowned, not with thorns, but with a ribbon of gold, symbolic of victory and sovereignty. The heavily veiled self-portrait anticipates the tragic virgin brides of the Lorca-influenced works *Así que Pasen Cinco Años/When Five Years Pass* and *A Bride for Lorca,* 1992. These images stem at least partly from González's fascination with Vermeer's *Glass of Wine,* ca. 1660 (Berlin, Gemäldegalerie, Dahlem), a painting in which a girl's features are obscured by the wineglass she has raised to her lips. González abstracts from the painting the conjunction of male and female and his favorite theme of the hidden face, arising from childhood years of secretly drawing female faces and perhaps from youthful memories of the cloaked heads of church sculptures, unveiled only on special occasions.

This work owes the greatest visible debt, however, to Medardo Rosso's sculpted head of a boy veiled in curtain folds, *Ecce Puer!,* 1906–7 (Collection of Lydia K. and Harry L. Winston, Dr. and Mrs. Barnett Malbin, New York), which was made after Rosso, visiting friends, glimpsed their young son hiding behind a curtain and spying on the adults.

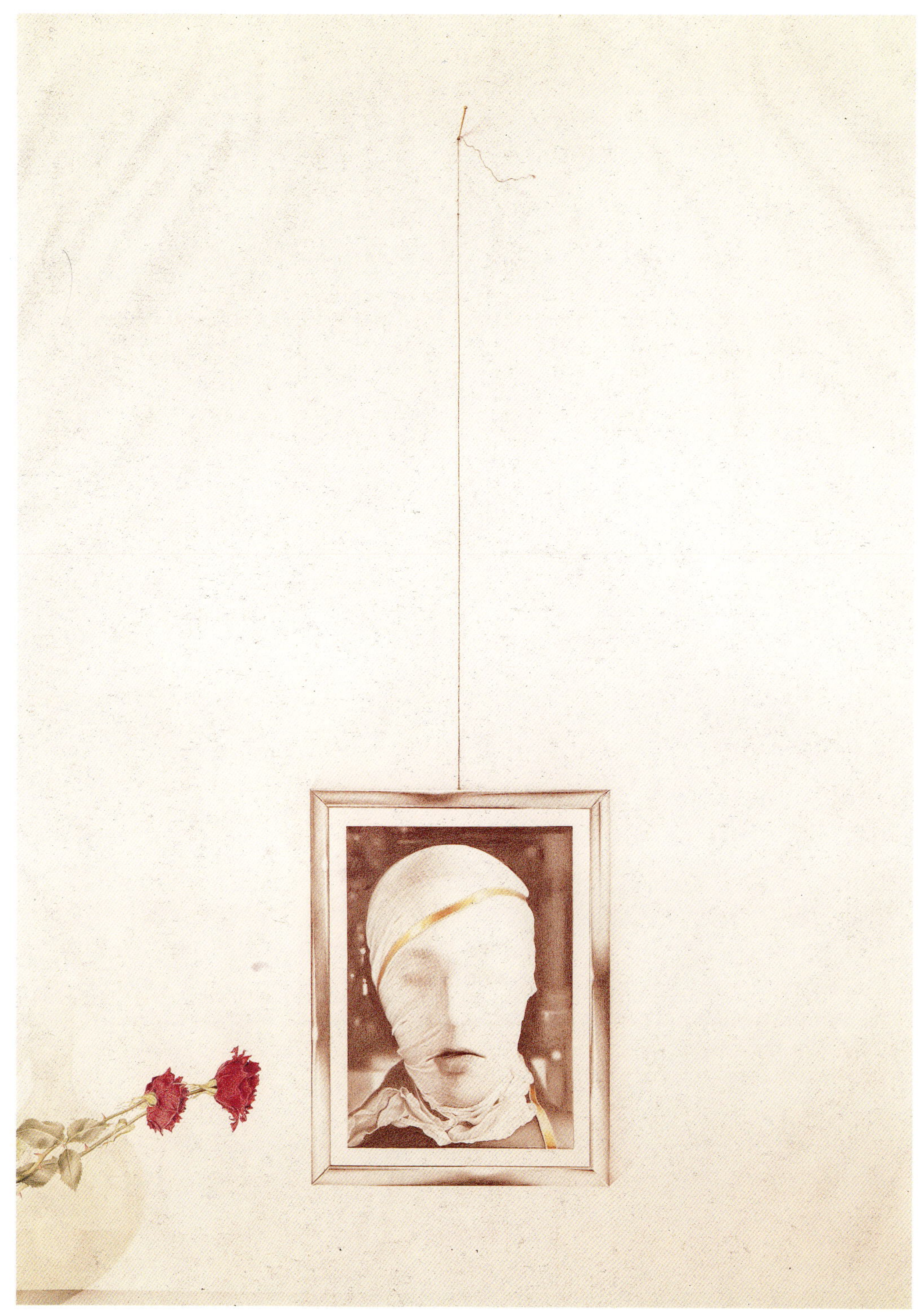

5 *Untitled (Divine Takes Off Her Dress)* 1973

Colored pencil on paper, 26½ × 21 inches
Mr. and Mrs. Marcos Pinedo

When González made this drawing of his own bare legs, he had in mind the poignant scene from Genet's *Our Lady of the Flowers* in which Divine (following a frustrating night out with Gorgui and Our Lady, who only have eyes for each other) goes behind a screen to take off her black dress and put on a pair of more becomingly colored green pajamas, in the vain hope of attracting amorous attention to herself. González adopts the role of Genet's androgyne male character Divine—the author's own alter ego—and combines the cast-off dress with the green pajamas, to seize on what will become a favorite symbolic color for him, green—an emblem of hope and the renewal of life and nature. The shedding of garments is also a sign of death of the old and birth of the new life in the empty fluttering shirts of *Ascension, El Cuarto en el Fondo del Pozo/The Room at the Bottom of the Well,* 1978, and in the artist's ritual removal of his shirt in *Nacimiento/Nativity,* 1979.

The dangerous-looking seagull below Divine and the pedestal she has ascended, with its waves of shimmering watery green fabric at her feet (from which issues an ambiguous touch of pink), suggest a quite different scene and space than Divine's apartment, however—a memory, perhaps, of Fernand Khnopff's naked *Sappho* from around 1912 (whereabouts unknown), contemplating suicide on her precipice above an ocean abyss, after she has been rejected in love. Divine's bare right foot is arched up as if she were about to step forward, and she is placed noticeably higher than the gull, implying that she stands on some high cliff or coastal ledge. Perhaps González is looking ahead to the end of Genet's history of Divine, in which, stripped of "every vestige of happiness," she attains "saintliness" and "ascension."[1]

The artist's positioning of Divine's bare legs above the ledge on which she stands also recalls the Crucifixion and the nailed feet of Christ, one foot usually raised above the other. Genet, too, had compared Divine's consumptive body to "the ivory body of Jesus on an eighteenth-century crucifix."[2] Inspection of the raised right foot in this drawing reveals one of medieval art's five wounds of Christ, in the real-life scar of a deep gash González sustained when he accidentally kicked a huge pane of glass in the studio, slicing the tendons of his foot. González here links the androgyne Divine with Christ in his Passion, as Johannes Thorn Prikker entwined his heavily veiled bride with Christ on the cross in the symbolist work *The Bride,* 1892–93 (Kröller-Müller Foundation, Otterlo, Holland), in which the bride's floral crown metamorphoses into Christ's crown of thorns as it winds sinuously from one head to the other.

Genet's book has held a lasting fascination for González primarily because of its unabashed lyricism. The artist admires most "those parts of the book where Genet retreats from the characters, speaks directly to the reader, and talks about how with lyricism you can be stronger, more daring—you can reach further. Genet says that Divine is a work of art—but that the difference between Divine and the artist is that she has her life written in her flesh, whereas the artist can retreat from it, and share the knowledge with others."[3] González's own work has been about controlling a powerful lyricism, never letting it get out of hand.

In this work González anticipates a strategy he uses in 1990 for *Rembrandt's Hands, Vermeer's Frame and the Passing of the Moth,* borrowing the creation of another artist and concealing a portrait of himself—or at least a recognizable part of his own anatomy—within an image of androgyny. In nominally portraying Genet's Christ-like androgyne Divine, González actually focuses on his own gashed foot, the very portion of his body in which, ironically, his life has indeed been "written upon his flesh."

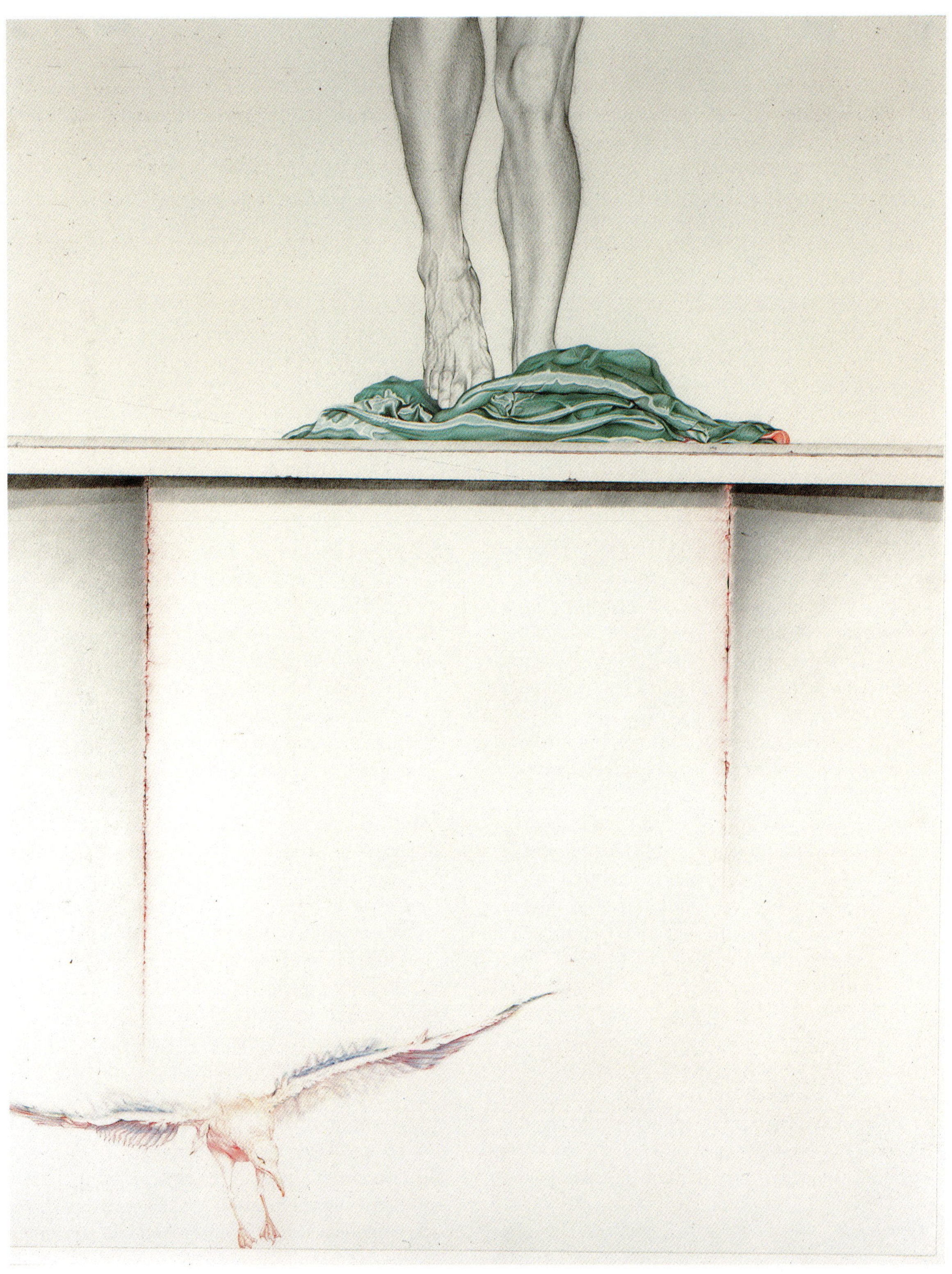

6 *Hot White Tennessee Williams* 1973

Colored pencil on paper, 16¼ × 27½ inches
Hoffman Greenwald Family: Nancy Hoffman, Peter Greenwald, Rebecca Hoffman Greenwald

González must have enjoyed drawing the gull. This drawing features a beautiful white bird with beating wings, trapped in a faded white room, casting its shadow on a theatrical scene painter's fantasy of a cracked plaster wall. The bird seems about to try a perilous escape out into the hot black summer night through the gauntlet of violently flapping black curtains, the movement caused, perhaps, by the approach of a summer storm. The white bird anticipates the mystic white bird of *Mar y Espejo* (Sea and Mirror), a bird of baptism and rebirth, emblem of the purified soul, emerging from the many birds of passage that flock through that triptych.

The most surreal element in the drawing is the pitch-black void of night veiled by the twisting curtains. Here is another white "wall" of paper, magically recessed. We gradually realize that within the frame of the window there is actually nothing of a real window, only empty space. The window disappears, as the door in *A.M.* disappears when we isolate the frame there. This curtained void looks forward to the recessed black square of death set within the linen-draped chest of drawers in *July 11, 1974*.

There is a good reason for the intense theatricality of this drawing. "I had just moved to New Jersey from Miami," remembers González.

> I had not been able to start working again for about a month, which was unusual for me. A friend invited me to see a production of *A Streetcar Named Desire* at Lincoln Center, with Rosemary Harris playing Blanche. The play had a tremendous effect on me, especially the scenes of Blanche's descent into madness. The things that the production did with the sound as her madness overtook her . . . ! I came home the next day and started work on this drawing, which is really about madness.

The curious title encompasses the white bird in the white room, the searing spectacle of Blanche's madness (her name, of course, meaning "white"), and González's obeisance to the author, Tennessee Williams. The drawing is a precursor of *The Sparrow and the Maiden*, 1975, in which a bird trapped in a similarly white room flies into its own mirror image (scrabbling at a door within the mirror that can never open, since it is only a reflected door), only this time the bird is accompanied by an apparitional white bride-doll, the glowing headless ghost of a lovely woman.

In *Hot White Tennessee Williams* González wanted to achieve "an effect of violent, blinding light inside a white space, to depict the moment of madness, the breaking point of Blanche du Bois, as if the light has caused her madness." This does not mean that González views Blanche's breaking point as a defeat. On the contrary, he feels, she has metamorphosed into the transcendent white bird rising above her persecutors and the meanness of her circumstances. She is now a soul in ascension, a creature filled with grace, like the pure white dove of the Holy Ghost.

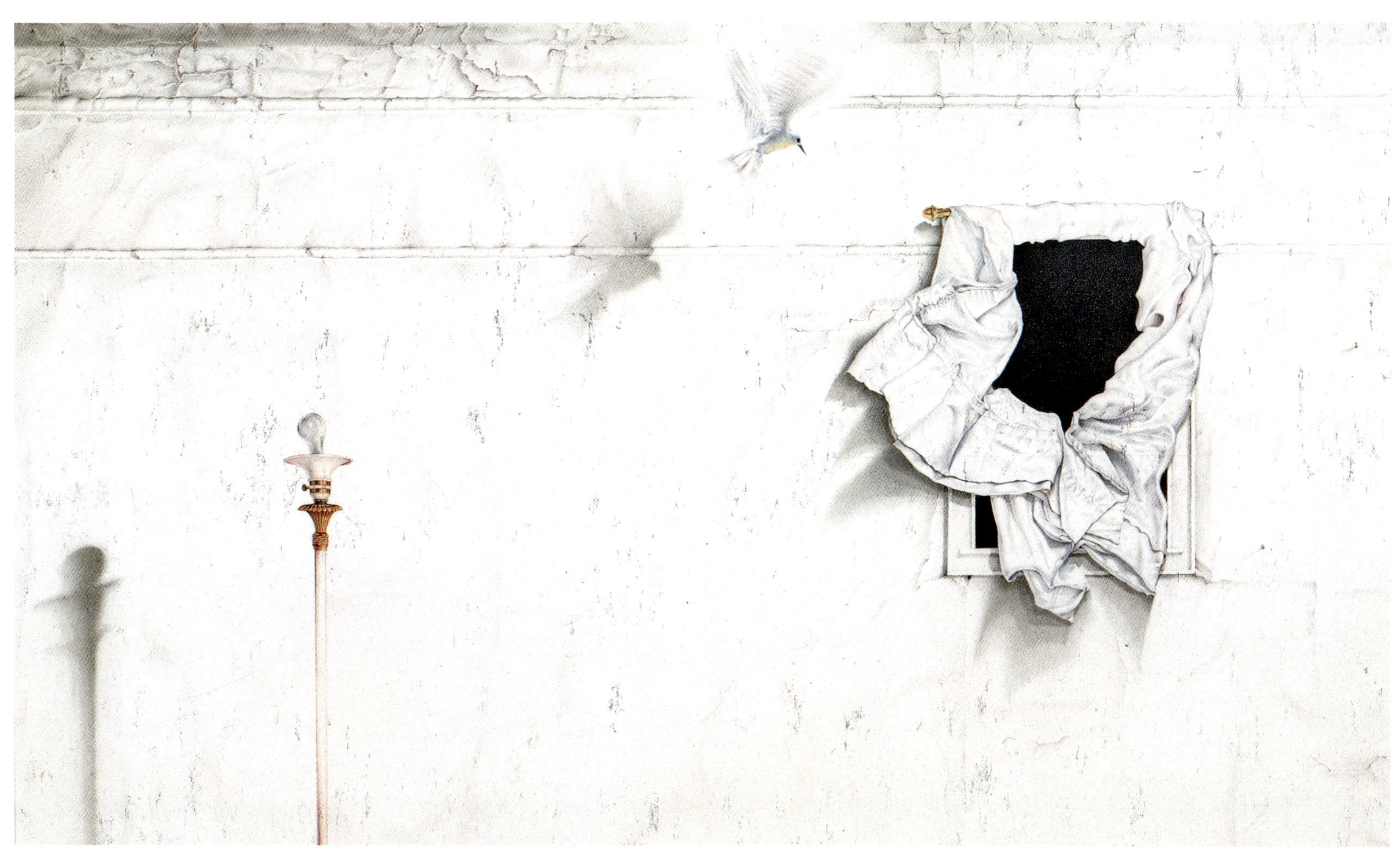

7 *Summer Flies* 1973

Colored pencil on paper, 25¼ × 24¼ inches
Collection of The Chase Manhattan Bank, N.A.

The title *Summer Flies* involves a double meaning. González refers both to the time during which he made the picture—summer—speeding by and to the large biting flies he encountered during his summer stay on Fire Island. He had wanted to make a still life that would explore and defy vulgar notions of "what we think of as ugly, and what we think of as beautiful." He had been thinking in particular about the way earlier artists had used life-sized trompe-l'oeil flies, adding them to their still-life paintings as *vanitas* symbols of death and decay: for instance, the big flies on the Master of Frankfurt's portrait of himself and his wife, one fly disturbingly poised on the snowy white veil covering the head of the artist's wife (1480, Musée Royal des Beaux-Arts, Antwerp).

González was delighted to be able to "catch a live fly—a really big fly—on Fire Island, and bring it back to the city. I kept it in a bottle in my home. I wanted to take away from the too obvious prettiness of my drawing, and I wanted the ugliness of the flies to clash with the beauty of the orchid. But after I started drawing the flies, I came to feel that they were really beautiful, perhaps more beautiful than the flower, because they're less obvious." These flies anticipate the dying frog in a hummingbird's beak in *Untitled (Birds),* the work that immediately follows this one, and the salamanders that appear in *The Sparrow and the Maiden,* 1975, as elements of the unexpected and the conventionally ugly, balancing and contrasting with the otherwise unadulterated lyrical beauty of the artist's drawings—part of the transformational magic that arises out of the willful conjunction of opposites in this artist's work. Finding beauty in the unconventional and unexpected is not merely an aesthetic strategy for González, but a ritual compulsion.

The obscure draped object in the center of the drawing is a pedestaled planter, mysteriously merging into the cracked plaster wall. A forked lightninglike vein of plaster shoots down dramatically to an ambiguously shaped loose knot of cloth, crowning a curtained void of soft shadow illumined by a segment of rainbow. The knot of cloth contains a single exotic orchid, recalling the double orchid tied in a sash to the hip of the supernatural androgyne under a starred sky in Fernand Khnopff's *Ein Engel* (An Angel), 1889 (private collection, Brussels), a sky González will remember years later in *A Bride for Lorca,* 1992. The flower highlights the fact that this white wall is magically metamorphosing into a veil of white fabric—a curtain opening onto a celestial, transfiguring rainbow, the same kind of barely visible glory glimpsed as a bar of bright colors beyond the white portal of *A.M.*

A second drama occurs in the top left-hand corner of the drawing. Just above the draped planter and a fly on the wing sits the pale horizontal ghost of a rectangle, the faint echo of a picture that once hung for many years on this faded New Jersey apartment wall. González himself had taken down the picture: "I was fascinated by the absence created when I did that. So *Summer Flies* is something I was trying to work in the name of an absence—showing the scar of an absence without becoming overly sentimental or romantic about it." Even more ingeniously, González had found a way to present the viewer with the image of an entire art work, frame and all, which the viewer will never be permitted to see, which will forever remain an authentic mystery.

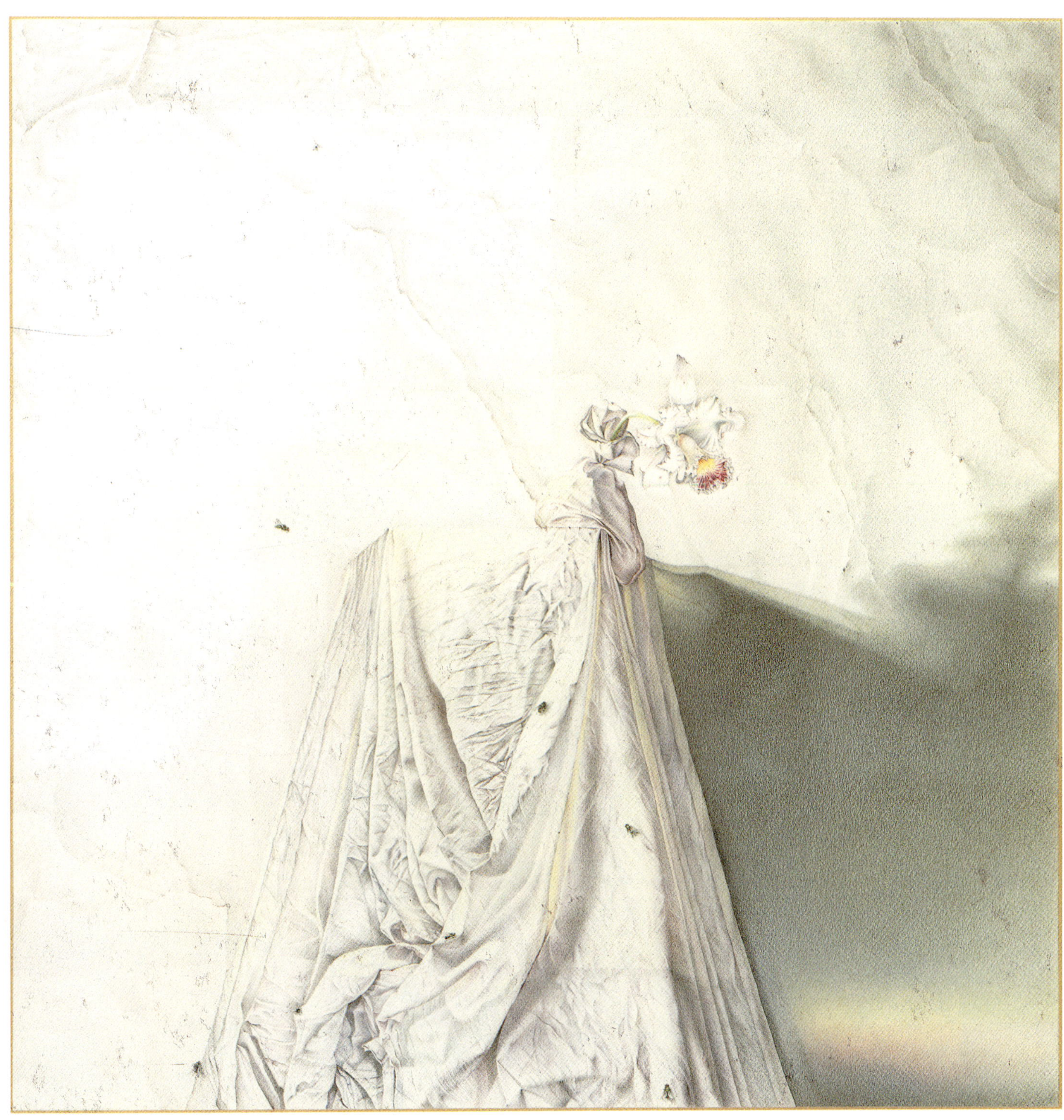

8 *Untitled (Birds)* 1973

Colored pencil on paper, 27½ × 22 inches
Joseph and Lannis Raffael

González dedicated this drawing to the artist Alice Neel, after admiring the psychological penetration and uncompromising honesty of her portraits, though, of course, this drawing bears no stylistic relationship to her work whatsoever. A lofty space is implied here, something like the shadowy interior of a bare, ruined warehouse or cathedral—a place perhaps only partially roofed, since massed birds have claimed a sanctuary here. We do not see the birds directly: we see their shadows. Most of the birds are strung horizontally, like a necklace of beads, across the top of the picture, in contrast to the strong compact vertical of the small niche at the bottom. Within the niche sits a clutch of eggs—emblems of the origin and mystery of being, of creation itself. Perhaps the niche reminds the viewer, too, of the stone ledge with its nest of eggs in René Magritte's soaring, petrified landscape of 1962, *The Domain of Arnheim* (Collection Mme Georgette Magritte, Brussels), a painting loosely inspired by Edgar Allan Poe's tale of the same title, evoking, like González's drawing, a landscape that exists only in the imagination—a dream landscape dominated by the image of the bird. Or perhaps González intended a reference to Francis Bacon's 1966 *Portrait of George Dyer Crouching* (private collection, Caracas), in which Dyer appears as a kind of squatting bird on an indoor diving board, the white oval of an egg below him in the brown nest of a circular sofa.

A zigzagging crack like seamed lightning opens a fissure in the wall over the window arch containing the eggs, possibly prefiguring what is to happen to the eggs beneath. The surface of the drawing is a wall of shadows, informing the viewer indirectly that this is an enclosed inner space inhabited by birds—spirit-messengers in conference. Radiant threads of light trace a mystic web of pattern across the dark lower end of the picture. Here and there within the veins of light, passages of pink occur, like the small pink-purple flowered forms embedded secretively in *Pink Wall,* 1972, an idea González had picked up from Genet's *Our Lady of the Flowers,* where the author observes that even the most dismal and severe part of the whole world is "entwined with marvels."

Only one "real" bird may be directly viewed in this wall of shadow birds. At the top center, a hummingbird shakes a long limp frog to death in its beak, another example in this artist's work of a cloudy, ethereal beauty shot through with the unexpected, even with the ugly—the artist refusing to acknowledge conventional expectations of what constitutes ugliness and beauty. The muzzy, apparitional quality of González's unified surface in any case renders the slightly shocking incident barely perceptible, setting it within the kind of Seurat-influenced life-and-death continuum that would later absorb him in *After Philadelphia,* 1982–84.

In the wall of shadows that functions as a mirror, reflecting birds that must inhabit the viewer's own space, González may also be drawing on childhood memories, when he and his father made shadow-box theaters from empty shoe boxes. González would meticulously cut out cartoon characters, which his father would then illuminate from behind with candlelight, making the cartoon characters spring magically to life. González remembers the intense thrill of staging evenings of shadow-box "movies" for younger cousins. These shadow-box theaters early predisposed him to appreciate the work of Joseph Cornell. In them lay the germ of González's finely crafted, multilayered, and artfully framed symbolist art works, which may often be viewed as tiny curtained theaters of magic—poetic landscapes or dreamscapes mirroring the enigma of his interior self.

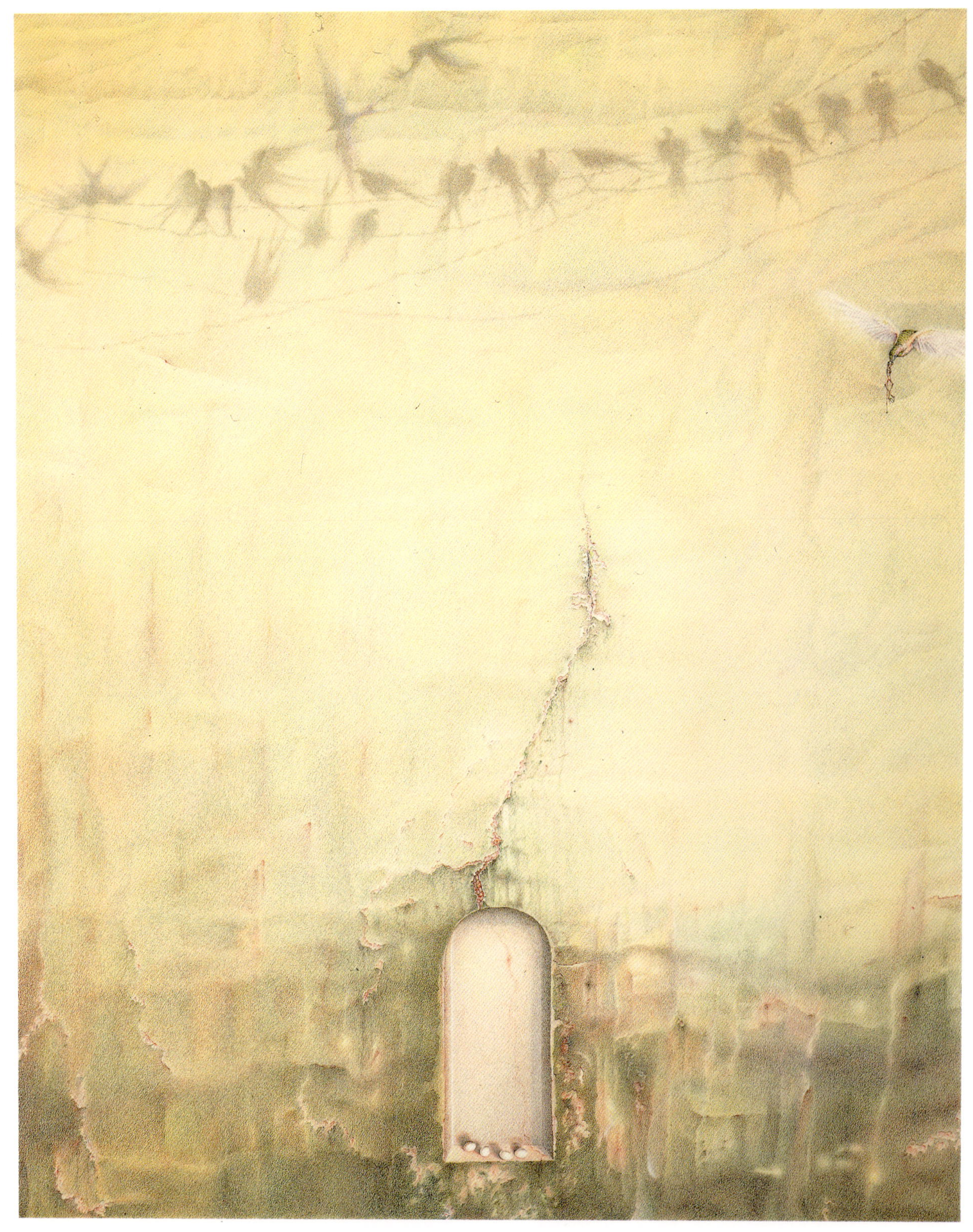

9 *Occupant, Port Authority N.Y.C.* 1973

Colored pencil on paper, 19¼ × 28 inches
Private collection, New York

González was living in New Jersey, traveling into New York several times a week, when he made this image of another radiantly web-veined interior wall—his richest, most painterly drawing yet. González was both fascinated and touched by the Port Authority bus station: "For me, as my entrance to New York, it was excitement. And I noticed these pigeons that were always there, summer and winter. So I made the two pigeons inside as a metaphor. The space inside, occupied by those two pigeons, is kind of exposed, so it's like the exterior space where the buses would let the people down. The pigeons are like the homeless people who hung around the Port Authority—people whose lives moved me, for whom I felt compassion."

The spectral white pigeons are like the white bird of *Hot White Tennessee Williams,* forerunners of the baptismal white bird of *Mar y Espejo* (Sea and Mirror), 1976. Birds in general in González's work, apart from Divine's predatory seagull, are symbols of liberation and ascension: "I think of things that fly as having to do with freedom," says González, who has unusually vivid flying dreams, "with overcoming the pull of gravity and the earth." In Catholic symbolism, the haloed descending dove with wings spread in benediction (looking like González's frontally viewed right-hand pigeon here—a bird that would not be out of place over the head of the Virgin in a fifteenth-century Annunciation painting) is the symbol of the Holy Ghost, the supernatural grace of God, of spirituality in man. González will place this magical bird next to his own figure in *New York, Year 1986* as a symbol of resurrection and redemption.

But González's Holy Ghost of a pigeon has a likely source in the childhood of Pablo Picasso and in Guillaume Apollinaire's poem "The Betrothal," dedicated to Picasso and containing the memorable image of "the pigeon who this evening seemed the Holy Ghost." After his sister Lola was born during a three-day earthquake, the traumatized three-year-old Picasso turned to his father, who encouraged him to sketch the pigeons in the plaza in front of the family apartment, pigeons Picasso's father himself was inordinately fond of painting. Later, terrified of attending school, Picasso was allowed to enter the classroom clutching one of his father's live pigeons—security that his father would return for him at the end of the school day: "To little Pablo, pigeons symbolized the security and protection his father offered against the outside world."[1] To González, pigeons symbolize not only the Holy Ghost but a tender, healing relationship between an unusually supportive, gentle father and a troubled son whose later success and fame in art history are without parallel.

The bus station is depicted as a surreal landscape. The extravagantly textured surface of the Port Authority's windowed wall is purely imaginary, the mass of dark, veined, organic-looking stones a boundary between mundane life (the strand of silhouetted pigeons we glimpse through the light-barred, translucent window) and González's interior space of transition or ritual initiation, embodied in the radiant pigeons the viewer can actually see. Swathed in a length of black lace and set with a softly rendered vase of flowers, a small table stands improbably in a yellow tide, the slabbed Port Authority floor awash in pale-edged waves like ocean surf lapping onto sand. This is magic water, invading the architectural frame as does the dark fluid of *A.M.,* the bus station a dream threshold of transition, the golden site of departure from the old life and rebirth into a new life.

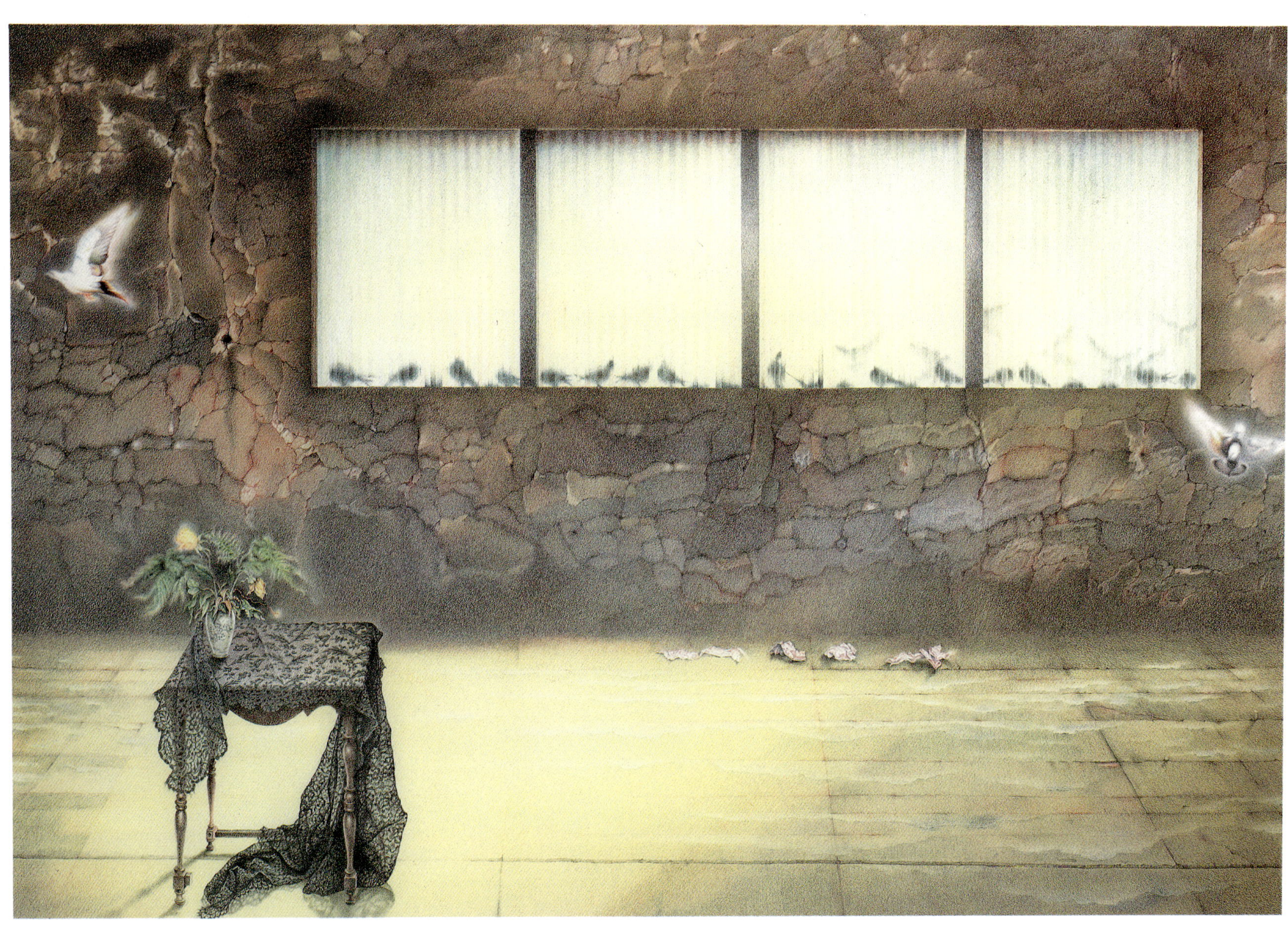

10 *Good Friday* 1974

Colored pencil on paper, 23 × 29 inches
Indianapolis Museum of Art, Roger Wolcott Fund, 74.542

Like Ascension Day, Good Friday is a Catholic holy day. Celebrated two days before Easter Sunday, it commemorates the day on which Christ was crucified and is thought of as "good" because on that day Christ sacrificed himself to redeem humankind.

No birds are apparent in *Good Friday,* yet there is certainly a kind of flight—and the dark form of what might be a tiny bird's nest terminating one strangely thick tree branch in the top left corner of the image. González has meticulously, even obsessively, worked the weather-stained, finely veined pink marble wall (which derives from the wall of the Metropolitan Museum of Art in New York) so that the stone takes on an almost living, pulsating quality. A winged being, a carved angel blowing a trumpet, is moored within the stone—a supernatural entity with the capacity, in González's mind, to bring the wall down: "I was thinking about the walls of Jericho, with people playing music and shouting around them. The drawing is about allowing people into this mysterious space. It's about the power of art, about believing that music can tear down walls." Trumpets and other musical instruments are common angelic accessories in art—but González himself delights in, and often refers to, music and musical instruments, particularly in works dedicated to or involving his older daughter, Maria. His love of music is passionate, and music is part of his daily ritual of working in the studio. The trumpet-playing angel, the first of González's many angels, has an obvious affinity with the artist himself.

The fact that one bar of a window in the prisonlike wall has been wrenched free of its socket and bent aside implies that some kind of escape or breakthrough has occurred, a flight toward freedom. And although the running man, drawn from a photograph of the artist himself, is not literally flying, the radiant twists of colored ribbons fluttering behind his back, intended to look like supernatural wings, certainly are. The attitude of the running man reflects the pose of an angel of Annunciation—bursting in upon the startled young Virgin. These associations create a direct relationship between the carved stone angel embedded in the wall and the liberated artist, flying his bright ribbons of color and satin texture behind him like magic wings.

There is also an affinity between the white bull terrier straining eagerly forward and the flying artist. The white bull terrier subtly quotes Lucian Freud's portrait *Girl with a White Dog,* 1951–52 (Tate Gallery, London), and represents

> the compulsion of the artist. I had never seen those dogs until I got to New York. I had a very close friend who was a photographer, and he had taken a photograph of this actual dog one Good Friday. I was fascinated by them, because I could barely bring myself to look at them. There was something so out-of-proportion and scary-looking about them. And then later, I found out that in Italy they were used as fighting dogs, and people would bet on them, as they bet on fighting cocks in Cuba.

The dog's whiteness, however, is a contradictory sign of grace and mystery—tripled in the three white bull terriers of *La Misa Blanca* (The White Mass). And here the dog is posed beneath an unidentified protuberance on the wall, veiled by a dark cloth, like the shrouded object confronting the sleeping girl in René Magritte's surrealistic *Ordeal of Sleep,* 1926–27 (Museo Civico, Briella, Italy). The white dog and the cloth-covered object both indirectly evoke the hidden presence of a young woman.

Art is González's compulsion, and he himself posed as the flying artist, an angelic intermediary between God and man with a divinely inspired message, his face veiled by his own raised hand, by making repeated short runs across a New York City rooftop in the biting depths of winter, while a friend photographed his ribbon-fledged flight—González feeling compelled to ascend to the freezing roof for a properly elevated imitation of flight, rather than being content to pose in the warmth and privacy of his apartment.

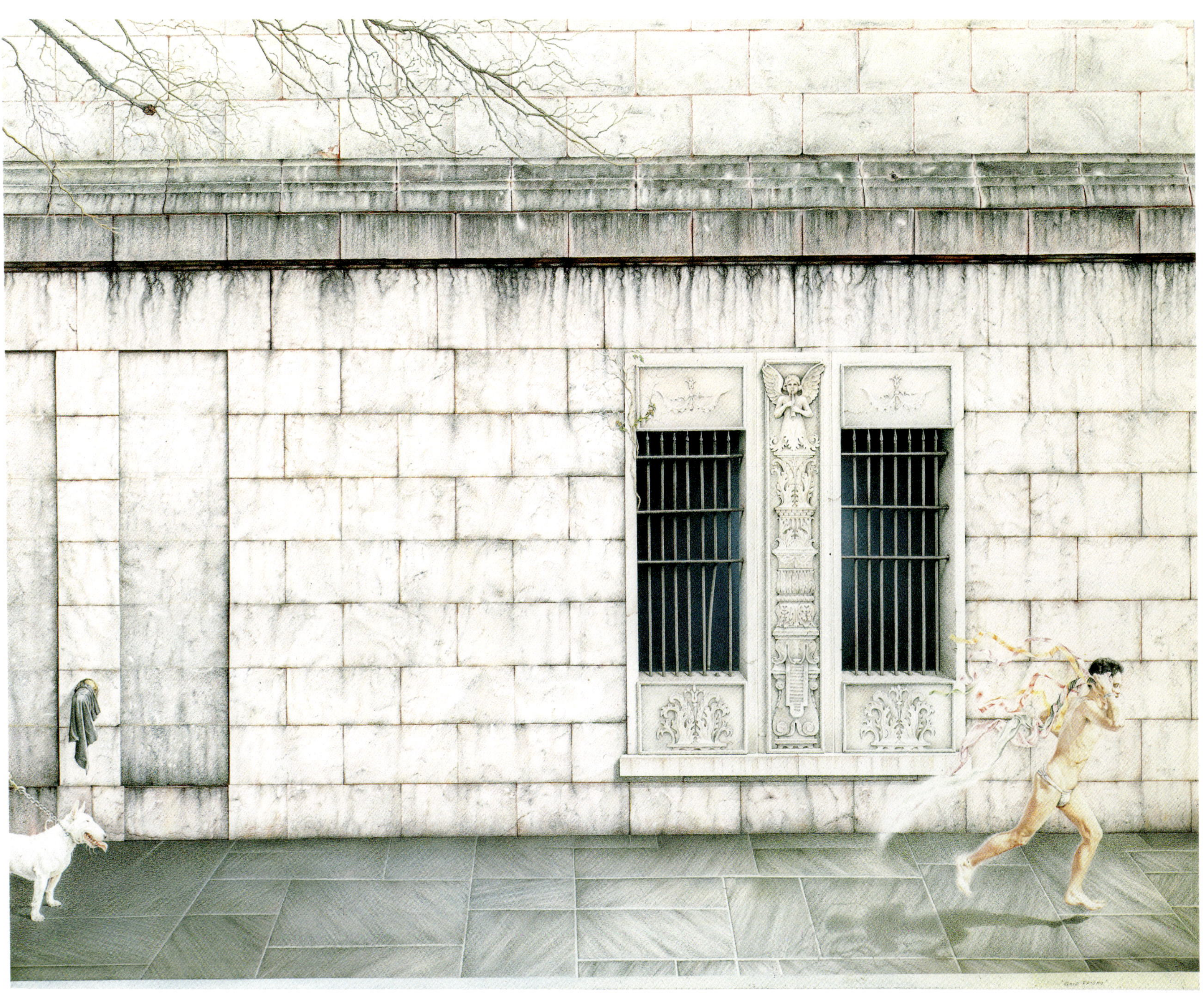

II *Untitled* 1974

Collage and mixed media on museum board, 17 × 20¼ inches
Maria and Daniel Schleifman

González considered this work, the product of an intuitive, collaged reworking of the artist's figure from *Good Friday,* in an attempt to say "something about the playfulness of art," so filled with private meaning that he preferred to keep it for himself. It is a mythic, doubled portrait of himself as Narcissus, and maybe the headless Orpheus too, though the separation of the head from the body may also be exploring the idea of the self divided between spirituality and sensuality.

Narcissus, the beautiful youth who was loved by both men and women yet who heartlessly rejected every suitor, fell in love with his own ungraspable reflection in the waters of a silver pool. Unable to possess his own beautiful image, Narcissus wasted away: "But when they sought his body, they found nothing, / Only a flower with a yellow center / Surrounded with white petals."[1] In the narcissistic vision of a headless self confronting a headless self in playful aggression, González for the first time introduces the idea of the mirror of self-knowledge, an idea he will develop in major works like *Mar y Espejo* (Sea and Mirror), hoping that the viewer will perceive his images "as though in a mirror," as if the image were an actual mirror portraying what exists in the viewer's own space, thereby implicating the viewer in what is happening in the art work.

If the striking narcissism of González's mirrored self is not sufficiently plain, a central element in the collage may settle the matter: the peacock, classic emblem of male beauty and vanity, poised in the window opening of the wall. González borrowed the bird from Ghirlandaio's *Last Supper* (1480), in the refectory of the Ognissanti, Florence. The space these headless figures inhabit derives from a sacred, exclusively male space: "I was thinking about this building in Florence that I really love," says González, "where Fra Angelico lived, San Marco. I was fascinated by the monks' cells, which were tiny, all painted that cream color, with this band of terracotta near the floor that enveloped the room and went up around the windows."

Why are the mirrored figures headless? A separation between the head and the body, and the disembodied head that is an obsessive theme of symbolist artists like Odilon Redon, will turn out to be a recurrent feature of González's work. Like Herbert Marcuse in *Eros and Civilization,* González associates Narcissus with the poet Orpheus, torn limb from limb by the women he had spurned, whose severed head, still magically alive and singing, floated on the poet's lyre down the Hebrus River and into the sea, where it traveled to the island of Lesbos, forever after celebrated as a source of music and lyricism. To Marcuse, Narcissus and Orpheus reflect one another. "The classical tradition associates Orpheus with the introduction of homosexuality," writes Marcuse, and Orpheus like Narcissus rejects

> the normal Eros, not for an ascetic ideal, but for a fuller Eros. Like Narcissus, he [Orpheus] protests against the repressive order of procreative sexuality. . . . Orpheus and Narcissus reveal a new reality, with an order of its own, governed by different principles. The Orphic Eros transforms being: he masters cruelty and death through liberation. His language is *song,* and his work is *play*. Narcissus' life is that of *beauty,* and his existence is *contemplation*. These images refer to the *aesthetic dimension* as the one in which their reality principle must be sought and validated.[2]

González's work is most comprehensible in terms of an Orphic Eros, a new reality on an aesthetic plane. Here in the narcissistic mirroring of his opposing selves, the artist enacts an ambivalent drama, transforming his own figure from *Good Friday* into something like the fighting men locked together in the second-century B.C. Greek sculpture of the *Wrestlers* at the Uffizi in Florence, or Francis Bacon's *Two Figures,* 1953 (private collection, England), a painting that memorably converts Eadweard Muybridge's photographs from about 1885 of wrestlers from *The Human Figure in Motion* into two men on a bed.

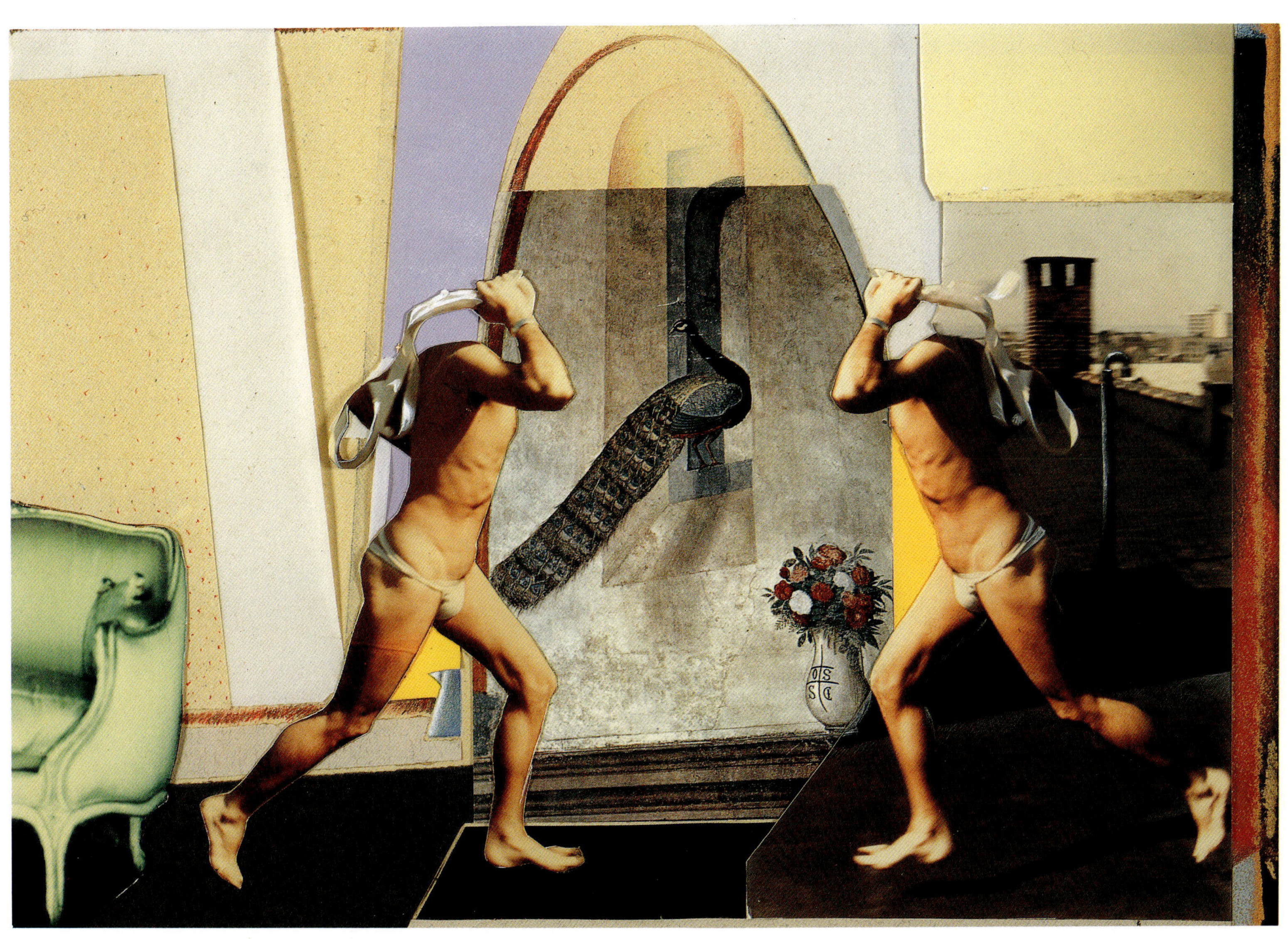

12 *The Sparrow and the Maiden* 1975

Colored pencil on paper, 24¼ × 39¼ inches
Mr. and Mrs. E. W. Nash, San Francisco

Like *Hot White Tennessee Williams* and *Occupant, Port Authority N.Y.C.* this drawing features a bird—or rather a *pair* of birds—in an interior space. Here, though, the bird has entered a frame-within-a-frame and, Narcissus-like, is trapped in an embrace with its own image as it flutters against the reflecting surface of a mirror. By this time González had thoroughly immersed himself in Flemish painting and had become aware of the concept of the painting as mirror, having closely studied and admired artists like Jan van Eyck.

From the white blank of the paper, González conjures forth a mysterious stage set, with elegantly minimal touches of the pencil constructing another wall, this time with a variety of openings onto a mysterious beyond: closet doors (the one on the right, like the door of *A. M.,* offering seductive rainbow glints of color in its depths); a reflected door on the other side of the room visible only in the mirror; and the ambivalent frame of the mirror, which might possibly be construed as the frame of a picture within this picture.

Like a cutout character from the shadow-box theaters of González's youth, a headless bride-doll appears—in real life a Barbie doll whose golden head had dropped off (the doll had been discarded by one of González's daughters). This headless bride, who surely bears some relationship to the headless artist/angel pair of the previous plate, is for González "a beautiful contradiction," reminiscent of the veiled self-portrait of 1973 and anticipating the veiled headless brides of *Mar y Espejo* (Sea and Mirror), 1976, and *Así que Pasen Cinco Años/When Five Years Pass,* 1991. The headless bride represents for the artist "veiled beauty and mystery, a miracle or an apparition. The viewer is denied the chance ever to see her face. She is a glowing spirit moving through the room—an announcing angel, which is why you see an aura around her, interrupting the baseboard behind her." Ultimately, she will become the bride veiled in dazzling light of *A Bride for Lorca* in 1992, revealing her source in the work of González's favorite poet.

This white room is based on a room González used for a studio in his New Jersey apartment. The room appears to be empty and white, yet it is full of tiny, bloodying touches of red, lending the piece a pearly pinkness. The mirror theme is extended to the floor, which partially reflects the mirror framing the bird. The ceiling of graphite suffused with rose holds a series of what González thinks of as "black pearls, burned-out light bulbs incapable of giving much light," studded across the top of the drawing like the stage lights of a theater. González remembers associating these lights with the lights recessed into New York subway entrances but also with bulbs in paintings by Francis Bacon.

He took the trapped-bird image from a scientific book on ornithology. This particular specimen, actually an enlarged image of a sparrow, derives from a photograph of a bird caught in a net trap. In odd places around the drawing, tiny salamanders appear, included, says González, "because I had a revulsion to them. They're creatures of the dark, so they add a necessary darkness to the drawing." The salamanders bring to the art work the essential element of the unexpected, a mystery and a perverse beauty, a layer of real and wild life.

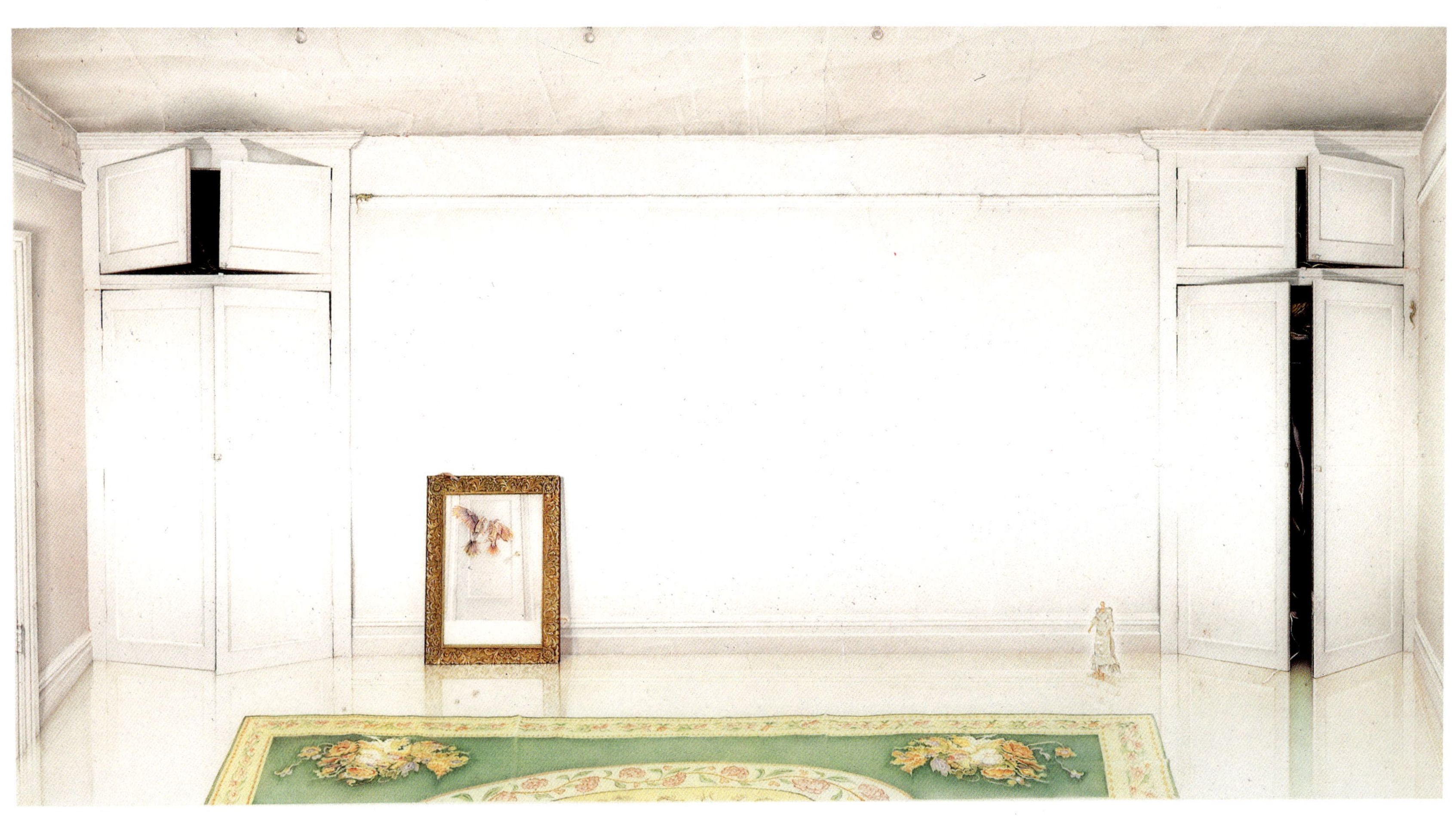

13 *Flor y Media* 1974

Watercolor and colored pencil on paper, 14 × 10 inches
Robert and Eva Vidor

The title *Flor y Media* (Flower and a Half) plays with the double meaning of the Spanish word *media,* which translates as both "men's socks" and "a half." So the title may be understood simply as "flower and sock" or as "flower and a half" (as in, "That's some kind of *super* flower"). González intended to signal that this was no ordinary still life. It is certainly true that most still lifes are not arranged, as this one is, on the gleaming porcelain lid of a toilet tank.

The flower jar, once a perfume bottle, holds a single spiked pink flower, whose bloom is mirrored in the rayed glass at the base of the bottle and doubled again in the spidery shadow on the bathroom wall. González used the perfume bottle as a traditional attribute of the Virgin, as a symbol of her Immaculate Conception. The uterine-shaped bottle is a well-known womb symbol in art. Perhaps the rather human-looking shadow cast by the bottle, crowned by the rayed halo of the flower-head shadow, may be interpreted as a Narcissus reference, the man who, dying, changed into a flower. Above the toilet tank hangs something ambiguous and rippling—a window blind, though it may also connote the blank space of an absent image, a mystery-laden picture within a picture.

The drama and beauty of the drawing lie in its imaginative contrasts: the antiseptic cleanliness of the bathroom and the seductive, velvety blackness of the soiled sock; the agitated surface of the window blind and the glacially calm surfaces of the toilet tank, the bottle of water, and the wall. *Flor y Media* is so limpid, so expressive of the watery context of the bathroom, that it is almost impossible to believe that these gentle yet dynamic effects were in the main achieved with the sharp pencils of an increasingly dexterous draftsman.

The spiked pale pink bloom in a predominantly pale blue space recalls the single chrysanthemums of Piet Mondrian, rendered in graphite, charcoal, and watercolor. Dating mostly from around 1908, these flower studies are evidence to some critics of an unexpected and hidden sensuality in the famously repressed and ascetic artist; to others, a symbolist statement about time and suffering and spirituality. González exploits all these associations and further pairs his Mondrian-inspired flower with its own slanted shadow-reflection, as he had doubled his own *Good Friday* figure in the headless pair of *Untitled* (1974).

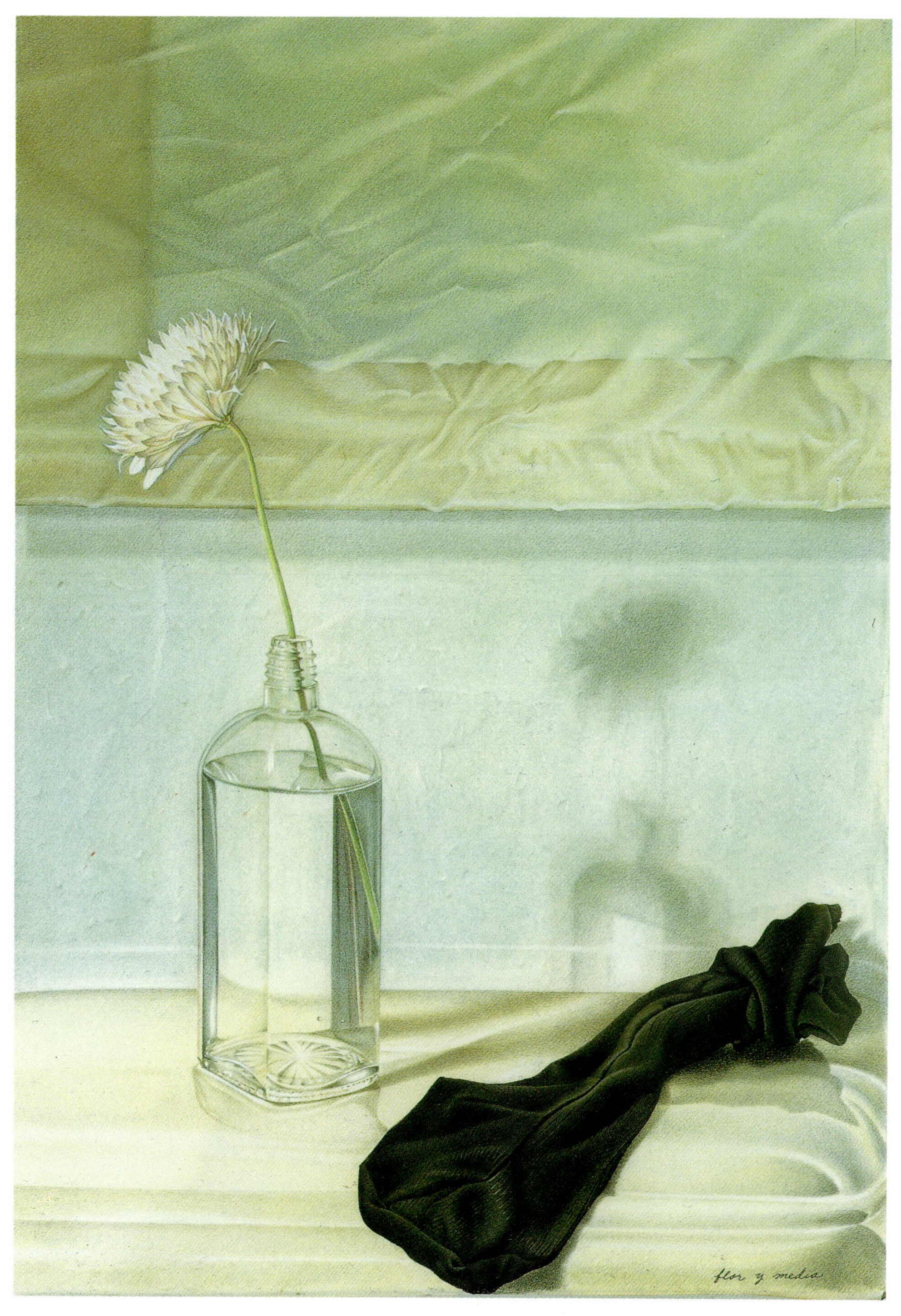
flor y media

14 *La Misa Blanca* 1974

Colored pencil on paper, 25 × 35¾ inches
Private collection

The sky of *La Misa Blanca* (The White Mass) is a celebratory mystery, a visionary veil or sheet (González took a hint from Robert Rauschenberg's 1955 disheveled *Bed* [Museum of Modern Art, New York], using a folded bed sheet for his model), ripe with poetic and symbolic significance, embodying both concealment and revelation—a curtain raised over the artist's private theater of art, faith, sex, and dream. The squared cloth registers the artist's excitement over the intense realism of Raphaelle Peale's *Venus Rising from the Sea—A Deception,* from 1823 (Nelson-Atkins Museum of Art, Kansas City, Missouri). Peale's illusionistic rendering of a cloth that prudishly covers the nakedness of the Venus, which he had borrowed from James Barry's rather more daring 1772 original, *Venus Rising from the Sea* (Municipal Gallery of Modern Art, Dublin), was intended to suggest that the only nude acceptable to prim Philadelphians was a heavily veiled one, innocuously displaying one arm and foot. González's ocean veil, raised over a view of the sea from Fire Island, is a more imposing affair than Peale's, though González had been charmed by the resemblance of Peale's illusionistic cloth to an overscaled handkerchief, concealing a miniature doll behind its folds and creases.

Perhaps the most startling element of this masterly drawing occurs in the colored pencils—a reference to the artist—which stab the sheet like knives from both sides, illusionistically penetrating the flat surface of the picture in two directions. The ferociously sharp, extended points of the pencils are no exaggeration, but completely realistic: "I always prepared my pencils like that," says González, "so I could get into the groove of the paper."

La Misa is the Spanish term for the Mass. A *Misa blanca,* or "white Mass"—the grandest, most stirring Mass—would be held at Christmas, Easter, the Ascension, and some saints' days, the altar and vestments in breathtaking cream or gold. The white bull terrier from Lucian Freud's *Girl with a White Dog* is repeated here in a Holy Trinity of whiteness, drawing the viewer's attention to the white ocean veil over the pink sea and emphasizing whiteness in this work. White is worn during Catholic sacraments as the outward, visible sign of inward, spiritual grace. The color of virgin saints and veiled brides, whiteness signifies purity and holiness, as the waters of baptism promise cleansing and rebirth. González's ocean veil specifically implies purification, since the artist was thinking of the purificator, the linen napkin used to cleanse the chalice, and the veil that covers the chalice after the sacrificial rite of the Eucharist, the partaking of the Body and Blood of Christ, which is the center of the Catholic Mass.

But as Charles Rycroft in *The Innocence of Dreams* points out, in dream symbolism the blank white sheet filled with light is akin to the mystic's vision of "nothingness," or to Freud's "oceanic" state, engendered by fantasies of fusion with the breast of the mother.[1] A deeper, more "oceanic" image than González has created here with his ocean veil can scarcely be imagined—a dream of water as mysterious as that envisaged in Edgar Allen Poe's *Narrative of Arthur Gordon Pym,* with its mystical white region and white creatures beyond "the vapory *white* curtain of the South." While completing this drawing, González had a brush with death on this ocean. The fallen flower, an impatiens, to the right of the central pencil in the veil depicts a real flower that drifted onto the drawing, part of a gift bouquet from a concerned friend following the day González could easily have been lost at sea, July 11, 1974.

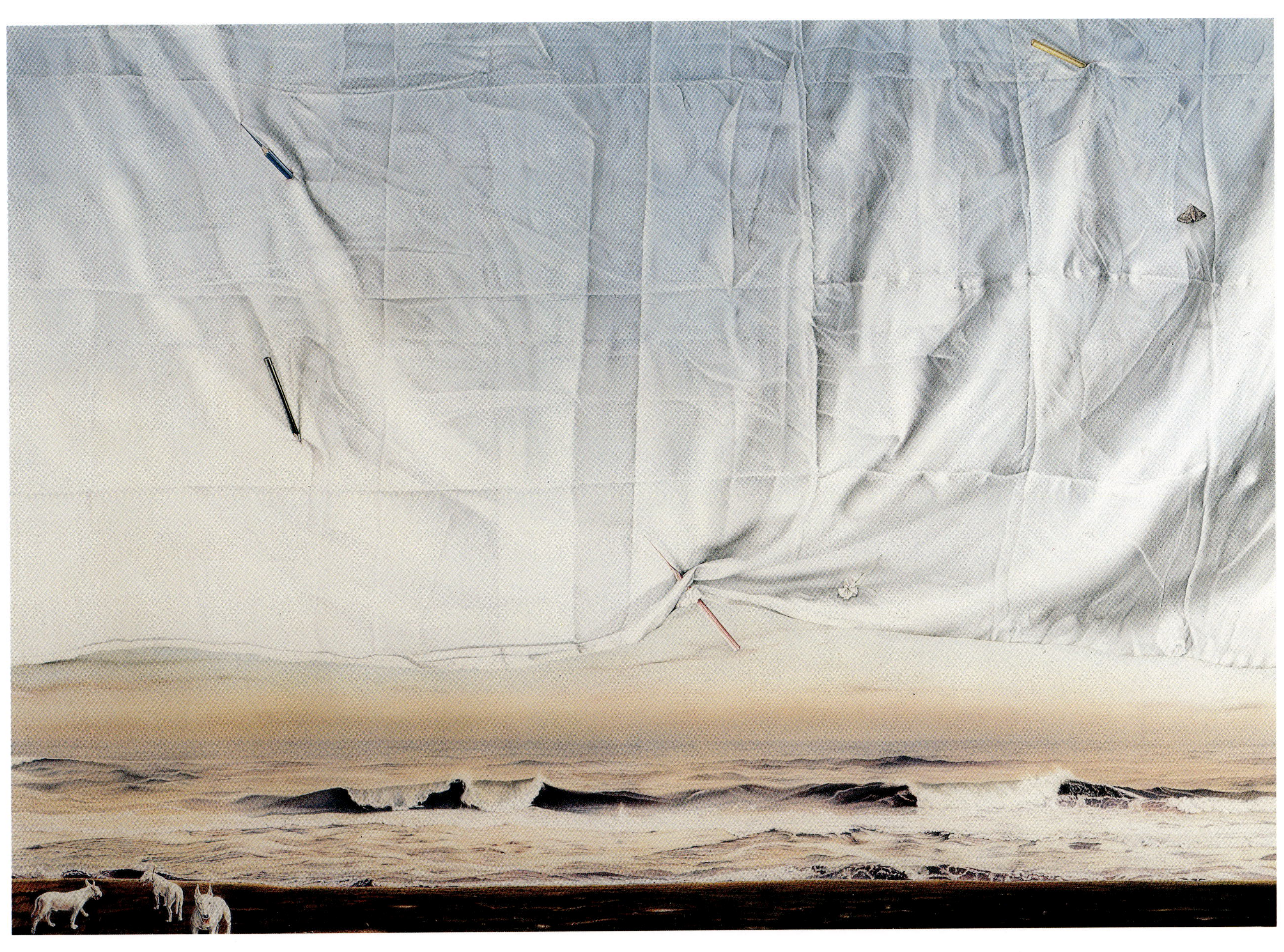

15 *July 11, 1974* 1974

Colored pencil and pastel on paper, 25½ × 19½ inches
Collection of Wally Goodman

González worked for the first time with pastels (sharpened almost to the needle point of the colored pencils, though the honing process was even more difficult to manage with pastels) for the exquisitely drawn and colored *July 11, 1974,* undoubtedly attracted to the medium by the fact that symbolist artists such as Odilon Redon and Fernand Khnopff had often used pastels.

González made this spectacular drawing after he returned from a day of being literally at the mercy of the ocean off Fire Island. While finishing *La Misa Blanca* (The White Mass), he was persuaded by friends to take a day off and go down to the beach. Lazing in the waves on a small white plastic inflatable raft, he suddenly found himself being swept out to sea:

> I couldn't manipulate the raft because the current was so strong. This happened around ten in the morning, and I didn't get back home until around seven in the evening. I was in international waters, on the high seas. It was like a roller coaster: the waves were *huge.* A helicopter would come, and then disappear again. They were telling me not to do anything, to just be calm, they would find a ship to come and get me. And the raft was so small I couldn't even stretch my legs out. The day before I had seen the Bergman film *The Seventh Seal;* and in the Sunday papers, I had read about a shark-fishing competition, how they'd caught about three hundred sharks here. So this drawing is all about what I was feeling when I thought that I was going to die. I remember the irony of being on the beach one moment, and bathing—then all of a sudden thinking, "I'm going to *die,*" and I looked back at the beach, and there were all these people suntanning themselves. Before I left the beach I'd been telling this friend about how I'd like to make some pictures of clouds to give to friends. Everything in the drawing is a memory of what happened on that day.

González intended the square black recess beneath the casually open chest of drawers to symbolize a gateway into the mystery of death. The drawer pulled out toward the viewer and the white-curtained black passage below it, leading the viewer into the illusionistic black hole in the flat plane of the picture, are dramatically effective.

The profusion of butterflies in the work might seem to be an unlikely surreal or symbolist embellishment, yet it is rooted in reality. González remembers butterfly migrations lasting at least two days before he was almost lost at sea: "They were everywhere. It was a real phenomenon. But still I'm using them here as symbols of metamorphosis and resurrection, of beauty and flying." There are willfully sinister touches in the drawing. One butterfly seems to have become entangled in an odd fold within the right-hand spill of cloth. Another butterfly has been half-concealed by the Magritte-like sky picture taped to the cracked white wall—a picture-within-a-picture contrasting inside and outside, the black hole and infinite space.

A red gladiolus, upside down in the rose-tinged vase, so that it appears to be bleeding and drowning simultaneously, provocatively converts another of Mondrian's flower studies, the *Red Gladioli,* ca. 1906 (Ruth and Bruce Dayton), to González's purposes. Even the Magritte-style wood-grained chest of drawers seems calculated to rouse memories of swelling waves with unimaginable depths.

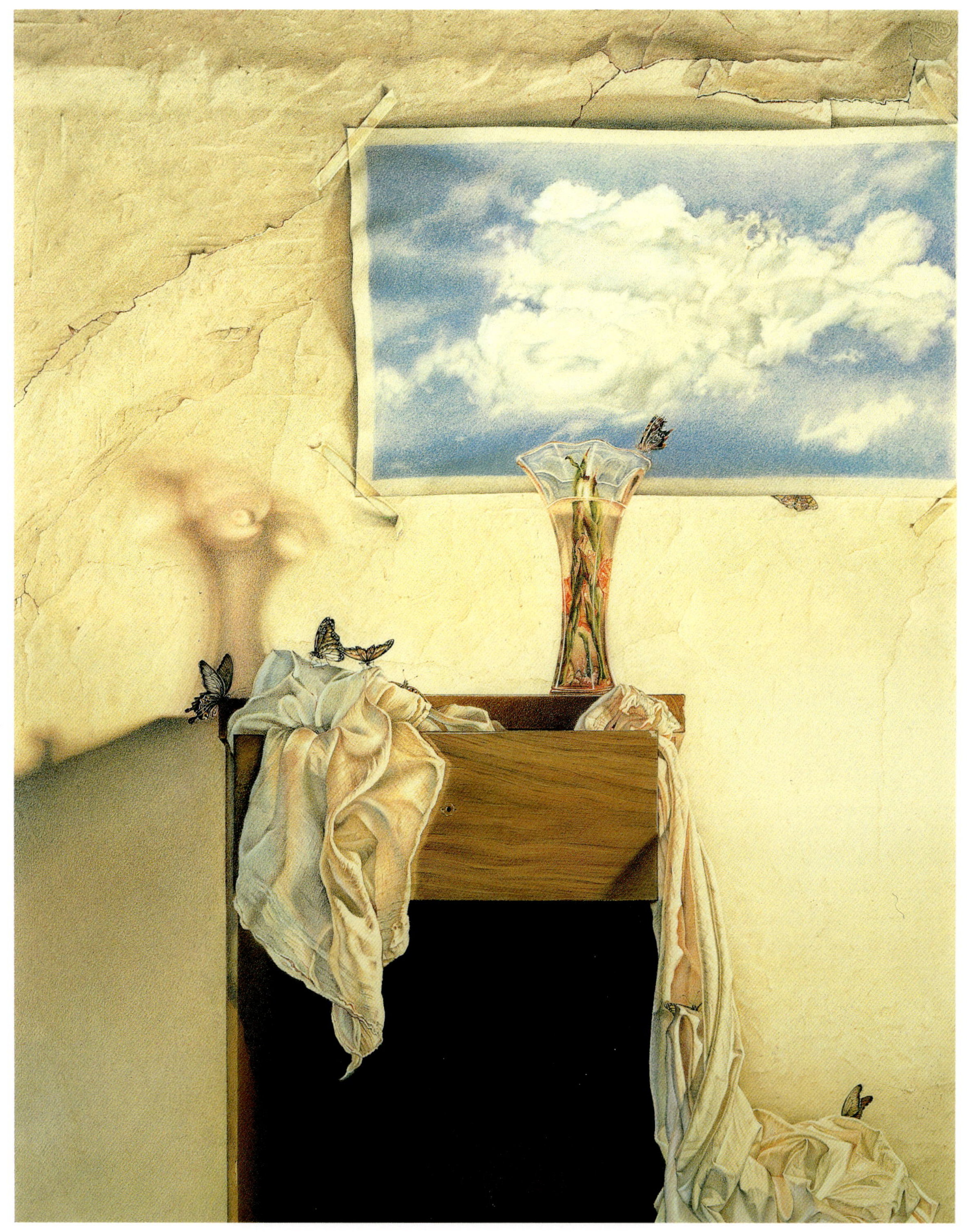

16 *Cuatro Pilares* 1975

Watercolor and colored pencil on paper, 15¼ × 17 inches
Teresa and Larry Katz

González began this drawing in a despondent mood. It represents a safe haven in a barren landscape. The exotic, baroque quality of the drawing, so different from anything else appearing on the New York art scene at that time, had the revitalizing effect of suggesting significant new directions for his art—directions in tune with his Spanish heritage and the baroque religious art that had surrounded him in youth.

The lamp from *Hot White Tennessee Williams* is repeated four times here, referring to the four corners of this wall-less room (a change from the period when González painted and drew almost nothing but walls), and to the "four pillars" of González's favorite childhood prayer—the four saints John, Peter, Martin, and Matthew being symbolized by the four corner posts or "pillars" of his Cuban bed. As a child, González was "fascinated by that prayer," completely subscribing to its efficacy as a prayer of protection, a magical invocation to ensure the safety of the sleeping child within the enchanted night space of the bed. Even today the theme of the magically protected sleeper or dreamer is profoundly appealing to this artist.

The figure in the floral Asian dressing gown, his back to the viewer, ushering us into the arid Tanguy-like landscape, is González himself, nursing a bandaged broken hand. He uses this figure viewed from behind again in *Nacimiento/Nativity,* 1979, *Songs for My Father,* 1980, *Roma,* 1985, *New York, Year 1986,* and *Rembrandt's Hands, Vermeer's Frame and the Passing of the Moth,* 1990. It is a favorite device, practically a signature, borrowed from an artist he greatly admires, Caspar David Friedrich (though, of course, González had also internalized Magritte's mysterious bowler-hatted men viewed from behind). Like González today, Friedrich was obsessed with symbolism and with death. In paintings such as *Traveler Looking over the Sea of Fog,* ca. 1818 (Kunsthalle, Hamburg), Friedrich depicts figures viewed from behind, engrossed in pantheistic portents of a radiant hereafter. Friedrich suffered bouts of gloom and madness until he died of a stroke in 1835, yet his paintings seem cheerfully reassuring compared with the bleak prospect that assails the viewer in *Cuatro Pilares.*

There is, however, the important protection of the four pillars. And the near-symmetrical twigs at the upper corners of the drawing, meant to evoke skeletons, also create an effect of theater, lending the scene an air of fantasy and transforming the artist into an actor. The parched landscape, expressing an unassuageable thirst, is based on a photograph of a drought in Nevada. The fearful whippet slinking around the antique couch was the artist's dog at this time, Papel: the name means "paper" in Spanish. "The reason I put Papel in the drawing," says González, "is because he seemed to reflect the way that I was feeling myself."

Water, usually so prevalent one way or another in the work of González, is present here only as dramatic absence. There is no "mirror," no reflected companion for this solitary Narcissus, excepting the dog with the blank, white name, Paper. In retrospect, the work uncannily prefigures the late series of González on this same couch, posing as the doomed Young Man, wounded by love, in *Así que Pasen Cinco Años/When Five Years Pass.* The figure viewed from behind is as elusive and mysterious as the veiled face of the masked self-portrait *Untitled* from 1973.

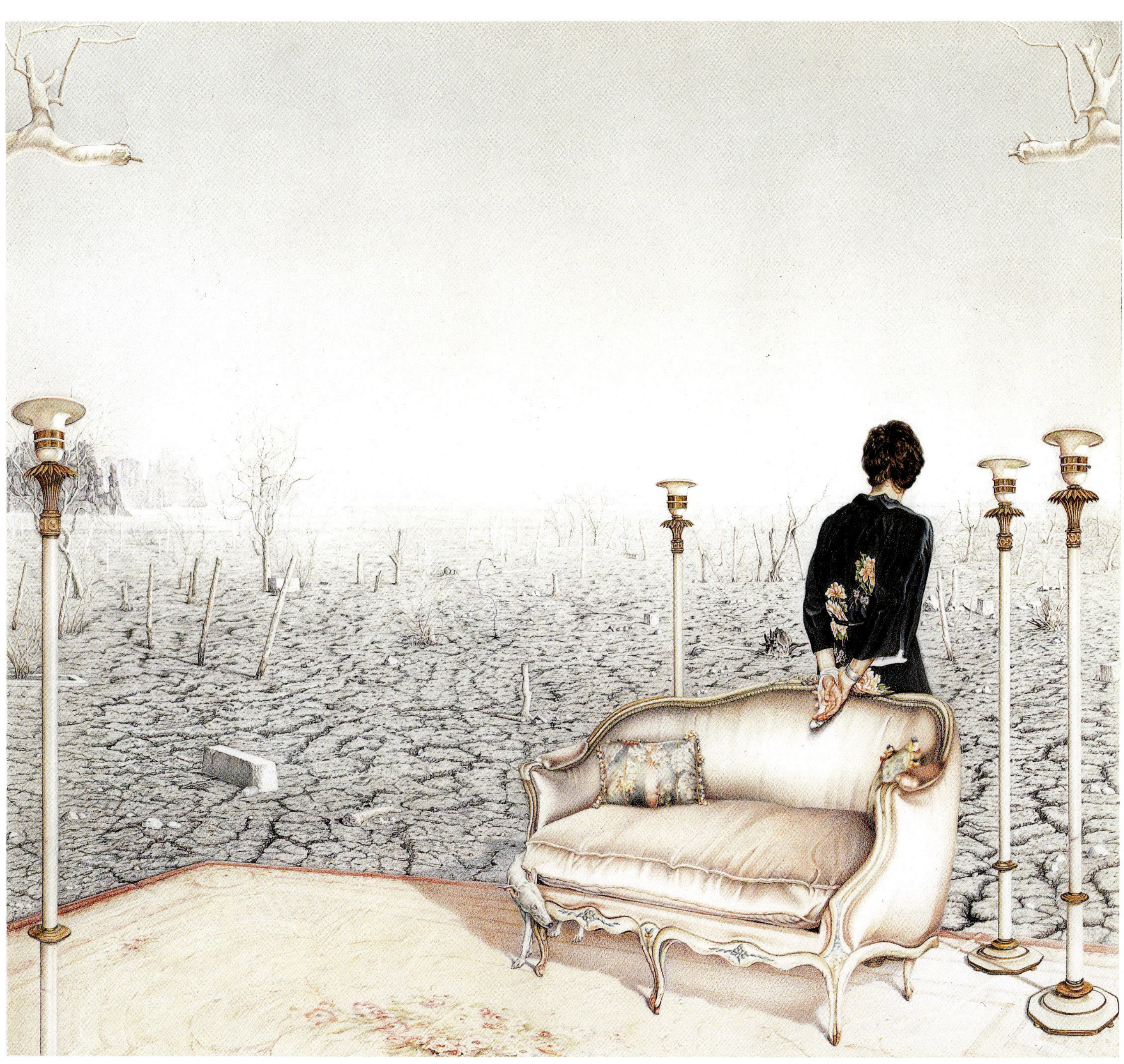

17 *Teresa* 1976

Colored pencil on paper, 5¾ × 5 inches
Teresa and Larry Katz

Teresa is a miniature portrait that represents a major breakthrough for González, his first attempt to capture the starry feminine beauty that had obsessed him in childhood drawings. After years of making idealized tourist portraits on Miami Beach, then undergoing formal art schooling, González had felt that he would never again be able to draw a portrait, "because all those years of trying to make people the way they *wanted* to look had cut me off from the real essence of drawing, which is to capture whatever you have in front of you."

At the same time, his daughters were growing up fast. González decided to attempt a birthday portrait for his younger daughter as she turned eleven—hence the eleven candles ranged in front of the girl. This work inaugurates the most joyful series of works in the artist's oeuvre, the portraits of his two daughters, who became the focus of his obsession with the perfect female face. Like González's first large painting, an untitled pop-art Venus in 1969, *Teresa* loosely quotes from Sandro Botticelli's *Birth of Venus,* ca. 1486 (Uffizi, Florence). Teresa's long tendrils of hair are whipped by sea breezes, and a shower of tiny roses is supplied by a patterned wallpaper behind the girl's head. Symbolic of Venus/Aphrodite (González further explores Teresa's pagan goddess qualities in the magnificent *Teresa en Verde* [Teresa in Green], 1985), the roses are also a reference by the artist to his daughter's fiery emotional nature, to the sparks he visualized flying around this volatile young woman.

The girl's sweater appears to be knit with thin tongues of flame, which have nothing to do with the birthday candles below, according to González, who loves to frustrate conventional expectations. The flames of the sweater are meant to symbolize the inner fire of Teresa, her zestful life force. The eighth candle appears to have lost its wick, signifying that González had left his home and family the year his daughter turned eight. The missing wick turns up between the last two candles—not gone for good, just blown a little distance away.

This magical miniature portrait bears the unmistakable influence of another of González's favorite artists, Joseph Cornell. It is placed inside a fairly deep white frame, made after González had experimented with sections of colored cardboard. The frame transforms the portrait into a small but substantial white box coming fully three inches off the wall. It becomes, moreover, a canopied box because of the trompe-l'oeil window blind, which, on the imaginative level at least, may be pulled down to protect the girl inside (the blind-pulling device is visible in the drawing). So this miniature portrait is a kind of guarded reliquary or shrine, possessing magical powers to protect its subject, as the four-poster bed protected González in childhood. And the making of the art work becomes a petition on behalf of a loved one, a conscious prayer. As González himself says: "I wanted to make a little shrine for her, and get the feeling that you could pull down the blind if she was in trouble or something. In any case, *compositionally* I always feel the need to separate the image from the viewer."

By separating the image from the viewer and emphasizing the physical nature of the art object itself, diminishing its pictorial illusionism, González transports the viewer's consciousness from the visual world into a realm of mystical ideas, a sacred inner space.

The candles and the faint grid continuing the parallels of the candles behind the girl's head imply for González the barred window of a prison, though the grid may also remind us of the *velo,* or reticulated net of Alberti, designed to place the forehead, nose, cheeks, and chin of the portrait subject accurately within parallel threads or lines.[1] In the curious vocabulary of González, being behind a barred window can mean being in a good, safe place—a protective enclosure. The chief mystery of the drawing, though, is that Teresa's wild hair does not appear to be confined within the same space as her shoulders and head. She is, like the free-spirited artist/angel of *Good Friday,* joyfully breaking out of her windowed wall, her magic mirror, or shrine.

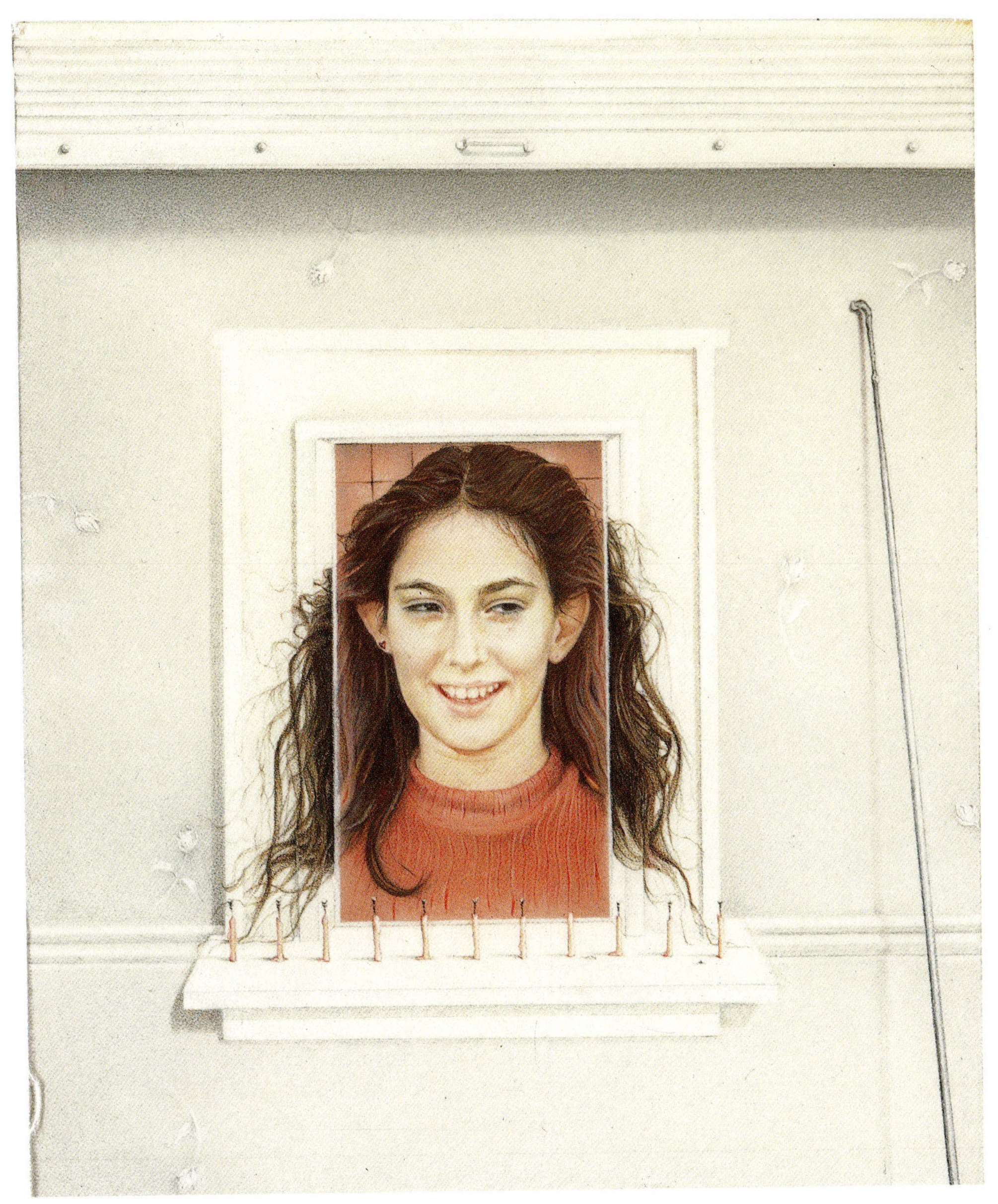

18 *Portrait of a Lady* 1976

Colored pencil on paper, 10¼ × 8 inches
Private collection, New York

Portrait of a Lady is an Ingres-influenced study from life of the mother of a friend: a concentrated drawing at the center of a sheet of paper, the subject contained and lightly framed by the soft contours of an armchair. The woman in the portrait was in crisis when González drew her, which explains the look of burned-out, dull-eyed suffering she wears. As his drawing *Hot White Tennessee Williams* indicates, González has always felt a keen sympathy for and identification with emotional vulnerability and instability. He made this drawing of a woman facing unbearable stress because, he says, "She had had such a rough life that I wanted to see how I could help her. She was divorced and lonely, with few friends. Dealing with the breakdown was tough. She was like somebody lost at sea." The drawing was an attempt to reach through the woman's blankness, and embrace her.

When he was a young man, newly exiled from Cuba and speaking barely a word of English, the only job González had been able to find in America was as warder of forty patients at Knoxville's Eastern State Hospital for the mentally ill, where he became

> very attached to the patients. I saw that the other warders could be cruel and mean—not just to the patients, but also to me. The patients seemed, by comparison with the warders, more gentle and less suspicious of me, so I developed friendships with some of them. But since I was one of the newer warders, I was made responsible for the electric-shock treatments of all the patients on my ward. I would have to hold patients down with a couple of other guys, and that was the most horrible part of my job. It was like being in a torture chamber: the *pain* you would see these people going through! I worked there for about eight or nine months, and it was a valuable lesson for me. I'd led a very sheltered life in Cuba. In Knoxville I learned about unkindness and injustice. There was a real innocence and nobility about a lot of the patients there. But it worried me, because I felt that the patients seemed to be the *normal* ones, and for me as a nineteen-year-old that was a really scary perception.

With an expressed intention of achieving an image that would be "humble, but intense," González depicts the exhausted face and figure of his friend's distressed mother, carefully placing her halfway between the shadow and the light, a real-life *Madre Dolorosa,* or Sorrowing Virgin.

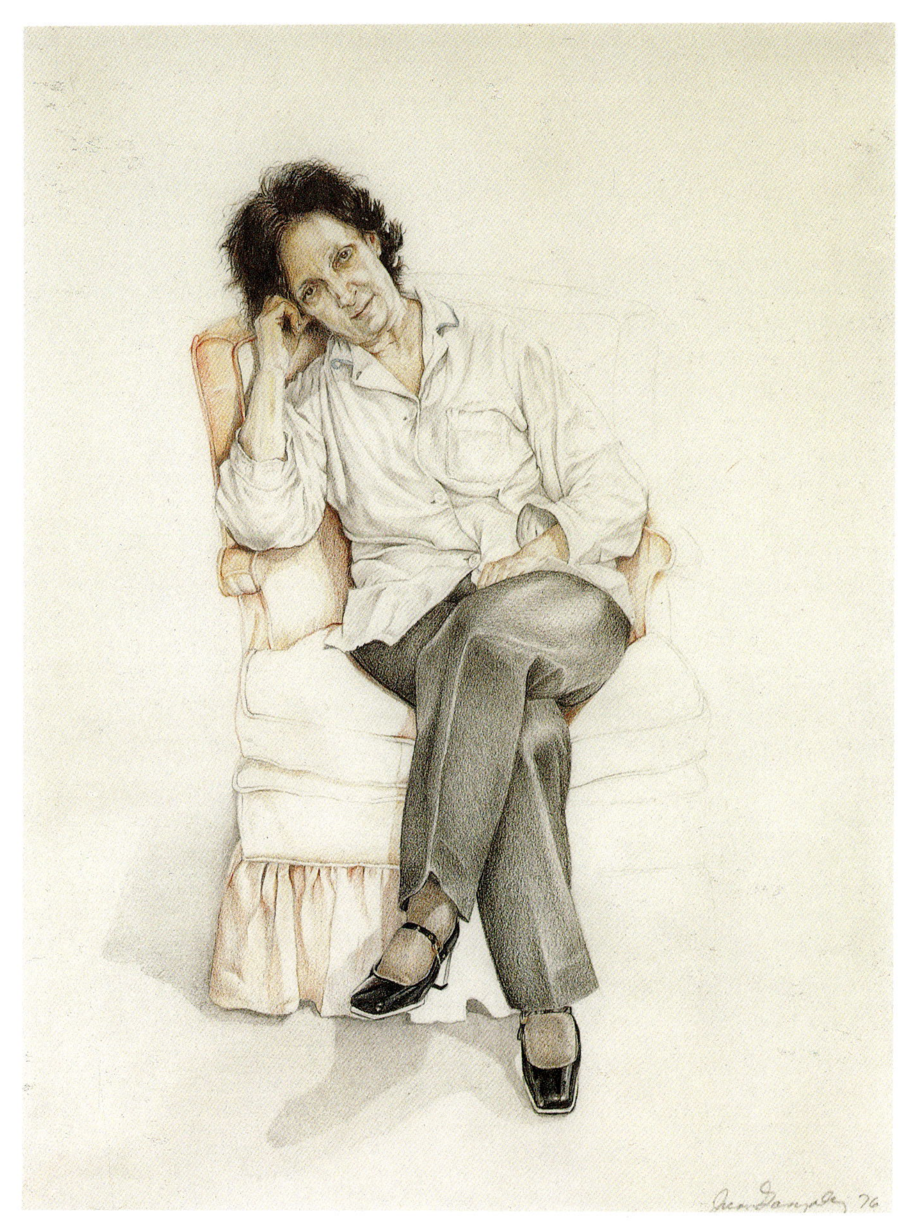

19a *Mar y Espejo* 1976

Watercolor, colored pencil, and pastel on paper, 28 × 20¼ inches
Private collection, New York

A symphonic, tripartite drawing that occupied González for a full sixteen months, *Mar y Espejo* (Sea and Mirror) draws on the colors and contours of the beach at Fire Island. The artist had noticed that the sea created an actual ledge of sand with a sharp edge, a steeply cut drop of five or six inches, which suggested to his eye the edge of a theater stage. He photographed this ledge and then enlarged it to create the enclosing wall of sand at the back of this triptych. He had become fixated on the ledge of sand because it reminded him of the rocky ledge in the foreground of Giovanni Bellini's *Transfiguration,* ca. 1475–80 (Museo di Capodimonte, Naples). González repeats the ledge in more rational scale at the edge of the sea, reoccupying the space it derived from, its curve forming a mirror reflection between the first and third panels of the triptych.

The three sections of this triptych are presented as panels of a mirror by means of an ingenious trompe-l'oeil beveled edge. The triptych, González is announcing, is the mirror of the artist's mind—his fears, loves, and dreams; his past, present, and future; beginning, middle, and end. The trompe-l'oeil beveled edges were modeled after a bathroom mirror with cracked edges González used at his New Jersey apartment.

The title of the triptych, *Mar y Espejo,* touches again on the myth of Narcissus, reflected in water, falling in love with his own likeness. Compounding ambiguities, González sets each of the beveled mirrors on a black trompe-l'oeil ledge containing objects that appear to be reflected in it. The triptych is exhibited on a *real* ledge of watery green glass, designed to exploit further the artist's vision of water and mirror as magical pools of self-reflection and self-knowledge. In front of this first mirror panel three birthday candles sit on the black ledge, implying that the sculpted boy on the beach is three years old.

What is the viewer to make of the stone boy with his strangely smiling *live* face, protectively turning away from the long-necked bird, a chained Cerberus beneath him, and the lilies growing around him in the sand dunes, one of them glass-stemmed? The impossible union of opposites implied by flowers growing in sand derives from González's favorite poet, Federico García Lorca. The flowers were not lilies, though they were certainly white: "Sand of the burning South / Seeking white camellias," wrote Lorca in the agonized poem "The Guitar."[1] In "Memento," the poet speaks of burying the dead moon "in a chalk-white rose . . . with a bright glass stalk."[2]

González's stone boy is a metaphor for himself in a Cuban childhood where he felt fundamentally displaced. He is mounted on a chained Cerberus—suggesting to the viewer that his childhood was a heroic struggle, that he has been to the gates of hell and back. But the drawing would also seem to reflect the artist's ongoing fascination with the work of Francis Bacon, who in 1976 completed *Triptych* (private collection, France), the central panel of which features the framed—possibly mirrored—image of a decapitated figure being attacked by a bird of prey.

Why the use of the mirror? As usual, González "did not want the viewer to look right into the landscape—I wanted it to be indirect and veiled." Paradoxically, this "indirect" transcription of the image heightens the mystery and drama of the work, since the image takes on a kind of immediacy—a magical *realism*—the artist playing with the notion that the art work has in fact become a mirror, reflecting the viewer's own space.

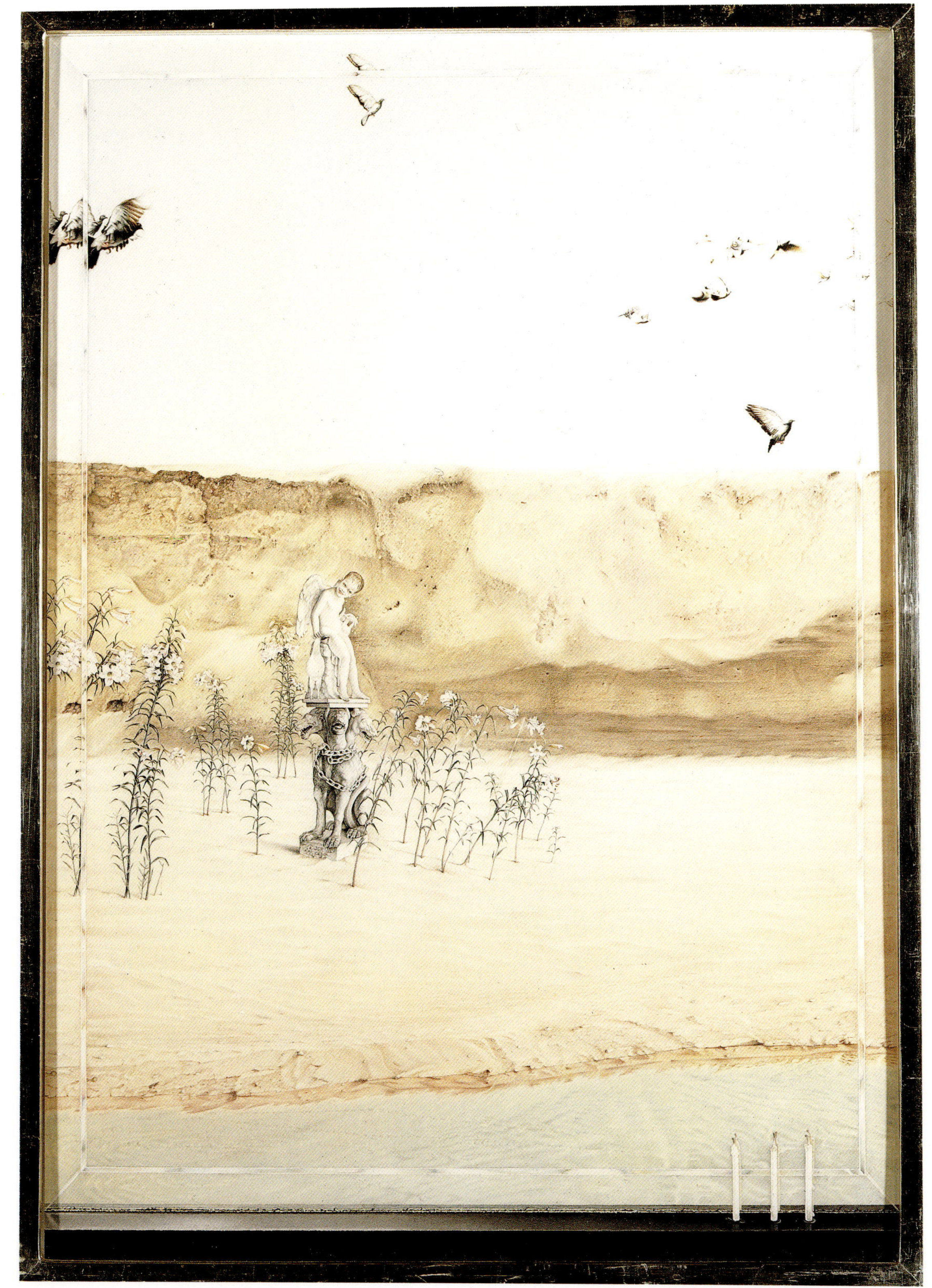

19b *Mar y Espejo* 1976

Watercolor, colored pencil, and pastel on paper, 28 × 20¼ inches
Private collection, New York

González intended the second panel of his tripartite mirror to be something of an homage to his wife and daughters. He reintroduces the headless bride-doll of *The Sparrow and the Maiden,* this time with apparently headless pigeons wheeling past her, their heads tucked beneath their wings. These mysterious pigeons are making a magical journey from left to right through the mirrored panels. They will land safely in the third and final section of this sea/mirror.

These pigeons are, as we have already seen, symbols of liberation. Here they pass through crystal walls implied by the beveled edges of the mirrors to reach their final destination—literally *flying through mirrors* to arrive at a new life, a new state. They have broken a barrier Narcissus could not break. The trapped lone bird of *The Sparrow and the Maiden,* scrabbling in vain at its own ungraspable mirror image, trying to enter the reflected door that would never open, is now *inside* the mirror, one of a host of birds flying free.

As a tribute to his ex-wife who loves pearls, González posts a magic wand of a pearl-topped hatpin on the black trompe-l'oeil ledge of this central panel. Pearls have traditional associations with the sea, with the feminine moon and the tides, with purity and spiritual grace. González would have been aware of Vermeer's fondness for painting glowing pearls as poignant, light-catching symbols of worldly beauty and the transient loveliness of woman.

González was thinking of Lorca again, however, in the curious gathering of wasps or bees he places on the headless bride's neck. In a popular translation of *Así que Pasen Cinco Años,* a forlorn Mannequin in a borrowed bride's dress poetically laments the fact that she will never marry and conceive a child: "The white pain of a bee/implants in my flesh its sharp caress."[1] The bee-stung Mannequin bride, together with the "sunken" mirrored ring of the third panel of *Mar y Espejo,* indicates that González was immersing himself in the imagery of *Así que Pasen Cinco Años* many years before he got the chance to design stage sets for that curious drama in 1991, depicting himself as the central character in Lorca's play, the tragic Young Man, the lover without hope.

The bees are the poet's and the artist's symbol of wounding love. No doubt Lorca knew of the classical account of Venus and Cupid stung by bees—how Cupid, stealing honey from a hive, was badly stung, and how, when he showed his wounds to his mother, Venus, she laughingly replied: "Aren't you like the bees, for small as you are, you too inflict cruel wounds?"[2]

The headless bride recalls the framed or mirrored headless figure of Francis Bacon's 1976 *Triptych,* evoked in the stone boy with a living head preyed upon by a long-necked bird in the previous panel of this triptych. But, as usual, González has transformed his sources, arriving at a personal image of transcendent feminine beauty—his prototype for the submerged ocean bride of *Así que Pasen Cinco Años/When Five Years Pass,* 1991, and the starlit *Bride for Lorca,* 1992.

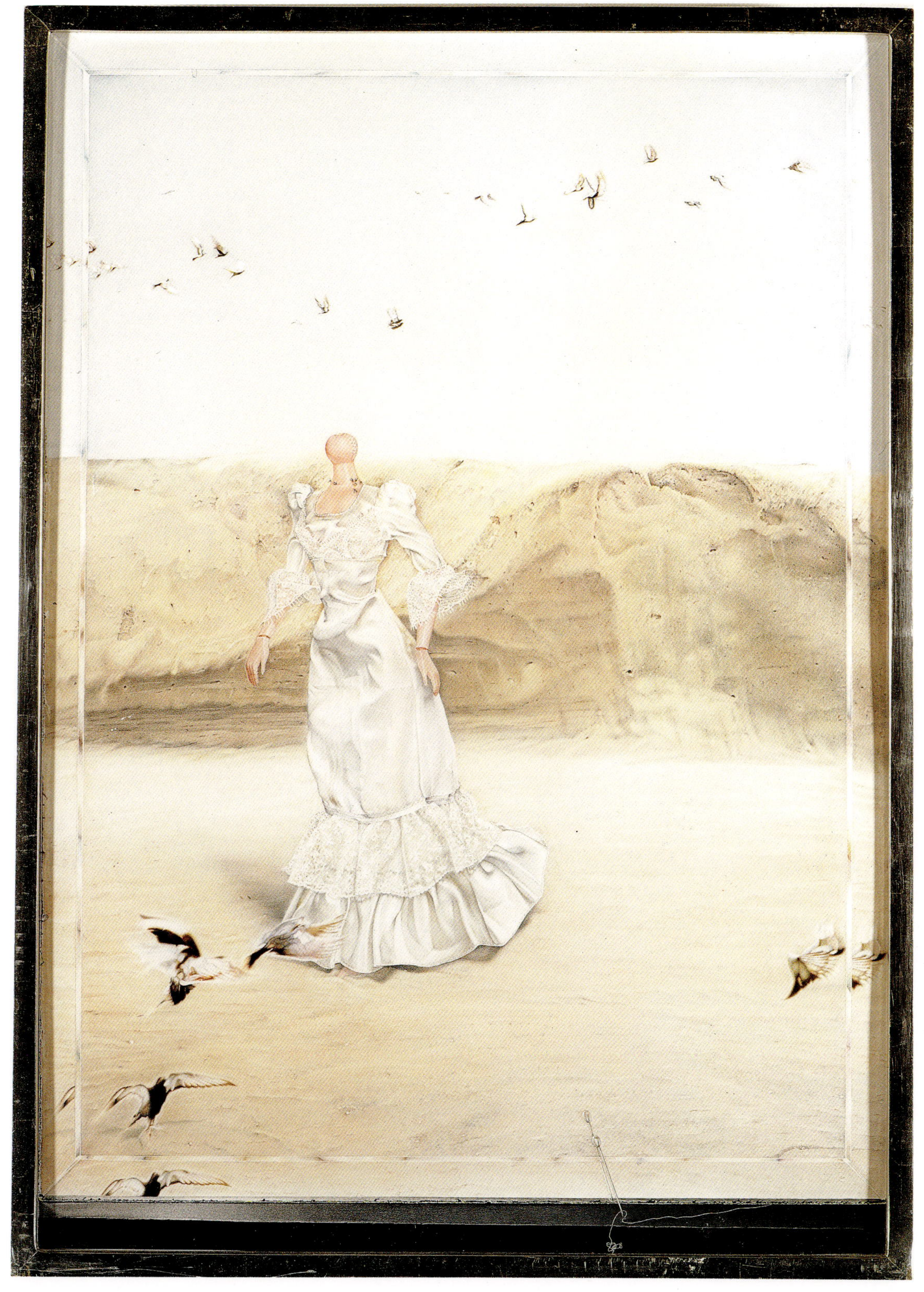

19c *Mar y Espejo* 1976

Watercolor, colored pencil, and pastel on paper, 28 × 20¼ inches
Private collection, New York

The color changes in the third panel, becoming a little brighter and clearer. There are no human figures. The pigeons have landed safely and strut between theatrical wings, a triptych-within-a-triptych comprising three blank veiled frames, which almost, but not quite, screen a dark door that has opened in the wall of sand at the back—the wall that is really the enlarged edge of the sand that meets the seawater, and that had reminded González of the landscape in Bellini's *Transfiguration.* This third panel celebrates González's own "transfiguration"—his realization as artist and creator of these three mystic screens thickly inhabited by pigeons, this triple theater of translucencies, all versions of the bathroom blind in *Flor y Media* (Flower and a Half).

The point is confirmed by the sacramental white bird, inspired by Piero della Francesca's cloudlike white dove of the Holy Ghost in *The Baptism of Christ* from the 1440s (National Gallery, London). González's white bird of baptism and rebirth has presumably emerged from within the three translucent screens or veils, to come down to the purifying water's edge, where it will enter the ocean. The white bird stands directly above a diamond ring given to González by an old school friend, the bird seeming to claim the ring as its crown of sovereignty or divinity. González will later combine a white seabird and a crown of lights in his *Double Portrait of Jimmy, N.Y.C.,* 1984. The door in the sand wall is symbolic of entry and passage, implying that the triptych as a whole may be viewed as a magical journey to a new state, the "sacred marriage" implicit in the ring. This mirror-imaged ring resting on its reflective black ledge also anticipates the scene in *Así que Pasen Cinco Años/When Five Years Pass,* 1991, for which González made a blazingly beautiful collage of an ocean floor. The broken-hearted Mannequin bride in that scene (whom Lorca, and González, at the end of the play portrays as headless and handless) cries out: "My ring, my ring, my golden ring! / Is sinking in the mirror's sand."[1] The line associates mirror and sand as interchangeable emblems of the passage of time and ruined hopes of love. González intended the ring in *Mar y Espejo* to be viewed as sunk at the bottom of the ocean.

The third panel incorporates a touch of white mystery in the top center of the mirror: a trompe l'oeil of human teeth dangling on pink threads. González had seen and remembered a sculpture of the sorrowing Virgin in Toledo, her anguished open mouth filled with perfect human teeth, each one volunteered by a young nun. Yet the dangling teeth also recall the hanging blind-cord prevalent in paintings by Francis Bacon—especially prominent, for instance, in the 1966 *Portrait of George Dyer Staring at a Blind Cord* (Collection Maestri, Parma).

The organization of the triptych is quirkily distorting. The three panels do not quite coexist on the same plane, though the viewer initially assumes that they do. The central panel appears to be closer to the viewer than the side panels, because the figure is enlarged and the water line has disappeared. Yet this central panel is actually set farther back on the green glass ledge than the side panels, so that it recedes by comparison with the side panels. And although the side panels sit farther forward on the ledge, closer to the viewer, their vistas seem to be more distant. As a whole, the triptych represents the distorting mirror of the unconscious, "oceanic" mind.

"Why was I born among mirrors?" cried Lorca in his "Song of the Barren Orange Tree." The poet's Andalusian obsession with death (death in *water* in particular), his emotionalism, his elegiac yearning for a love that can never be, epitomized in the barren brides of his poems and plays, his Spanish flair for extracting spiritual and poetic beauty from pain, all struck a deep chord of familiar feeling in González.

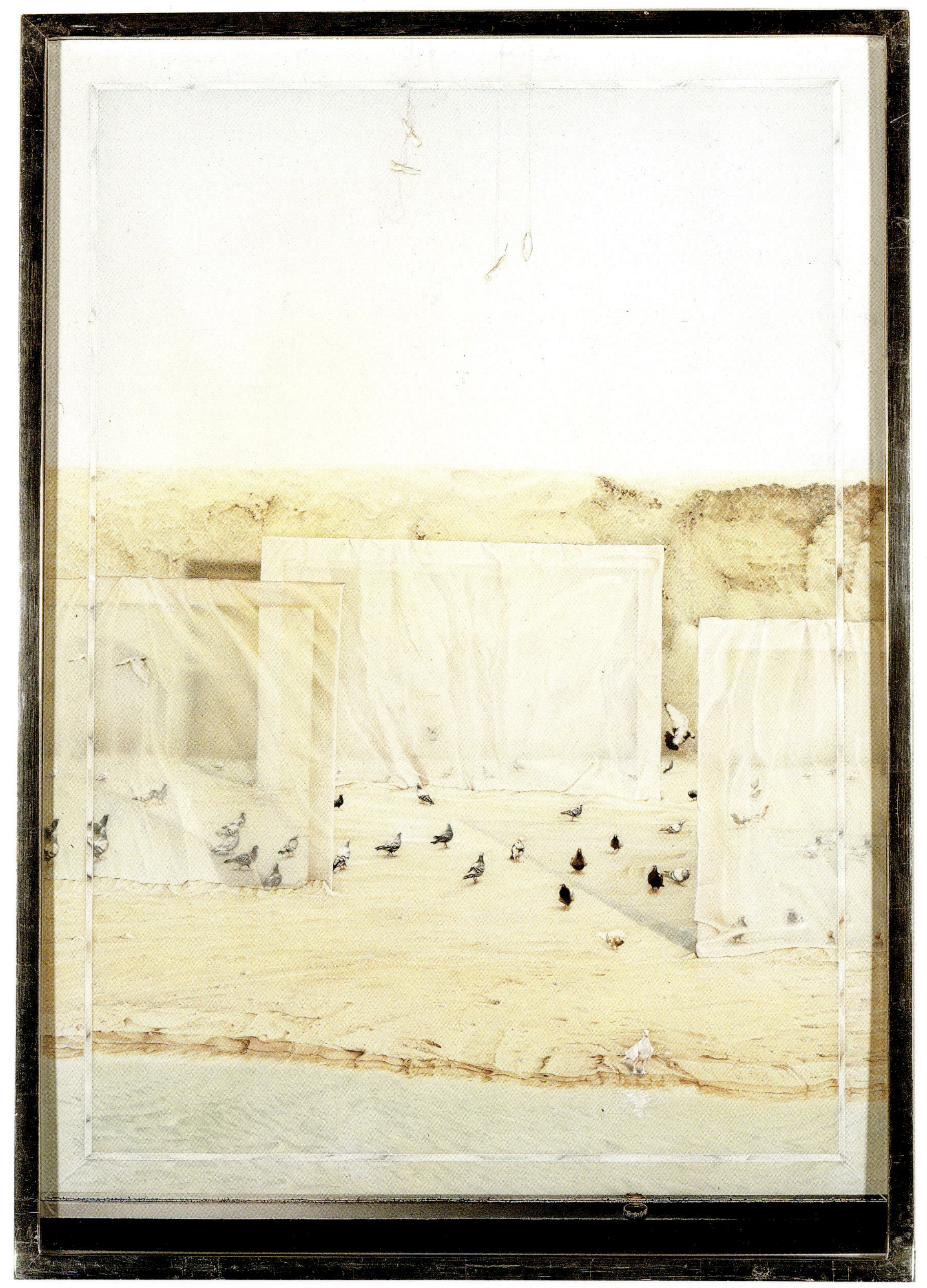

20 *La Cuna/The Cradle* 1976

Watercolor and colored pencil on paper, 18 1/16 × 14 3/16 inches
The Caren and Walter Forbes Collection

Purifying whiteness and protective translucencies, walls that are veils around a mirrored and veiled floor, are the enchanted essence of *La Cuna/The Cradle*. González had wanted to work in a minimalist way after the epic endeavor of *Mar y Espejo* (Sea and Mirror). Here he reworks the three veiled stretchers from the final panel of that work as a "cradle" room or womb, in which the scale is deliberately ambiguous.

The linen handkerchief, a sacramental veil reminiscent of the folded white bed sheet of *La Misa Blanca* (The White Mass), floats like a gridded cloth or veil on the surface of a still pool. Behind the central wall of fabric, at the right-hand corner of the cradle, stands an unlit pink birthday candle—an almost concealed symbol with a salient connection to the womb, involving the idea of the soul's preservation in the darkness of womb or tomb.[1] *La Cuna/The Cradle* is a kind of abstract portrait of a soul shrouded in darkness, protectively hidden.

The idea of a mirrored floor within a cradle or womb is fascinating, since it raises the mythological issue of the hero's "water birth,"[2] or exposure at birth to waters upon which he is likely to perish, after being removed from, or rejected by, his true parents. Saved from the waters, the hero is usually then raised by simple folk, different from or inferior to his true lineage, growing up with a consequent sense of displacement and a lingering dream of some royal or magical origin. González remembers that this drawing "came out of a conversation I had with a cousin I grew up with in my grandparents' house, a girl. She was a writer—very smart. We were very close, and one day she told me that she had been suffering since she was a baby. She said she remembered being cold and terrorized in her cradle. Her mother was very protective of her, but still my cousin was never able to operate in Cuban society."

Cuban society expected and demanded the conventional, and González's cousin was duly required to conform, to adopt a false self—an imposition González himself, quietly and in an interior way, resisted. Empathizing with his cousin, and seeing in her a reflection of his own feelings, González has here created a luminous, crystalline, interiorized image of birth upon water—suspended above a magical spring of light, a mirror of self-knowledge and spiritual perfection.

The artist luxuriated in this deceptively simple image, taking pains to make the cradle as exquisite and sumptuous as possible, aiming for a texture like fine silk, the individual threads showing up with hallucinatory sharpness and clarity. In the notion of a mysteriously empty white cradle succeeding the white ocean-bride and white bird or Holy Ghost of *Mar y Espejo,* and in the magical conjunction of the artist and his girl cousin, uniting the fundamentally opposite principles of male and female as the artist had united himself with Anne Minich in the white portal of *A.M.,* González achieves what Jung, after the alchemists, would call the *coniunctio*—the marrying of opposites resulting in the birth of the androgyne, the child or new being with a capacity for wholeness, discovering and redeeming what was previously submerged or unconscious in the personality.[3]

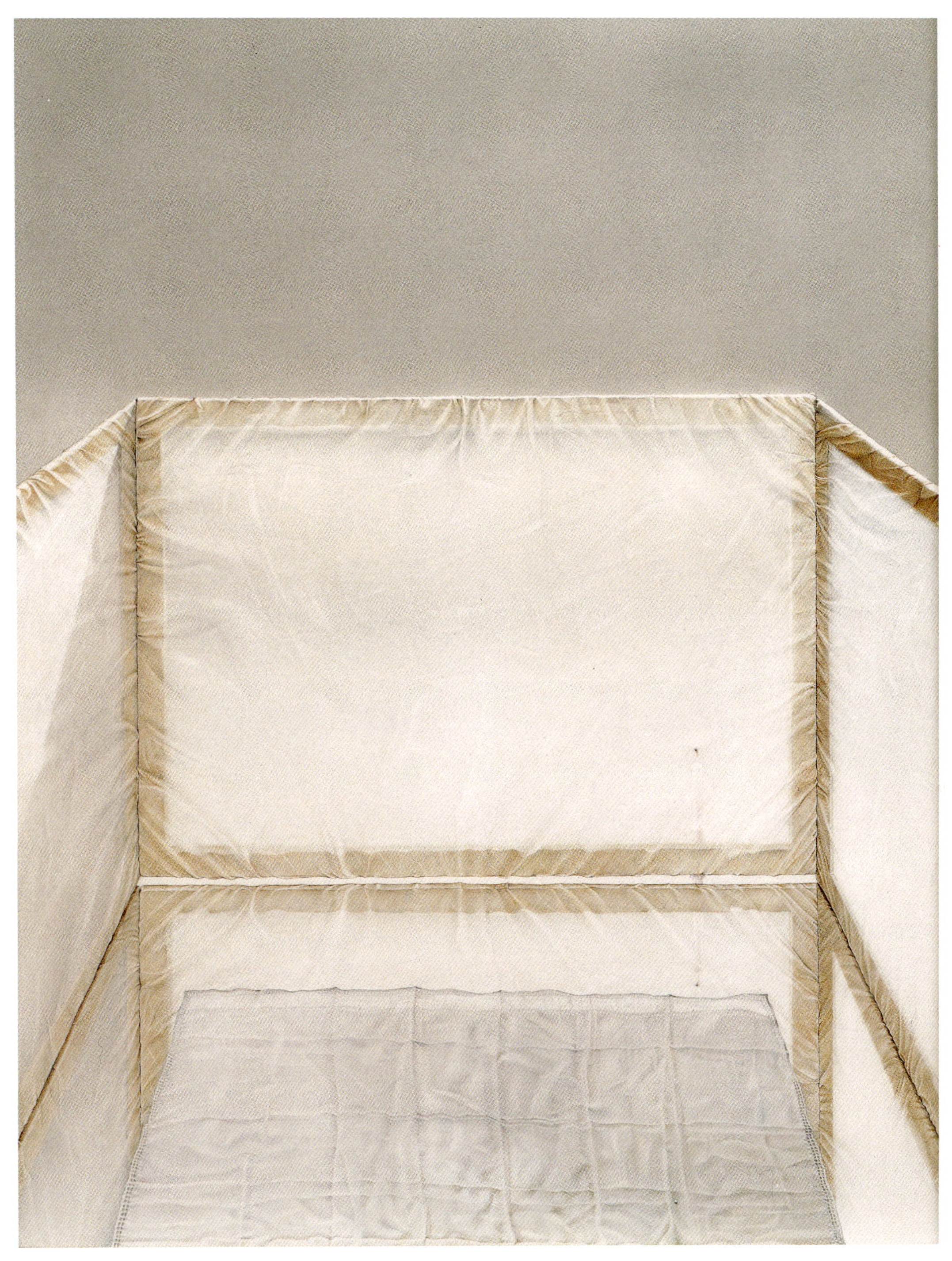

21 *The Warning* 1977

Watercolor, colored pencil, and pastel on paper beneath etched glass, 28¼ × 20 inches
Nancy and Sanfred Koltun

The Warning is a premonitory shadow box, an apparently serene "white" stage set that is also a window of warning: the glass pane that covers the art work and separates the image from the viewer is actually, physically etched, as though it carried the electric-foil alarm tape familiar on New York City store windows: break the foil and a warning bell will sound. González is here taking to magical extremes his penchant for the protective veiling of the art work, literally sealing it off from mundane reality and transforming it into some kind of ancient ritual or drama with invocatory powers.

Behind the protective pane are a ledge upon which stands an assembly kit of toy soldiers, a mountain of salt, which the artist calls "a reference to Sodom and Gomorrah," and, at the bottom corner of the picture, two Annunciation stamps. One is a section of Botticelli's Uffizi *Annunciation* with the angel holding a lily. The other, cites the artist, "is an angel from a Fra Angelico *Annunciation* at San Marco that was always really mysterious to me, because the angel had stripes of different colors and a blue circle in the middle of the wings, like a butterfly."

These *Annunciation* fragments and the pink-tipped matches provide bright sparks of color amid the harmony of grays in this fastidious, refined work, composed in a surprising variety of media, as contemporary a conception of still life as *Flor y Media* (Flower and a Half). Around this period, González began to get restless working in pencil alone, especially when he worked for a substantial length of time on any one piece, as he often did. He is used to committing himself twelve hours a day for months at a time to most of his works. To stay fresh and to keep the image alive, he will switch media at whim.

Above the ledge with the toy soldiers hangs a grand Greek temple of an empty bird cage, its roofline cut by the top edge of the picture. Its weight and position in the composition remind us of the ruined temple that occupies the top half of Botticelli's *Adoration of the Magi,* ca. 1470 (National Gallery, London). The empty bird cage symbolized for González a fateful feeling of being resigned to an inescapable way of life. The cage and the shadows it complicatedly throws are drawn and colored so that the cage becomes the most fully realized entity in the piece—though the etched alarm glass that separates the cage from the viewer jolts us out of our perception of it as all but three-dimensional, awakening the viewer to the artist's purpose in this symbolist still life, his attempt to convert and transform feelings of foreboding, laying them to rest within this sealed and etched window.

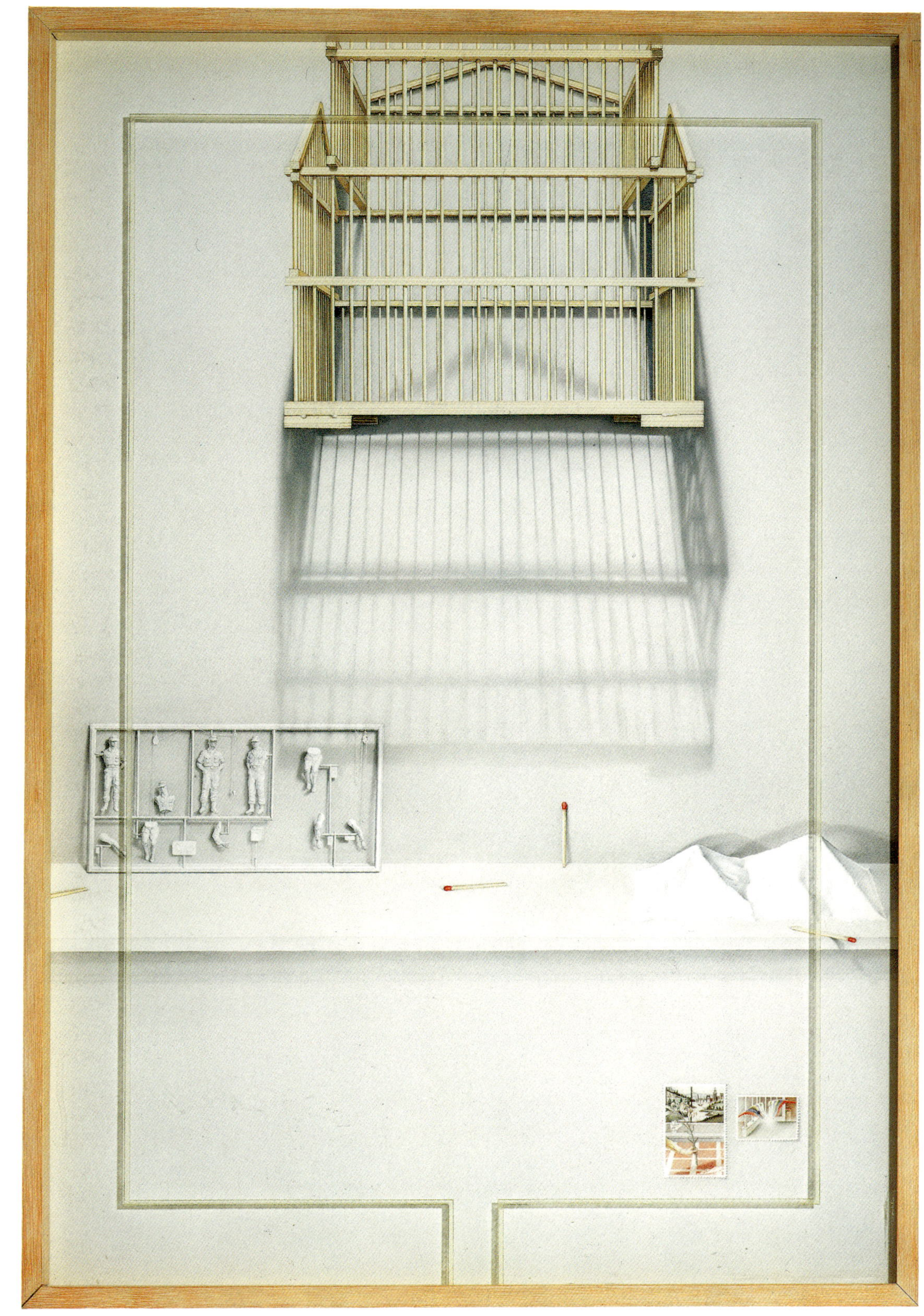

22 *P. M. Times* 1977

Watercolor, pastel, ink, and colored pencil on paper, 12¾ × 18 inches
The Frances Lehman Loeb Art Center, Vassar College, Poughkeepsie, New York. Purchase.
The Barbara Doyle Duncan, class of 1943, Fund for Contemporary Latin American Drawings. 1978.18

"P. M." refers both to the initials of a friend's name and to time, suggesting that this delicate work marks and celebrates time spent with him. The piece is once more arranged like a triptych or an altarpiece, translucent graph paper recalling the triple "veils" or screens of *Mar y Espejo* (Sea and Mirror) and *La Cuna/The Cradle.* At this period, González says, "I was very interested in balance, movement, geometry, and in the metaphysical quality of the still life. The drawing has to do with light and transparencies. There are these very frail elements, like the toothpicks, which I also use as a compositional device. And there's a white top, and a black top, again relating to time—night and day—but also to good and evil, and life and death."

Three charred toothpicks lean on the left panel. González burned these toothpicks with matches before posing them in the still-life group from which he drew this composition, also charring a fourth match for the opposite side of the triptych, where one white and one black toothpick repeat the contrast of the black and white tops, one suspended, one grounded. As we study the play of the toothpicks in conjunction with their shadows, a series of triangles emerges. We notice, too, the predominantly triangular shapes of the tops and the puzzling peaks of shadows that lack explanatory toothpicks in the foreground—evidence of toothpicks leaning on the other side of the translucent graph paper.

This evidence of unseen things *behind* the sheet or wall of paper repeats the movement of the sharp pencils that interpenetrate both sides of the ocean veil or sky curtain of *La Misa Blanca* (The White Mass) and the veil-obscured candle of *La Cuna/The Cradle,* visual equivalents to the spiritual element González perceived in Tennessee Williams's otherwise earthy and real short story, "Two on a Party": "in between the lines, these mystical suggestions of things."

A lightly delineated large triangle emerges almost directly over the white top, its apex at the upper inner corner of the right-hand panel, reiterating and crowning the lower series of triangles and providing a protective pyramidal tent over the white top.

The mystic tripleness of the composition seems clear in this triptych of triangulations or "trinities" evoking a spiritual world, emblematic of the Holy Trinity of Father, Son, and Holy Ghost. But the quiet restraint and emphasis on balance and geometry typical at this period of González's work have more to do with a self-imposed discipline—the artist restricting and repressing his baroque compulsion toward richer imagery, in an attempt to address the minimalism of the day.

The tops, introduced here for the first time, are a characteristically romantic and whimsical touch, however. They suggest the plumb line, and González certainly had one in mind: "I love that plumb line at the Smithsonian in Washington, which marks the time and place where you are." But the tops primarily represent a personal memory, being a childhood toy of the artist's in Cuba. He returns to the tops again in *El Paisaje del Rey/The Landscape of the King, Prisma y Prisión/Prism and Prison,* and *El Cuarto en el Fondo del Pozo/The Room at the Bottom of the Well,* all 1978. Like Joseph Cornell, González places toys in his art for associative and poetic reasons, most especially to promote a wistful sense of nostalgia for the lost charm and innocence of childhood.

Finally, injecting a note of spatial ambiguity into this gossamer still life, a single wire hangs high to the right of the triptych—intended to evoke the kind of wire a trapeze or high-wire artiste might use to ascend to the topmost heights of a circus tent, a minimalist token of spangled heroism and the artist's dream of flight.

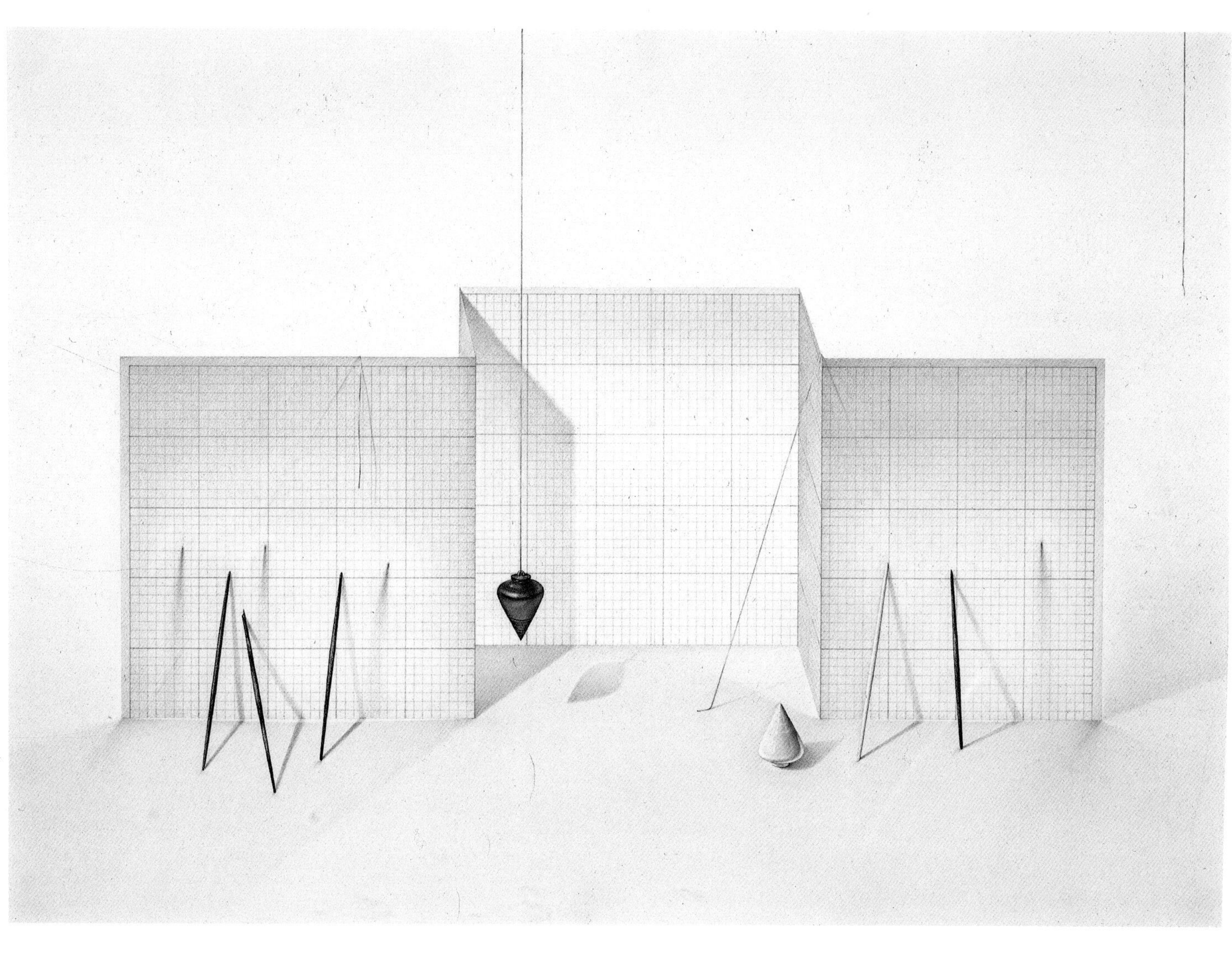

23 *Sara's Garden* 1978

Graphite on paper, 22 × 18 inches
Glenn C. Janss Collection

González had a friend called Sara Necee, who lived in a carriage house in New York with an attached plot of earth, where "every year she would plant hundreds of lilies, so they would be blooming at different times. She was very devoted to her garden, and quite wonderful." The fine threads, the little pearls or beads, the air of mystery about the beautifully conceived flowers, are all vintage González. But the drawing, which is a kind of reverse drawing, more involved with surface than anything he had yet done, marks an exciting new departure for the artist, since the surface of the paper itself is transformed into a dark burnished mirror.

"What triggered that drawing was that there had just been an exhibition of young Spanish realist artists in New York," González remembers.

> And they were experimenting a lot with graphite and turpentine. They were able to get a surface that was fascinating to me, because at that time I was already involved in trying to develop a new kind of surface myself. So for the entirety of the black surface in this image, I used a ruler to fill in line after line, and then I bathed it with turpentine, to make the graphite *soak* into the paper. And then I'd go back and repeat the whole process all over again. By the time the drawing was finished, the black space looked like a metallic mirror, or polished brass, because it had a built-up six or seven layers of graphite, a very flat, even, lead surface. It took a long time, and a lot of equilibrium, to make, because I had to draw in such a way as not to touch or smudge the paper, and spoil the white areas. The flowers are the white of the paper, dominating the dark space around.
>
> It's a very important thing for me, to discover ways of creating an unusual surface, so that people have no idea how the image was made. With this drawing, it wasn't calculated, but once I had the idea of filling up the black background like that, there was no other possible way for me to go. The surface looks so strange and beautiful, so perfect and uniform, and yet you can see the lines. Even though they're on top of each other, you can feel the *rhythm* of the lines.

Around the outer limits of the drawing González has imposed vertical and horizontal lines, the direct result of his infatuation with Richard Diebenkorn's *Ocean Park* paintings.

González here introduces a favorite theme, the garden. At the same time, with the abstraction of a cross in the background, he anticipates the lily-crucifixion of the next image, *El Lirio Cuadral* (The Square and the Lily), and the great Easter lily, emblematic of Christ's resurrection, from his *Untitled* drawing for Nancy Fried, 1991–92. The lily, like the rose, is traditionally a symbol of the Virgin Mary, specifically of her royalty and purity. But González is most fond of the Easter lily, with its promise of Christ's resurrection. Here in *Sara's Garden,* the white lilies evoke a transcendent light in darkness, a spiritual illumination shining out of the dark mirror of the background.

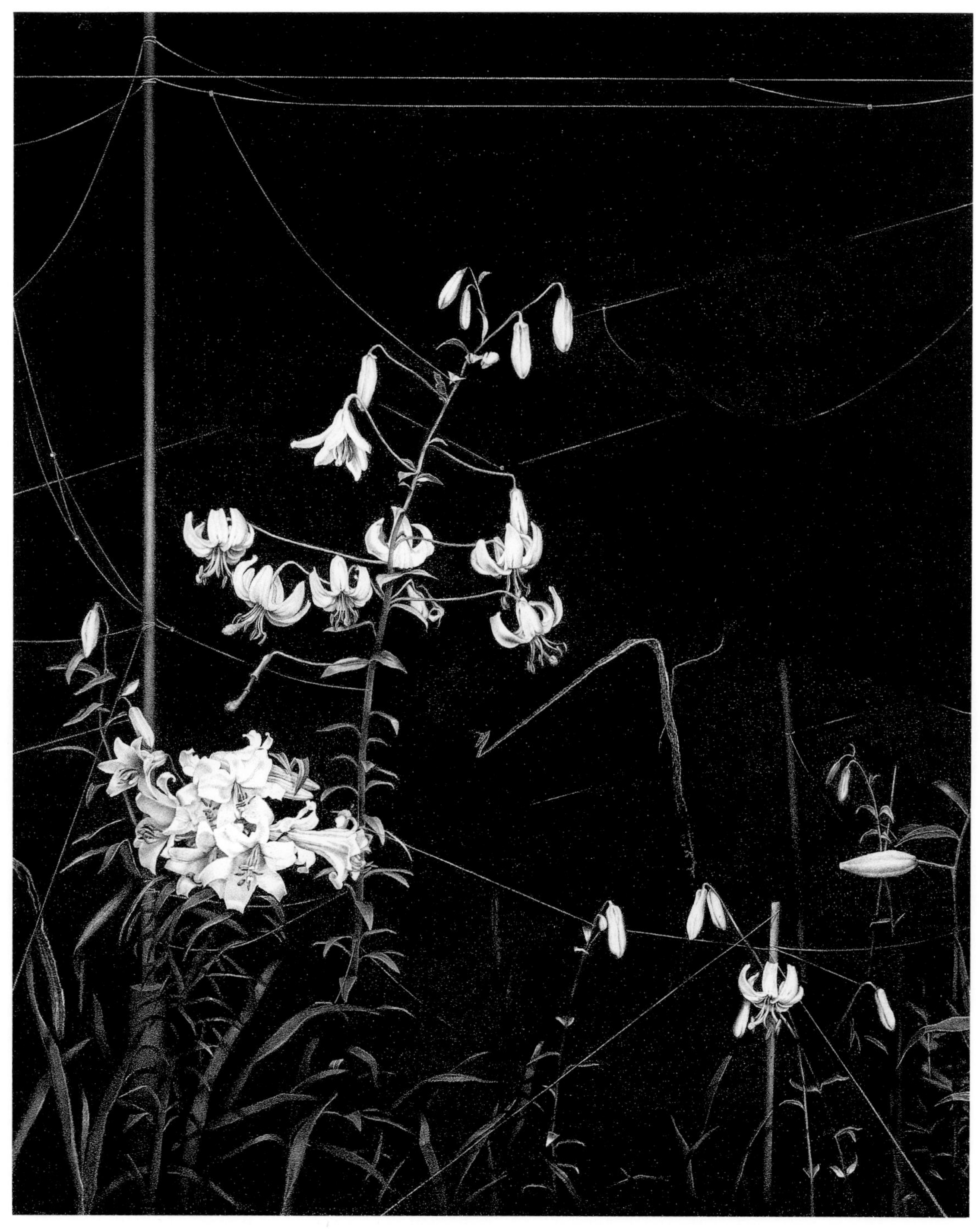

24 *El Lirio Cuadral* 1978

Colored pencil and watercolor on paper, 10 × 15¾ inches
Collection of Mr. and Mrs. Graham Gund

González describes *El Lirio Cuadral* (The Square and the Lily) as "a Crucifixion, set against a tiled bathroom wall made of pale blue-white tiles. I have these altar lilies ranged at the bottom of the drawing, with one single lily set higher above the rest, backed by a square of wet tissue paper, which is sticking to the tiles so that it frames the single lily." The damp sheet of tissue paper clinging to the tiled bathroom wall is both a frame for the tall lily and another translucent veil, the artist's poetic response to and transformation of the minimalist grid, adding a magical-realist layer to González's obsessive theme of the wall. The drawing of the wall here is encased so as to resemble an actual segment of wall carved out and set up, Joseph Cornell–style, within a white cabinet two or three inches deep, a strange specimen of wall and flowers clinically preserved. The cabinet appears to have been whitewashed inside and out and takes on the presence of a miniature theater of redemption and resurrection, a bleached reliquary for a forgotten ritual.

González modeled the structure of his bathroom-tiled Crucifixion scene on an unusually restrained Crucifixion by that grand master of obsessive fantasy and dream gardens, Hieronymus Bosch. Perhaps the great fantasist's earliest known work, dating from around 1480–85, *Christ on the Cross with Donors and Saints* (Musées Royaux des Beaux-Arts, Brussels) intrigued González by virtue of its atypical simplicity. Parallels may be drawn between the arrangement of donors and guardian saints below Christ on the cross in the Bosch painting and González's closed lilies ranged below the tall, unfurled lily with its abstract suggestion of a crown of thorns.

Perhaps, too, the horizontal top bar of Bosch's T-shaped cross has something to do with the trompe-l'oeil imagery of stiff brass wires (three horizontal, one not), which tie the central flower to the outermost edge of González's drawing. The longest brass wire, piercing at least one side petal and probably the whole center of the flower, is certainly symbolic in intent, González reworking an idea he had already used in the untitled masked self-portrait of 1973: "I was thinking of the Roman soldier who drove his spear through Christ's heart," says the artist.

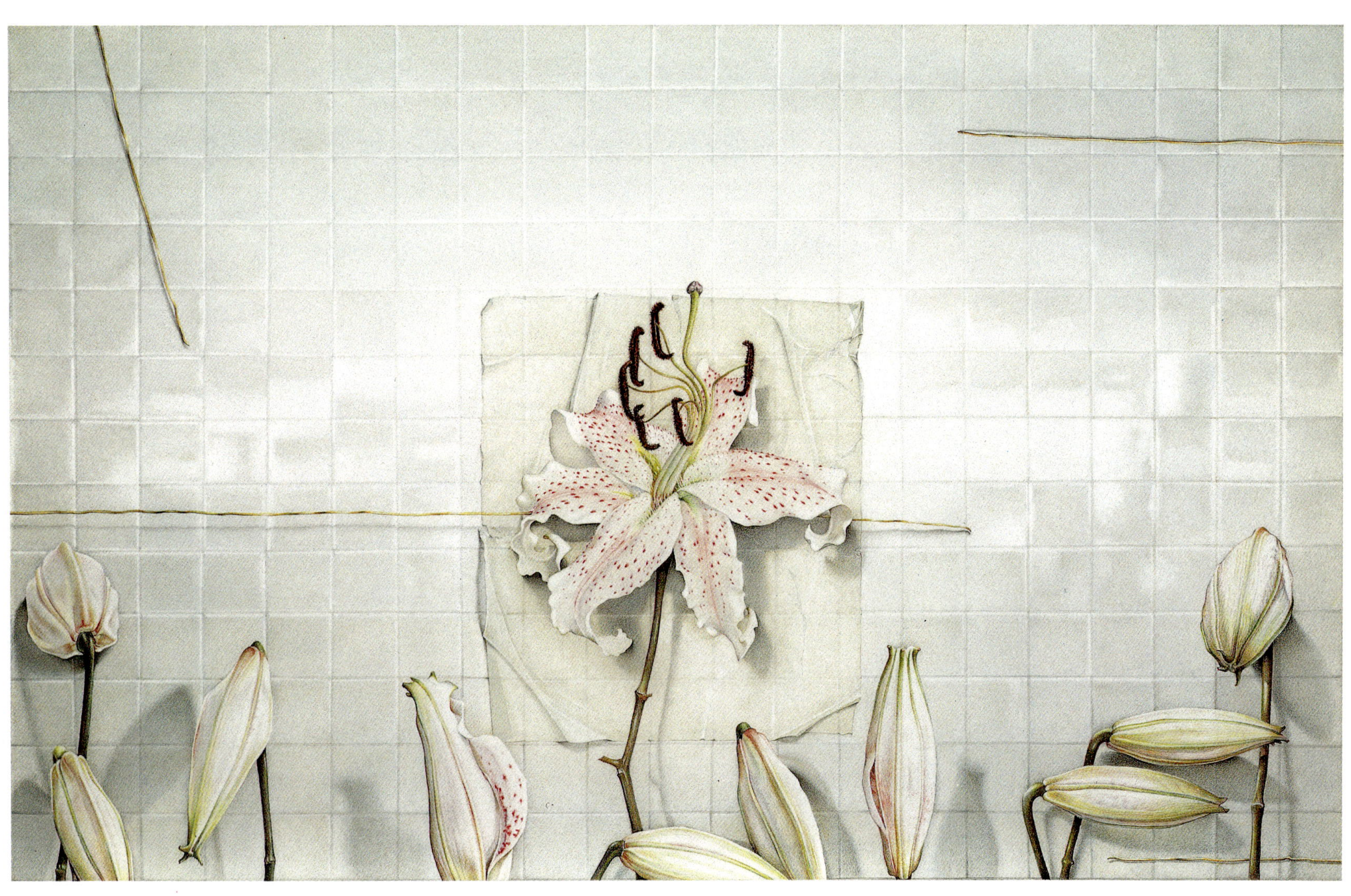

25 *El Paisaje del Rey / The Landscape of the King* 1978

Acrylic, graphite, ink, and colored pencil on board, 20 × 40 inches
Mr. and Mrs. E. W. Nash, San Francisco

The title of this superbly illusionistic drawing derives from the myth of Oedipus Rex. González's aim was to try to capture some of the mystery of a son's difficult relationship with his father—a relationship examined and transformed through art but made to feel startlingly real, immediate, and intense through deployment of trompe l'oeil, controlled color, and a balance of disparate elements. As usual, spatial ambiguity—for instance, in the contrasting proximity and distance of the green glass ledges, both drawn on the flat surface of the paper—heightens the mystery.

The true "king" to whom González pays tribute in this piece, however, may be Alberto Giacometti, creator of a famous surrealist sculpture of 1932–33; González ardently admires *The Palace at Four A.M.* (The Museum of Modern Art, New York). Giacometti was fascinated by the human face and figure and often placed his figures within simply drawn frames, sealing them inside a living space within the drawing. González views these figures sealed in space as "serene, Egyptian," and reveres Giacometti for his capacity "to dream, to find a refuge." González's folded skeleton of a bird on the lower of the two green glass ledges has an obvious affinity with the flying skeleton of *The Palace at Four A.M.,* while the bottom half of a toy soldier's torso (one of the kit soldiers of *The Warning*) occupies an area of upper space roughly parallel to the framed space inhabited by the flying skeleton of *The Palace at Four A.M.*

In the corner of the upper green ledge, González has placed a small white figure of himself beneath a twig tree within an enclosing white frame, translating Giacometti's near-abstract drawing of 1949, *Figure under a Tree* (Collection Gérald Cramer, Geneva), into a naturalistic equivalent as full of poetry and mystery as the original.

High above the Eadweard Muybridge–inspired horse and rider is a floodlit circus tightrope, while between the green glass ledges a high-wire artiste's balancing pole, drawn as a brass wire, rests on two white verticals—a kind of portrait-in-absence of a tightrope walker, perhaps someone like Giacometti's 1943 *Woman on a Tightrope* (Estate of Pierre Matisse, New York).

Of course, there is much that is purely personal to González, like the black top from *P. M. Times,* emblem of childhood and of creative and generative forces, the vortex. There are blank white sheets (translucent and opaque) pinned illusionistically to the wall. A taut thread slices through a trompe-l'oeil square of frayed red silk, evoking yet again the lancing of Christ at the Crucifixion and that perennial theme of the Latin American artist, here abstractly treated, the Sacred Heart. Five white ceramic tops, perhaps symbolic of the five wounds of Christ, are tinged blood red.

From the top of the white frame behind the small tree and figure hangs a crimson detail described by the artist as "a thorn dipped in blood," a famous emblem of Christ's Passion, and the symbolic antithesis of the rose. The trompe-l'oeil color photograph below the green glass ledge reveals the direct source of this red "thorn" in real life: a light bulb draped in a red bandanna, viewed through a doorway from González's bed, in the last apartment he had in Miami.

González here introduces the smiling stone angel of Rheims, whose face is dissected like the scrap of red silk, the Bleeding Heart of Jesus, by a slicing thread: the artist will strongly identify with this angel in future works as a type of androgyne self-portrait. The dissected face of the stone angel echoes Bacon's 1969 dissection of Lucian Freud's face within the linear cube in *Three Studies for a Portrait of Lucian Freud* (private collection, Rome)—Freud, of course, being the grandson of the famed proponent of the Oedipus complex, Sigmund Freud.

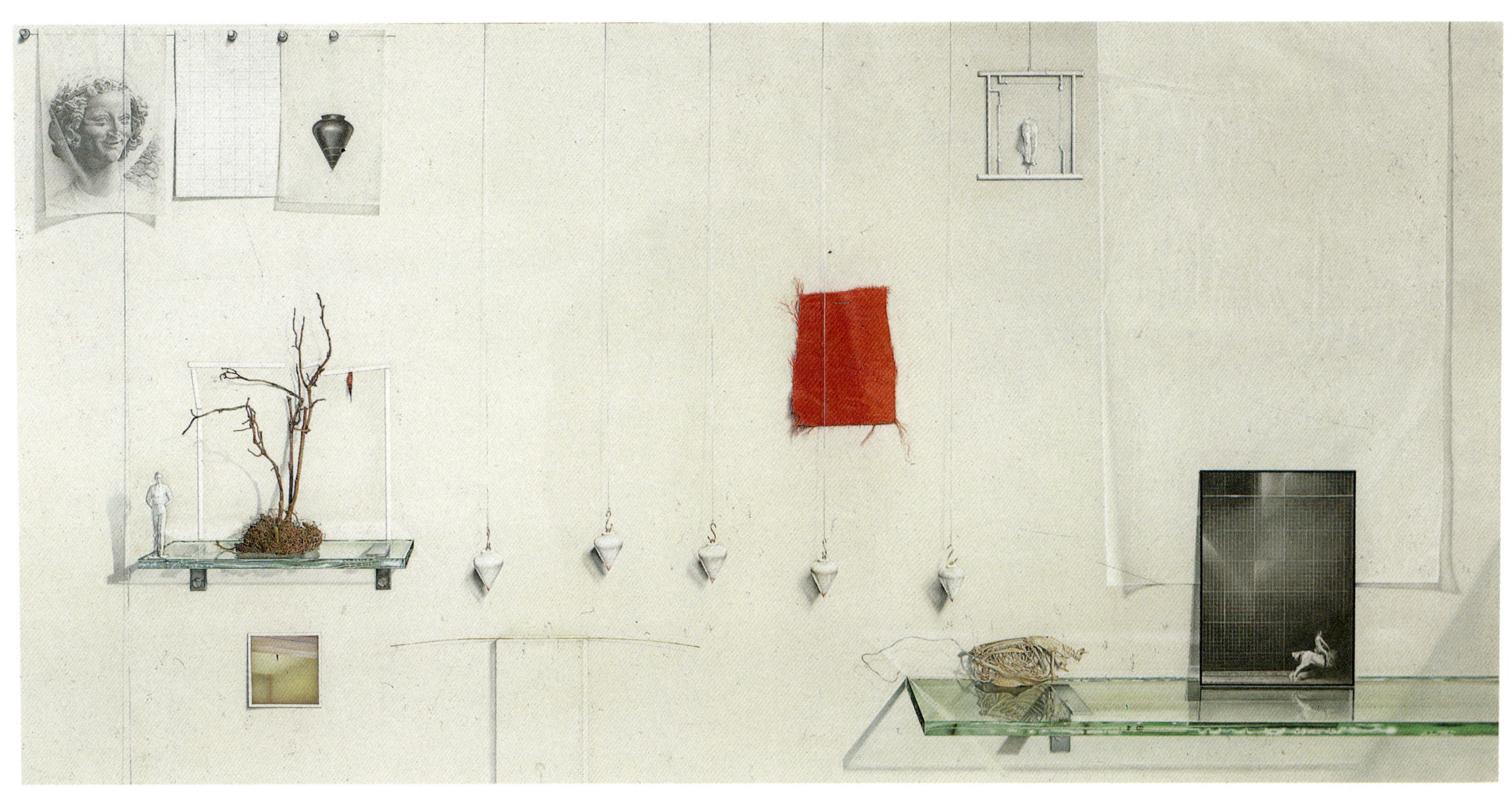

26 *Mari in the Shadow Box* 1978

Watercolor and colored pencil on paper beneath etched glass, 18½ × 29½ × 4 inches
Collection of Mr. and Mrs. Graham Gund

Using lessons learned about the centrality of the image in *Portrait of a Lady,* this first portrait of the artist's daughter Maria (whom he has always called, Cuban-style, "Mari") succeeds in presenting her as a majestically enthroned young Madonna, backed by a contemporary version of the cloth of honor favored by the Venetian *Madonnieri,* or painters of the Virgin Mary, in the grid of a soft black leather armchair: "In Titian, Giorgione, and Bellini, the Virgin is almost always protected with a panel in the back, and I wanted that sense of a protective destiny for her," says González. (González refers to the cloth of honor even more deliberately in *Portrait of Mari,* 1981.) The work is a four-inch-deep shadow box, a miniature theater in which Maria is as grandly elevated as Giorgione's Madonna at the cathedral of Castelfranco.

Directly in front of Maria, González has set up a mirrored altar of votive offerings, a hopeful symbolist landscape to conjure beneficent magic for the girl's future. Maria's denimed legs cast a blue reflection in this mirrored landscape, with its glassy surface like a pool of water. The elements have been selected with love and pride. The young woman had become a student of architecture in Miami by the time this portrait was conceived. A metronome evokes the pyramids of Egypt, examples of vast public architecture (though this metronome will later be used as a symbol of learning in another work dedicated to her, *El Recuerdo para Mari/Memories for Mari,* 1980. A diminutive birdcage next to it suggests a cell or some other unassuming dwelling. A potted plant, its contours flowing into Maria's, represents a lofty tree, and a tiny horse and rider posit a virile cowboy to carry her off. Scattered seashells float across the reflective surface of the crate tabletop, associating Maria perhaps with Venus (though usually González tends to associate his other daughter, Teresa, with the classical goddess, and Maria with the Virgin Mary). Certainly the shells are meant to imply the feminine principle: the moon and virginity; love, marriage, and fertility. González thinks of the glassy tabletop as "the romantic Nile." Often in his art he leans toward a hieratic style—an art bound by religious structure like the stately art of ancient Egypt or Renaissance paintings of Christ, the Madonna, and angels.

A protective veil between subject and viewer is provided by the etched glass of the pane that covers the image like the glass of *The Warning.* An inverted L on either side of the glass evokes theater wings, architecture, and perhaps even a hoped-for opening of doors for the young woman. The etched glass casts real shadows, deftly intertwining with pencil-drawn shadows, the real fused with the illusionistic.

A specifically Cuban reference to both the feminine and the architectural is embodied in the splayed fan: "In Cuba there were these stained-glass windows that face an interior courtyard, that generally had a semicircular shape," says González. And in Spain, "in Granada or Seville, all the women carry fans to church." With this simple device, González traces his daughter's Cuban and pre-Cuban roots (the artist's grandparents were Spanish, on both sides), while also presenting her as the essence of the feminine—and as a young architect. The fan is a rich symbol harmonizing with every element of this work: representing the unfolding life, widening experience, the warding off of evil forces—and the winged flight of soaring birds (corresponding to the empty birdcage on the table). Above all, González's white fan salutes the dignity and power of his daughter as she faces her destiny.

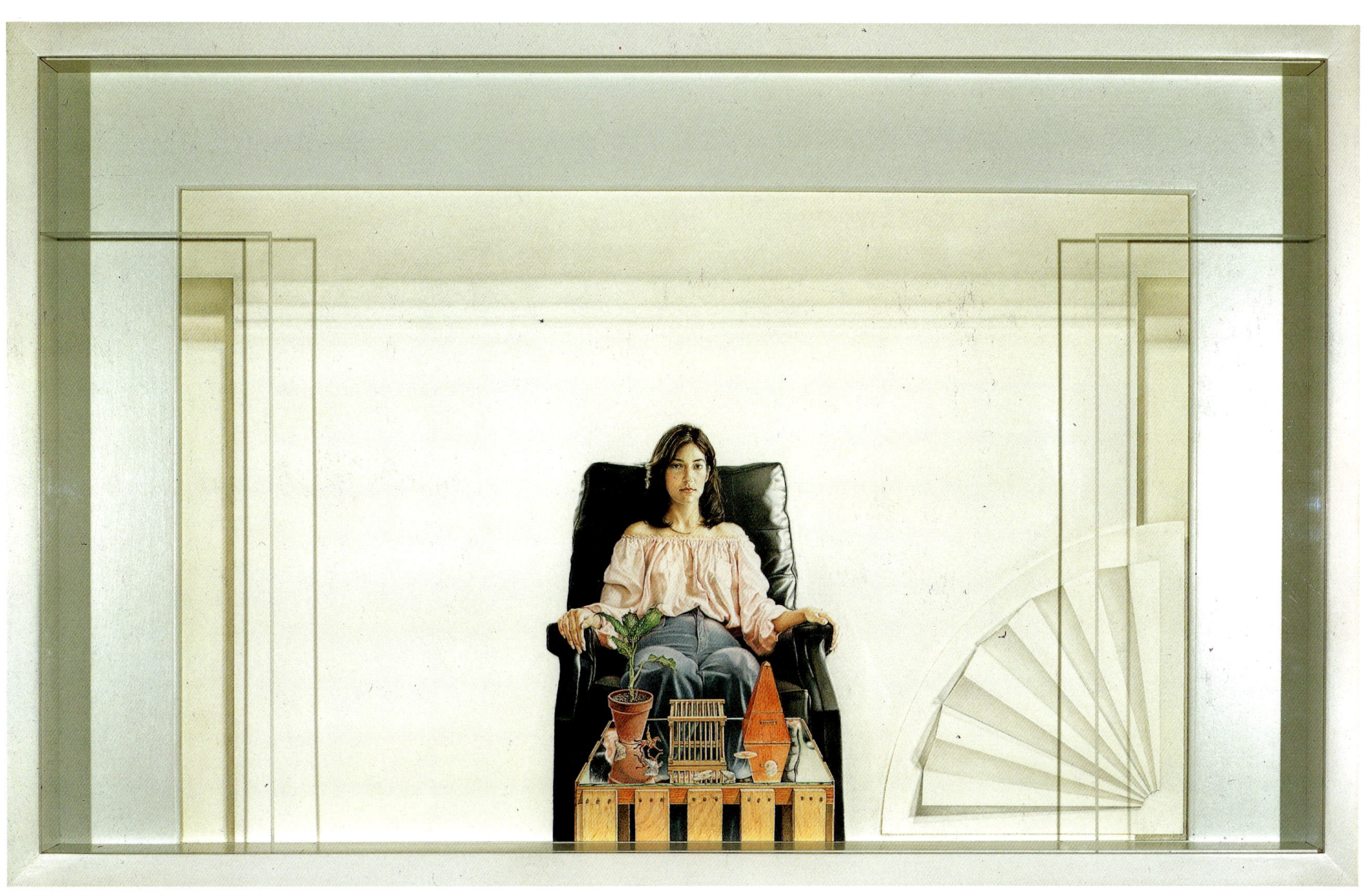

27 *Prisma y Prisión/Prism and Prison* 1978

Mixed media, 18¾ × 33½ × 6 inches
Private collection

The title of this exquisitely balanced and controlled piece plays on the similarity of the words *prism* and *prison*. The word *prism* refers to the triangular form in crystal, its shape reminiscent of González's top, having three or more faces parallel to an axis, with the capacity to refract a ray of light into seven separate colors: red, orange, yellow, green, blue, indigo, and violet. *Prison* refers us back to González's ambivalent and obsessive cage. In combination, these words seem to evoke the idea of being trapped in and at the same time protected by glass. The issue is complicated by the mirrored floor of this six-inch-deep glass case, reminiscent of the glass floor in *La Cuna/The Cradle*. The clear glass ceiling, studded with seven rows of nails that look like tiny crosses, is also as reflective as a mirror, like the closet ceiling of *Ascension*. This cool, glittering interior space represents the artist's mental landscape.

Snugly framed within a central niche, the fragmented angel of Rheims appears caged or veiled behind threads and is reflected, like Narcissus, in the mirrored floor. The red thorn from *El Paisaje del Rey/The Landscape of the King* reappears in the upper-right corner of the angel's niche, as it appeared to the upper right of the figure of González himself in the earlier work. No one who has read Lorca closely could look at this work without thinking of the poet's famous line in the "Gacela of the Dark Death": "I am the immense shadow of my tears."[1] The pearly, glazed ceramic tops tinged with blood like those in *El Paisaje del Rey/The Landscape of the King,* shed on wall and floor a shadowy and reflective rain, which the artist describes as "drops going down into some kind of abyss," though paradoxically, they also present an image of ascent.

A single Tiffany glass prism, which González has lightly misted with a rainbow blush of color, rests before the angel, slightly to one side, where it is also reflected in the mirrored floor of the glass case, crystal layered upon crystal. The tightly strung threads from which the ceramic tops hang cast a phantom array of bars over the graph-papered back of the case.

The most perceptible influence here is that of Joseph Cornell, arch-poet of crystal cages and mirror-lined boxes. A catalogue statement by Cornell in 1948 reads almost like a motivating outline for this work: "Shadow boxes become poetic theaters or settings wherein are metamorphosed the elements of a childhood pastime. The fragile, shimmering globules become the shimmering but more enduring planets—a connotation of moon and tides—the association of water less subtle, as when driftwood pieces make up a proscenium to set off the dazzling white of seafoam and billowy cloud crystallized in a pipe of fancy."[2]

González's childhood tops most certainly carry connotations of time and tide, especially when they are arranged, as here, in seven rows: "I always use mystical numbers if I have something that repeats in my work," affirms the artist, "like seven, nine, or twelve. The seven, for instance, represents the Seven Sorrows of the Virgin, the Seven Virtues or Gifts of the Holy Spirit, the Seven Cardinal Sins, the days of the week, and phases of the moon that put us in touch with the tides."

González's veil or reticulated net of parallel threads between the subject and the viewer has never been utilized as magically as it is here: the serried ranks of crystal beads run seven layers wide and four layers deep, the hermetic space within the glass case sliced by threads and lines in every direction, setting up a visual music of ascending and descending intervals on the back wall of the case—a vivid sense of spiraling forces moving around and above the angel in the double-helical rhythm symbolic of the androgyne.

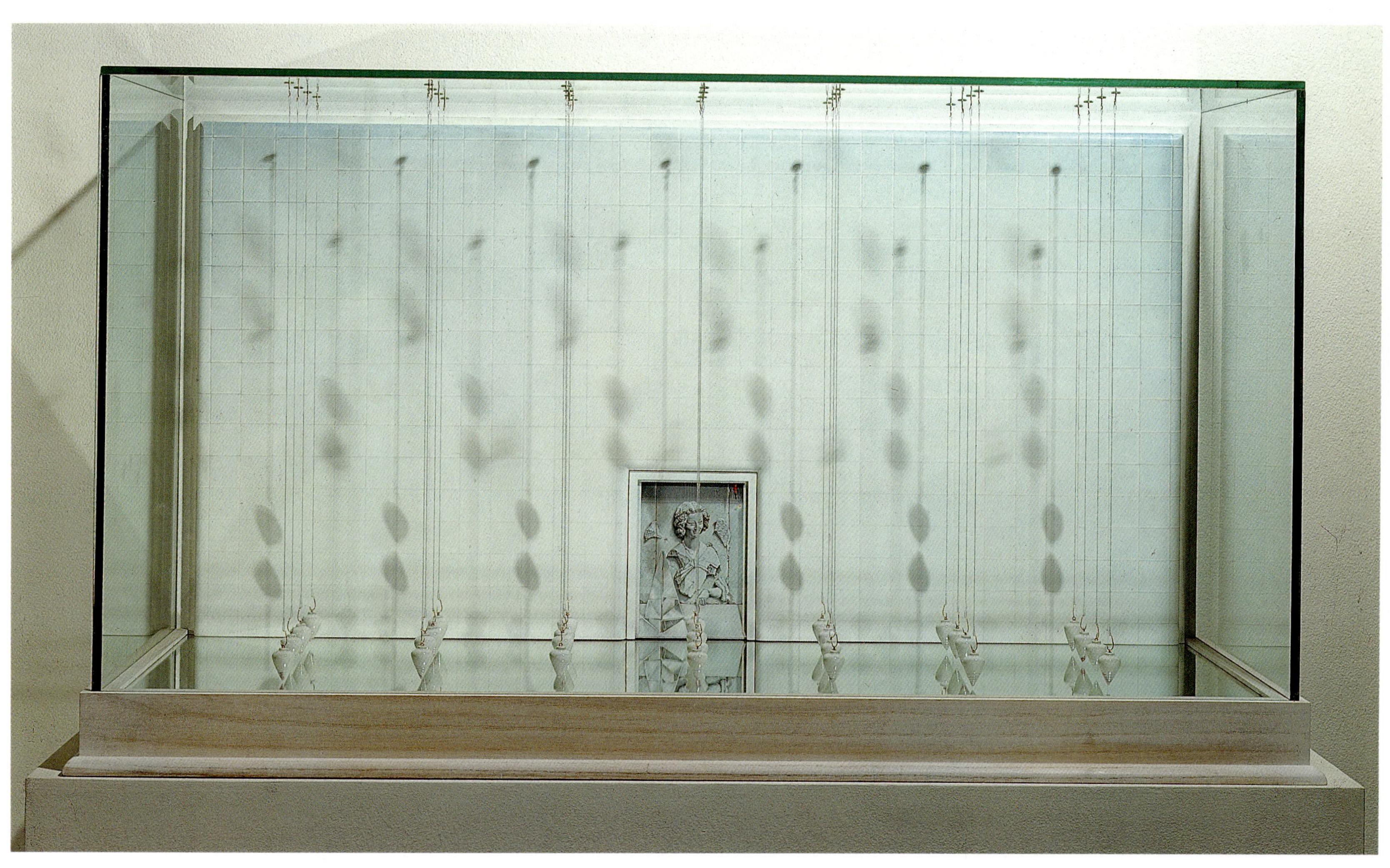

28 *El Cuarto en el Fondo del Pozo/ The Room at the Bottom of the Well* 1978

Mixed media, 18¾ × 28 × 6 inches
Teresa and Larry Katz

The color red and its associations with passion and death saturate the six-inch-deep glass case of *El Cuarto en el Fondo del Pozo/ The Room at the Bottom of the Well.* The red silk used for the background is reflected everywhere in the gleaming surface of the case. A square red niche, or recess, cut out of the graph paper on the left-hand side has been transformed into the red cell of a small birdcage on the right-hand side. Its solid red converse in the graph paper harks back to the Sacred Heart, the scrap of red silk in the center of *El Paisaje del Rey/The Landscape of the King.* The split red and white sections of this image present two warring halves of a divided self, oscillating between earthly passion and spiritual purity, ultimately unified.

The floor of the glass case is graph paper masked beneath layers of graphite, somewhat like the layered lines of graphite flooding the background of *Sara's Garden,* with its effect of a metallic mirror. The floor of this case incorporates an actual small mirror like a trapdoor, directly below the single suspended black top in the right foreground corner of the case (the black top is like the one from *P. M. Times*). The top and its mirrored trapdoor present the viewer with a dark spiral entering the vortex of its own self, the caduceus, or double-spiral, shape of the androgyne, symbolizing opposites united in the two-way action of ascent and descent, good and evil, life and death—dualities exemplified in the split red and white halves of the work.

On the white wall of graph paper, a mystic seven toothpicks of varying lengths ascend and descend at intervals around a solitary chair with a fluttering, moving shirt draped over the back of it, a shirt as filled with supernatural motion as the shirt of *Ascension.* González places a drawing of himself at the bottom center of the white wall of graph paper, beneath the red "heart," a naturalistic rendering of himself as one of Giacometti's *Standing Woman* series, perhaps in particular the *Woman in a Cage* of 1946 (Estate of Pierre Matisse, New York); the figures are quite alike in their tense stance within framed space. González's trinity of blank white "bed sheets" on the left of the wall of graph paper traces a path down to this self-portrait in a "room at the bottom of the well." To the artist, this work was "an image of deep isolation, expressing my inner state. I felt unable to really connect with anybody."

The white androgyne figure of himself—the magical conjunction of the artist with a female opposite implicit in the quotation of Giacometti's *Woman in a Cage*—is a sharper, clearer self-portrait of the Oedipal white figure on a glass ledge of *El Paisaje del Rey/The Landscape of the King,* while the red and white "mirrored" halves of this work relate back to the Bleeding Heart scrap of frayed red silk depicted in the earlier work.

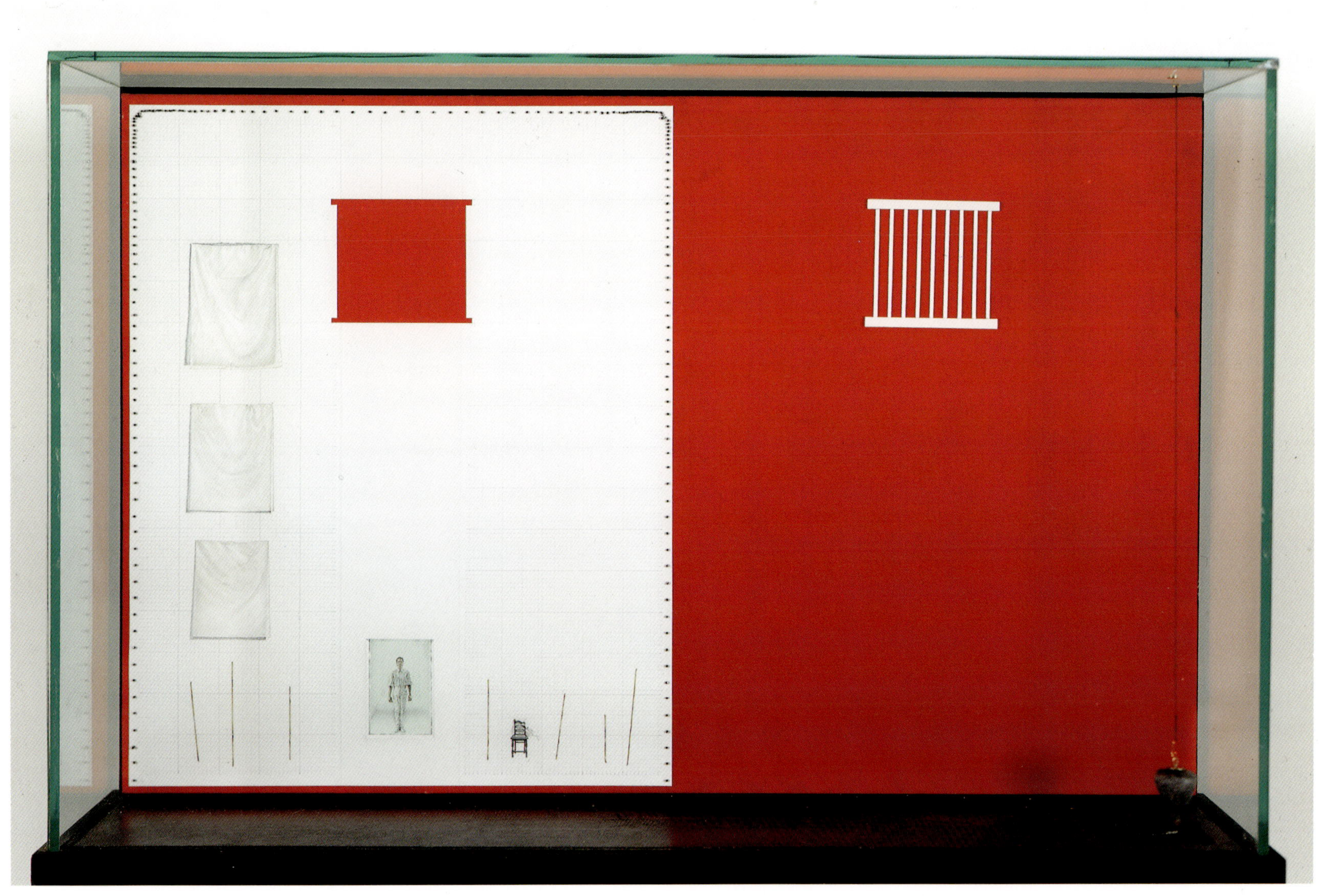

29 *Untitled* 1978

Tempera, gold leaf, and oil on board, 11 × 12 inches
The Carnegie Museum of Art, Pittsburgh, Pennsylvania, The A. W. Mellon Acquisition Endowment Fund, 81.106

This intensely colored miniature portrait of a friend repeats the theme of the cage. The pale trunks of palm trees set up a surreal wall of bars in a dream synthesis of an upstate New York fall-foliage landscape and a tropical Cuban treescape; the palms are an ideal or symbolic projection of González himself into the landscape. González is aware that palms are emblematic of victory and spiritual conquest, of Christ's triumphal entry into Jerusalem, commemorated every Palm Sunday. Palms are also self-creating emblems of the androgyne—of perfection, wholeness, and paradise regained. Yet it was once again with the drawings of Giacometti uppermost in his mind that González created this cage of palms to frame the slight, elongated, strolling figure of his companion.

At the top of the painting, the crescent-shaped blue mound (actually a mountain, though it looks very watery and pool-like) occurs because the artist was "always surprised in the fall that the upstate mountains would be blue." This blue mound is reminiscent of the mounds in early paintings like *Pink Wall* and the chest mound of *Self-Portrait in Black Wrapping*. The sky over the blue mound is pure gold leaf, influenced by an art work that had enchanted González on a recent trip to Europe, Martin Schongauer's 1473 *Madonna of the Rose Hedge* (Church of Saint Martin, Colmar).

The artist reverses the trick he used in *Mar y Espejo* (Sea and Mirror) to create a short but abrupt drop in the foreground of the picture—a miniprecipice like the front edge of a theater stage. This low ledge is a dreamlike condensation of the towering walls of cut stone that rise on either side of many upstate roads, the roads slicing right through the core of mountains. Instead of enlarging the edge, as he did for the wall of sand in *Mar y Espejo,* González here reduces it, to dissect the foreground of his composition and to separate the spectator from the dream stage in the image.

A lizard, unseen by the oblivious strolling man, basks on the rocky ledge, which now offers the double drama of precipice and reptile. The lizard is like the salamanders of *The Sparrow and the Maiden*—a perverse touch of dark realism in a glowing landscape of the imagination, a serpent in the Garden of Eden. It is also a uniquely Cuban touch. Cuban children played with small lizards, either pulling their tails off or wearing them as earrings. González remembers: "They used to have the lizards bite on their earlobes. The lizards were very aggressive when you caught them; they would hang on for a few minutes—but I could never do it. I've always had a kind of primeval reaction to lizards. I look at them, and I feel terror and revulsion."

The image of the unseen lizard has its art-historical counterpart in Caravaggio's *Boy Bitten by a Lizard* (c. 1592–97, private collection), in which a young Bacchus, posed with a vase of roses and some scattered fruit (including paired cherries, symbolic of love), recoils with a cry as an all-but-hidden lizard bites his middle finger. Possibly painted after Caravaggio had suffered a disappointment in love, the lizard represents an allegorical warning of the pitfalls of romance.

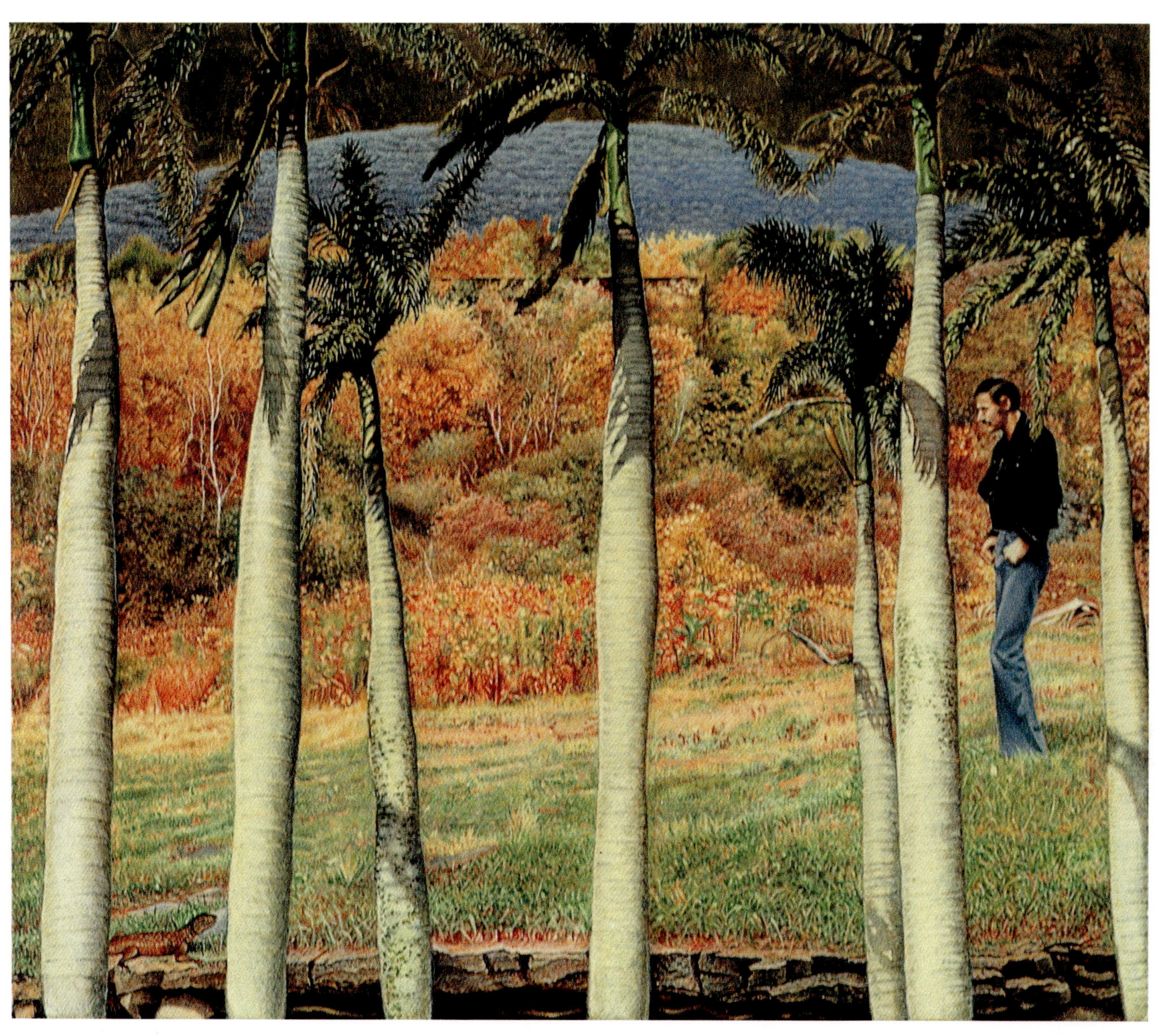

30 *Nacimiento/Nativity* 1979

Watercolor on paper in a wooden cabinet, 14¾ × 15 × 10¾ inches
Collection of Hal and Susan Einstein

Nacimiento/Nativity, a wooden cabinet nearly eleven inches deep, is a Cornell-inspired box, a miniature theater of memory quoting a dazzling array of art works González had viewed on a summer trip to the Uffizi in Florence. The kneeling angel, the vases of flowers, and the scattered petals are drawn from the huge *Portinari Altarpiece* of Hugo van der Goes, ca. 1476–78. The white-railed terrace transformed into a theater stage was inspired by Giovanni Bellini's *Sacred Allegory* of Purgatory and Paradise, ca. 1490. The artist's youthful mother (based on a photograph taken many years before, just one day prior to her wedding) is veiled by a windowpane of watery green glass, a fallen "handkerchief" at her feet, actually a translucent gauze fold extrapolated from the angel Gabriel's filmy overrobe in Botticelli's Cestello *Annunciation,* 1489–90. The angel's gauze fold may announce the artist's mother as the Virgin, yet it also fantastically fuses her with Francis Bacon's 1967 *Portrait of Isabel Rawsthorne Standing on a Street in Soho* (Nationalgalerie, Berlin), part of whose arm and dress also escape from or are dissected by Bacon's linear cube around the figure, and at whose feet there is also an ambiguous smeared splash of white paint, repeated at hip level, where González transforms the white paint into the pure white head of the sacrificial lamb, Christ.

Though the artist's mother is enthroned in the foreground, the pane of glass that covers her seems to be attached to or confluent with a curious wooden frame, set back in the middle ground of the stage, at the depth of the black curtain. The architecture of the curtained terrace is dream architecture, irrational, with the artist's mother being brought to the foreground of the painting, where she looms unnaturally large for the background structure that supposedly contains and frames her. *Nacimiento/Nativity* was created, like most of the early works, with the aid of a jeweler's lamp and magnifying glass. González spent well over a month working obsessively on his mother's face alone, "trying to get at some psychological truth about my relationship with her. I just couldn't let go until I felt I had that, even though the face is so tiny." This was his first and last portrait of her.

Meanwhile, smaller, more distant, and older, the artist's father, painted from a photograph taken much closer to the time when González made this work, muses complacently over his Good Shepherd crook, or crozier, here modeled on a device for extinguishing candles in church. The bawling infant in this strange nativity—the artist's symbol of the human condition—is ignored by all, with the exception of the red-socked, bare-chested man standing next to González's father, who is the same friend who appeared in the previous landscape with a lizard. The adult artist himself, garbed in baptismal white, is viewed from behind, surveying the lost Cuban landscape of his past. He is also the young man standing at the front of the stage, concealed from his family by a curtain of Mantegna gold, a veil that might theoretically be drawn at will across this theater of bittersweet memory. The young artist doffs his shirt "like a snake shedding his skin," according to González—expressing the old life cast off, the new life embraced.

Setting a seal of liberation over this miniaturized interior are a flamboyantly colored tropical parrot[1] flying free in the sky overhead and a pair of fiery wings emblazoned in the top center of the wooden box—the sign of the Holy Ghost.

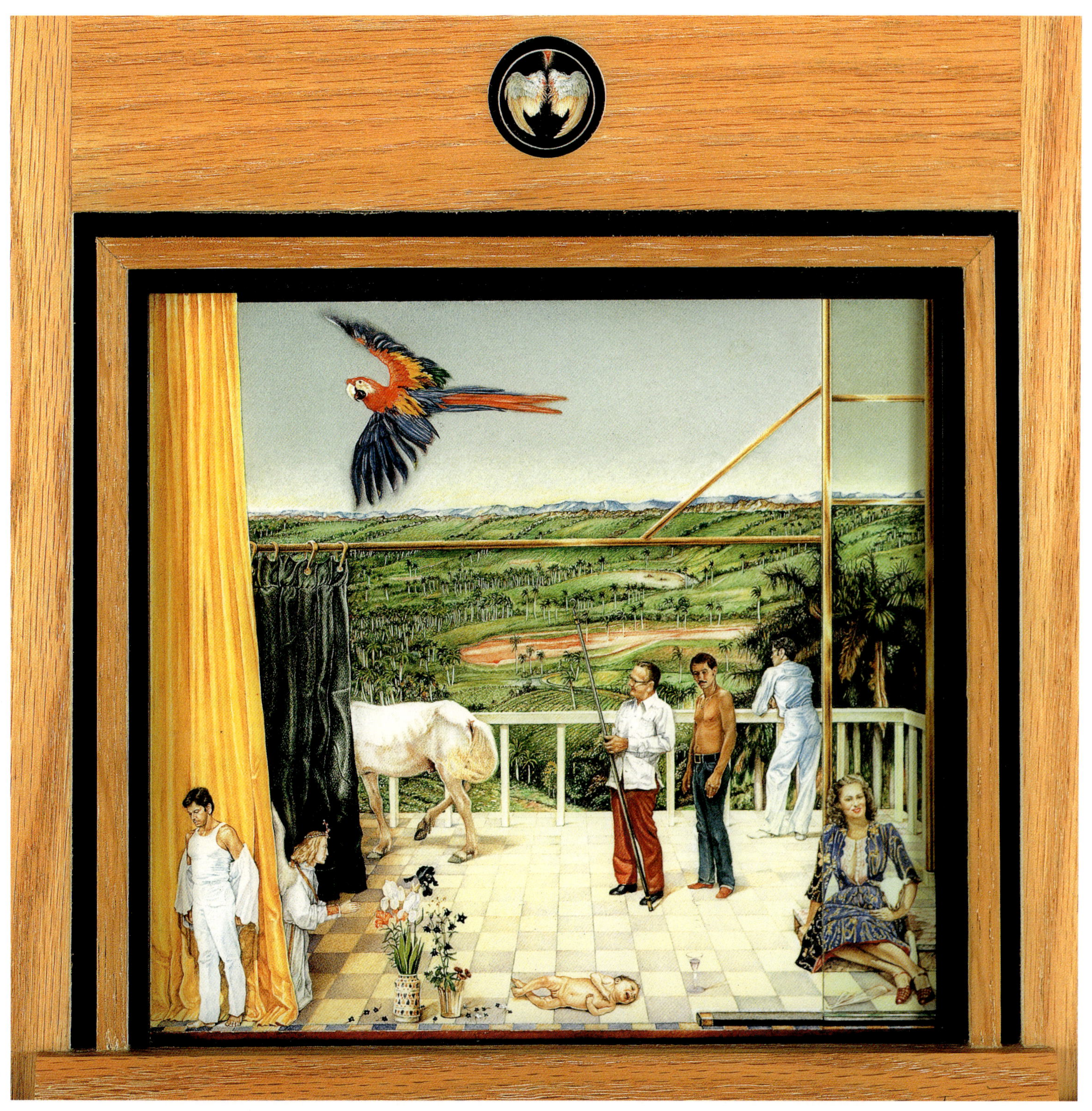

31 *Irish Red (Portrait of Patrick)* 1979

Pastel on paper, 19¼ × 26 inches
Collection of Stephen S. Alpert

Patrick McDonough was one of González's closest friends until he died in 1986, the year González dedicated the painting *New York, Year 1986* to his memory. Of Irish heritage, Patrick aspired to be a poet. He had written a poem about Narcissus, and González decided to use images from the poem "to surround him. I was thinking about the way the Pharaoh sits in Egyptian tablets—with a border of hieroglyphs and symbols all around him. I was using that stately structure to surround Patrick with his own poetry, to *adorn* him with the images of his own poem."

González recalls that Patrick's now-lost poem on the theme of Narcissus incorporated the image of a spiral shell and a reflection of the moon on the surface of still water, suddenly disrupted by creatures moving through and disturbing the water. Perhaps González's memories of Patrick's poem have meshed with memories of poems by Lorca—for instance, "Snail": "They have brought me a snail. / Inside it sings / a map-green ocean. / My heart / swells with water, / with small fish / of brown and silver. / They have brought me a snail."[1] Equally valid may be the reference to the crescent-horned moon goddess and the broken surface of water in Lorca's "Reflection," a poem from the *Mirror Suite:* "Lady Moon. / (Did someone shatter the quicksilver?)."[2] González's image incorporates the Lady Moon, the snail, and small fish emerging from a surrealist void between Patrick's room and the L-shaped symbolist frame above and to one side of the room.

The most dramatic element of the painting, however, and the source of the title, is the way Patrick's head is backed and in a sense framed by an area of bright red like a skewed cloth of honor, signifying passion, energy, and danger. In this red area is an image of red-vested whirling dervishes, a gift from one of Patrick's uncles. Members of a Sufi order of beggars (the Turkish "dervish" and the Persian "darvish" both mean "poor man"), the dervishes are fixed in Western consciousness as "whirling" owing to the possessed dance they perform, dramatizing the spiraling of the planets and revolving cycles of existence. This dervish painting has everything to do with the helical configuration of the snail shell, symbolic of the ebb and flow of energy in nature, the waxing and waning moon, and the turning earth. These dancers characterize the whirling motion of the black top of *P. M. Times,* ritualizing a vision of an engulfing and irresistible vortex.

On the purely visual level, the composition presents the viewer with a series of diagonals—in the fish, the moon, and beneath the snail shell—underscoring the radical nature of the red diagonal behind Patrick's head, where the whirling dervishes personify the remorseless pull of the aspiring poet's compulsions and dreams.

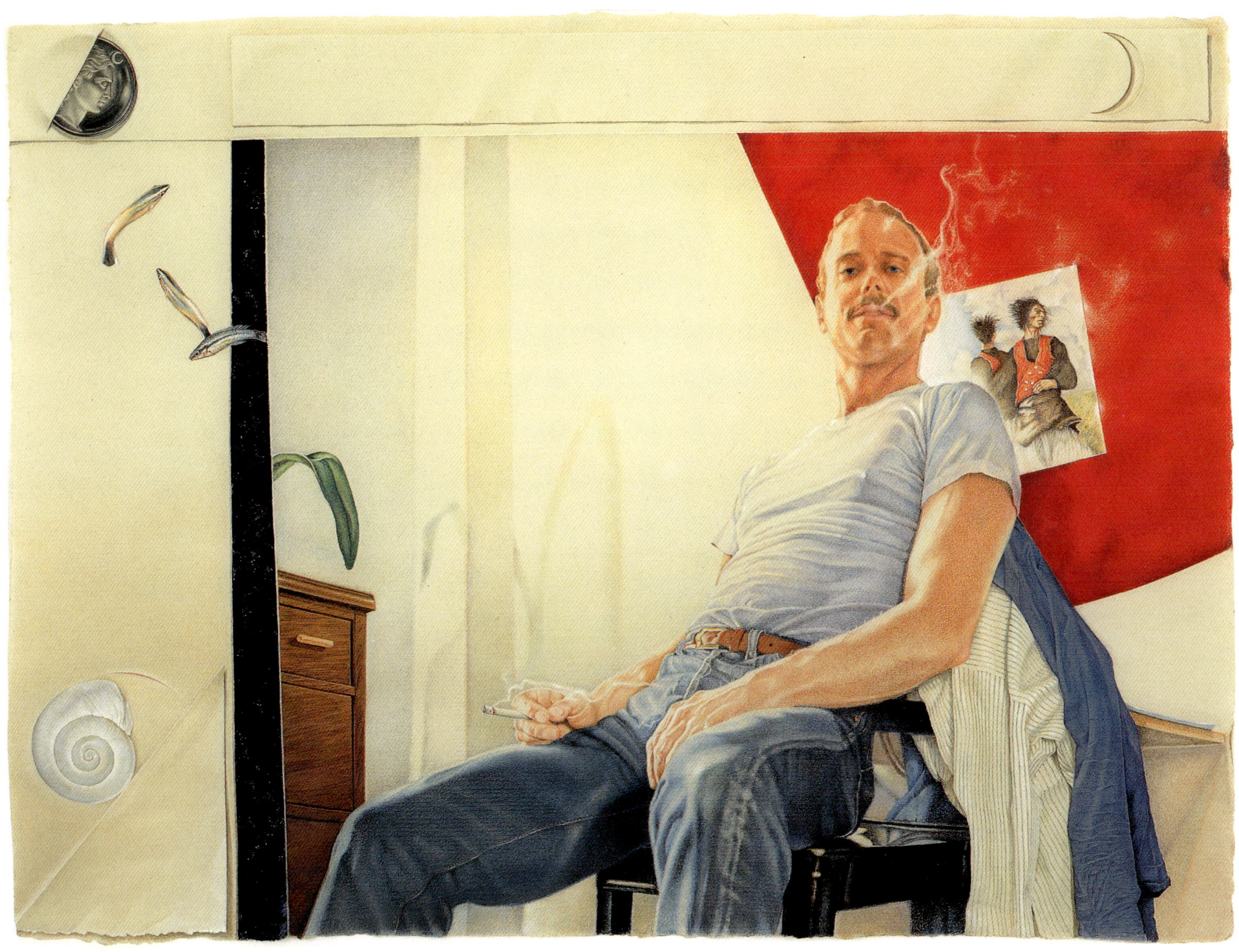

32 *Songs for My Father* 1980

Watercolor and Conté crayon on board, 22 × 42½ inches
Private collection

González further pursues the idea of music, magic, and symbolism in this highly personal and mysterious dreamscape, entitled *Songs for My Father,* as if it were a collection of Old Testament canticles. At the surreal center of the painting is a blazing golden yellow bed, bouncing light back out of the picture at us. This vibrant gold is the color of the stage curtain in *Nacimiento/Nativity*. In *Songs for My Father* González is more strident in his use of the symbolic color in contrast to a predominantly monochrome backdrop: the pictorial space resembles, as ever, a theater stage with veiled entrance and exit wings. The golden bed has the power and presence of a heap of glittering treasure in a dark cave, a fairy-tale emblem of spiritual treasure, enlightenment, the hero's hard-won sense of his own true nature and identity. González intends the bed to be viewed as visual poetry: "a lyrical statement of an electrifying way of looking at the world." The sensational color and satin texture of the bed arises once again from the artist's determination to find a lyric beauty in unexpected quarters. González took the triumphant gold of the bed from the work of Mantegna, after admiring its use in juxtaposition with black in paintings like *The Virgin of Victory* of 1495–96 (Louvre, Paris) and *The Death of the Virgin,* 1461 (Prado, Madrid). González uses the color again in paintings like *El Soñador/The Dreamer,* 1982, *Still Life in Red for Manuel,* and the all-yellow garden *Il Giardino delle Sorelle* (The Garden of the Sisters), both 1987.

Songs for My Father portrays the artist traveling back by stages to his own infancy. He is the young child held in the warm embracing arms of his father, González using the same photograph on which he based the very different image of his father in *Nacimiento/Nativity*. González crowns his father here with a consecrating tonsure, turning him into a contemporary counterpart of Saint Anthony holding the Christ Child, one of the artist's favorite devotional images—also recalling Francis Bacon's 1956 painting *Man Carrying Child* (private collection, Paris), in which a robed Moroccan man carrying a child in his arms has an oddly domed white elevation to his head. Perhaps, too, the strange conjunction of the bed and the beach umbrella here exotically reworks Bacon's reclining bathers under black umbrellas in paintings like the 1974–77 *Triptych* (estate of the artist).

González himself is the young boy in blue who confronts the viewer. He is likewise the adult who, viewed from behind, spreads his hands like a pair of bird's wings to form a bizarre crown over the boy's head. Finally, his is the ambiguously smiling face that peers out at the viewer from over the artist's shoulder, as though the artist were reflecting his image back to us from a black mirror. González's trinity of miniature self-portraits inhabits an art-historical context, designed to evoke the small-scale worshipers who kneel supplicatingly beneath the vast dark mantle of Piero della Francesca's *Madonna of Mercy,* 1460–62 (Museo Civico, Sansepolcro), though the diaphanous white robe of González's towering Madonna of Mercy (only partially visible) is noticeably tinged with the blood of passion and sacrifice.

One of the most fascinating aspects of this profound work is the appearance of the sky—as peculiarly visionary as the sky of *La Misa Blanca* (The White Mass). Based on a flawed laboratory print of one of the artist's photographs, the sky is traversed by what might be an unfurling cloth, or the swell of an incoming tide, looking something like Christo's 1976 *Running Fence,* dropping into the ocean at Bodega Bay, in Northern California. Above this mystery derived from mundane reality, González has placed a Holy Trinity of white clouds, forming a downward-pointing triangle in contrast to the upward-pointing white triangle of the open umbrella. Stranger yet are the repeated segments of ocean, keying off four pale leaping waves (more ebb and flow, or ascent and descent) behind the artist's father, roughly parallel with the pier railing. González had been encouraged to order nature in pattern after studying Martin Johnson Heade's dozen or so subtly changing but nearly identical studies of twilight on the Plum Island River, for the way they show "the power of the artist to record and manipulate nature according to his needs."

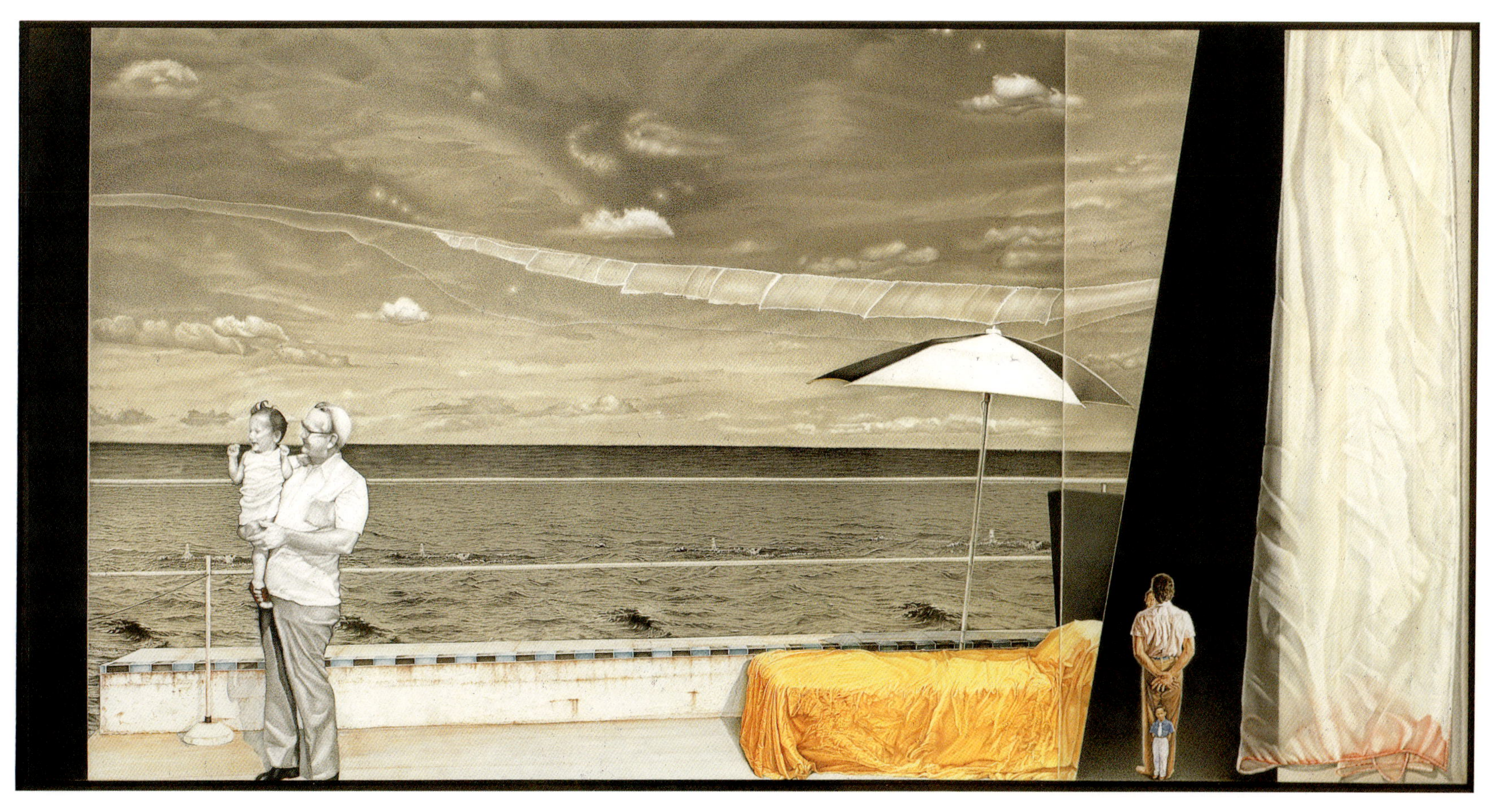

33 *El Recuerdo para Mari/Memories for Mari* 1980

Watercolor and mixed media on handmade paper, 23½ × 20½ inches
Maria and Daniel Schleifman

Another birthday gift for Maria, *El Recuerdo* juxtaposes a view of the child Maria dressed in Easter finery, walking in an enclosed courtyard—a pyramidal metronome before her, as it was in *Mari in the Shadow Box.* The metronome is a quote from Matisse's 1916 *Piano Lesson* (The Museum of Modern Art, New York), González drawing a parallel here between the intimidating exercise of learning the piano and the fearful descent into the unknown that life often entails. Placed alongside her like an Annunciation angel is the "caged" and mirrored head of the smiling stone angel of Rheims, familiar to the viewer from *El Paisaje del Rey/The Landscape of the King* and *Prisma y Prisión/Prism and Prison,* where the angel's face was also dissected by vertical lines or threads, reminiscent of Francis Bacon's dissection of Lucian Freud and Isabel Rawsthorne within the linear cubes that frame and surround them.

Here, as in *Prisma y Prisión/Prism and Prison,* the dissecting threads over the angel's face are actual, physical threads tied to the cutout window through which we view the girl and the angel. The artist has strung these threads with tiny pearls, which may be slid up and down, expanding his obsession with spiraling forces in ascension and descension unifying polar extremes, first broached in the shadow rain of drops moving up and down threads in *Prisma y Prisión/Prism and Prison.* At the same time, he capitalizes on traditional associations of the pearl with the moon (which it resembles in miniature form); with ocean waters (where it resides, hidden deep); with the luminous and the feminine; with beauty, purity, and spiritual grace. Perhaps the artist has in mind the parable of the " 'pearl of great price,' for which man must dive into the waters of baptism and encounter dangers,"[1] the pearl of saving wisdom and spiritual enlightenment. Below the cutout window, attached to the pale green wall of the picture, is an abstract black springboard and a pale green abstract diver flying off the board, down to unseen ocean depths. González claims this pale green (the color of the handmade paper he uses here) as a symbolic color particular to his vocabulary as an abstraction of ocean depths, encompassing a wealth of meanings such as baptism, death, and rebirth. This same color is used to stunning effect in *Bathers of Blenheim,* 1982, and *Teresa en Verde* (Teresa in Green), 1985. But the diver may also remind the viewer once again of Francis Bacon's Muybridge-based 1966 *Portrait of George Dyer Crouching* (private collection, Caracas)—in which Dyer squats on a kind of diver's springboard, over the center of an ambiguous circular sofa, a brown "nest."

The stone angel of Rheims is the veiled portrait of González himself, metamorphosed into imperishable stone, an androgyne conflation of the stone angel and flying artist of *Good Friday.* This carved angel is doubled, occupying two spheres, the real and the mirrored. A trompe-l'oeil mirrored wall, echoing the crystal walls implied by the beveled edges of *Mar y Espejo* (Sea and Mirror), separates the artist from his daughter; they turn away from one another, each unable to see the other. This angel/artist revolving in reflective glass is a type of petrified Narcissus, isolated but immortalized in art.

The red threads framing the diver and springboard are in trompe l'oeil, but the three red wax seals in the box at the bottom of the piece are as material as they seem to be, intended by the artist to "seal a contract or covenant" with his daughter.

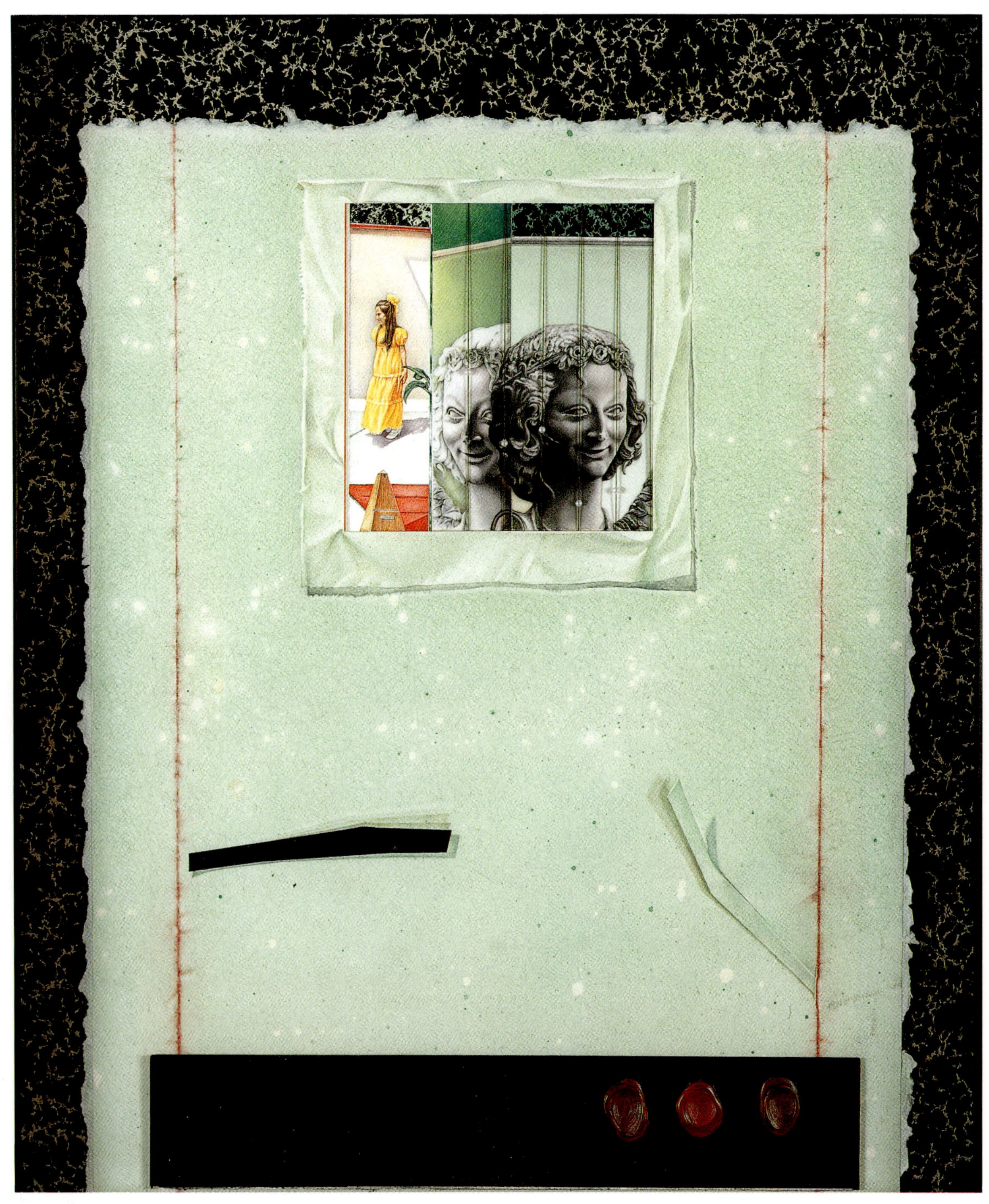

34 *Miércoles de Ceniza* 1980

Watercolor and collage on paper, 23¾ × 25 inches
Stuart Handler Family Collection, Evanston, Illinois

The first day of Lent, the season of penitence climaxing in Holy Week in the Catholic church, is called "Ash Wednesday" because on that day the foreheads of the congregation are crossed with ashes, in symbolic reminder of mortality and the ritual words of interment: "earth to earth, ashes to ashes, dust to dust; in sure and certain hope of the Resurrection to eternal life, through Our Lord Jesus Christ." Inevitably, the title of this work reminds us of T. S. Eliot's great poem "Ash Wednesday" and the "time of tension between dying and birth." *Miércoles de Ceniza* (Ash Wednesday) is about recognizing one's own mortality—though the rough bands of deep green at the top and bottom of the image are undoubtedly intended to signal hope of redemption in Lent and the Resurrection.

A slightly flawed memory of Lorca's letter of May 1918 to the futurist poet Adriano del Valle informs the flowered background of this piece. The poet had described himself miserably to his friend as "a poor impassioned and silent fellow who, very nearly like the marvelous Verlaine, bears within a lily impossible to water, and to the foolish eyes of those who look upon me I seem to be a very red rose with the sexual tint of an April peony, which is not my heart's truth. . . . Sadness of the enigma of myself!"[1] González has turned the rose into a carnation but nonetheless acknowledges this letter as the symbolic basis of the back cloth in *Miércoles de Ceniza,* his idea being, like Lorca's, to contrast the cool purity and innocence of the white lily, symbolic of the Virgin, with the overt passion characterized by the red flower.

González remembers that the visual source for his half-length portrait against a back cloth was the 1499 *Portrait of Oswalt Krel* (Alte Pinakothek, Munich), the young Albrecht Dürer's first great portrait painting, depicting a sharp-eyed young merchant posed against a dramatic red cloth background (the back cloth in both the Dürer and González works intersects the subject's right shoulder at exactly the same point). Perhaps, too, Dürer's half-length 1493 *Self-Portrait With Eryngium Flower* (Louvre, Paris) is remembered in the black fabric folds bordered with red, which function almost as theater curtains or wings at the sides of this work, conveying a sense of self-revelation: Dürer wears a dark red–bordered tunic loosely open to the waist in his self-portrait.

Yet *Miércoles de Ceniza* undoubtedly alludes to a couple of González's own paintings—from the stiff and shiny black curtain in the middle ground of *Nacimiento/Nativity* to the artist's enigmatic *Self-Portrait in Black Wrapping,* in which a plasticlike black material similar to the curtains here opens around the artist's naked foreshortened torso, to dramatize the unveiling of the self. It is worth remarking, too, that with these black curtains, González has brought the Madonna's cloth of honor (used in his portraits of Mari) into the foreground, dividing its comfortingly solid expanse into two torn halves, which lie at the outer sides of the painting, rather than taking up the center.

Most strikingly of all, the artist has here for the first time created a true and masterly self-portrait—interiorized and removed from the viewer though it is, presented to us in a magic mirror in space. Ingeniously, too, the artist implies a flat, reflected mirror image, which subtly slides into a mysterious ledge or pedestal projecting out toward the viewer, which is covered with a filmy purple fabric. "In Cuba on Ash Wednesday all the saints in the church would be covered with a purple material, until the Sunday of Christ's Resurrection," comments González. This purple cloth, which appears to cling damply as much as to fall in drapes over the ledge or pedestal, rises like a fluid element around the artist's mirrored torso, placing him chest-deep in a pool of purple, a ghost in the watery world of the mirror.

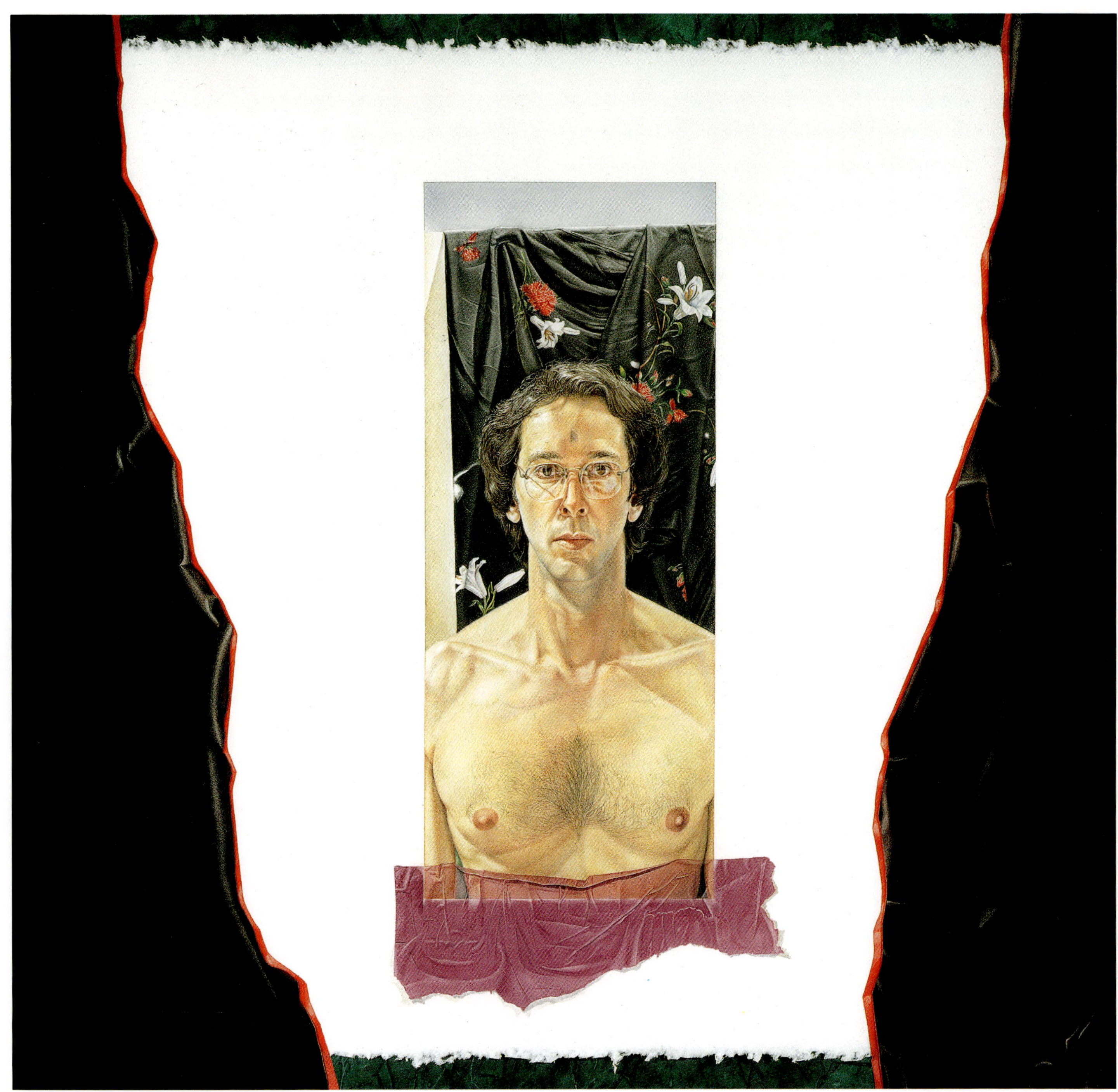

35 *A la Cabeza del Bautista en Sevilla/ To the Head of John the Baptist in Seville* 1981

Charcoal, gouache, pastel, and Conté crayon on handmade paper, 29 × 23 inches
Collection of Gloria Manney

González made this huge, mostly monochrome study of the head of his friend Patrick on a plate partly in reaction to the intensely colored miniaturism of *Nacimiento/Nativity,* using Conté crayon sharpened to an extreme point to achieve a rich range of values and dark atmospheric ground—a veiled yet detailed surface alive with the suggestion of hidden forms moving beneath the surface of the drawing.

The massive scale of the head, about three times life size, was in response to the huge Head of Constantine the artist saw in Rome (ca. A.D. 315, Palazzo dei Conservatori), though he had also been deeply affected by Juan de Mesa's life-sized polychrome wooden head of John the Baptist of about 1625 exhibited in Seville cathedral—an unusual piece in that it was apparently designed to be shown upright, whereas other Baptist heads were displayed lying on one side.

The initially disturbing notion of the severed or disembodied head was a favorite theme of symbolist artists in paintings of John the Baptist or Orpheus—common in works by Gustave Moreau, Lucien Lévy-Dhurmer, Jean Delville, Fernand Khnopff, and Odilon Redon. Redon in particular, in drawings like the charcoal *Head of a Martyr,* 1877 (Rijksmuseum Kröller-Müller, Otterlo, Holland), and the 1913–16 pastel *Orpheus* (The Cleveland Museum of Art) among others, was obsessed with the severed or disembodied head. Robert Delevoy, in *Symbolists and Symbolism,* suggests that for Redon the disembodied head likely represents "the mind surviving after the death of the body; . . . it may be an image of Orpheus, tortured by his unsatisfied passion. . . . It may be associated also with the age-old dream of human flight, and with related images of the sphere of the heavens. . . . It recalls the mystic representations of the Ascension."[1]

González's portrait of Patrick is, like the earlier *Irish Red,* "a portrait about his poetry," says the artist, "because he was always frustrated that he could never find the time to write." It is a portrait of Patrick colored by associations with Orpheus as well as John the Baptist, a portrait of the poet rejoicing in the immortality of art, transforming Patrick into the Orpheus he dreamed of becoming.

The head rises above water, appropriately enough for both the Baptist and Orpheus. González has placed Patrick's laughing head on a mirroring plate presenting a burnished, liquidly reflective surface, like a rippling pool of water. The gridded background, which the artist worked from a photograph of a Robert Rauschenberg image, incorporates fluid runs of white primal matter to the right of the subject. This white splash nods yet again in the direction of Francis Bacon, who splattered white pigment onto his 1966 *Portrait of George Dyer Staring at a Blind Cord* (Collection Maestri, Parma).

Bright touches of coral pastel (aside from the green line of resurrection in the rim of the plate, almost the only other sparks of color in the monochrome composition, a lesson learned from Khnopff) enliven the finches fluttering in a halo or crown around Patrick's head (González and Patrick actually kept pet finches in a mirrored aviary constructed by the artist). A single finch hovers at Patrick's ear, offering the poet inspiration.

An electric tuft of hair standing up on Patrick's head may imply ascension, though the Seville head of the Baptist is itself notable for what Maria Elena Gómez Moreno in *The Golden Age of Spanish Sculpture* describes as "a Baroque feeling of form with its wavy hair piled up on the forehead."[2]

González began work on this portrait from life, after Patrick received a brutal new haircut. The portrait is subtly contemporary—the bespectacled head ends in a roll-neck sweater and sports a pink contusion in piquant reference to the Baptist and Orpheus.

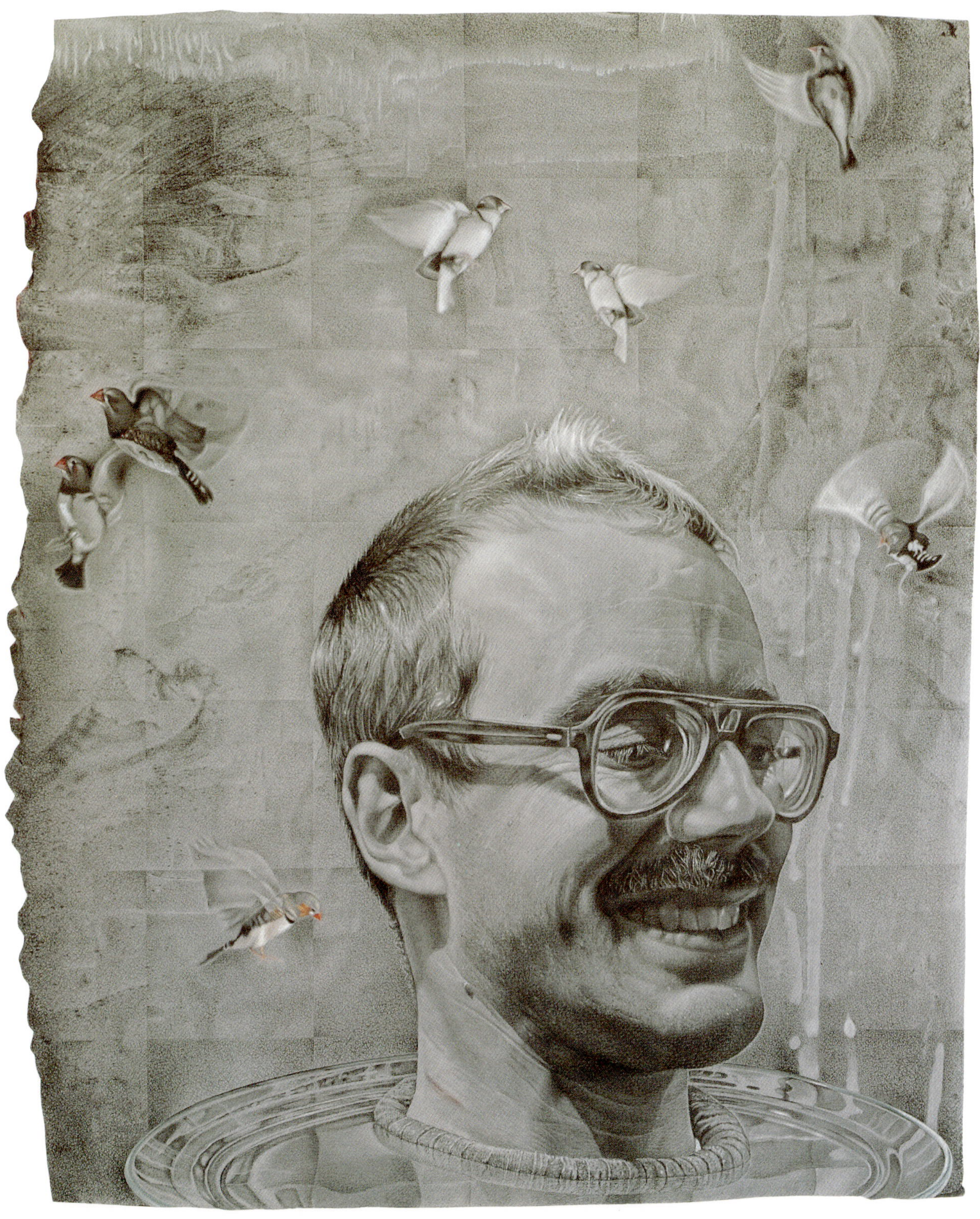

36 *Portrait of Mari* 1981

Oil on linen, 8 × 8 inches
Collection of Laila and Thurston Twigg-Smith

With this small, finely glazed portrait of his daughter Maria (González had been intensively researching the technical secrets of the Venetian and Flemish painters), and with the next work, *Whistler,* and *El Soñador/The Dreamer,* completed in 1982, González returned to oils for the first time in about fifteen years, working on all three paintings concurrently. The perfectly square *Portrait of Mari* enlarges the face at the center of *Mari in the Shadow Box,* both portraits being based on a single photograph taken by the artist. In the former work, González had had in mind the paintings of Bellini, Giorgione, and Titian—Madonnas enthroned with protective and ornamental fabrics at their backs, reinvented by González as the grid of a soft dark leather armchair. The idea is elaborated on in this painting: the gold-edged red cloth with a grid of creased folds above the leather armchair is directly inspired by the background of Giovanni Bellini's *Madonna and Child,* 1510 (Brera, Milan), though reversing the colors of Bellini's cloth of gold edged with red.

To the right of the gridded cloth is something like a window-view of a Cuban landscape, positioned much like the blue-skied mountain landscape of Giorgione's *Madonna and Child,* 1503–5 (private collection, Bergamo). To the left of González's leather-throned Madonna is a shadowed fragment of an architectural drawing, emblem of Maria's profession. The arch to one side and the treescape to the other side of the cloth of honor are reminiscent of Dürer's *Madonna with a Siskin,* 1506 (Staatliche Museen, Berlin-Dahlem), while placing Maria calmly and majestically between past and present, light and shadow, framed within a protective grid of softly undulating lines.

González returns again and again to images of his daughter Maria as the Virgin Mary. She is the incarnation of his childhood dream of a perfect female beauty, his personal embodiment of the divine. She is also a living mirror image of the artist—through familial resemblance, ethereal personality, and art-oriented profession—his anima and muse.

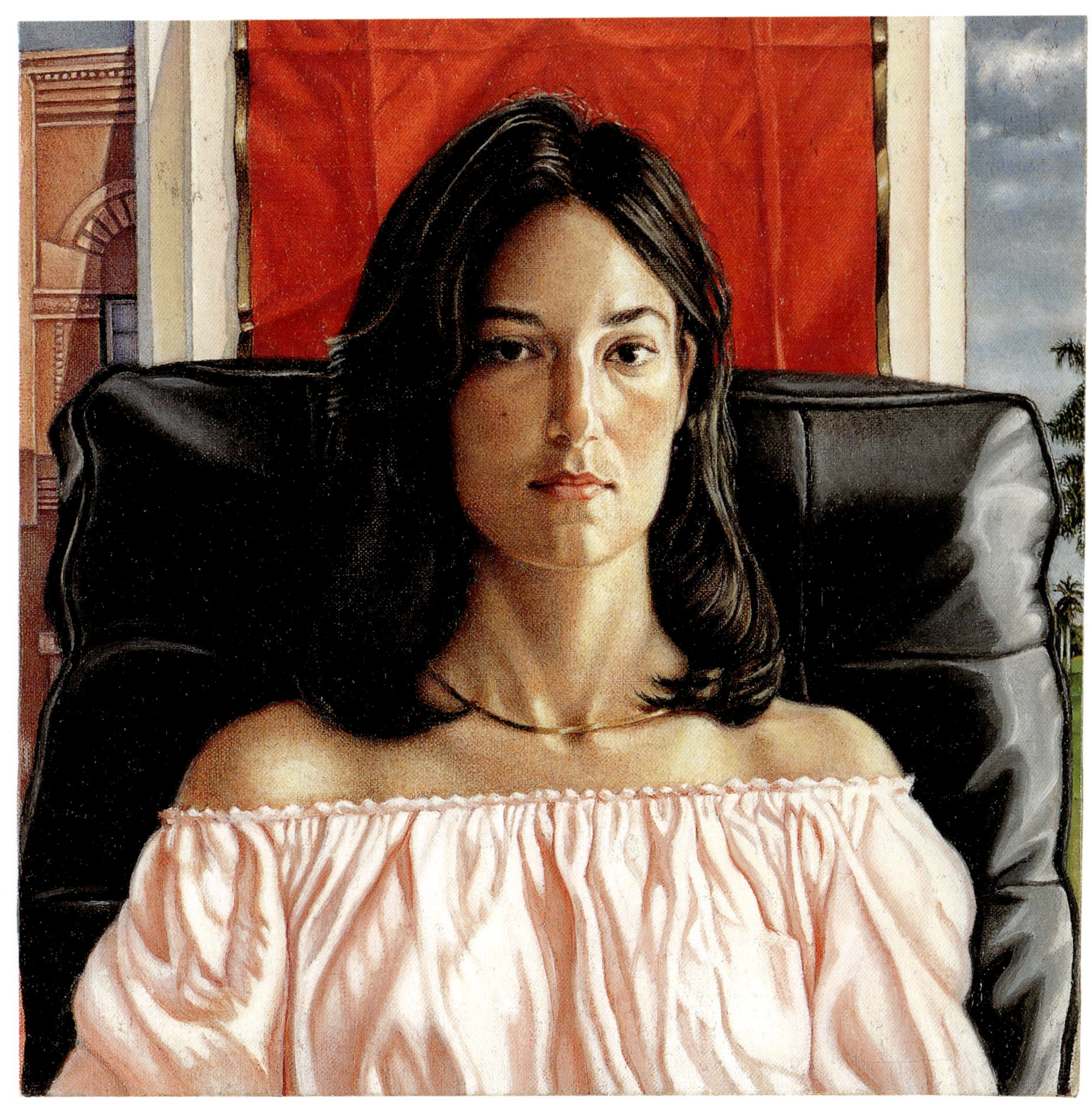

37 *Whistler* 1981

Oil on Masonite, 7 × 6 inches
Private collection

González began this self-portrait by drawing himself from life, in the mirror of his room at the American School in Morocco, rented by the New York School of Visual Arts for the summer. He had been teaching drawing and painting at the school since 1976 and spent the summer of 1980 in Morocco as a painting instructor for the school.

This small, tightly hemmed-in painting, with its frenetic surround of barred Islamic geometry, was intended to convey a sense of "entrapment," according to the artist. "The architectural center of the image is actually enclosed, because this is a dead-end street. I wanted to evoke that private fear of looking at myself in a mirror—trying to grasp the truth of who I was, and how I looked. I wanted to confront my fear of being cornered by myself. Around the time I painted this, I had started to purse my lips that way, to change the way my face looked in the mirror as I grew older." González had had in mind a fragment of Truman Capote's *Other Voices, Other Rooms,* recording Joel Knox's daily discomfort as he studies himself in the mirror: "Looking in the hand-glass became an ordeal: it was as if now only one eye examined for signs of maturity, while the other, gradually of the two the more attentive, gazed inward wishing him always to remain as he was."[1]

Art-historical precedents contributed to the structure of the composition. The tightly framed head of the artist recalls Giacometti's obsessive studies of his brother Diego's head in framed space, from around 1950. Francis Bacon's *Head III* (private collection), a head with intense eyes turning back over a shoulder toward the viewer, is an influence, together with the same artist's *Head VI* (Arts Council of Great Britain), both 1949, in which Bacon arrives at the linear cube framing and concentrating the isolated, screaming pope in claustrophobic space.

Though *Whistler* is undoubtedly an image affected by modern art, expressing an existentialist view of the human condition, the artist's strangely pursed lips may also remind the viewer of Rembrandt's *Self-Portrait in a Cap, Open-Mouthed,* 1630, in which Rembrandt theatrically makes a round O of his pouting lips, to achieve a look of shock or wonder. In 1990 González would paint his own hands over the brocaded abdomen of Rembrandt's *Isaac and Rebecca (The Jewish Bride),* ca. 1666 (Rijksmuseum, Amsterdam), and entitle them *Rembrandt's Hands,* identifying himself with the great painter of psychologically revealing self-portraits. Rembrandt's idea of the painter as costumed actor, reflecting and embodying human passion in the mirror, clearly appealed to González, who also imagined himself as Christ imprinted on the veil of Saint Veronica in *Letter to Veronica,* 1983.

González here interprets himself as anxious modern man, his head filling the imprisoning frame of the mirror. Yet he is not quite alone, not quite as isolated as he was in *El Cuarto en el Fondo del Pozo/The Room at the Bottom of the Well.* A miniature Moroccan man on a ladder in the distance—a tiny, hopeful image of man in ascension—looks toward the artist and the viewer as he plies his brush. He is a painter of houses, not pictures, yet a link is implied between the two types of painting, and between the two men. González tried "to make him very sensual. Morocco has so many sensual-looking people. I have him there as a companion in this space that is a cage."

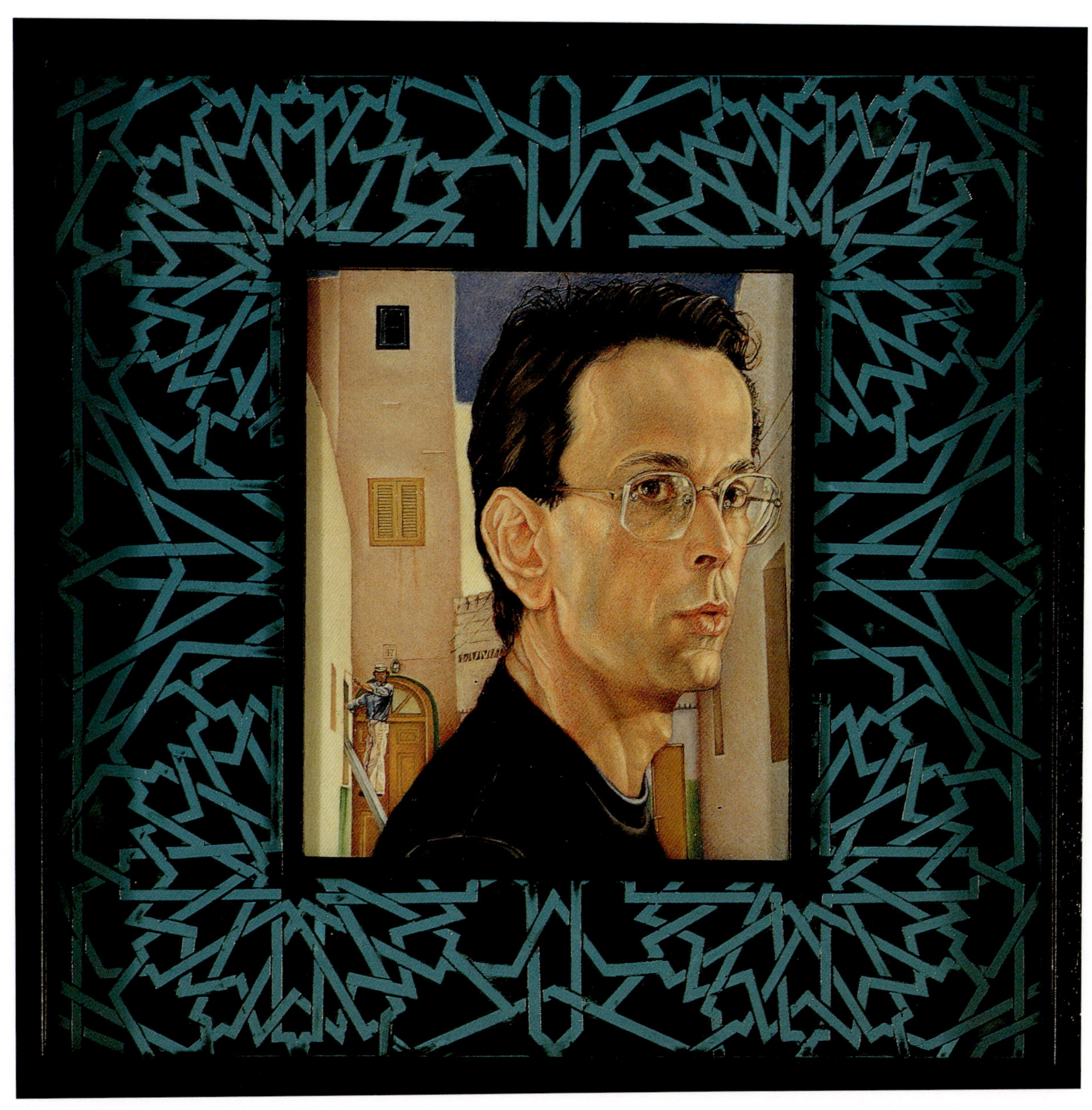

38 *Self-Portrait in Tangier* 1980–82

Pencil and pastel on paper, 16 × 12 inches
Collection of Jalane and Richard Davidson

As if to break out of the tightly framed mirror-vision of himself in the previous small oil painting, González, in this substantially larger work, places an identical self-portrait, drawn rather than painted, against a light, wide-open pastel sky, its soft tints ranging from evanescent yellows through pinks to blues at the very top of the drawing (balanced in the artist's shirt at the bottom).

The view from his room in Tangier is spread out in a low horizontal below the sky, a distant miniature city contrasting with a vast vertical sky and with the monumental head of the artist, which has entered the sky in the same way Patrick's head entered the symbolic red zone of *Irish Red.* In this image of ascension, the artist's black *Whistler* shirt has metamorphosed into a shirt of sky blue, emphasizing the artist's kinship with the heavens above (González will further push the low horizontal of a distant landscape to the very bottom edge of the drawing in *Cultivo una Rosa Blanca* [I Grow a White Rose], 1988, placing a skull at the top of the picture, for an extreme image of ascension). Here, González makes a seemingly mundane self-portrait, drawn from absolute reality, address a religious mystery—Christ's last appearance on earth and ascent into heaven forty days after Easter. The artist finished the drawing in the United States, adding two authentic but romantic features from the New York City night sky of the period: a crescent moon and the star of Venus (the star was unusually bright in the night sky when González finished this drawing).

As consecutive self-portraits and "mirror-images," *Whistler* and *Self-Portrait in Tangier* together create a dualistic effect like the opposed yet complementary halves of *El Cuarto en el Fondo del Pozo/The Room at the Bottom of the Well. Whistler* expresses the artist's Catholic sense of being caged in his sensual earthly body; while the subsequent *Self-Portrait in Tangier,* depicting the companionless artist beneath a cosmic sky, expresses the spiritual orientation of a more ethereal nature. With these two "identical" self-portraits, so frankly opposed in their psychological implications, González demonstrates that the context—the frame—in portraiture is everything.

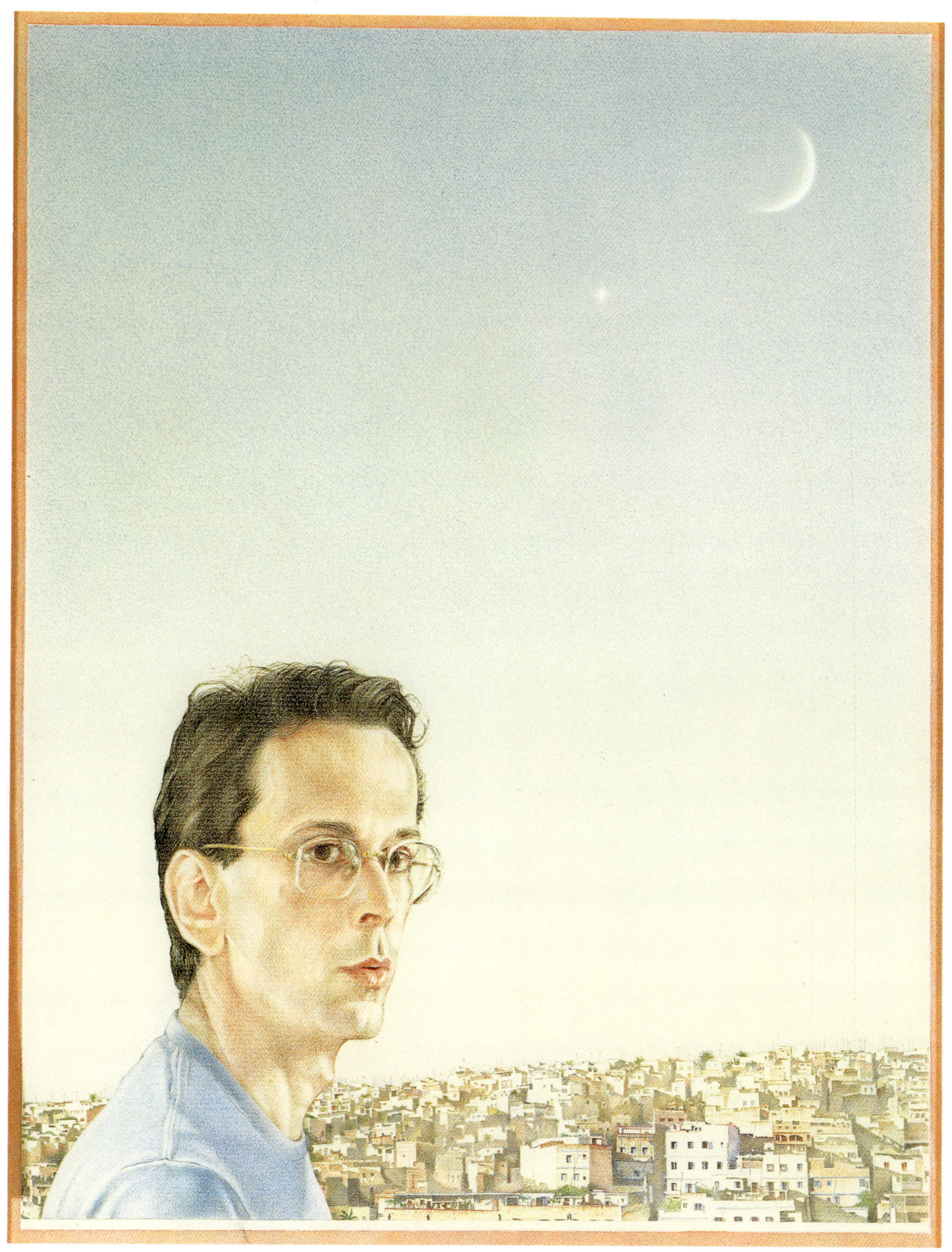

39 *El Soñador/The Dreamer* 1982

Oil on linen, 40½ × 36 inches
Private collection, New York

It is impossible to contemplate González's stunning *El Soñador/The Dreamer* without recalling Nicolas Poussin's Narcissus in *Echo and Narcissus,* circa 1627 (Louvre, Paris), since the disposition of Poussin's prostrate Narcissus and this contemporary sleeper are so remarkably alike.[1] Yet a host of other visual sources underpin the image, according to the artist: Henri Rousseau's *Sleeping Gypsy,* 1897 (The Museum of Modern Art, New York), one of the artist's favorite paintings; Piero della Francesca's canopied, dreaming Constantine (1460–62) at San Francesco, Arezzo; and the sculpted sleeping body of a stone saint in a Barcelona church. The common charm of these varied sources for González is the notion of a magically protected eternal dreamer locked in blissfully secure self-absorption—his "sleep" reflecting the deep introspection of the artist. The pointedly symbolist organization of the three gladioli in *El Soñador/The Dreamer* reinforces these associations, recalling the trinity of lilies that guard the subject of Fernand Khnopff's 1891 painting *I Lock My Door upon Myself* (Neue Pinakothek, Munich).

But *El Soñador/The Dreamer* is also dazzlingly self-referential: the red gladiolus placed in ritual and symbolic centrality before the sleeper, an emblem of his sensuality, inevitably recalls the drowned red gladiolus of *July 11, 1974,* commemorating the day on which González was almost lost in the ocean off Fire Island, while the tiled floor here recycles the tiled terrace of *Nacimiento/Nativity,* itself related to Bellini's sea-view terrace of the *Sacred Allegory,* ca. 1490. The rumpled satin of the bed is an ivoried version of the golden bed by the sea in *Songs for My Father.* And the artist's perennial dream of flight or ascension recurs in the black, starred sky stretching into infinity beneath the raised theater curtain or window blind. The artist further intended this curtain or blind to yield a bird's-eye view of the rumpled bed sheet, like the ocean-veil bed sheet of *La Misa Blanca* (The White Mass). The splendidly illusionistic white gladioli, complete with trompe-l'oeil shadows that flank the sleeper, will later find a counterpart in the pure white roses flanking the submerged diver beneath the subtle folds of a sky curtain in *The Diver's Journey,* 1989, an image of death and transcendence.

Even the artist's lifelong passion for the poetry of Lorca again informs a key element of his work. A famous line from the Spanish poet's "Ode to Walt Whitman" (a work in which Lorca pictures his personal idol Whitman, the lover of "virile beauty," sleeping eternally on the banks of the Hudson River) actively inspired the image of the needle piercing a circle in the pure expanse of the white sheet above González's sleeper. In the "Ode," Lorca celebrates Whitman with the curious observation, "you moaned like a bird / with the sex transfixed by a needle."[2] Yet González is also aware of the circle as a Jungian symbol of completeness in the magical union of opposites, a conjoined sun and moon. The circle and needle may also be viewed as a contemporary abstraction of a crown of thorns above the body of Christ.

El Soñador/The Dreamer weaves together the artist's most important themes, most especially his awareness—akin to Poussin's—of the ambivalent symbolism of water as, on the one hand, the purifying, baptismal fount of salvation and rebirth and, on the other, the source of delusion and destruction, of a consuming self-absorption.

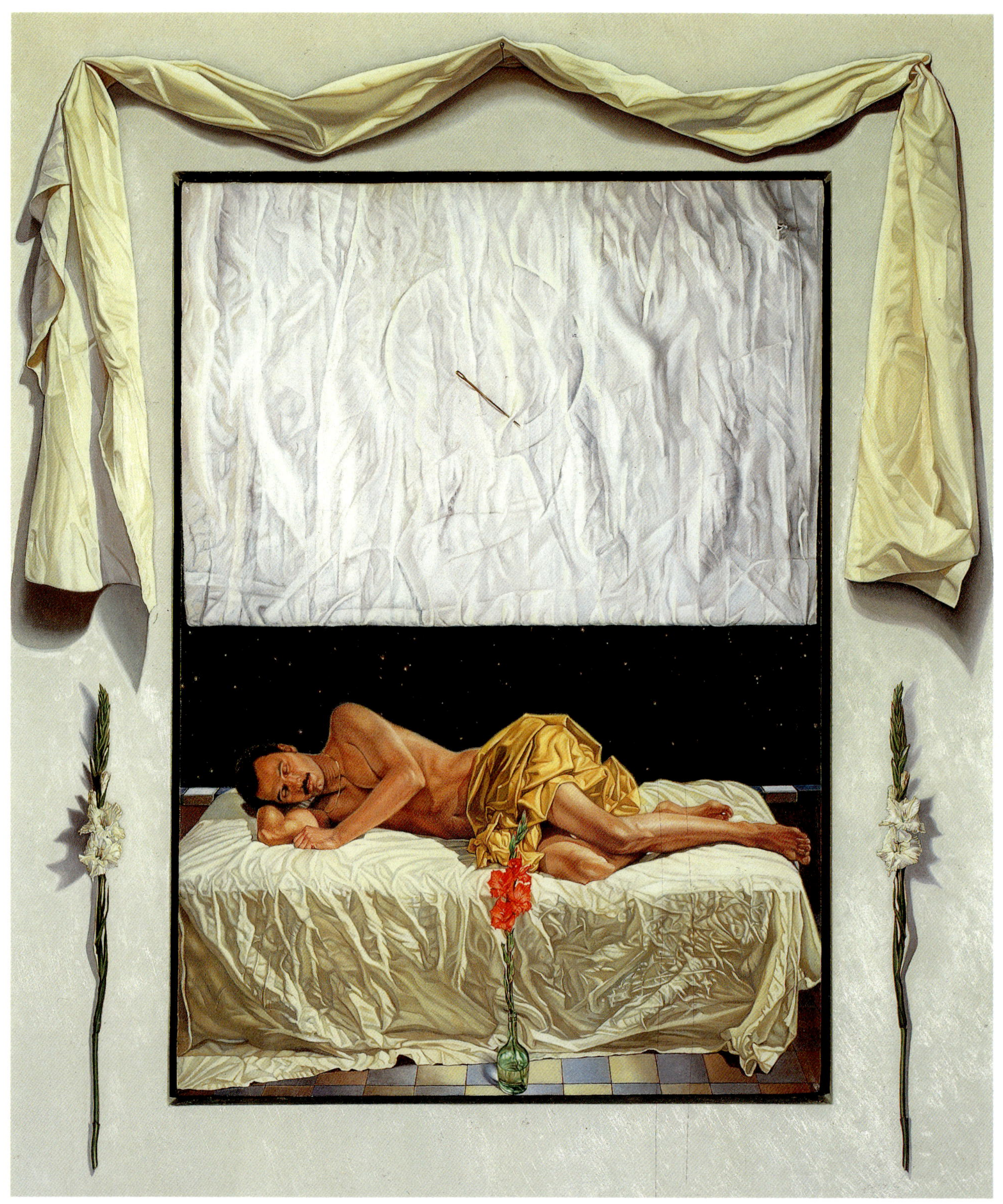

40 *Bathers of Blenheim* 1982

Charcoal and wash on paper, 11½ × 16½ inches
Courtesy of Capricorn Galleries, Bethesda, Maryland

González was staying at Woodstock in Oxfordshire, England, when he drew this tranquil Garden of Eden inhabited by two male bathers under a hovering sculpture standing on a column high over the trees, the miniature figure of Marlborough atop Blenheim's Column of Victory. The bathers emerge from the water that mirrors the trees, in a lush pastoral idyll replete with grazing sheep. González sat every day for a month at Blenheim to draw this scene on pale green paper—paper he no doubt chose for its suggestively watery beauty, as he had earlier chosen it for *El Recuerdo para Mari/Memories for Mari,* with its diver and pearls. Later, staying with Anne Minich in Philadelphia, he completed the image with framing passages of trompe l'oeil: a border of shining green ribbon symbolizing nature, hope, and resurrection, worked around the monochromatic image of the bathers; a fine twine garland with wild rose to the right (a single leaf spotted with twin dewdrops like pearls) and a sprig of Virginia bluebells to the left. He was charmed with the bluebells as emblems of metamorphosis, passing time, and fleeting youth or love, since the flower is pink in bud and bright blue when it opens in tubular blossom.

Bathers of Blenheim exploits a play of contrasts between the chromatic and the monochromatic, the real and the fantastic. The ribbon, twine, and flowers are in luminous trompe l'oeil, while the charcoal monochrome of the landscape seems more like an old photograph or distant memory of some ideal time. This striking opposition is reminiscent of the fifteenth-century Sienese painter Giovanni di Paolo's flowered side panels, contrasting a white rose on the left side with a red rose on the right side, flanking the old-fashioned narrative representation of *Saint John the Baptist Retiring to the Desert,* ca. 1454 (National Gallery, London): González admired these matched yet dissonant flowered side panels so much that he double-quoted them for an elaborate frame-within-a-frame in the untitled 1988 collage for his friend David Shapiro. Perhaps they have contributed to the symbolic contrasting of red and white flowers in González's work—for instance, in *El Soñador/The Dreamer.*

The clarity and realism of the framing flowers certainly heighten the oneiric quality of the central image. The bathers are also strangely diminutive figures by comparison with the distant trees and considering their foreground location—an anomaly that would once again seem to owe some measure of influence to Giacometti's figures in the landscape in drawings like the 1949 *Figure under a Tree* (Collection Gérald Cramer, Geneva). The folded scrap of paper bearing the title is a device borrowed from Giovanni Bellini, to be used again in works like *Still Life in Red for Manuel* and *In His Silence:* in these later paintings, González will even attach the scrap of paper to a Bellini-like predella, the platform or uppermost step of an altar. Though Zurbarán and many others used the device, González remembers this particular scrap of paper as quoting the folded paper in Bellini's *Portrait of Doge Leonardo Loredan,* ca. 1501–5 (National Gallery, London), as not merely an occasion to show off with a passage of trompe l'oeil but as having "something to do with personalizing and claiming the painting," in effect announcing that the painter himself is one of these Blenheim bathers (Patrick McDonough is on the left, González is on the right).

The lavish trompe-l'oeil frame suggests a subtle separation between inner idealism and outer realism, fantasy and fact, though external "fact" here in the illusionistic flowers and twine is as gorgeous and sensual as any fantasy, while the internal "fantasy" is presented in mundane monochrome. The mirror-imaging of the trees echoes the twinning or near mirror-imaging of the two naked male bathers, in a Paradise before the Fall. In the work that followed this, an epic monochromatic study of a town in flood, González explores the darker side of water symbolism.

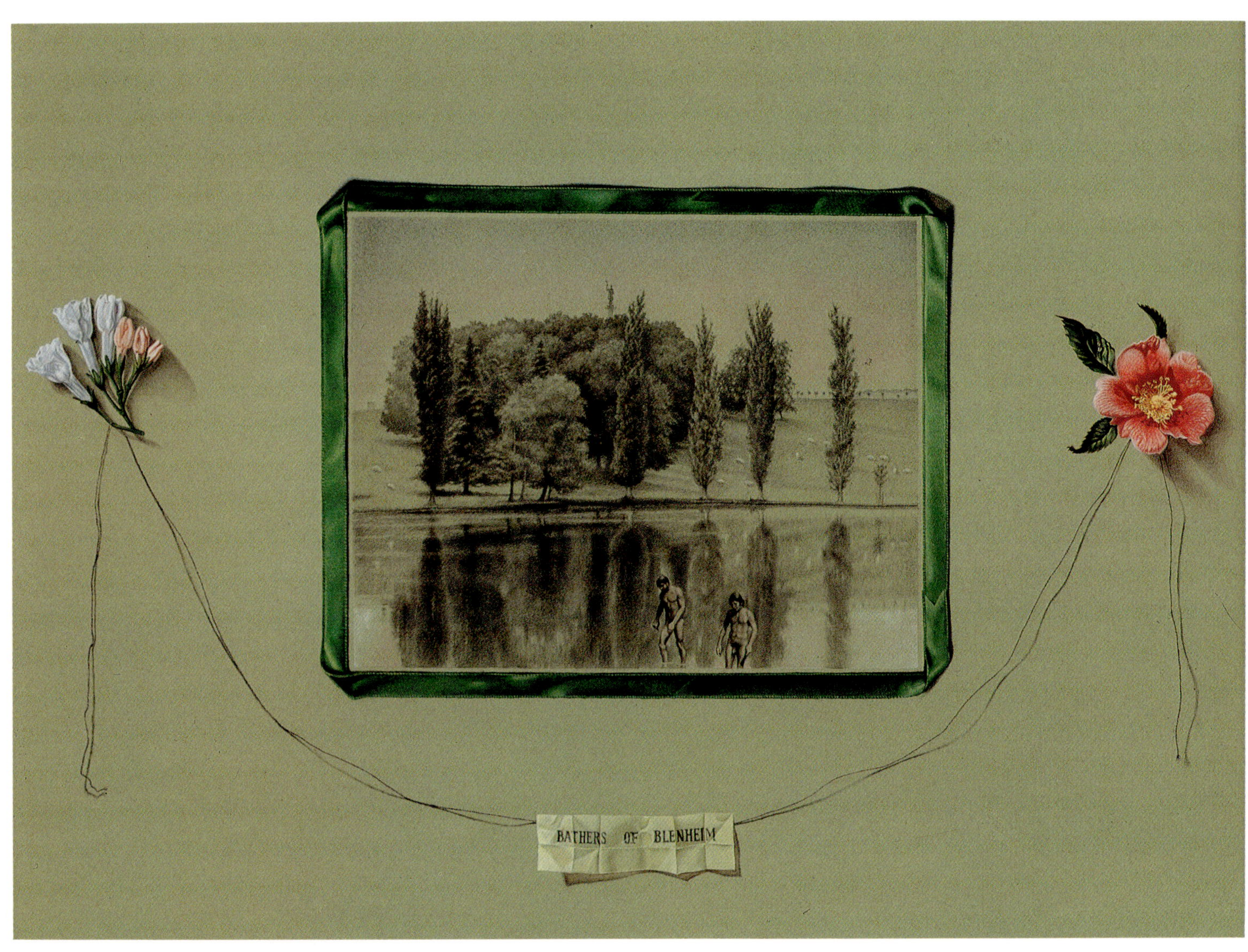
BATHERS OF BLENHEIM

41 *La Educación de Maria* 1984

Oil on canvas and wood, 26½ × 23½ inches
Mr. and Mrs. Richard Aron, Stamford, Connecticut

As usual with his works, González had a deep-seated personal reason to make this painting. Maria had been telling her father "people were discouraging her, telling her that architects never really get to do what they'd like to do. I felt so pained and hurt that I could hardly respond—because I'm very close to my daughters. So I made this Annunciation: what happens to the Virgin at the Annunciation is that you see her glory and her pain all at once."

Three great paintings fueled this new and complex vision of the artist's daughter as the Virgin. Francisco de Zurbarán's *Young Virgin Praying* of about 1632–33 (see page 14) prompted the theatrical arch of fabric through which the viewer sees the Virgin, though González has created a cloth arch in a symbolic green, unlike the luscious pink of the original. Zurbarán's painting likewise influenced the meticulous still life on the "forestage" of the table in front of Maria: González's vessel of purity and fecundity, an ordinary glass bottle of water, occupies the same position as Zurbarán's vase containing virginal lilies and the roses of love. González's blue glass plate teeters dramatically on the edge of the forestage ledge, just as Zurbarán's superb little sewing basket does. Zurbarán's youthful seamstress has a pair of scissors; González's Maria, a young architect, has compasses. The box of tissues carefully covered over with a single white tissue refers to the veil that covers the chalice and its divine contents during Mass.

The crumpled red-and-white-striped fabric of Maria's casual cotton top, the soft length of white linen that winds behind the girl's head, and the dark green drapery at each side of her softly embracing, green velvet wing chair, all arise from the famous female nude by Ingres, his *Bather of Valpinçon* of 1808 (Louvre, Paris) (see page 14). In the Ingres painting, the nude bather has the red-and-white-striped fabric twisted around her head, dark green drapery to her left, a white curtain and white bed linen to her right and under her.

The tilt of Maria's head, her bare shoulders, closed eyes, even her plucked eyebrows, bear an astounding resemblance to the bather of Odilon Redon's *Closed Eyes,* 1890 (Musée d'Orsay, Paris) (see page 14), whose head and right shoulder rise out of a pool of water, the subject appearing to be lost in a mystical reverie. González, like Redon, implies a watery environment for his Virgin, the seven blue ribbons like rivulets falling on the green waves of the fabric arch. With *Closed Eyes* Redon threw himself into color, pulling away from the dark pessimism of the *noirs,* his visionary black lithographs. As Redon oscillated between color and monochrome for a decade, so González insists on a similar freedom, moving from the rich darkness of *After Philadelphia* through the color and clarity of this painting, to the somber self-portrait on a "lithograph stone" of *Letter to Veronica,* its sacred theme dear to both Zurbarán and Redon.

The artist's sensitive assimilation and synthesis of art-historical sources and obsessive conversion of such material into visual autobiography make González a unique contemporary artist. In this painting, Maria becomes both an Annunciate Virgin and a dreaming, introspective artist preparing for a difficult career—while González expands on the implications of the Giacometti- and Friedrich-inspired miniature figure of himself viewed from behind in *Songs for My Father* as a supplicant donor beneath the mantle of Piero's *Madonna of Mercy*. Here he has become a spiritual messenger to his daughter: "the invisible annunciating angel Gabriel, whom Maria cannot see." He stands before the backdrop of a Cuban landscape by day—a postcard view propped up on the box of tissues. The view swells and repeats above Maria's head in another magical union of opposites, a conjunction of night and day.

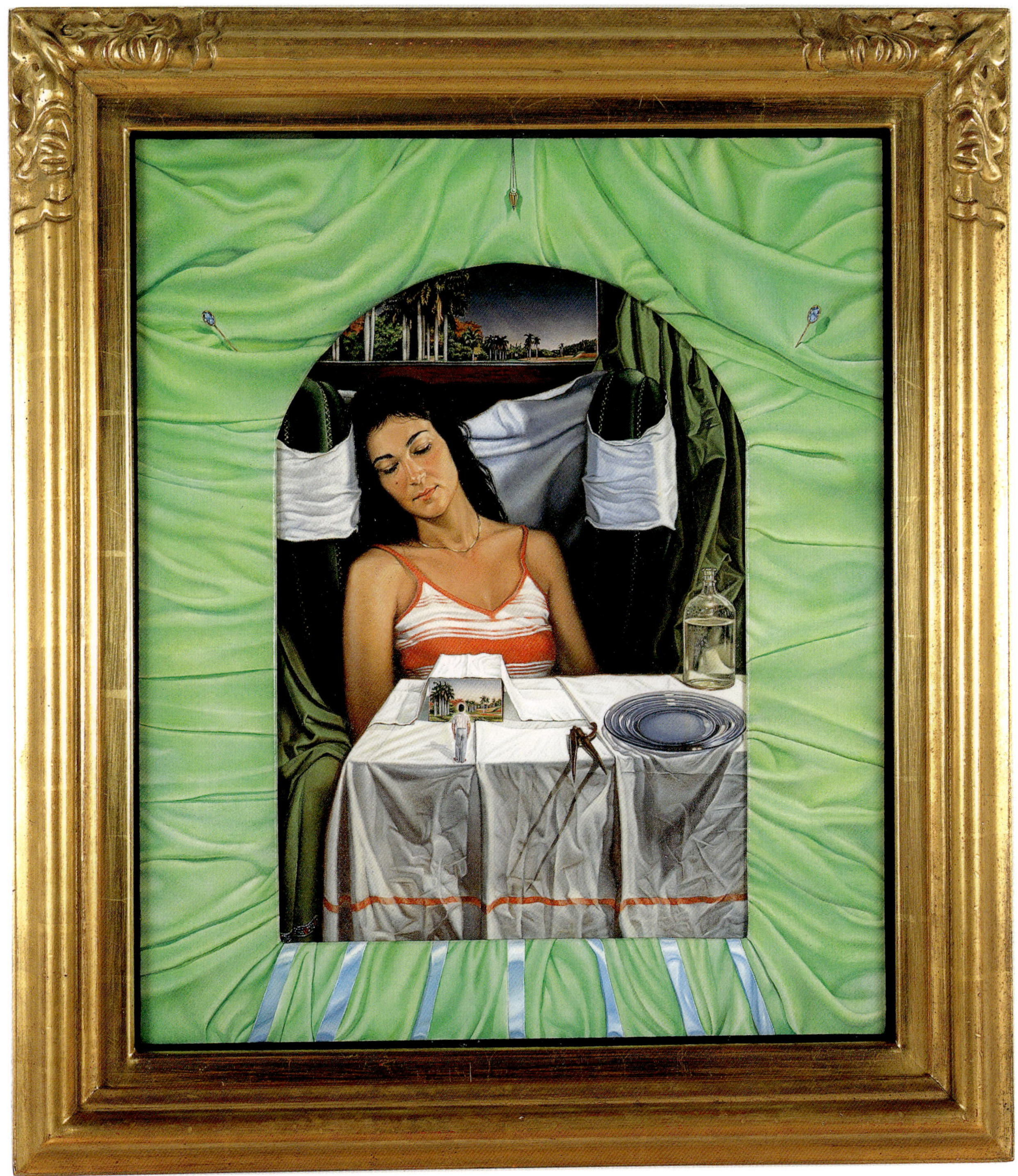

42 *Letter to Veronica* 1983

Gesso, graphite, and acrylic with cast-cement frame, 20 × 16¾ inches
Fred Jones Jr. Museum of Art, The University of Oklahoma, Jerome Westheimer Acquisition Fund Purchase

Fashioned as a companion portrait to the image of Patrick's head on a plate, this work ought to feature an imprint of another disembodied head, rather than a mirror image of head and shoulders combined. In Christian legend, Saint Veronica braved the Roman soldiers to wipe the bloodied face of Christ with her veil, whereupon the face of the Son of God (the *vera icon,* or "true icon," which gave rise to the name "Veronica") was miraculously transferred onto the veil. This legend may have been the artist's initial inspiration, but the grid of Patrick's portrait and the sheet of *La Misa Blanca* (The White Mass) recur here, not simply as background for the head but *interwoven* with the face and shoulders of the artist, recognizing the grid drawn on the surface of the mirror into which the artist is gazing as he makes his miracle self-portrait on a "veil."

González wanted to rework El Greco's *Saint Veronica with the Sudary* (Museo de San Vicente, Toledo), in which the image of Christ's face does not realistically fall into the folds and pleats of the fluttering veil in Veronica's hands. He must also have remembered Zurbarán's stunning trompe-l'oeil veils of the Saint Veronica series; the finest of five examples, circa 1635, at the Nationalmuseum of Stockholm, is frequently reproduced in books on Zurbarán. It is entirely possible, too, that González at some point before making this image came across Odilon Redon's poetically conceived lithograph *It Was a Veil, an Imprint* in the *Dreams* album of 1891.

With his face caged in a grid of folded cloth, González ingeniously picks up where Zurbarán and Redon left off, working toward an imaginative combination of lithograph stone, mirror, and veil to secure this "graven" image. The artist has haloed himself with an extraordinary substitute for the crown of thorns, in a Holy Trinity of contrastingly colored finches on an overhead wire. Two white finches hang upside down, which to González's sensitive perception represent "complete insanity—it has the effect on me of an electric shock." One black finch sits tortuously upright, his head stretched back so that his beak touches the top dead-center of the gridded "veil." The rough cement edges of the frame mimic the lithographic stone, one means of artistic printing or "reflecting." The stone reflects González as Christ in the midst of his Passion, on a gridded or folded sheet that has the effect of introducing faint lines that lightly splice the center of the artist's face and body. González drew his face several times, whitewashing over the image each time, to create a fragile, fugitive ghost of a self-portrait.

It is the idea of the self-portrait as *object* that is most radical here, however, pushed to an extreme conclusion in the cast-cement surround and the concept of the self-portrait as an image on a lithographic stone. Perhaps González had admired Piet Mondrian's 1918 stone block–like *Self Portrait* in charcoal (Gemeentemuseum, the Hague). Certainly he was aware of Zurbarán's tendency to create theatrical, frozen still lifes, into which he introduced the Virgin or saints like dolls or puppets. As Julián Gállego in his illuminating discussion of Zurbarán still lifes points out, "Zurbarán's Saints are true objects, almost still lifes, very real and quite petrified at the same time, which is what gives them their mysterious majesty."[1]

There could scarcely be a better term than "petrified" to describe this self portrait on "stone," or, for that matter, any of the other self-portraits beginning with *Mar y Espejo* (Sea and Mirror), in which González portrays himself as partially or wholly turned to stone, or assuming the guise of a church sculpture: the angel of Rheims, the bust of *Miércoles de Ceniza* (Ash Wednesday), the polychrome baby Jesus of *Memory Piece,* or the pietà on the sofa of *Así que Pasen Cinco Años/When Five Years Pass.* In the artist's next painting, the tiny baroque figure of an infant Saint John the Baptist is depicted as a figure in a still life, an object on a tabletop.

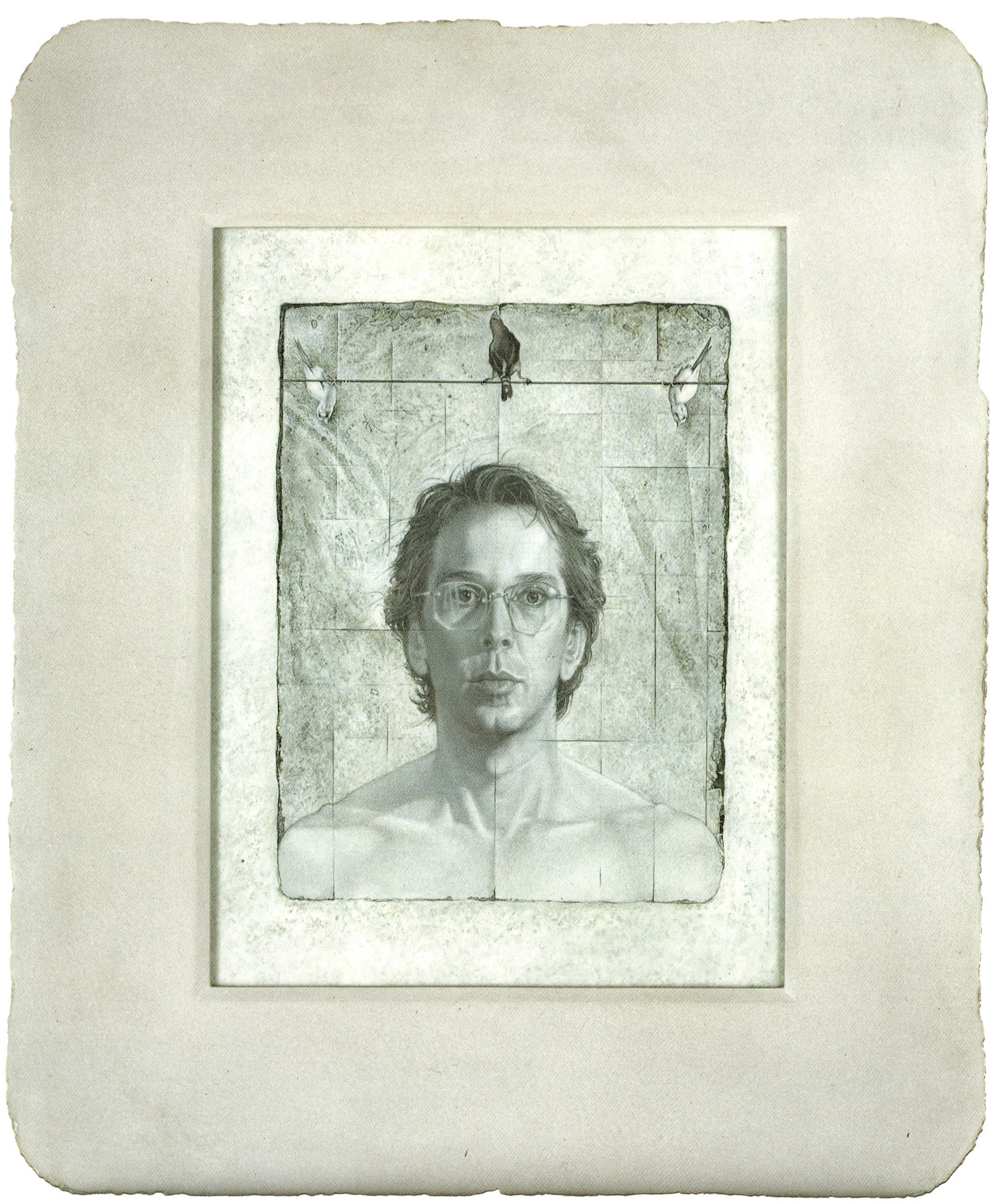

43 *After Philadelphia* 1982–84

Watercolor and Conté crayon on paper, 18 × 52 inches
The Metropolitan Museum of Art, New York, Purchase, the Eugene and Estelle Ferkauf Foundation, Aron Foundation, and Nancy Hoffman Gallery, Inc., Gifts, 1986

González spent six months in Philadelphia, staying with his friend and comrade-in-art, Anne Minich, while renovations on his New York apartment were completed. Fascinated by a newspaper photograph of a southern town hit by a flood, he began drawing it, tinting a long horizontal of paper with a light wash of blue on two sides (evoking the past, memory, and his love of Joseph Cornell's blue glass panes over portraits), leaving the center untouched so that it would radiate a clear white light. The work looks monochromatic, yet it is a triumphant symphony of blacks, grays, and blues on white paper. He worked intensively on the drawing over a two-year period—literally the period "after Philadelphia," though the title also implies a sense of "after the Flood," a time of disaster.

Why would a muzzy newspaper photograph of a flood so grip the imagination of this artist? A strong hint may be found in the upper left-hand corner of the drawing—a tribute to Georges Seurat in the form of a tiny boat appearing at roughly the same point in the composition as Seurat's little boat in *Sunday Afternoon on the Island of La Grande Jatte,* 1884–86 (The Art Institute of Chicago). Close by González's boat are the flaring twin headlights of a pickup truck, the artist's symbol of rescue or salvation, uncannily reminiscent of the twin lights of candles flanking the Redeemer on the cross in Seurat's 1887 Conté crayon drawing of his aunt on her deathbed.[1] In the grainy realism of the newspaper's snapshot of the flood, González found not only a brilliant metaphor for the disaster of AIDS but also a naturalistic equivalent to the atmospheric light-dark continuum of Seurat's Conté crayon drawings, so pregnant with phantom apparitions, revealed yet at the same time concealed—like the veiled symbolist portraits that had earlier obsessed this artist. Form and content are especially suited to one another in *After Philadelphia,* since Seurat's drawings so richly demonstrate "the precariousness of human existence, its suffering, and the patience required to bear it."[2]

The work is full of personal and symbolic elements, such as the artist's securing his two daughters in a boat in the center of the drawing, protected by a triangular tent of fine lines. Anne Minich, solitary but compassionate survivor of the disaster, wades through the water with her head bowed in sorrow. A fleeing, bare-chested boy in a haze of red, at bottom center—the only brightly colored element in the image, inspired by a little figure above a frescoed portal in the Belvedere (the fortress just outside Florence) and intended as a self-portrait of the artist—runs toward a Muybridge rider, emblem of masculine sexuality in the vocabulary of this artist, while an ominous line travels from the dark eyes of the horse to strike the head of the boy. Seven pigeons fly from the top-right corner down to the bottom left of the drawing, their flight reversing the joyful flight to freedom of the pigeons in *Mar y Espejo* (Sea and Mirror). In memory of the lancing of Christ's side at the Crucifixion, a pale line transfixes the heart of the seventh pigeon, which recoils like Magritte's bloody, shot bird plummeting through the air in *The Murderous Sky,* 1927 (Musée National d'Art Moderne, Paris).

The scratched lines that cover the work are an intriguing late addition, connecting and making narrative sense of symbolic elements. First suggested to the artist by the cracked seams of age he had admired on the surface of Fra Angelico's *Burial of Saints Cosmas and Damian,* 1438–40 (San Marco, Florence), they finally conjure up the image of a scratched pane of glass. In truth, González *literally* scratched lines over the surface of his drawing. Yet surely these lines are also a compulsive reaction to the drawing-by-modeling entailed in the artist's epic exploration of Seurat's world of darkness.

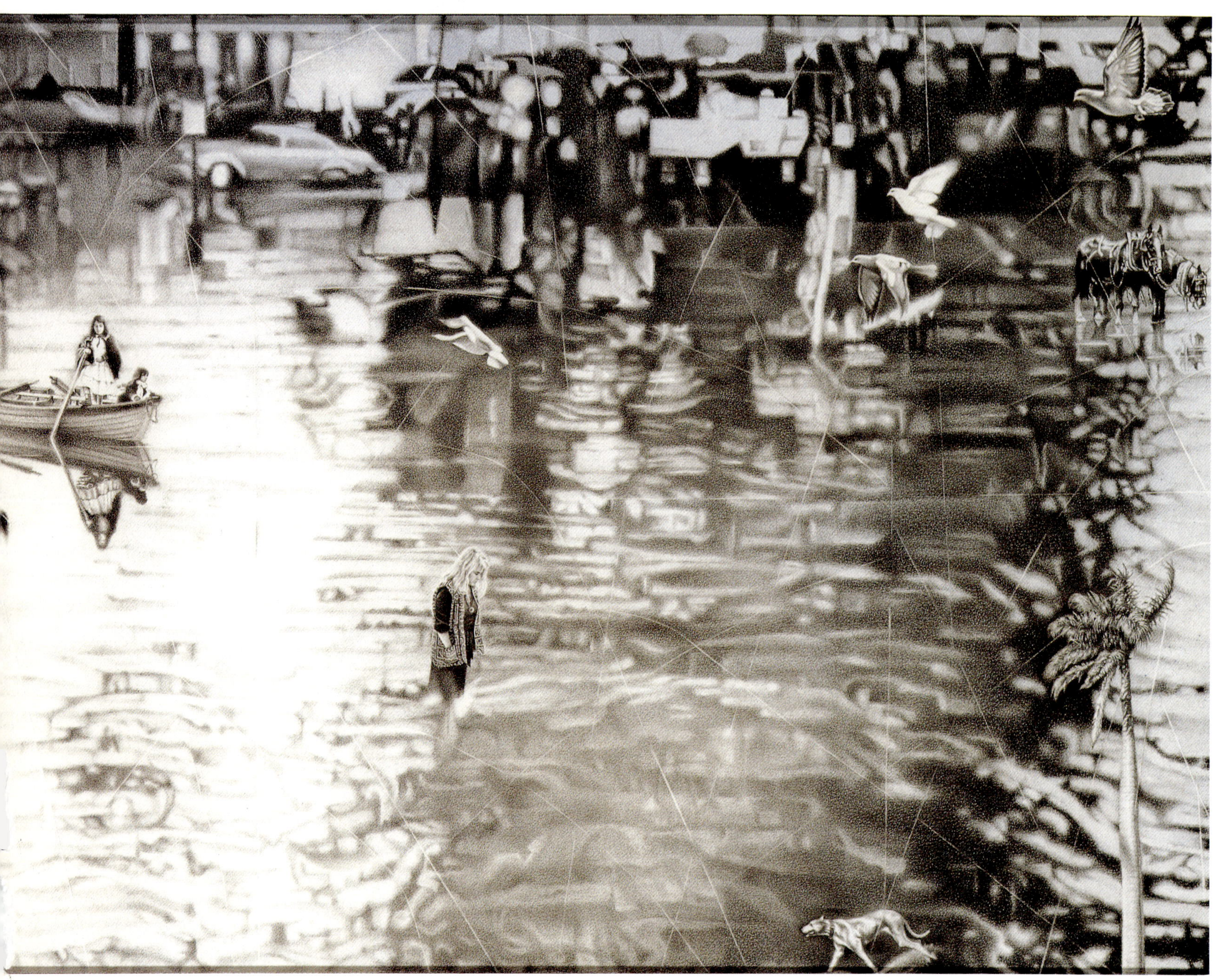

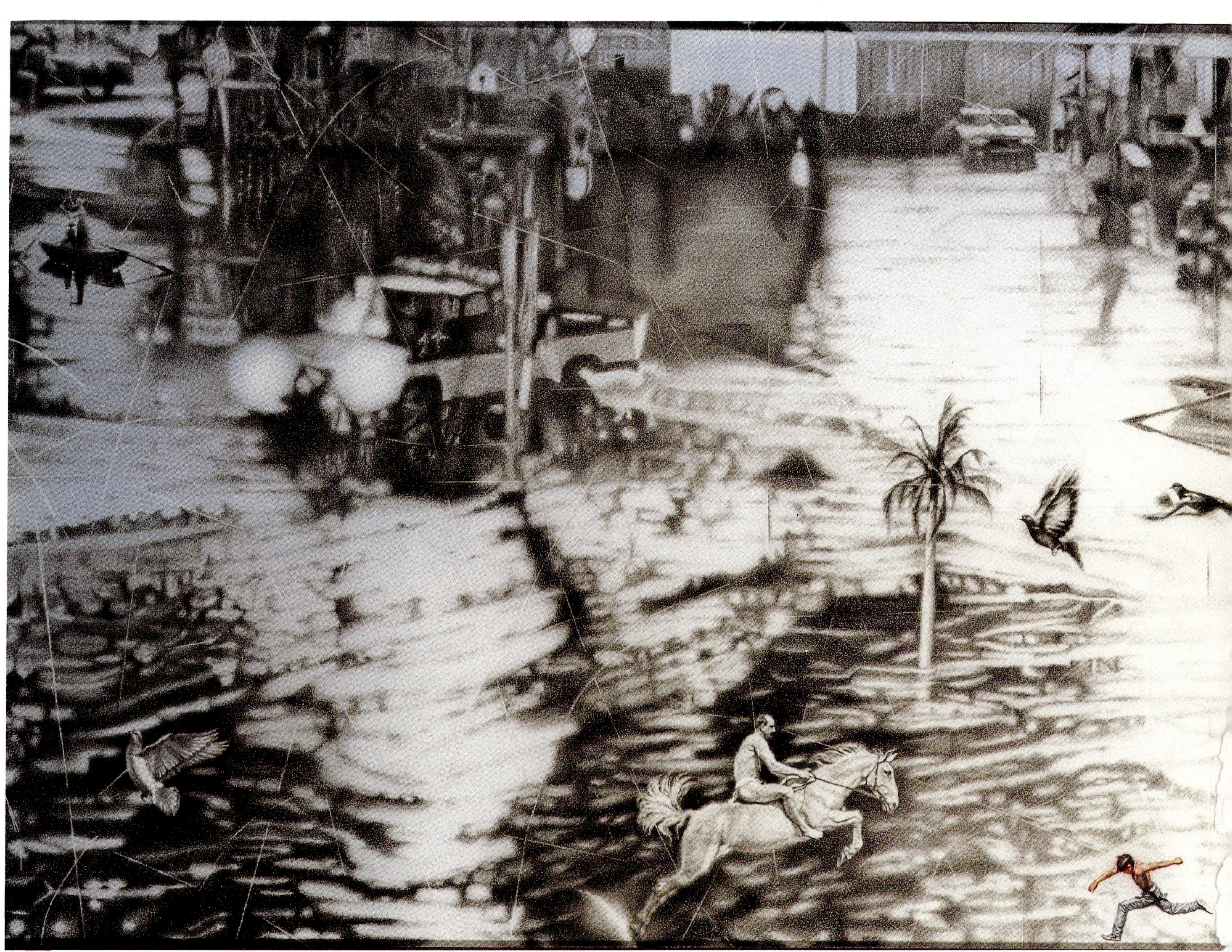

44 *El Niño* 1983

Oil on canvas, 19½ × 23 inches
Private collection, New York

In *El Niño* (The Child), González once again yields to the compulsion to split the image down the center, adding a pivotal sacred figure at the center bottom of the painting. González had seen the life-size model of the infant Christ or Saint John the Baptist in Seville—perhaps the infant Christ made by Juan Martinez Montañés for the Confraternity of the Sanctuary at Seville, carved in the nude so that it could be dressed in a variety of costumes. The childhoods of the Virgin, Jesus, and the Baptist were extremely popular subjects in baroque Spain. González is always sensitive to the kitsch aspect of these pieces, but the theme has an overwhelming personal attraction for him, engendering memories of a devotional sculpture he had cherished in childhood:

> I had joined the Society of the Little Jesus of Prague. Every other month they would bring me this little mahogany shrine that had two doors you could open and close, and the sculpture of the little Jesus would be behind them. I loved the whole idea of this little Jesus in his own space. He had really beautiful robes, and a crown, and a globe of the earth in his hand with a little cross on top. It was really a seductive image! That whole idea of the mahogany shrine and the little Jesus perhaps has something to do with my cages and enclosed spaces. I was so affected by that sculpture coming to my house for a couple of days every other month.

On the simplest level, *El Niño* is a still-life painting, an exercise in values after Vermeer, whom González was studying with heartfelt admiration at this period. But González chose to miniaturize the sacred infant, to interpret it specifically as the Baptist, and to split the still life in two by inventing a dark mirror to frame and reflect a vase of flowers at the unseen opposite end of the table, a mirror parallel to the picture plane and defined by light-glinting beveled edges. The oil lamp adjacent to the mirror is depicted in a subtly slanted open space, in delicate reference to the tilted planes and baroque amor of Cézanne's *Still Life with Plaster Cupid,* ca. 1894 (Courtauld Institute Galleries, London). The visual mystery of the mirror reflecting the flowers at the *opposite* end of the table is reminiscent of the mirror that reflects the king and queen of Spain in Velázquez's *Las Meninas,* 1656 (Prado, Madrid), González implying that the viewer must be somewhere in the vicinity of the reflected flowers.

The Baptist has been planted immediately in front of one corner of the mirror, at the bottom of the beveled mirror edge filled with reflected color, a vertical shaft of spiritual ascent. He has symbolic attributes in the red oil of the lamp and the water of the flower vase: oil is traditionally used with water in baptism. In the mirrored side of the painting is "water"; in the nonmirrored side, the oil lamp provides a richly beautiful emblem of Pentecostal flame.

Religious symbolism aside, the placement and tiny scale of the Baptist are obsessive hallmarks in the work of this artist, reaching back to the Giacometti-inspired figure of the artist balanced on the corner of a glass ledge in *El Paisaje del Rey/The Landscape of the King,* or to the running boy "self-portrait," smaller than the pigeons, at the bottom center of *After Philadelphia.* Tiny figures on or at a ledge will occur again and again in later works—in *Roma,* 1985, *New York, Year 1986, Still Life in Red for Manuel,* 1987, *Cycle,* 1989, and *Vermeer's Frame,* 1990. These figures are evidence of the artist's lingering fascination with the cutout figures in the shadow-box theaters of his youth, his admiration of modern artists like Giacometti, Cornell, and Bacon, and his abiding passion for the polychrome sculpture of seventeenth-century Spain and the religious paintings of Zurbarán, whose curtained dramas of enclosed interiors, theaters of perfectly painted still life into which saints have been introduced like objects, have justifiably been compared with "the puppet booth, the sacrarium, the shrine."[1]

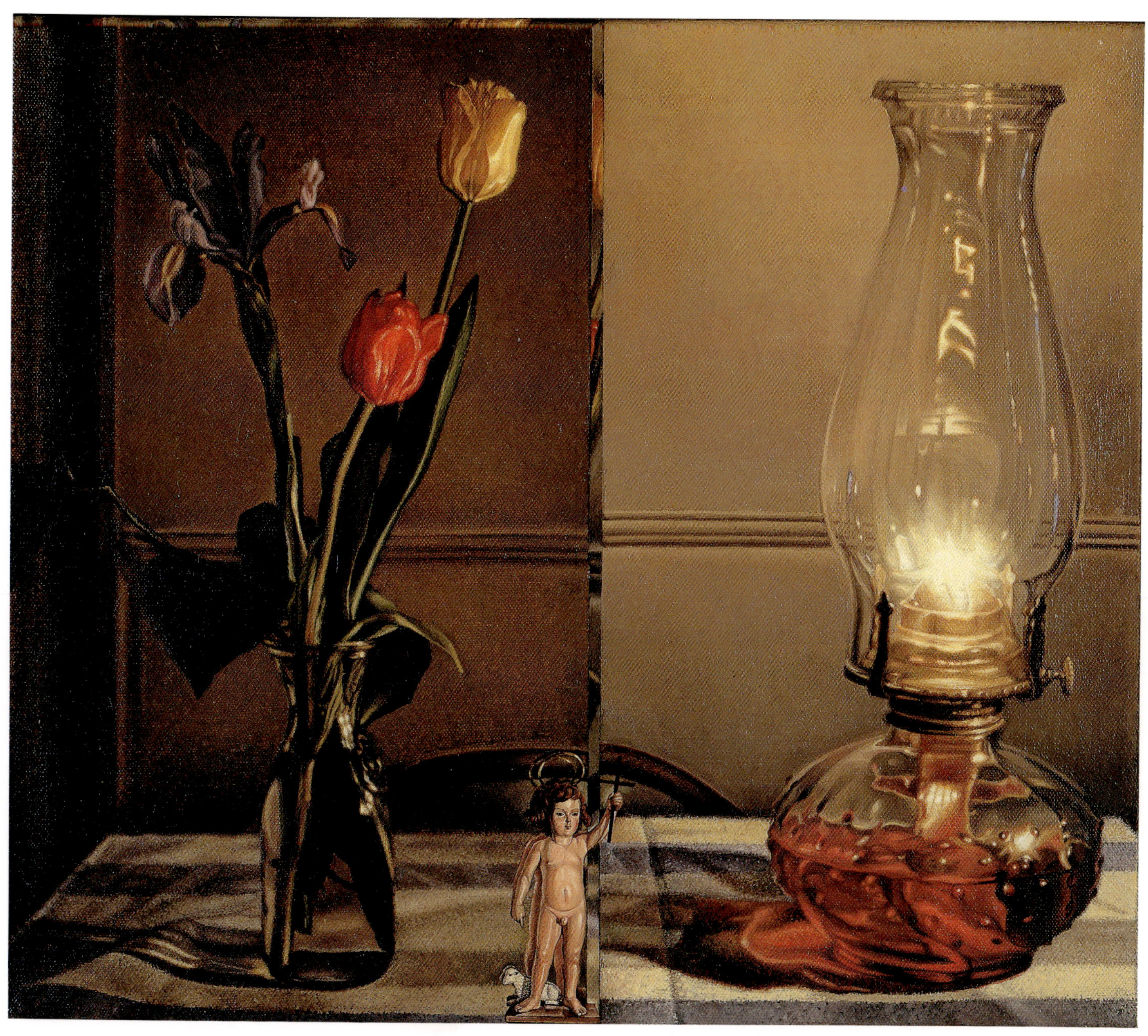

45 *Double Portrait of Jimmy, N.Y.C.* 1984

Watercolor on paper, 23 × 33¾ inches
Muriel Karasik Collection

The sense of a puppet booth that is also a shrine has never been more potent in González's work than it is in this gauzy watercolor full of theater wings. Jimmy had wanted to be an actor in New York.[1] In this doubled, mirroring portrait—which is an interesting permutation on the headless and opposed figures of the artist in *Untitled,* 1974—González creates a soft, fabric-walled and -floored environment like that of *La Cuna/The Cradle,* a toy-circus-arena-cum-cradle. Jimmy enters from the wings on both sides almost as though flying, though precedent for this portrait in profile may be found in Odilon Redon's *Portrait of Madame Redon with Ari,* ca. 1900–1903 (private collection, Netherlands), in which Redon's adolescent son enters the mother/son portrait sideways, making him seem strangely disconnected from his mother.

A circle of glasses holding lit candles (rounded out by an unlit candle in one of the green glass candlesticks, upon which is propped a postcard detail of a painting) forms a supernatural crown of lights around the head of the white bird enthroned on the inverted glass in the foreground—a glass that casts a trinity of shadows, emblem of the three-in-one mystery of the Catholic church. The small bird and giant flower are in homage to Martin Johnson Heade and his series of massive exotic orchids and tiny hummingbirds. An even more pointed reference to Heade occurs in the postcard detail of *Storm over Narragansett Bay,* 1868 (Amon Carter Museum, Fort Worth, Texas), in which a young boy looks out over dark water at a sailboat beneath a forked vein of lightning. González thought of Jimmy as "a boy in a storm. He was from the Midwest—from a very, very poor family. He had a sister who had just died of cancer and had nothing to leave him, except a little bell with a bird sitting on top, from a wedding cake, which is why I have the bird sitting on the inverted glass here."

The radiant amaryllis is clearly influenced by Mondrian's dramatic watercolor sketches of red amaryllis against a blue background, cruciform emblems of suffering and triumph, martyrdom and redemption. This silent theater of magic and dream is a space for the calm working out of the artist's strong, tender feelings for the "lost child" that Jimmy represents to him: "The crown around the bird's head implies that some kind of ritual is going on in the little theater. You find that crown in so many Spanish paintings." The crown-as-circle also implies a Jungian concentration on the center, a containment of opposites or an image of integration, like the circle or crown in the canopy above the dreaming sleeper of *El Soñador/The Dreamer.*

The pleated valance of translucent white cloth at the top of the picture, casting a trompe-l'oeil shadow below, is reminiscent of the pleated refectory tablecloth in Zurbarán's 1641–58 *Saint Hugo in the Refectory* (Museo Provincial, Seville). The trompe-l'oeil apron of linen hung over the central lower edge of the "theater" is meant to evoke the fair linen of the Catholic Mass, the purificator and the veil, as two tiny crosses embroidered in red at the corners of the cloth indicate. Folded crisply in the center, the cloth seems to point yet again to the artist's compulsive need to express a sense of splitting or duality. González had intended the cloth surround or frame to suggest Japanese architecture, a serene and spare interior. The dark veil hanging center stage, stranded with threads of gold, represents an obscure darkness flashing intermittent light. The mysterious shadow of the amaryllis rising from an empty blue vase is an element González describes as "a miracle," a magic-realist displacement, the fantastic embedded in the artist's idea of everyday reality.

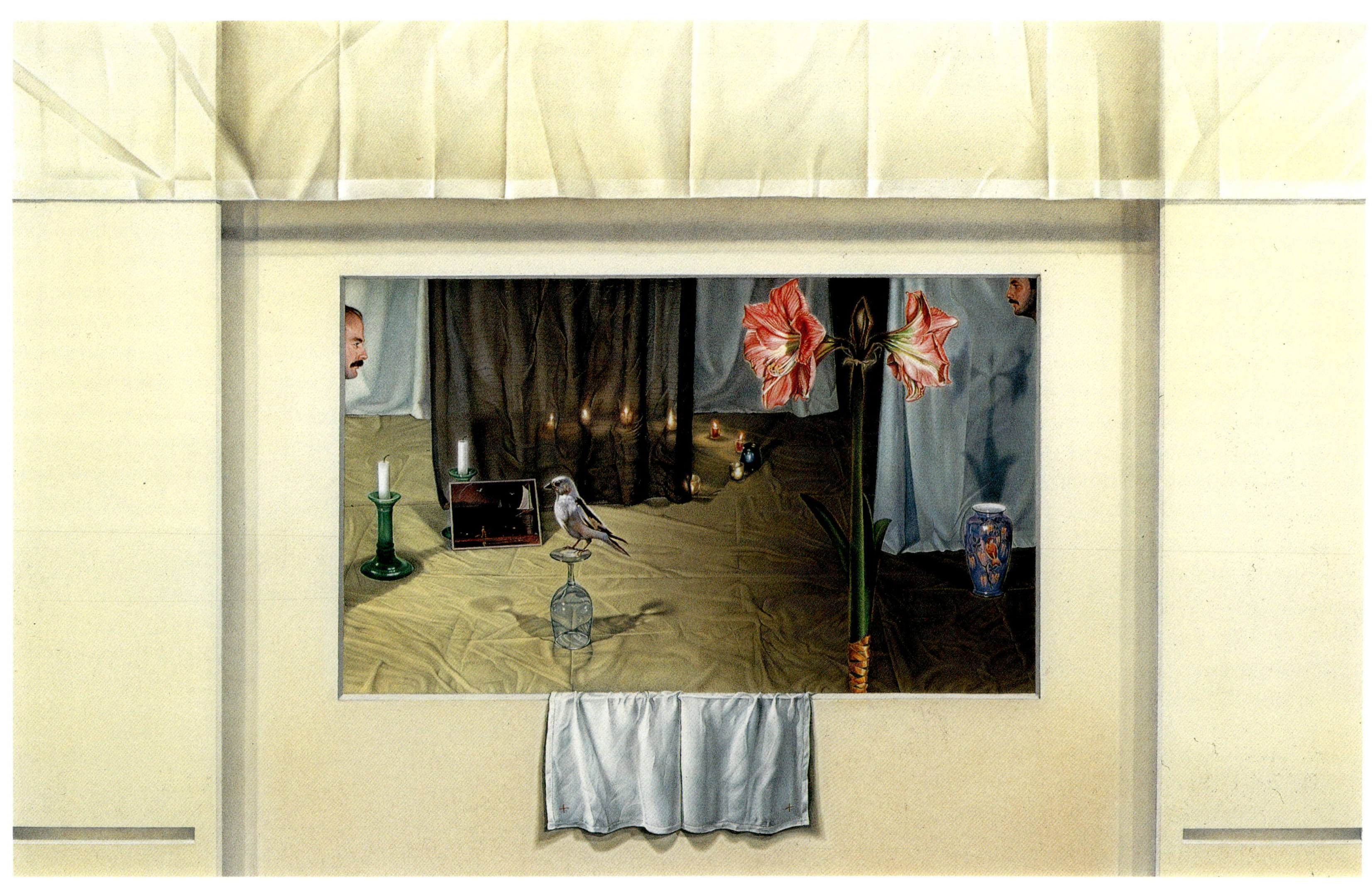

46 *El Palmar de los Locos* 1985

Tempera on handmade paper, glass gems on frame, 26 × 32 inches
Courtesy of the Danforth Museum of Art, Framingham, Massachusetts

In a sardonic mood, González takes up the theme of madness in this Byzantine jewel of a painting. "En el palmar de los locos" (In the palm grove of the insane) was a slang phrase used a great deal by the artist's mother in Cuba: "As a kid I remember the meaning was a place that was so wild, so far out, that you would never want to go there. I felt that the slang expression never really worked—that there just couldn't be a place that you wouldn't ever want to go to."

The work was to some extent a response to the handmade gray paper that González purchased because "it looked like stone," reminding him, no doubt, of the effects he had achieved in *Letter to Veronica.* He made a broad frame for the picture, cut with four perfectly square windows to frame his face viewed from four different angles, discovering an ingenious way to integrate the self-portrait and the grid, along with a new rationale for miniaturizing and multiplying the disembodied head, placing it at the top, bottom, and sides of the work, rather than in the usual center of the image. These superb little self-portraits generate a feeling of "foursquare" integrity and morality, a sense of the totality of the "four corners" of the earth. They are ritually positioned so as to mark out stages in the gesture of making the sign of the cross, touching first the forehead, then the chest, the left shoulder and the right shoulder, while uttering the words, "In the name of the Father, and of the Son, and of the Holy Ghost."

At the actual corners of the image, the artist set square mounts for large dark blue egg-shaped "gems." In making the miniature self-portraits, González was thinking particularly of

> a black room at the Villa of the Mysteries in Pompeii, where all the panels are a graphite color, finished with a built-up line, and in each corner of the panels is a little head or mask. I had loved that room for a long time, so when I started working on this handmade paper that looked like stone, I decided to reflect the way I felt about those panels at the Villa of the Mysteries. On the other hand, while I was working out the frame, I did a lot of research on Byzantine reliquary and Gospel covers, which are usually inset with portraits of the apostles and adorned with precious metals and stones.

The self-portraits have a nimbus, or aureole, of radiant spiritual light around them. The artist's closed eyes imply the searching inner vision of the mystic—appropriately enough, since the heads were inspired by masks on the walls of a villa where mystery cults practiced their Bacchic rites, symbolizing the redemption and eternal triumph in the afterlife of the initiates.

The artist has beautifully converted the speckled surface of the handmade paper, lightly touching it with white to evoke a cosmic field of stars, a rushing infinity. A fine white line likewise accentuates the window through which we view the interior landscape, this stormy memory or dream of the artist's Cuban past. To deepen the recessed, cutout quality of the central image, González has crosshatched somber bands of trompe-l'oeil shadow to contrast with the delicately drawn white edge of the illusionistic mat, intending the center drawing to be "like an apparition."

The moonlit fantasy landscape is seductive in its wonderful use of color, the blue-gray Cuban grass resembling a sea of waves under a sky of writhing clouds and gale-tossed silver and gold palm trees. One way of looking at the landscape is to compare it with the miniature daytime landscape of a palm-"caged," golden-skied upstate New York in *Untitled,* 1978, to which this is a kind of nocturnal pendant.

González's final elegant art reference in the image occurs with the lettering of the title, borrowed specifically from the portraits of Hans Holbein—suggesting that the landscape is, in fact, a portrait of the artist's inner vision behind closed eyes.

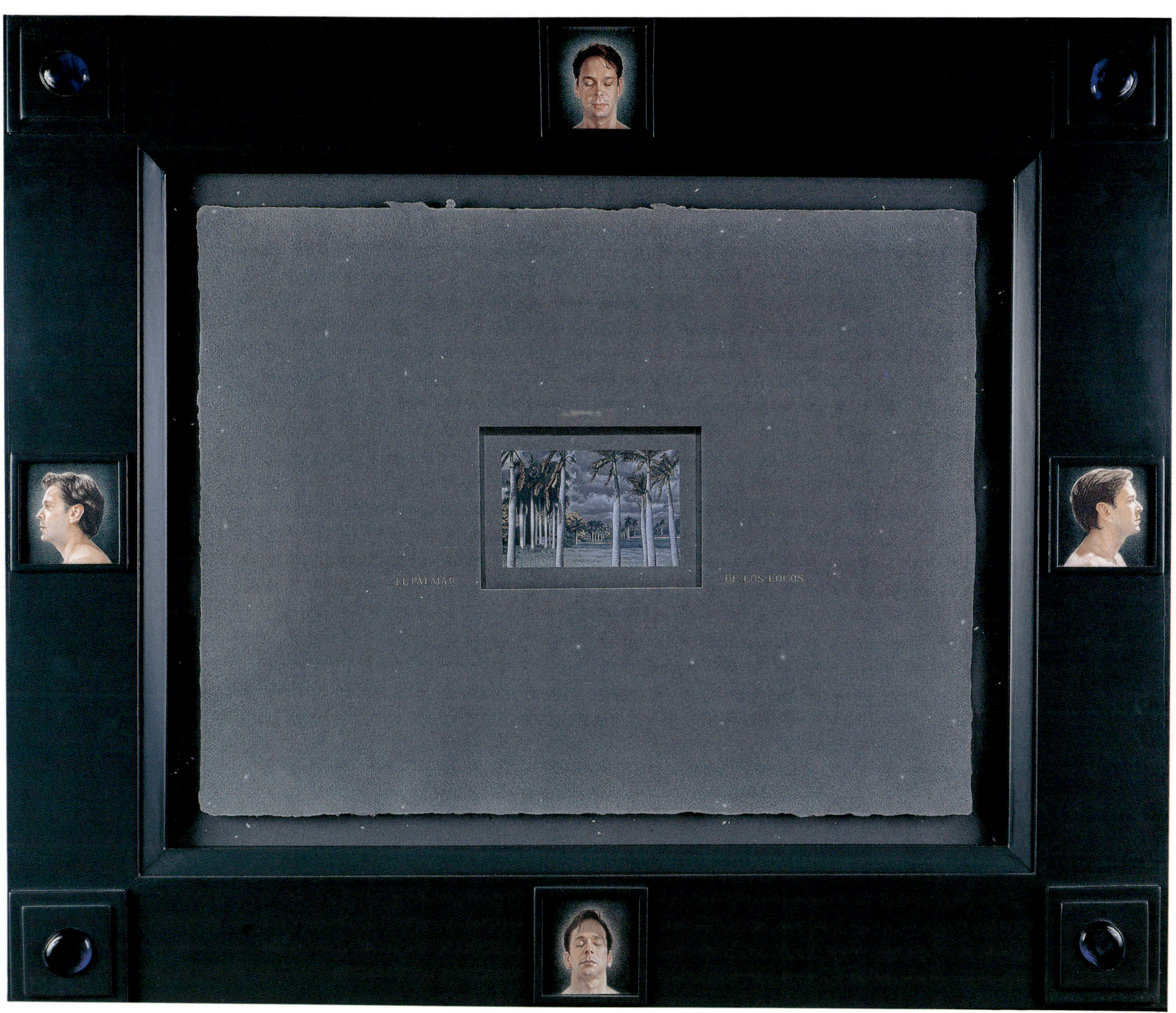
EL PALMAR
DE LOS LOCOS

47 *Pensamientos* 1985

Tempera on paper, glass gems mounted on gold, 12¼ × 12¼ inches
Private collection, New York

"*Pensamientos* is an image of thinking about death," says González. "My friends and people that I knew were getting ill and dying of AIDS. There's an edge to the frame of the image, a black line referring to the funerary announcements you see in places like Venice. The red stone is meant to suggest both the Holy Spirit and a drop of blood, or the Body and Blood of Jesus Christ. I believe in Holy Communion; I still try to remember what I felt when I was an adolescent and I thought that the Body and Blood of Christ was in *me*. And I made the frame of *Pensamientos* to suggest an aerial view of a pyramid, with the portrait on the summit."

Pensamientos (Thoughts) resembles the *Self-Portrait in Tangier*. In both portraits the viewer senses that there is no way to go but up, like the wheeling crows and pyramid implied by the white frame of *Pensamientos*.[1] *Pensamientos* moves the lateral miniature portraits with closed eyes of *El Palmar de los Locos* (The Palm Grove of the Insane) to the exact center of the painting. In this perfectly square format, González presents the viewer with his bird's-eye view of a pyramid, the artist's face imaginatively dissected by the apex of the pyramid—the pinnacle occurring at a point just between the artist's closed eyes, about where we might expect the "inner eye" of spiritual vision to be placed. In the 1943 self-portrait *Thinking of Death* (private collection), Frida Kahlo paints a circular image of a miniature skull and bones at precisely the same point on her forehead. In the similarly morbid 1946 *Self-Portrait Dedicated to Marte R. Gómez* (Collection Marte Gómez Léal, Mexico City), Kahlo transforms her eyebrows into a black swallow stretched above her weeping eyes, its beak pointing upward to the middle of her forehead. Like Kahlo, González seems to paint his own portrait almost as a way of conquering death.

González chose to introduce the black crows after admiring Hubert and Jan van Eyck's Ghent *Altarpiece*, arguably 1432 (Cathedral of St. Bavo), specifically the Annunciation scene with its minutely observed turreted townscape viewed through a window—a townscape remarkable for its tiny, distant inhabitants and flying or resting birds. To study the Van Eyck Annunciation scene is to realize that González has here created an Annunciation for himself: the great black crow that crowns him with its widespread wings (as the child González is crowned with hands spread like bird's wings in *Songs for My Father*) replaces the white dove of the Holy Spirit above the head of the heavenward-gazing Virgin in the Van Eyck *Annunciation*. This is the artist's own moment of "pain and glory," of deep insight into his mortality and divinity.

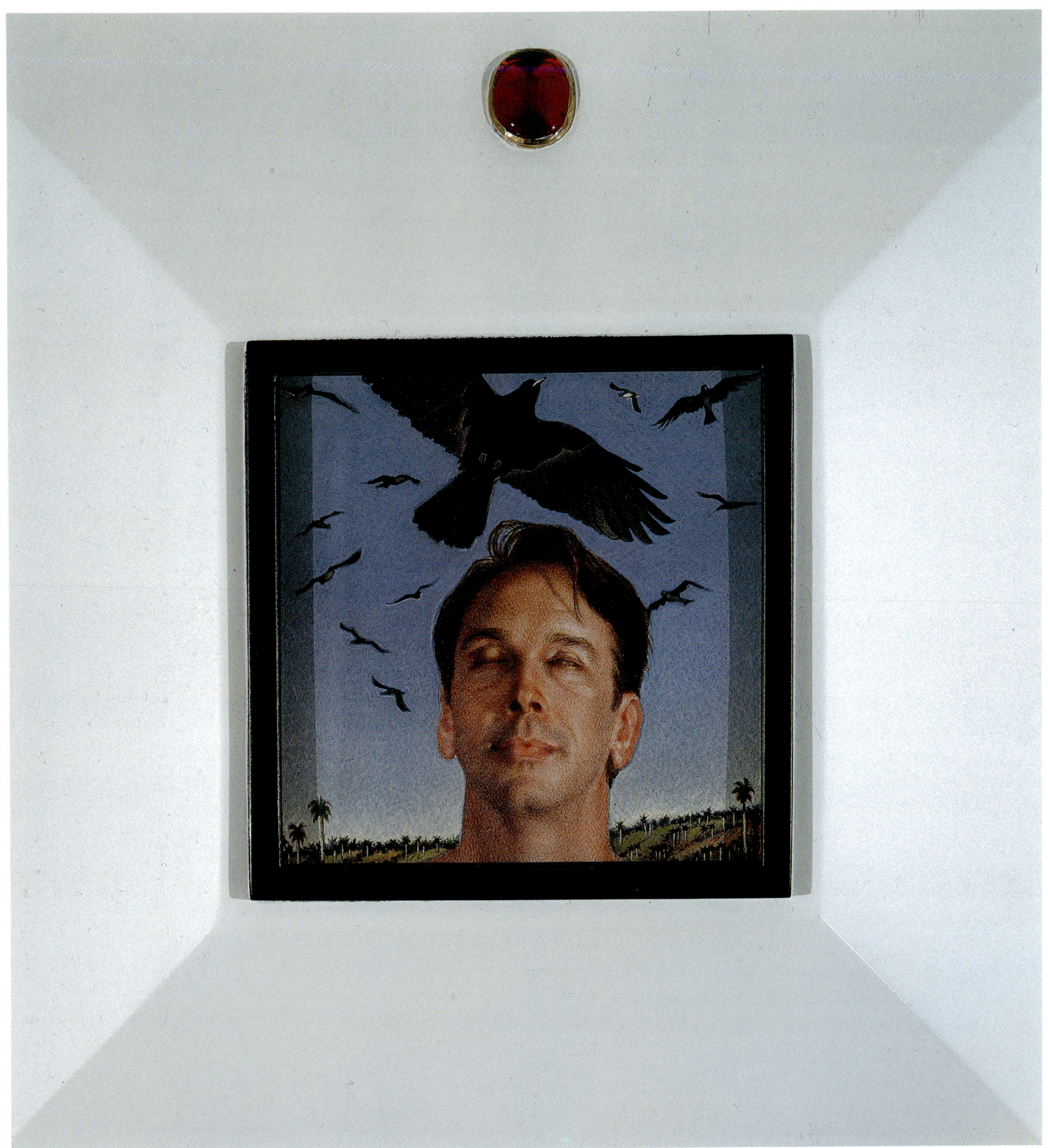

48 *Teresa en Verde* 1985

Watercolor and Conté crayon on paper, 54½ × 31¼ × 3 inches
Anne and Ronald Abramson

Raphael's tiny but charming painting of *The Three Graces,* 1505–6 (Musée Condé, Chantilly), a favorite image of the artist, contributed to this magnificent, larger-than-life portrait of his younger daughter, Teresa, a golden apple raised in her hand. As González had converted portions of Hugo van der Goes's massive Portinari altarpiece into a miniaturized Nativity, so here he departs from a small-scale work (*The Three Graces* is only 6¾ × 6¾ in.) to generate a truly monumental image—yet another example of the artist's ambition to seek out opposites, like the closed and open portraits of himself in Morocco, the sun and moon of *El Soñador/The Dreamer,* or the night and day landscapes of *La Educación de Maria* (The Education of Maria).

Another diminutive but modern source for this drawing is Giacometti's *Standing Woman in a Cage,* 1950 (private collection), scissored into the same silhouette of a shrine that frames Teresa here—though González did not construct his Giacometti-inspired frame until after he had also studied Greek stelae at the Metropolitan Museum for their "grace and beauty."

The poetic title of the work has everything to do with Lorca's *Sleepwalking Ballad:* "Green, how much I want you green," goes the opening refrain, a refrain repeated like a magical incantation throughout the poem. "In Spanish," comments González, "the sound of *Verde que te quiero verde* brings you into a greenness that is like a green wall. It is one of the greatest lines in all Spanish poetry." Christopher Maurer, in his edition of Lorca's *Collected Poems,* offers the author's own explanation of the poem as expressing "Granada's longing for the sea," but adds that the poem may also tell the tale of a gypsy girl who, while waiting at night on a balcony for her smuggler lover, falls or throws herself into a rainwater tank and drowns, hypnotized by the moonlit water below her.[1] Certainly "green" becomes a rich, encompassing symbol for Teresa, the daughter González remembers for her passionate yearning to experience love and motherhood.

González's portrait is a spellbinding union of opposites: the monochromatic and the chromatic, the precisely delineated and the fluidly dappled, the drawn and the painted. Watercolor lights the work with pale, watery greens and provides the sparkling gold of the apple and pink blush of the girl's belly and the mother-of-pearl button on her shorts (González intended the button as a friendly salute to the girl's mother, his ex-wife, Josefina Camacho, who loves pearls). The drawing is so finely detailed, so alive, that the viewer can see pores dotting the fresh young skin of the nubile girl.

The light green cast of the composition is reminiscent of the paradisal *Bathers of Blenheim.* Teresa appears to wade through water, González having inlaid the lower inside edge of the drawing with a roughly three-inch-deep mirrored ledge to reflect the girl's knees, placing her in an imaginary pool. The watery environment is confirmed by the scallop shells carved on the shrine above and below her, symbol of both the pagan Venus/Aphrodite and the Virgin, the *stella maris,* or "Star of the Sea." This marine goddess anticipates the Virgin Bride on the ocean floor of *Así que Pasen Cinco Años/When Five Years Pass.*

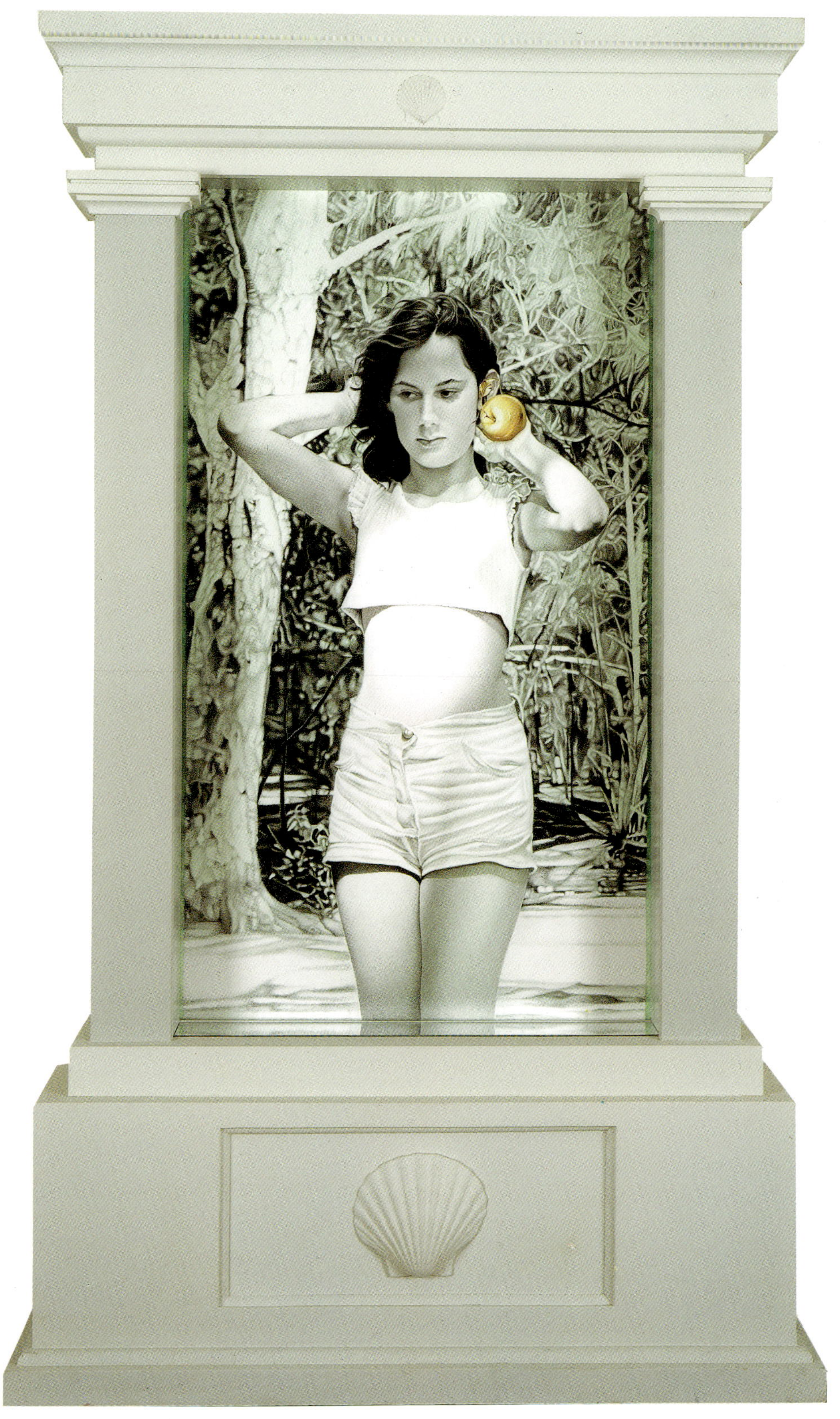

49 *Roma* 1985

Pastel on paper, 43¾ × 22¾ inches
Robert C. Woolley

González had visited an artist friend in Rome, Frances Cohen Gillespie, whose name is inscribed at the top right of the entablature in this image. She had persuaded him to stay and work in the city, giving him her bedroom to use as a studio, where he began this drawing from life: "I had a wonderful terrace, which had this view of Rome. I finished the picture in New York, surrounding the view with sculptures of Rome. The sculptures had impressed me more than the paintings, which you could hardly see in the dark churches—while the sculptures were glorious. I went to the Vatican, where I saw the sculpture of the boy and bird; then I went to the Campidoglio and the Palazzo dei Conservatori, where I photographed the Head of Constantine and this very classical female head."

The artist remembers the boy at the top of *Roma,* an imperial marble copy of a second-century B.C. Greek bronze, as "Amor or Love, a sculpture of a boy like the Greek Eros, wrestling with a bird." In fact, the marble depicts a three- or four-year-old boy strangling a goose in an excess of affection; he is reminiscent of the stone boy victimized by the bird of *Mar y Espejo* (Sea and Mirror), only now the boy has mastered the bird and is playfully hugging it to throttling point. In *Memory Piece,* 1990, a transcendent infant Christ will serenely display a fluttering bird on a length of string. The evolution of this boy-and-bird symbolism is deeply personal and not entirely explicable, though it is undoubtedly a reference to the artist's private self.

González quotes a pair of nearly but not quite symmetrical "mirrored" angels from the baroque facade of a church near the Ara Pacis. He quotes from the monument itself in a segment of the famous frieze of garlands and heads of sacrificial cattle, recalling Augustus's stupendous Altar of Peace, erected in 9 B.C. to celebrate the end of twenty years of civil war. González uses the frieze to frame the boy and goose and to "crown" his art work. The angels kneel in celestial niches cut out of the columns flanking this prospect. The weighty stone frieze rests on thin air, as if it were levitating. And a tiny stone saint carrying a child (most probably Saint Anthony of Padua once again), carved onto the facade of an old building, hovers in the low center of González's cityscape, beneath someone's flapping laundry, as he floats upward in eternal ascension, looking toward the miniature figure of the artist.

González calls this "a more objective piece than most of my work. I was really responding to the beauty of Rome. The only drama in it is my relationship to Constantine and the female. I thought about that while I was working, and I suddenly realized that they were a portrait of my mother and father." Like Redon's portrait of Ari in profile, as his mother looks straight ahead toward the viewer, the grouping and direction of the heads in *Roma* depict a physically close yet emotionally distant family.

The artist portrays himself dwarfed in vast space. Though the scale of the colossal Head of Constantine has not been exaggerated, the scale of the "window" through which the artist viewed Rome certainly has. So has the scale of the imposing female head. Perhaps the real "Father" González is thinking of is God.

The surface of the image confounds the viewer: is it painted or drawn, watercolor or pastel? In fact, *Roma* was done entirely with sharp pastel crayons, effectively conjuring up the earthy brick colors of Rome, baking beneath the sultry heat of a rose-horizoned cobalt sky.

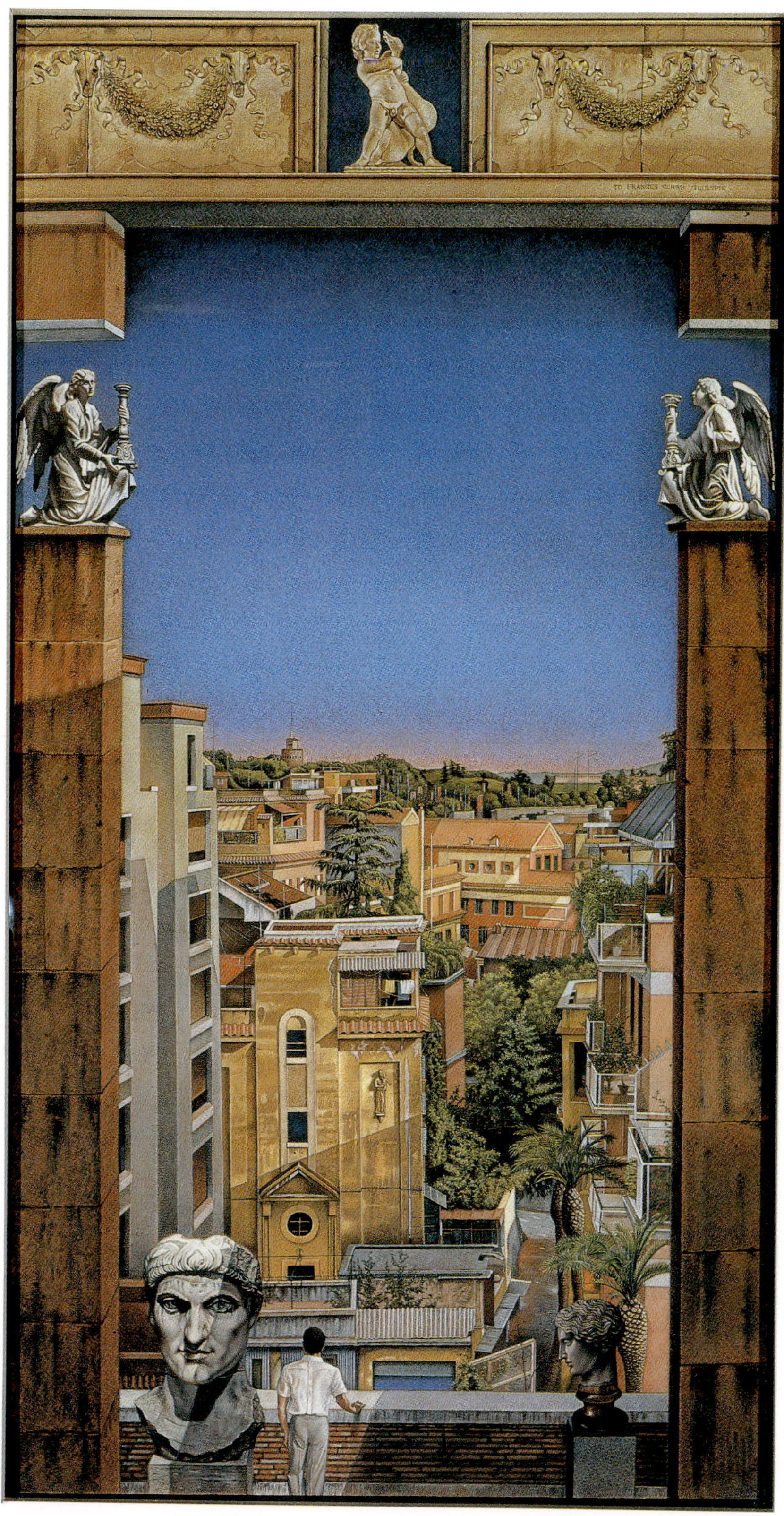
TO FRANCES COHEN GILLESPIE

50 *New York, Year 1986* 1980

Watercolor and gouache, 49 × 29 × 3 inches
Private collection

In 1986 González's great friend Patrick, subject of *Irish Red* and *A la Cabeza del Bautista en Sevilla/To the Head of John the Baptist in Seville,* died. González dedicated this painting to his memory, and to the city that has become his true hometown. The stormy, rain-soaked view that we see here is the encyclopedic view González has from his New York City apartment roof, encompassing buildings from 17th Street all the way to the World Trade Center. This work is in a very real sense the artist's ultimate stage set, with the Friedrich- and Giacometti-inspired cutout of himself positioned at low center stage, surveying the landscape of his life.

The nearly symmetrical stone angels of *Roma* (to which this is a darkly antithetical companion painting) have been displaced by a pair of bare-chested young men seated high in the turbulent sky, images of ascension enthroned on twin green columns of oxidized copper. Radiant pigeons flutter around the figure of the artist, and the keyboard of a piano is implied in the multi-windowed building immediately below him. The pigeon to the right of the artist, wings spread wide, is an emblem of the Holy Spirit, of annunciation or baptism.

Above the stage set of New York is a sky that metamorphoses into a theater curtain lifting over a rain-washed city—a curtain folded or gridded like the aerially viewed sheet of *La Misa Blanca* (The White Mass). In place of the circle and needle symbolizing the sun/moon or crown over the dreaming sleeper of *El Soñador/The Dreamer* is a crown or wreath of white roses. The sheet and crown are a triumph of realist painting serving a fantastic vision, the crown of white roses symbolizing love and martyrdom, innocence and transcendence. In this work, González's most personal and powerful symbol, the rose, reigns majestically over the image and initiates a major series of rose paintings, all in one way or another connecting roses with the idea of the enchanted sleeper or dreamer, as safe as a marble sculpture in eternal rest: the roses in the red, reflective water of *Il Giardino delle Sorelle* (The Garden of the Sisters), 1987, with its tiny, sculpted figure of the artist; the roses in the mirror above the dreaming head of the artist asleep on the ocean horizon in *Mar de Lágrimas/Sea of Tears,* 1987–88; the boy dreamer in roses of *Jardin de un Sueño* (Garden of a Dream), 1987–89, *Cycle,* 1989, and *To the Dream of the Apples,* 1990; the red roses of death contrasting with the white roses of transcendence in the Paestum diver series; and the Lorca-inspired Dead Boy in a crown of white roses in the *Así que Pasen Cinco Años/When Five Years Pass* collages, 1991. With *In His Silence,* 1988, the Falguière sculpture of a little-known boy martyr is converted into an image of Saint Sebastian, eyes closed as he leans eternally against the "column" of his thorned rose cane. The white rose of innocence and transcendence appears like the face of Christ on the cloth in the sky over Cuba in *Cultivo una Rosa Blanca* (I Grow a White Rose), also 1988.

The flowered crown of martyrs and saints is everywhere in art history, most especially in the work of Spanish artists like Zurbarán. Perhaps most suggestively of all for its influence on the work of González, Zurbarán painted a boy Christ inspecting his bloodied fingertip after pricking himself on a premonitory crown of thorns in *The Child Jesus with a Thorn* (Manuel Sánchez Ramos, Seville). González's symbolist favorite, Odilon Redon, during a five-year period of personal difficulty, repeatedly drew Christ in thorns in images like *Christ with Red Thorns* (private collection, France). González reinvents the rose crown of the Spanish painters and the red thorns of Redon to create a visual miracle—a royal crown of grace—for a city suffering from AIDS.

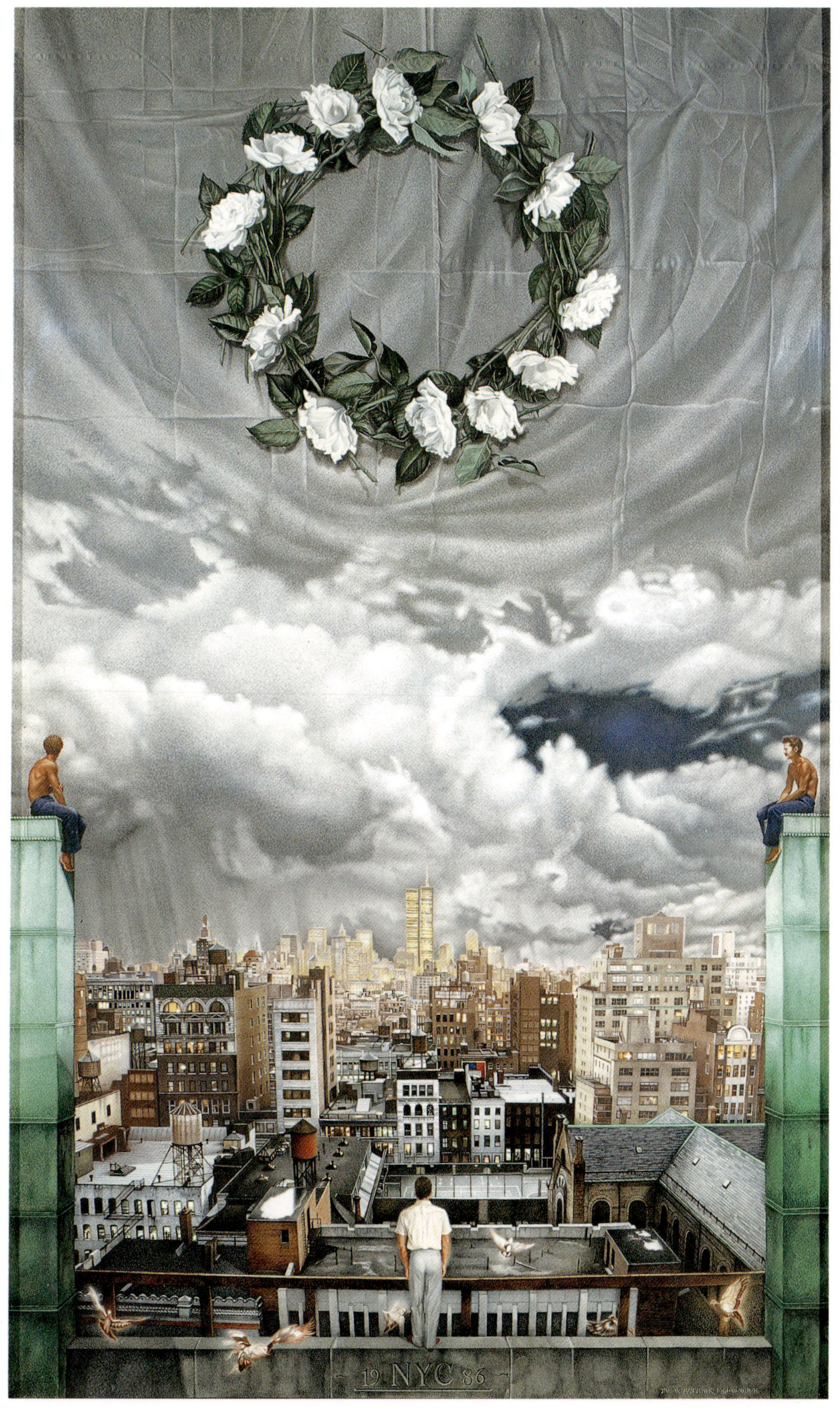
19 NYC 86

51 *Still Life in Red for Manuel* 1987

Watercolor and gouache on paper, 23½ × 16 inches
Collection of Manuel E. González

Still Life in Red for Manuel is remarkable for the economy of means with which González brings together his favorite techniques and themes in one modestly scaled, deceptively spare composition. The work was a gift for a friend called Manuel, who is not, however, the subject of the painting. The young man in swimming trunks, laughingly poised on the edge of a precipitous ledge, was a one-time student of the artist's at the School of Visual Arts, who mailed greetings to González together with the holiday snapshot of himself upon which this painting is based.

The bare light bulb hanging above the young man provides the clue that González is paying tribute to Francis Bacon—specifically to the black triptychs that followed the death of George Dyer in 1971; in *Triptych* (May–June 1973; Collection of Mr. and Mrs. Saul Steinberg, New York) and *Triptych* (March 1974; private collection, Madrid) the bare bulb hangs first above Dyer, then above a twisting athlete, like a dark omen of death in the black void behind and around them. The bare light bulb hangs over each of the heads in the *Three Portraits* of 1973—the *Posthumous Portrait of George Dyer, Self Portrait,* and *Portrait of Lucian Freud* (private collection)—as the lower bodies of the three men liquefy in a black, seeping meltdown of mortality, just as life drains out of González's tulips from *El Niño* (The Child), which are now only a shadow of their former colorful selves. The stark blocks of color isolating the figure of the young man quite likely owe something to Bacon, too. As impressed by Bacon as this artist undoubtedly is, however, he is also far less pessimistic—not the godless existentialist Bacon was. González is always inclined to a deep religious faith in beauty that nothing in his life has ever seemed able to shake. The tulips of *El Niño* may be drained of color, yet they are finely differentiated one from another and richly bordered with a fine band of gold.

Painstaking skill has been expended on the trompe-l'oeil scrap of paper attached to the ledge below the figure. This scrap of paper and the ghostly apparition of the tulips reveal the miniature scale of the laughing figure to the viewer, making the young man in red shorts a tiny figure in a still life, an ultralifelike yet eternally frozen statuette, a flesh-and-blood counterpart to the sacred infant in the still life of *El Niño.* As he stands on the ledge in his swimming trunks he is also, of course, a diver—a breezier, more cheering cousin to Bacon's diver squatting pitifully on his coffee table diving board in *Portrait of George Dyer Crouching* (private collection, Caracas).

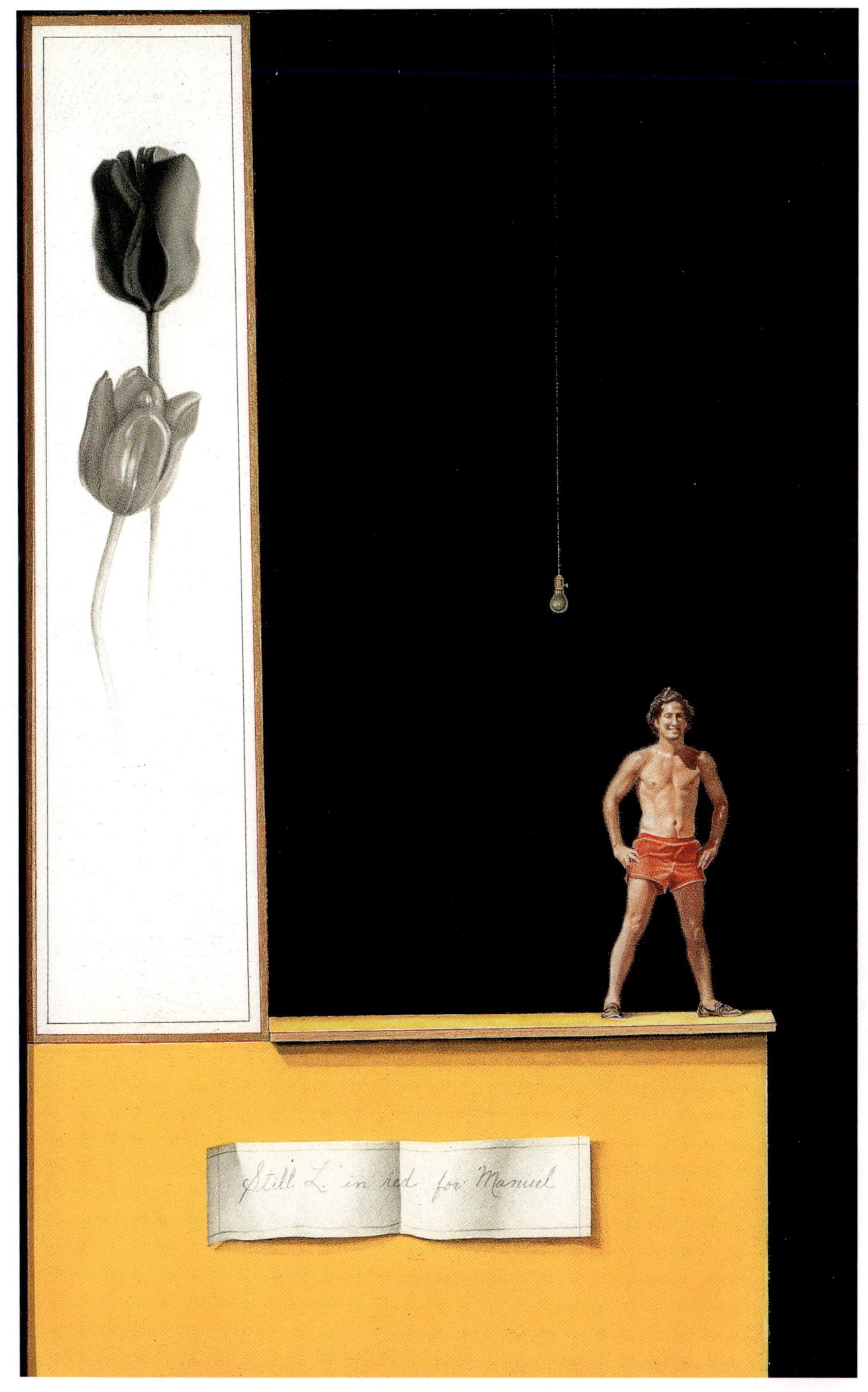
Still L. in red for Manuel

52 *Il Giardino delle Sorelle* 1987

Watercolor, pastel, and Conté crayon on paper, 50¼ × 37½ inches
Corporate Collection, Bacardi Imports, Inc.

In this epiphanic vision of the Royal Plaza Park in Palermo, Sicily, González returned to the colored pencil of his earliest drawings, to create a "yellow environment" communicating a sense of "looking into the sun." One of the figures strolling in the garden, apparently the focal point of attention for the promenading park visitors, resembles a sculpture in shorts who seems to have come to life. This "petrified man," as González calls him, is a tiny portrait of the artist, eternal and serene in his enchanted garden of sun and gold. Traditional symbolic associations of the palm—with the sun, with fame, triumph, the self-creating androgyne, and the martyr's victory over death in resurrection—are central to this celebration of the talents of those memorialized in the dark subdued palette of *New York, Year 1986.*

González had wanted to paint a yellow environment after admiring Vincent van Gogh's yellow-on-yellow study, *Basket with Lemons* at the Rijksmuseum in Amsterdam. Giacometti's drawing of palm trees, *Paesaggio,* 1953 (Collection of Franco Russoli, Milan), may further have influenced this work, along with González's memories of Cuba and his father's beautiful, trained fighting cocks: "The palm trees make me think of birds fighting, and feathers flying in the air." Early "poetic" memories of getting delightfully lost in a fairground hall of mirrors and an adult fascination with the theory and symbolism of the Rorschach inkblot test's mirrored-image puzzles of perception brought about the complicated structure of *Il Giardino delle Sorelle* (The Garden of the Sisters), though González was certainly thinking again of the line from Lorca's "Song of the Barren Orange Tree": "Why was I born among mirrors?" (a line the artist understands as a reference to narcissism). Perhaps González also carried into the composition a memory of the more playful Lorca poem entitled "Narcissus," which opens: "Boy! / You'll fall into the river! / Deep down there's a rose / with another river inside."[1] The mystically glowing, mirrored roses of love and blood in the artist's red pool would seem to confirm an acquaintance with the latter poem. The red water is described by the artist as "a reflection of a reflection, because the landscape—which is mirrored at the sides—is also reflected below, in the pool. The only thing that unites the two is the bench, which is a place for the eye to rest—and then the title at the bottom, where I write *Il giardino delle sorelle*."

But the "mirroring" of *Il Giardino delle Sorelle* is all deception. Compare the split halves of the composition and the superficial symmetries fall apart. Few other images by González so deliberately express the profound ambivalence of narcissism, its double-dealing. The all-yellow environment of *Il Giardino delle Sorelle* is further remarkable as a vivid example of Marcuse's notion that narcissism, "usually understood as egotistic withdrawal from reality," may paradoxically express oneness with the universe. "In other words, narcissism may contain the germ of a different reality principle: the libidinal cathexis of the ego [one's own body] may become the source and reservoir for a new libidinal cathexis of the objective world—transforming this world into a new mode of being."[2]

González has written the title of the image in red ink on a banner reminiscent of a Frida Kahlo banderole. Though the artist perhaps initially incorporated text in the image after examples in Bellini and Zurbarán, the banderole looks quintessentially Latin American—purely in the tradition of the small religious paintings on metal that Kahlo collected, which thank Christ, the Virgin, or the saints for divine assistance and carry written descriptions of the illnesses or crises depicted in the paintings.

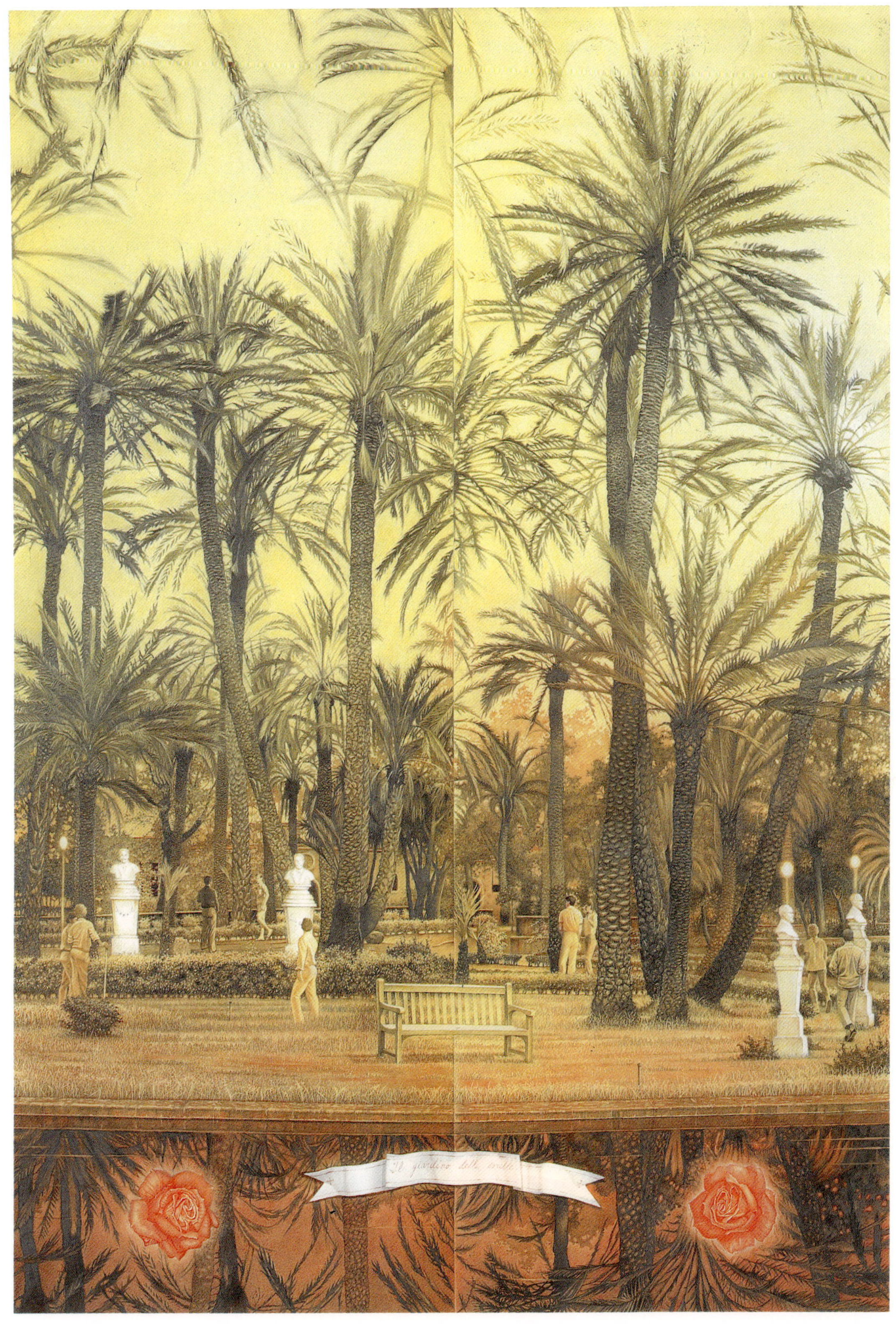
Il giardino delle

53 *Jardín de un Sueño* 1987–89

Tempera, acrylic, oil, and gold leaf on panel, 16½ × 37⅛ inches
Collection of Laila and Thurston Twigg-Smith

González lingered for two years over this tender vision of his two daughters in an Andalusian *carmen,* an enclosed and fragrant garden of paradise—the only occasion upon which he has painted Maria and Teresa together. The two young women express differing sides of the artist: Teresa, in the distance, watchful, alert, actively confronting the viewer; Maria, with the closed eyes of the dreamer, a withdrawn and introspective creative spirit. Maria's inclined head and closed eyes mirror the attitude of the blue-veiled sleeping boy in the small right-hand panel, whose head is borrowed from Jean-Baptiste Carpeaux's touching nineteenth-century sculpture group at the Metropolitan Museum, *Count Ugolino and His Sons.* González intended the sleeping boy as yet another symbolic portrait of himself as a sculpted dreamer. The two end panels appear to mirror each other: the canopy of moonlit roses is the same in each panel, yet the left-hand panel omits the sleeping boy, echoing the ambiguous "mirroring," or false symmetry, González consistently plays with, most notably in works like *Il Giardino delle Sorelle* (The Garden of the Sisters).

The blue portrait of the sleeping boy salutes Joseph Cornell's blue-glazed *Medici Slot Machine (Bernardino Pinturicchio)* of 1943 (Collection of Mr. and Mrs. E. A. Bergman, Chicago). Blue is a color that increasingly comes to connote a wistful sadness or nostalgia in González's work, culminating in the 1993 self-portrait titled *Blue*. González would certainly have been aware, during these years, of Lorca's rose symbolism, since he was working on the *Blood Wedding* collages in 1988. The tragic Bride of *Blood Wedding,* unable to resist her mad love for Leonardo, protests to her dark lover: "I can't listen to your voice. It's as though I'd drunk a bottle of anise and fallen asleep wrapped in a quilt of roses. It pulls me along, and I know I'm drowning—but I go on down."[1] González fills his *Blood Wedding* stage sets with crosses and crowns of roses, observing and expanding on the poet's direction that the Bride's home should feature "a cross of large rose colored flowers."[2] These crosses and crowns of roses symbolize a compulsion to love, even at the cost of life itself.

If the artist's boyish alter ego in blue sleeps beneath roses, his cherished daughters are crowned like Madonnas, their heads haloed with flowers as they silently coexist in a serene and timeless magic garden. This lovingly crafted piece is framed to imply that the viewer is looking at the painting through the contours of a bridge, or at a safe passage over dangerous waters. Seven opalescent studs, like moonstones, evoke the moon, water, and the passage of time.

Every blade of grass, every tiny blossom, appears to have been individually brushstroked into place, producing a landscape of hallucinatory sharpness at ground level, turning to a misty golden haze at the level of the trees and sky in a loose pyramid of ascension. The end panels are inlaid with gold borders and are spangled with shimmering crosshatched gold leaf. Two vertical garlands, bought from a company specializing in architectural ornament, embellish the sides of the frame. The purpose of making this second Garden of the Sisters, says the artist, was to "send my daughters a spiritual message of protection and a good future."

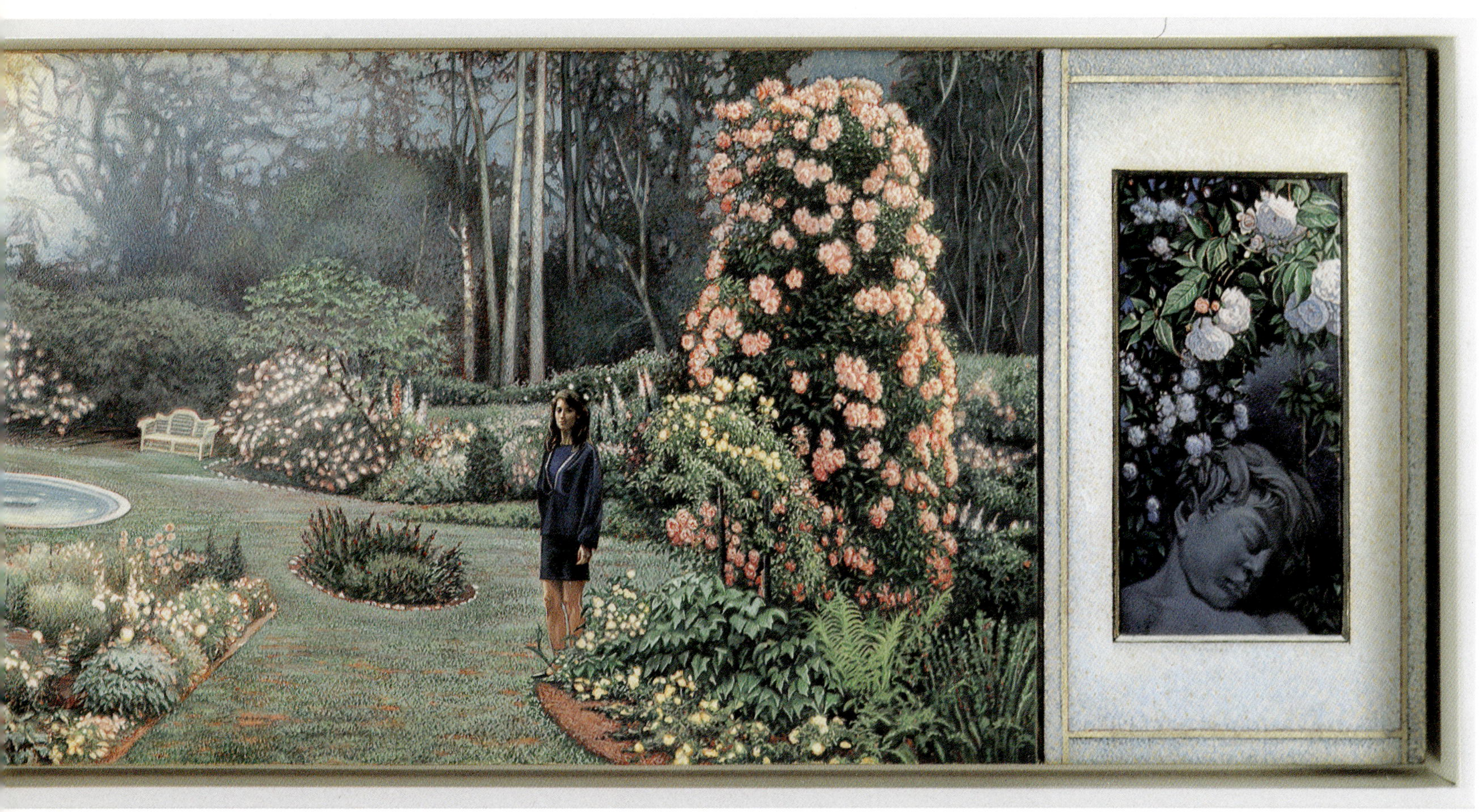

54 *Mar de Lágrimas/Sea of Tears* 1987–88

Watercolor and gouache on paper mounted on board, 27½ × 43¼ inches
Private collection, New York

The evolution of *Mar de Lágrimas/Sea of Tears* is amply documented. González has on file a manila envelope filled with the research materials he gathered for this work: a gridded photograph of the Sea of Japan (his metaphoric "sea of tears"); a colored reproduction of Fitz Hugh Lane's atmospheric *Ship Starlight* (Butler Institute of American Art, Youngstown, Ohio); bouquets cut from magazines from which have been scissored a pair of red roses; photographs of himself and friends bathing; and a half page torn from a *National Geographic* illustrated article about a dozen men of varied nationalities, preparing to brave a fierce Icelandic river in canoes, inaugurating their expedition with a communal bath in underground geothermal springs.

In the manila envelope with this multiplicity of visual references are a couple of rough pencil sketches by the artist, figuring out the structure of the composition. Initially, the seven red roses at the top of the work numbered eleven, and they were mounted on a curtain rod: in the empty right-hand panel, a translucent curtain hung, reversing the left-hand position of the curtain in *Nacimiento/Nativity*. Ultimately, González settled for a sacred and complete seven roses. He dispensed with the curtain in favor of the brilliant illusion of a bevel-edged three-paneled bathroom-cabinet mirror—playing with the notion of an old-fashioned Cuban drilled-glass mirror, fixed with plastic flower-capped screws to a back panel of wood. The sky in this dark mirror recycles the Holy Trinity of white clouds from the earlier *Songs for My Father,* while the idea of a triple-paneled mirror that is a "sea" relates back to the triptych *Mar y Espejo* (Sea and Mirror).

González had at first placed his own head resting on its side in the central panel, above and slightly to the left of the miniature bathers at the bottom of the image. The skull, intended to be part of the narrative, occupied its own little box high in the left panel. But in the finished work, González moved his head through the beveled edge of the mirror and into the left-hand panel. He transferred the skull to the right side of the work, where it has ascended up and out of the picture into the silver-leaf frame, becoming a piece of architectural ornament outside the image, leaving the right panel to blank sea and sky.

A variety of art-historical sources contributed to this head of the artist pillowed on a dark night sea: Rousseau's 1897 *Sleeping Gypsy* (The Museum of Modern Art, New York), Redon's 1890 *Closed Eyes* (see page 14) and his numerous heads of Orpheus floating on the waters; Constantin Brancusi's oval dreaming head, the *Sleeping Muse,* 1906 (Museum of Art, Bucharest); perhaps Auguste Rodin's ca. 1911 marble muse *Sleep* (private collection); and very likely, the horizontally displayed Spanish baroque head of John the Baptist at Seville cathedral. González flirted with the concept of a head that is immortal, a painted or sculpted head that may come alive at any moment—hence the real-looking tear that courses down the artist's cheek, in itself a familiar and poignant touch in polychrome sculpture and in the self-portraits of Frida Kahlo. But the head is self-referential, too, a companion "in the mirror" for the dreaming Narcissus of *El Soñador/The Dreamer.*

An image of dashing lyricism from a Lorca poem González loves, the "Gacela of the Dark Death," had a great deal to do with the conception of the painting: "I want to sleep the dream of that child / who wanted to cut his heart on the high seas."[1] The first line of this same poem—"I want to sleep the dream of the apples"—stayed with González for years, resulting in 1990 in the painting *To the Dream of the Apples,* with its horizontal head of a sleeping boy angel against a backdrop of roses. The "sea of tears" cried by the artist is a sea of death, but also eternal life. "All must know that I have not died; / that there is a stable of gold in my lips," proclaims Lorca in the poem. González seeks the same immortality in his painting.

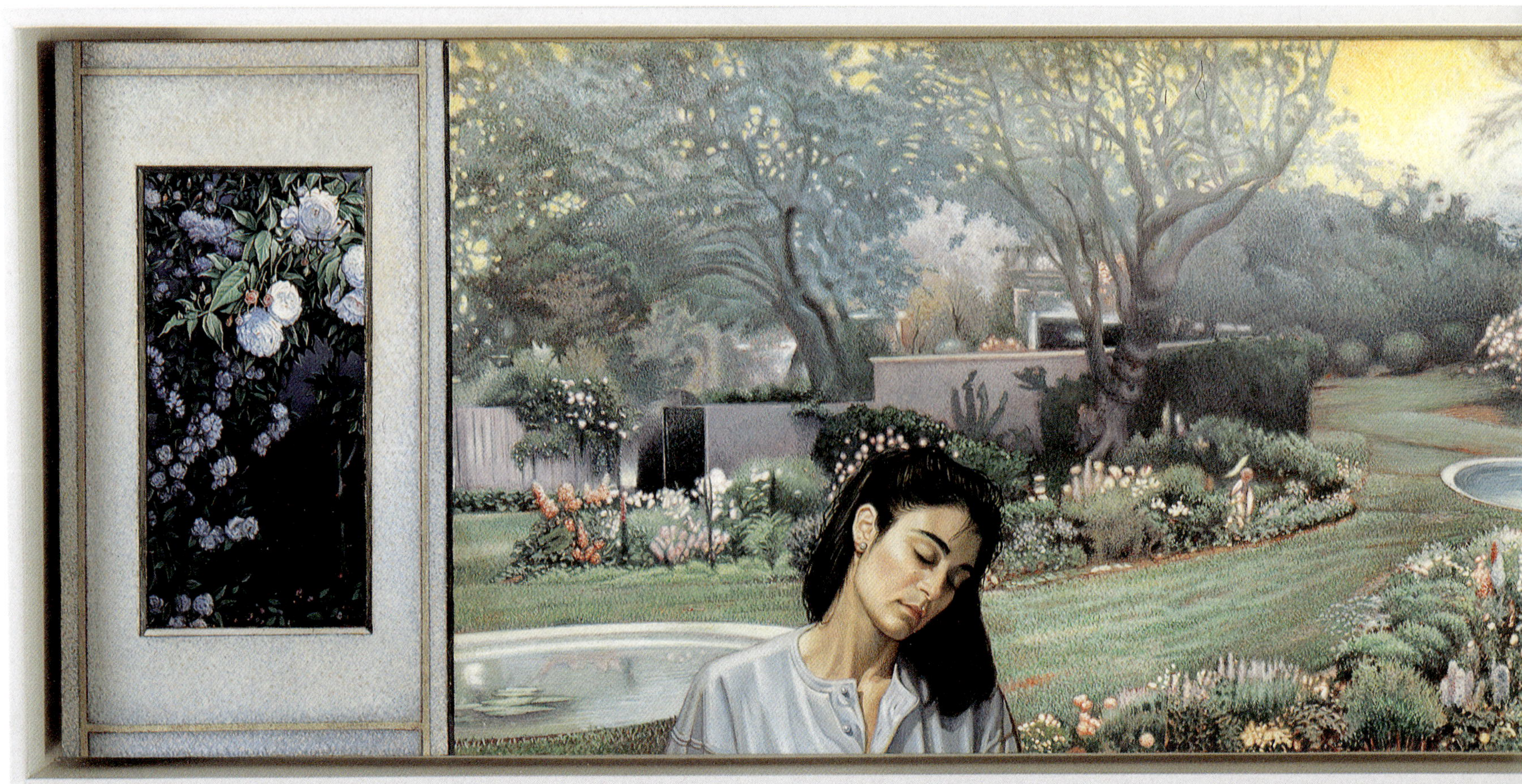

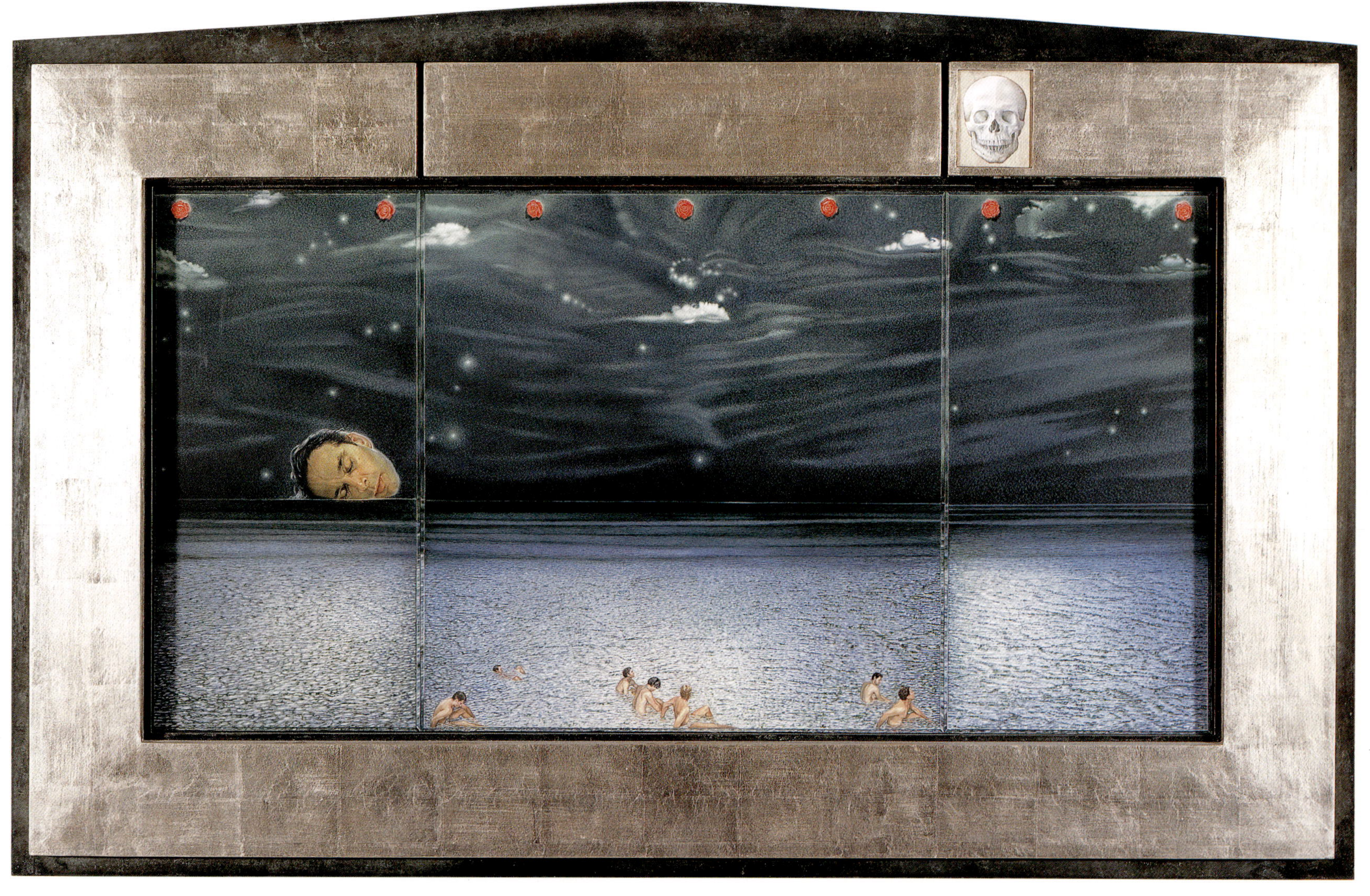

55 *Cycle* 1989

Mixed media on Gator board, 24½ × 15½ inches
John P. Axelrod, Boston

González immersed himself for this work in Rodin's tragic vision of modern life, *The Gates of Hell,* commissioned in 1880 and partially derived from Dante's *Inferno.* From Dante, Rodin took such elements as Ugolino and his sons, incarcerated and starving to death; the Three Shades; and the famous *Thinker*—who may have been intended as a portrait of Dante himself, or as a combination of the poet and the artist, the creative seer. In *Cycle,* González improvises his own "gates of hell," while simultaneously honoring the chiaroscuro in sculpture of Rodin and his model Carpeaux, the baroque tendency of Rodin's figures to slip in and out of their architectural frames, the startling changes in scale of figures throughout *The Gates of Hell,* and the dramatic power of Rodin's burdened Adam/Shade.

The sleeping youngest son of Carpeaux's Count Ugolino, whom González had first placed in an end panel of *Jardín de un Sueño* (Garden of a Dream), here reappears as a companion to the figure González thinks of as Adam, though it is actually one of the Three Shades crowning the top center of Rodin's portal (the Shades were variants of *Adam* or *Creation*). The large scale and prominent position of the Shades above the thorned vine that crowns *The Thinker* and suffering humanity fascinated González—who himself had crowned the portal of *Roma* with the *Boy Embracing a Goose* and would go on to crown *Memory Piece* with Rodin's *Kiss.* Unlike Rodin, who was obsessed with the entire family group of Carpeaux's *Ugolino and His Sons* (his *Thinker,* of course, being clearly influenced by Carpeaux's agonized father), González focuses once again on the poignant vulnerability of the innocent sleeping boy, placing a loose halo of roses above his head and a thorned rose cane to one side, almost like a ladder of ascent or descent for the Adam/Shade. With the conjunction of the thorned rose cane and the blue "quilt of roses" inspired by the fated Bride of *Blood Wedding,* González arrives at antithetical symbols of passion and suffering, martyrdom and victory.[1] The image of the boy sleeping among roses, practically *lost* in roses since both are drowned in blue, surely reflects, too, the famous lullaby in act 1, scene 2 of *Blood Wedding,* sung by the Mother-in-law of Leonardo, the tempestuous horseman who has been riding all night to court his far-flung lover, the Bride. "My rose, asleep now lie, / for the horse is starting to cry," runs the Mother-in-law's thrice-repeated refrain.[2] If there is a single fragment in all of Lorca's poetry that with its lyric strength and poetic irrationality moved González above all others, the refrain contrasting the sleeping rose of a baby and the tormented horse crying in the river because "he didn't like water," would be it: "The image seems to me so fantastic and unexpected, and at the same time sad and gentle," says González. It is an image that in some profound way "freed" the artist.

From the sleep of death, prefigured in the long, quiet spell of deep introspection and concentration of the artist, comes struggling life—Adam, the Creation. The title of this piece expresses the idea of a cycle of death and rebirth played out in a romantic, Cornell-inspired theater of dreamy, moonlit beauty and fantasy. Vivid life is embodied in the exciting warm red of the Zurbarán-like curtain canopied above the boy in his bed of roses. The separate stages in the life cycle of a moth unfold from top to bottom of the image, as the moth, finally color-drained, descends to the forestage of the blue-lit theater. To Cubans the moth is a symbol of death, "a creature of the night." González depicts a similar moth fluttering over the blue head of a sleeping boy angel against a golden quilt of roses in *To the Dream of the Apples,* 1990.

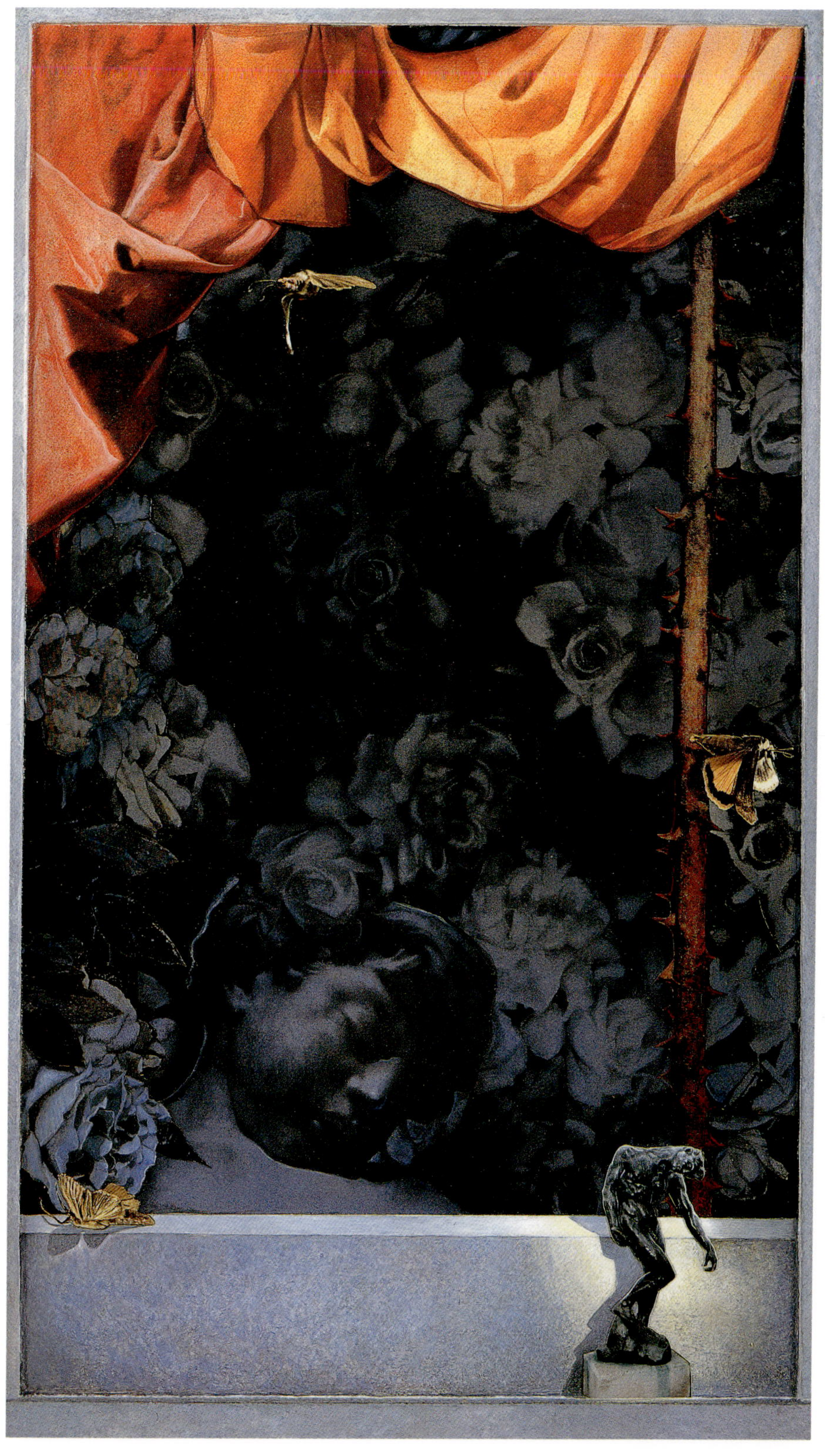

56 *Untitled* 1988

Mixed media on Gator board, 17¾ × 24½ inches
Collection of David Shapiro

Sienese paintings have often appealed to González for their magical objecthood, the way in which the *frame* is endowed with as much importance and drama as the picture. A work by the fifteenth-century Sienese painter Giovanni di Paolo, *Saint John the Baptist Retiring to the Desert,* ca. 1454 (National Gallery, London), in particular cast a lasting spell over González: in this untitled collage the artist recreates the contrasting white and red roses of the gilt-edged side panels flanking that quaint narrative scene. González had been fascinated by the repetition of the two roses, and by the way the white rose turns a little away from the viewer, nodding into the black void of the side panel. He was also influenced by the repetition of the two figures of the saint, who is depicted as emerging from a city portal, then heading into the barren hills, still carrying his knapsack over his shoulder.

This doubling or mirroring of the saint's figure, miniature by comparison with the roses, has everything to do with González's diminutive male figures (derived from the photographs of Eadweard Muybridge), juggling large red balls from one side of the inner frame to the other, describing a trajectory connecting the two figures. The red ball is for the artist "an emblem of the juggling that relationships require and of the difficulties inherent in any prolonged and meaningful contact with another human being."[1] González also repeats or mirrors the flowered frame of the Sienese painter—making it smaller, more recessed and distanced (though the landscape irrationally becomes larger), lighting it with a faint aureole of golden light breaking through the gilt inner frame from a sky transformed to gold, a toy-theater-within-a-theater that anticipates the little baroque theater in the woods of *Así que Pasen Cinco Años/When Five Years Pass,* 1991.

The artist thinks of this work as one of his first full-blown collages, paving the way for the collage series of *Blood Wedding* stage sets he was about to undertake, and linked in his own mind with the mirrored repetition of the two headless *Good Friday* figures playfully opposing one another in *Untitled,* 1974. The image is full of dissonant symmetries in the nude figures, in the Zurbaránesque loops of rose-colored Annunciation curtains, and in the repeated gilt frames. The palm-treed horizon line within the inner frame is only roughly contiguous with the palm-treed horizon line set within the outer frame, a Magritte-style visual trick suggesting for the artist "a dislocation within a gigantic mirror. I made the landscape to imply a reflected landscape, with the horizon lines of the inner and outer frames purposefully not quite matching."

The total effect of the composition is like the sum effect of *Bathers of Blenheim,* a work in which the artist also presents the viewer with a lush pastoral interior vision or idyllic memory, set within out-of-scale framing flowers, like a treasured photograph embellished with pressed flowers. In that earlier work, the artist also used a pale green ground, in his symbolic vocabulary evoking water.

In the twin male nudes that have stepped out of their black flowered niches—reminiscent of the angel and Virgin who break out of their frames in Jan van Eyck's diptych *Annunciation* (Thyssen-Bornemisza Museum, Madrid), leaving only a ghostly reflection of their silhouettes behind them in the dark mirrored ground of their niches—in the repetitions and watery-looking expanses of grass, in the concept of the image as a "gigantic mirror," González subtly but determinedly raises once again the issue of the Narcissus myth and the exploration of the self through art, the mysterious ways in which art can accommodate the introspective vision.

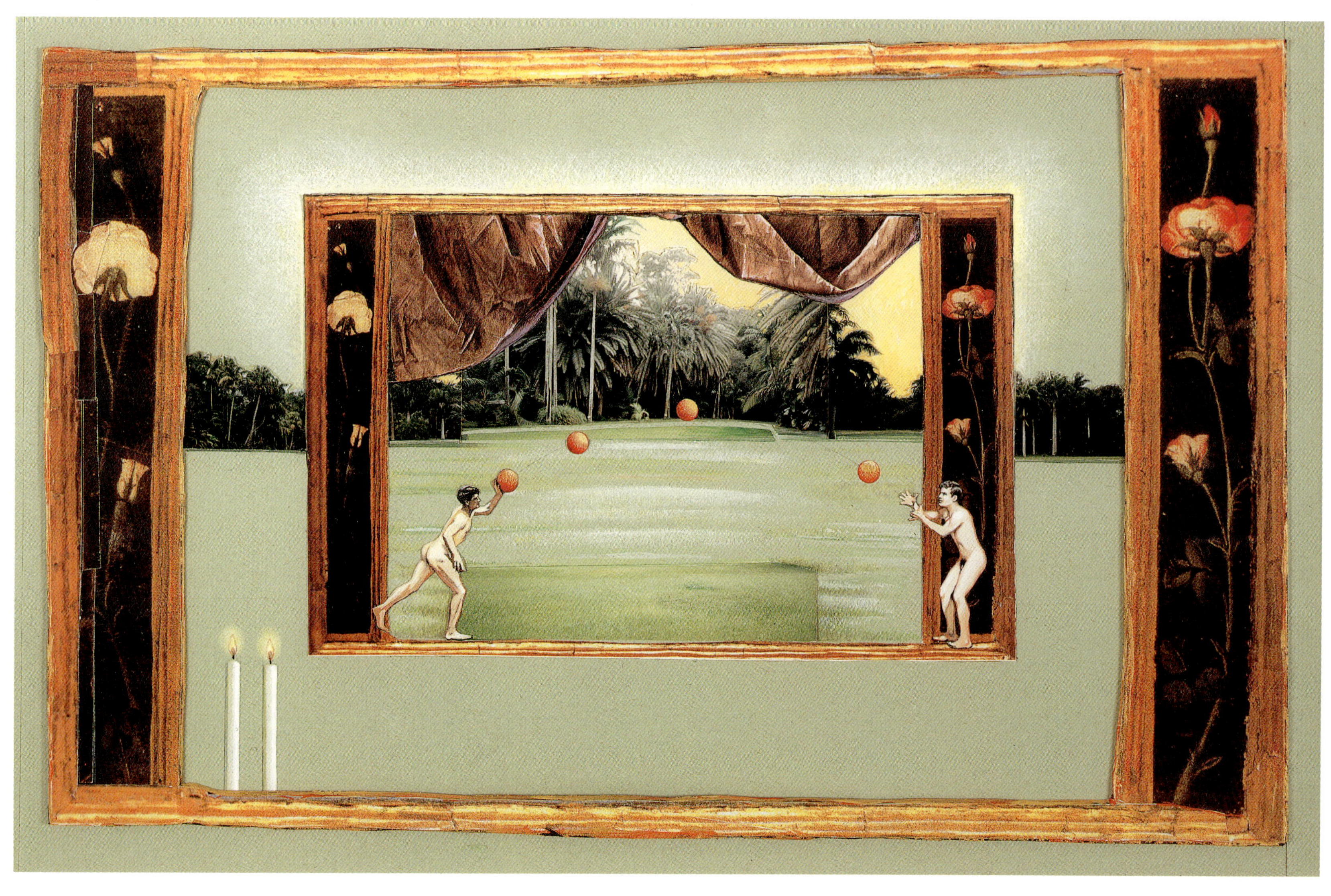

57 *In His Silence* 1988

Watercolor and gouache on paper mounted on museum board mounted on honeycomb panel, 12½ × 21½ inches
Glenn C. Janss Collection

González borrowed from Odilon Redon's *The Crown,* 1910 (Musée d'Orsay, Paris), the idea of a displaced crown or halo to one side of the subject's head. The artist thinks of his subject as "Saint Sebastian," placing arrows in mosaic side panels to underline the identity of the saint who survived the arrows. In fact, this stone boy, whose shoulder at least appears to have the magical glow of living flesh, is based on Alexandre Falguière's 1867 boy martyr *Tarcisius,* a sculpture González also remembers seeing at the Musée d'Orsay.

The scrap of paper draped over the wooden ledge or predella bears the handwritten message *a Angel,* or "to Angel." The boy martyr memorializes Angel, a friend of the artist's, who González learned in a phone call from New York had died of AIDS, just after the artist had visited the works by Redon and Falguière. González glorifies Angel as Saint Sebastian, the beautiful favorite of the emperor Diocletian who died for his faith, tied to the highly original column of the thorned rose cane—personalizing and updating the image of the saint in a unique way. (Sebastian is the saint to whom prayers have been addressed in times of plague.)

The intense, fiery color of the piece is unusual for González. Luminous, rich midnight blue trompe-l'oeil mosaics—the outcome of a trip he made to the dazzling tomb of Galla Placidia in Ravenna—unify the three panels. With the wooden insets and ledge, González was "making a reference to the cross of the Crucifixion—and I wanted the wood to feel completely *real* to the viewer. The ovals are something you really do find in plywood, but I was playing them off against the halo. At the same time, the ovals have a symbolic logic: I debated for a long time where I wanted those shapes to go, because I wanted them to be *ascending.* Yet the oval patterns in the wood also suggest curtain fabric, something like moiré." Use of the halo in Christian art is coeval with the mosaics of Ravenna. The oval shape occurring in González's flaming halo and in the plywood is the mandorla or vesica, the almond- or fish-shaped oval of light expressing spiritual radiance in sacred art, since the fish had been one of the secret signs of Christianity among the early believers and martyrs. The oval often surrounds or contains sacred figures in art—for instance, the fiery mandorla that frames the Virgin and Child in the sky of Carlo Crivelli's *Vision of the Blessed Gabriele* of about 1489 (National Gallery, London). González depicts his friend Angel attaining the transcendent light of sainthood.

Sacred geometry gives way to a contemporary touch in the tape-looped message of the central mosaic medallion, designed to roll on into perpetuity: "En su silencio . . . en su silencio . . ." (In his silence . . . in his silence . . .).

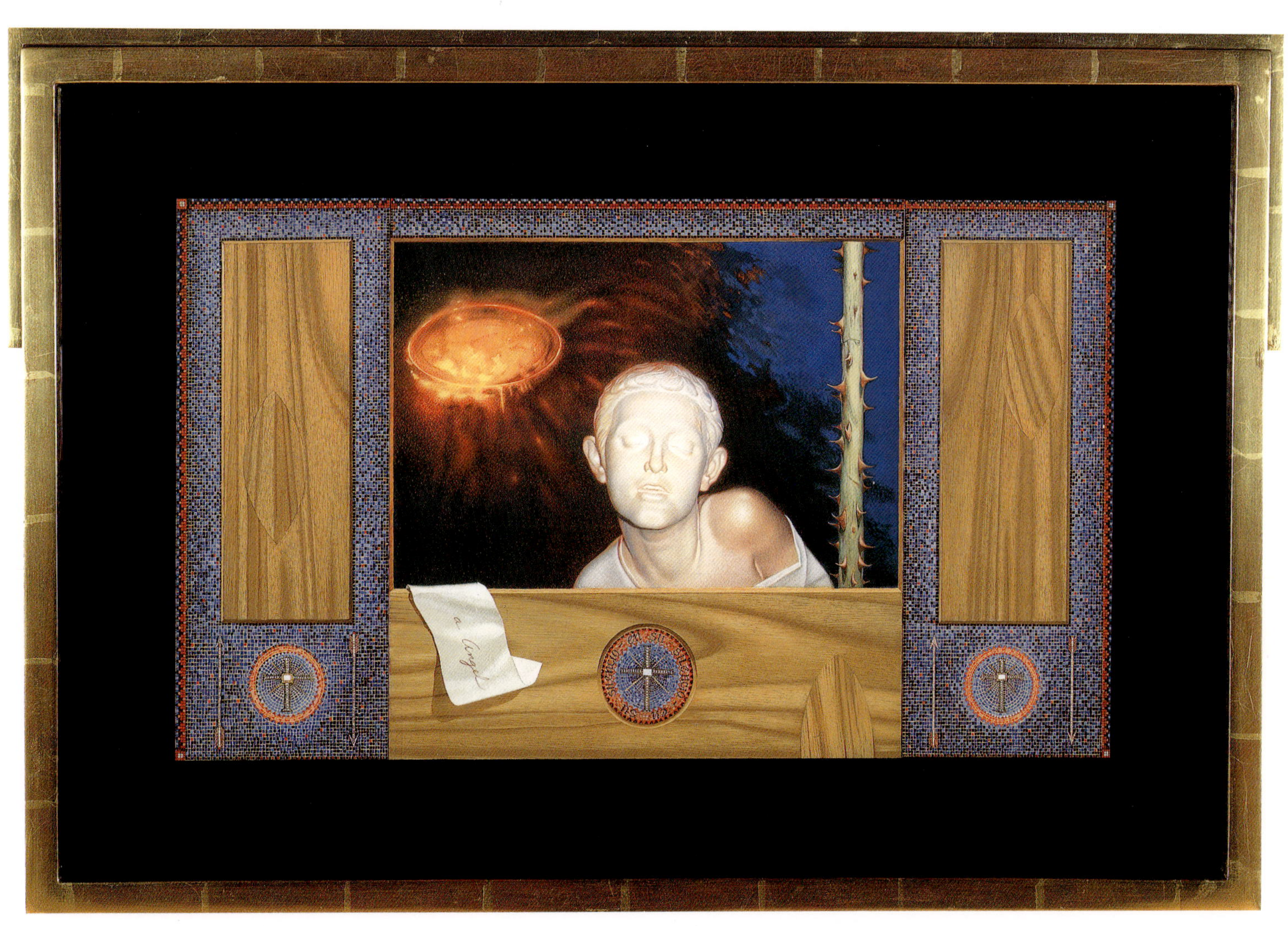
a Angel

58 *Cultivo una Rosa Blanca* 1988

Watercolor and gouache on paper, 30 × 22 inches
Collection of the Chase Manhattan Bank, N.A.

González moves to a polar extreme of color, mood, and light in the contradictory white space of this work, following the rich blaze of the night theaters depicted in *Cycle* and *In His Silence.* The trompe l'oeil of the white cloth projecting toward the viewer from the white picture plane is strikingly reminiscent of the earliest drawings on white paper in such works as *A. M., Hot White Tennessee Williams,* and *The Sparrow and the Maiden.* Thematically, of course, the work is the culmination of the series of rose paintings initiated in the white rose crown of *New York, Year 1986.* With this image González's world has turned a still, silent white. It would not be going too far to say that González reveres the sheer white blank of the paper—the sheet or wall that with the perfect minute strokes of the brush or pencil is transformed into a symbolic trompe l'oeil or a still life with a divine theme, like the white veil over the ocean of *La Misa Blanca* (The White Mass).

Here, a coastal landscape in Cuba, pushed to the extreme low edge of the image and miniaturized into the far distance, provides a point of departure—a vast white sky—for the trompe l'oeil of the white cloth suspended above it. The cloth is imprinted, not with Veronica's miraculous face of Christ, but with the thorn-stemmed white rose of innocence and transcendence. High above it, at the top, is the skull of *Mar de Lágrimas/Sea of Tears.*

This austere white work, carefully balancing horizontal and vertical elements, is described by González as "an arrangement of symbols that are free association. What was in my heart was the horror of what was happening around me and my friends—the horror of AIDS." The title is taken from the famous Latin anthem by the Cuban nineteenth-century martyr to independence, José Marti, who wrote: "Cultivo una rosa blanca, / en julio como en enero, / para el amigo sincero / que me da su franca." González explains the meaning of the lines as " 'In bad times and in good times, I grow a white rose for friends and enemies alike.' It's the idea of putting a good face on things, making the best of them."

Cultivo una Rosa Blanca (I Grow a White Rose) may stand as an effective summation of González's entire output and method—his Latin aesthetic of pain transformed into exquisite ornament, a beauty that veneers agony, in a sublimating meditation on death. The image of the white rose in the sky is also peculiarly Dantesque, following hard on the heels of the *Inferno*-inspired Adam/Shade in *Cycle:* in the *Paradiso* (Canto 30), Dante and Beatrice are conveyed into the Empyrean, a heaven revealed to Dante as "a round sea of light, above which Paradise is discovered as a vast white rose," inside which the angels and the redeemed dwell blissfully in two separate courts. It would be like González to combine Dante's vision of paradise as the "Celestial Rose" with the earthy realism of a rose stamped on a trompe-l'oeil cloth hung on a wall—to overlay a contemporary Cuban verse with the pre-Renaissance mysticism of Dante.

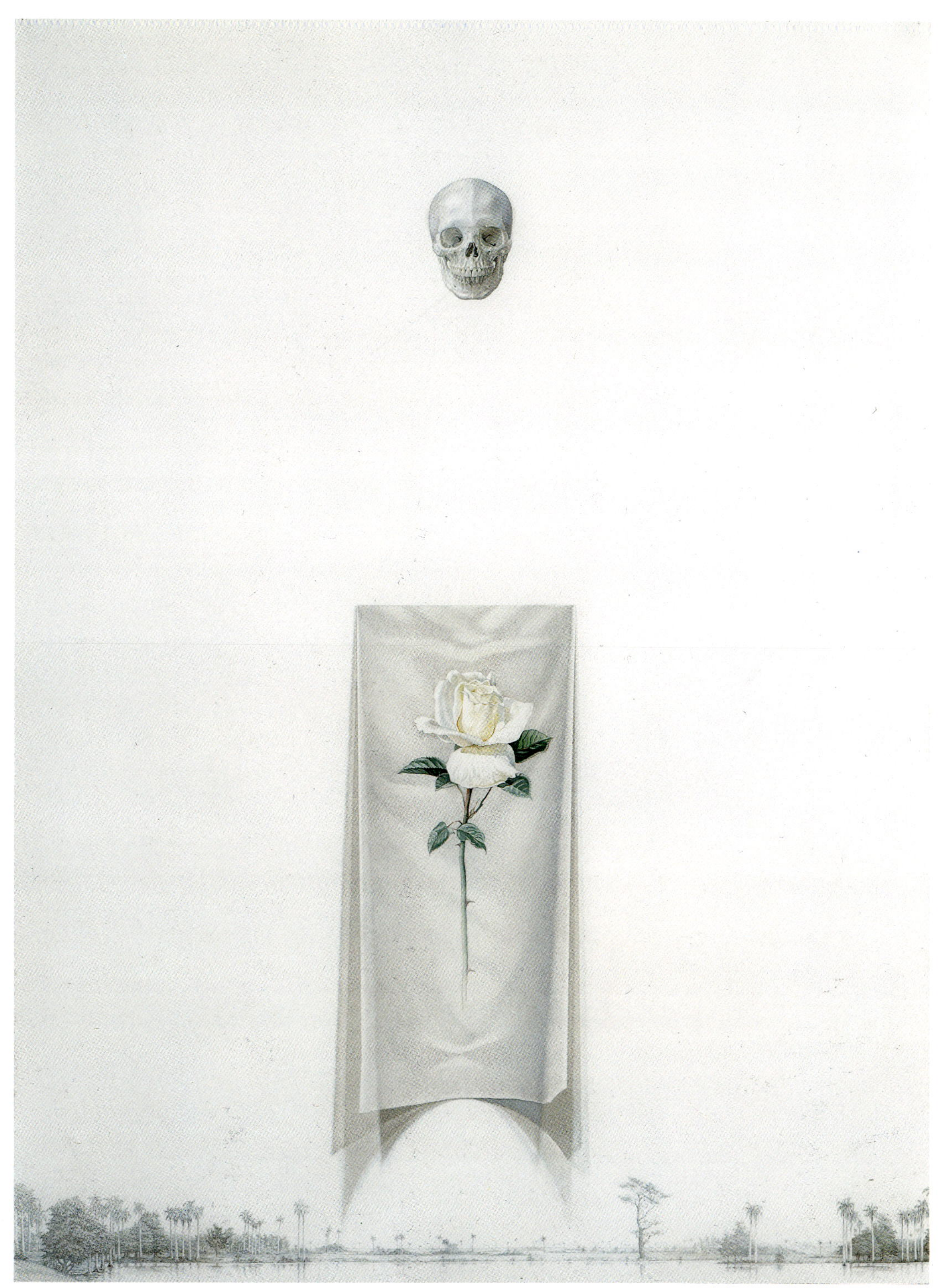

59 *Blood Wedding: Act 1, Scene 1* 1988

Mixed media on Gator board, 28¼ × 40¼ inches
Glenn C. Janss Collection

In 1988 González produced a set of mixed-media set designs for the Lorca tragedy *Blood Wedding,* to be staged at the Great Lakes Theater Festival in Cleveland, Ohio, that fall. He was free for the first time to respond fully to the vision of his favorite poet and adapt that vision to his own vocabulary.

Lorca had been inspired to write *Blood Wedding* after engrossing himself in newspaper accounts of a shooting before a wedding in Almería, Spain. The murder victim, a lover of the bride, had eloped with her on horseback the night before the wedding was to take place. To avenge family honor, an outraged cousin of the groom shot the lover dead. In ongoing newspaper reports of the tragedy, Lorca scented the theme, perennial with him, of a secret and fatal love. But the poet made some significant changes, inventing a dark, mysterious forest in which the groom and the impassioned lover (whom he called Leonardo—the only character in the play he named) knife each other to death. Most radically, as Ian Gibson points out, Lorca marks Leonardo as "the victim of ineluctable fate, the youngest in the line of a family of killers who have already reduced the Bridegroom's family to its last male." And in the third act of the play, the poetic inspiration of Lorca reached "one of its finest flowerings when, in the wood scene, everyday reality is transformed as the moon comes to preside over the sacrificial deaths of lover and groom."[1]

González's artful setting for the first scene of *Blood Wedding* faithfully follows the poet's stage direction, conjuring up a yellow room, redolent of the early morning and the gathering heat of the sun. The Bridegroom is on his way to the vineyard, demanding a knife with which to cut his breakfast grapes. His widowed Mother speaks bitterly of the husband and son she has already lost to the knives of Leonardo's clan. González adheres to all these details: the Bridegroom, the vineyard, and the premonitory Knife, which he aptly turns into a third character, enthroning it on a tall stool at the front of the stage. Giant bunches of grapes hang over the characters' heads, grapes of the Communion wine, commemorating the mystery of Christ's sacrifice—though they also refer to Lorca's repeated references to land lust (the wrongheaded reason for the arranged marriage that precipitates the tragedy of the play) and to the giant vegetation that for the poet symbolized passions running out of control. For González, the outsized grapes frame and define the miniaturized scale of the figures in the still-life "landscape" of this triple-paneled theater of yellow, where an angry mother waylays her fatherless son. They are also the "realistic," trompe-l'oeil frame that authenticates even as it distances the fantastic art-historical characters on the stage—as the flowers around the *Bathers of Blenheim* confirm in the present the fond but far-off memory of the central image.

The twin domination of this scene by the Mother and the Knife is emphasized by the wooden stakes that pierce the floor of the stage, tethering a spider's web of imprisoning ropes or lines around the characters, ropes that noticeably strike at the two empty chairs of the murdered father and brother of the Bridegroom, like the scratched lines striking symbolic targets in *After Philadelphia.* This network of lines deftly blends González's preoccupation with cages and the wounding threads of destiny, with Lorca's notion of an ineluctable fate for these driven characters. González borrowed his "spidery" Mother, a far-from-injured innocent in the plays, from Goya's *Marquesa de la Solana,* ca. 1794–95 (Louvre, Paris). The Bridegroom in swimming trunks derives from one of Picasso's two young bathers in *The Pipes of Pan,* 1923 (Musée Picasso, Paris). The ghostly silhouettes behind the Mother and the Bridegroom—the self echoed and tripled like Rodin's *Three Shades*—are intended to evoke "their spirits, and their movement," according to the artist.

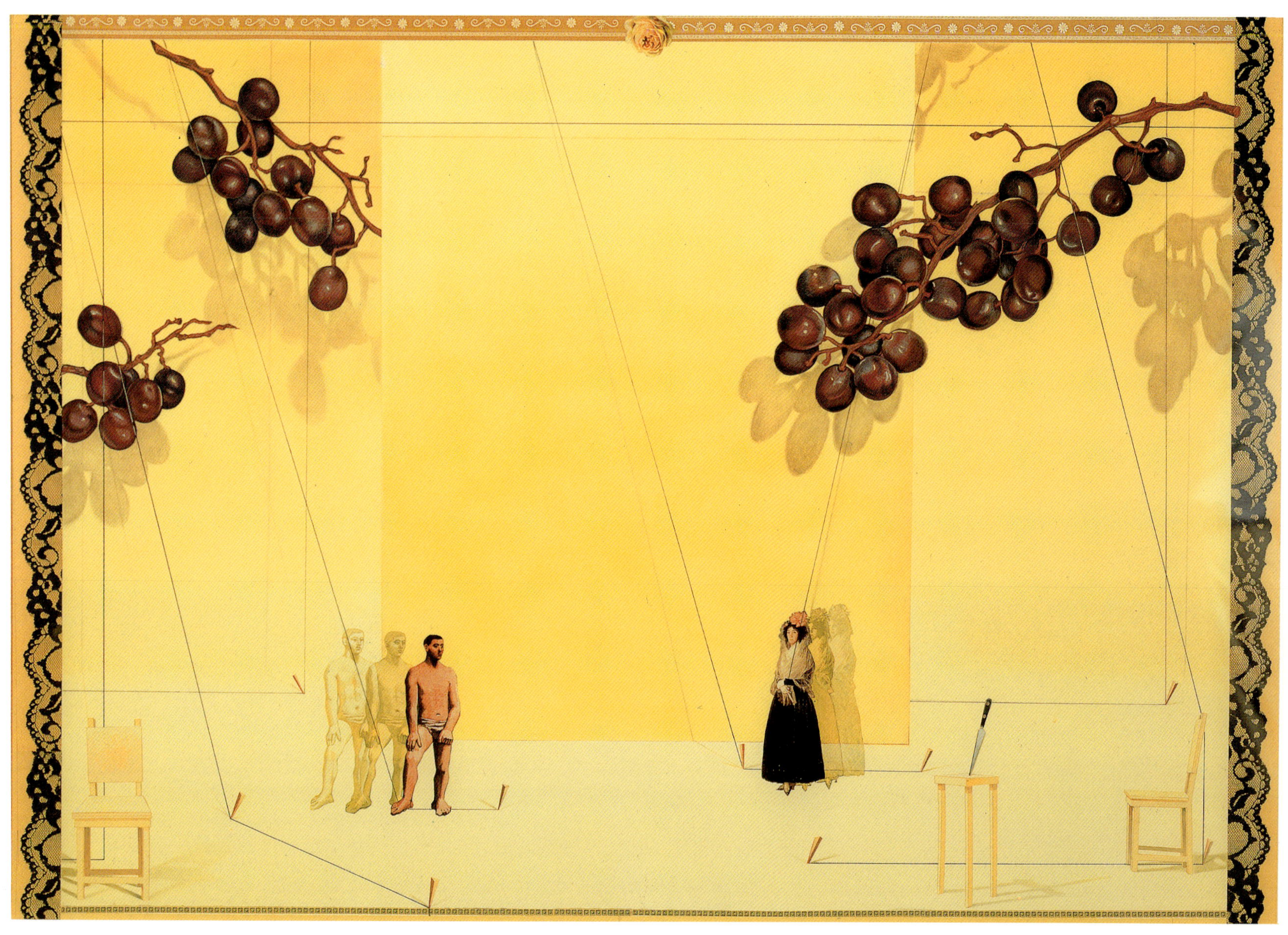

60 *Blood Wedding: Act 2, Scene 1* 1988

Mixed media on Gator board, 30 × 40¼ inches
Dorothy and Lewis Cullman

"The entrance hall of the Bride's house. A large door in back. It is night," stipulates Lorca in his stage-direction notes for this scene.[1] The Bride is having her hair dressed by a Servant in preparation for her wedding, both of them suffering in the sweltering heat of the night. The Servant makes a wreath of orange blossoms for the Bride's hair, which the unhappy Bride hurls aside. Leonardo unexpectedly turns up (ahead of the wedding procession, traveling by moonlight to beat the blistering sun of the day) and demands admittance to the Bride, to declare his guilty passion for her. They will elope, and the wedding will be consummated with the blood of Leonardo and the Bridegroom.

A lovely, shadowy river of tree branches laces the floor of the stage, vividly evoking the perfumed beauty of a Mediterranean night. In the giant citron vine that rambles over the enclosing wall of the Andalusian cave dwelling of the Bride, González once again draws upon dramatic dualities, opposing levels of scale and reality. With the *Blood Wedding* stage sets, the artist creates theaters or puppet booths that are also still lifes, into which he inserts miniature figures, realizing his Giacometti-derived dream of "measuring man against his mysterious landscapes."

González borrows his Bride from Picasso's monumental *Woman in White,* 1923 (The Metropolitan Museum of Art, New York) and his Servant from the same artist's *Three Women at the Spring,* 1921 (The Museum of Modern Art, New York). His Leonardo beneath a bull's mask, a ghostly mirror image of himself concealed within the texture of the wall, also recalls Picasso, yet the figure was actually drawn from Muybridge, like the figures in the wedding procession at the top of the picture. Perhaps, too, González had remembered some lines from a favorite Lorca poem, "Lament for Ignacio Sánchez Mejías," a gored bullfighter friend of the poet: "Death has covered him with pale sulphur and has placed on him the head of a dark minotaur."[2] The Picasso-inspired dove over the Bride's head recalls the lanced seventh pigeon of *After Philadelphia.*

This gorgeous image, vibrating with chromatic energy in the contrasting warm amber hues of the citron vine and the chill, silvered blues of the starred sky and cave home of the Bride, is one of the most voluptuous night scenes González has ever crafted—a seductive landscape above which the shape of the doubled moon anticipates the silver cutting instruments that will consume the lifeblood of Leonardo and the Bridegroom. The end of the drama is present in the dark Annunciation of the impaled dove, whose specter is recalled in the final scene, when the Bridegroom's grimly satisfied Mother announces, "of my dreams I'll make a cold ivory dove that will carry camellias of white frost to the graveyard."[3]

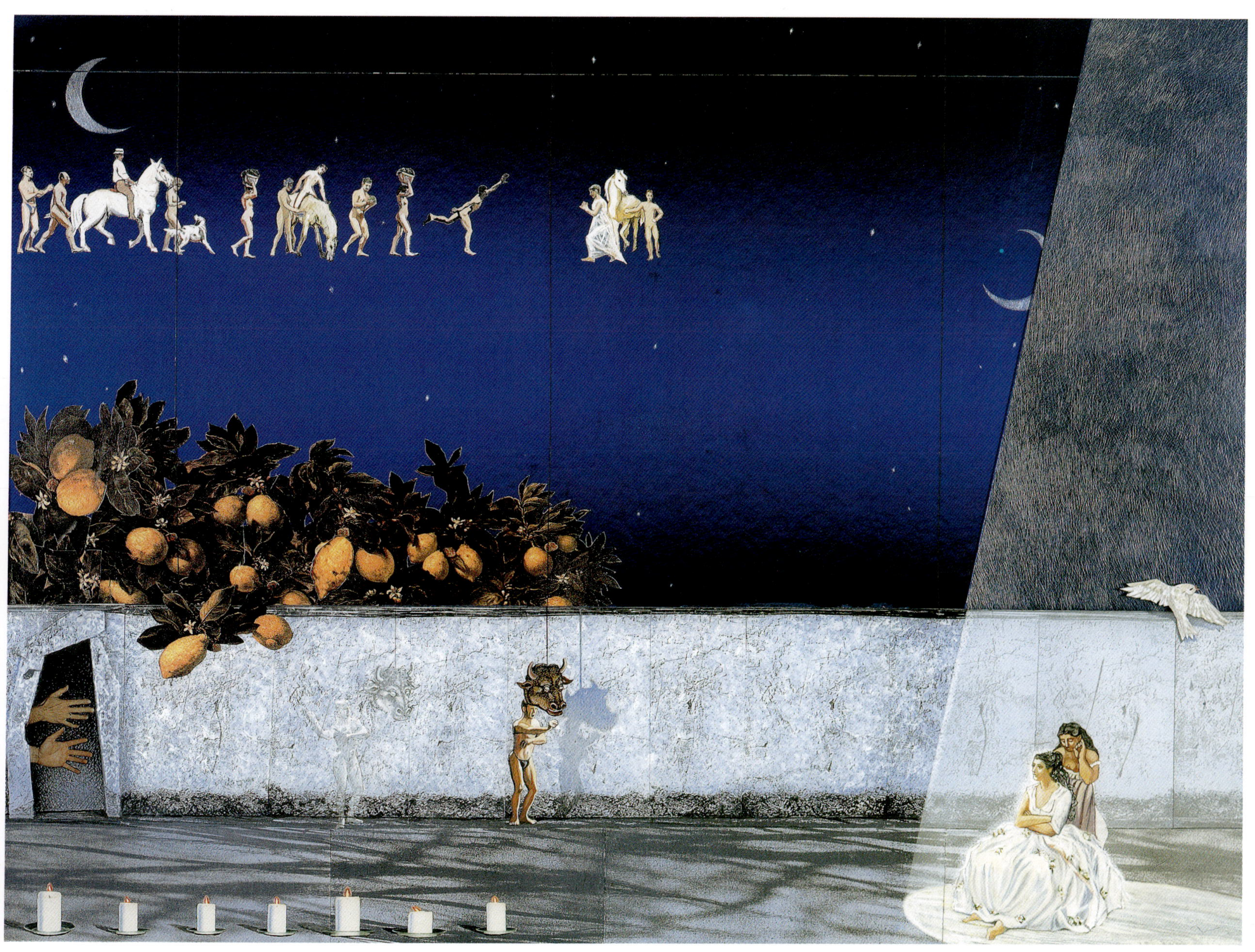

61 *Blood Wedding: Act 2, Scene 2* 1988

Mixed media on Gator board, 19 × 32 inches
Teresa and Larry Katz

In this rather free interpretation of Lorca's stage directions for the wedding scene, González has dispensed with the poet's cactus trees and panoramas of tan tablelands "in white, gray and cold blue tones"[1] outside the Bride's cavern home. The artist has brightened and intensified the blue of Lorca's imagined sky, reduced the cast of characters to the Bride and Leonardo, and turned the exterior of her home into a matador's bullring. The sacrificial ritual of the bullring vividly illustrates the Spanish concept of *duende,* the awareness and acceptance of mortality, which is then transformed into a source of deep emotion and inspiration—anguish, mystery, wonder, and beauty all springing from an elegant confrontation with death. The central characters of *Blood Wedding,* the Bridegroom, the Bride, and Leonardo, have *duende,* a quality important to Lorca. And considering the comparison of the wedding to a rising bull, and the bloody fight that follows the wedding, González's interpretation of the wedding scene as a bullring is apposite.

The artist sets a canopy or crown of roses over the wedding scene. Paying a Christmas visit to Lorca's village just outside Granada, González had been entranced by the sight of a forty-foot-wide Christmas wreath strung with flowers, lights, and shimmering fabric, hung in the sky above the village plaza. The crown of roses in this wedding scene is not simply a favorite symbol repeated, but a reference to the poet's village and to the commemoration of the sacrificial birth of Christ. Purely as a symbol of secrecy, the crown of roses is apt in this drama of hidden passions: "If a rose was painted or sculpted on the ceiling of any room it always signified that talk and discussion held there was confidential. The expression *sub rosa* was virtually synonymous with 'secret,'" observes Gerd Krüssmann in *The Complete Book of Roses.*[2]

González has scored the sky with thin lines, much as he scored the surface of *After Philadelphia*—the network of lines suggesting the skeined trap of inexorable fate, perhaps, as well as reverting to earlier works by the artist in which the sky is transformed into a gridded cloth or veil, notably *La Misa Blanca* (The White Mass) and *New York, Year 1986.* Perhaps there is a suggestion here of nets that trap birds in the sky. Beneath this netted sky, the Bride elopes with Leonardo—who will die before they can consummate their guilty passion.

González is focused wholly on the Bride and Leonardo. The Bride is tripled: she is the dancing figure in a diaphanous drape at center stage and also the two female figures in flight from the wedding—one running down a flight of steps to the white horse and rider, the other (reminiscent of the running boy of *After Philadelphia*) about to take off from a top ledge where her arms and head have already entered the crown of roses. This tension of irrational oppositions, embracing the inconsistent, is echoed in the duality of the cantering black Spanish horse and rider outside the bullring, tightly framed in a divided archway, with the white horse and rider standing inside the bullring, waiting in white space.

González's X-acto knife–cut baroque theater curtain, drawn back to reveal the unfolding drama, assumes the form of an ominously black fretwork of cutout leaves, in counterpoise to the tender pink tones of the rose crown, while the photocopied strip of lace at the lower edge of the image denotes the forestage, framing and containing the scene within the limits of the *retablo,* the Spanish word that signifies both the painted screen or panel behind the altar and the portable stage of the puppet theater.

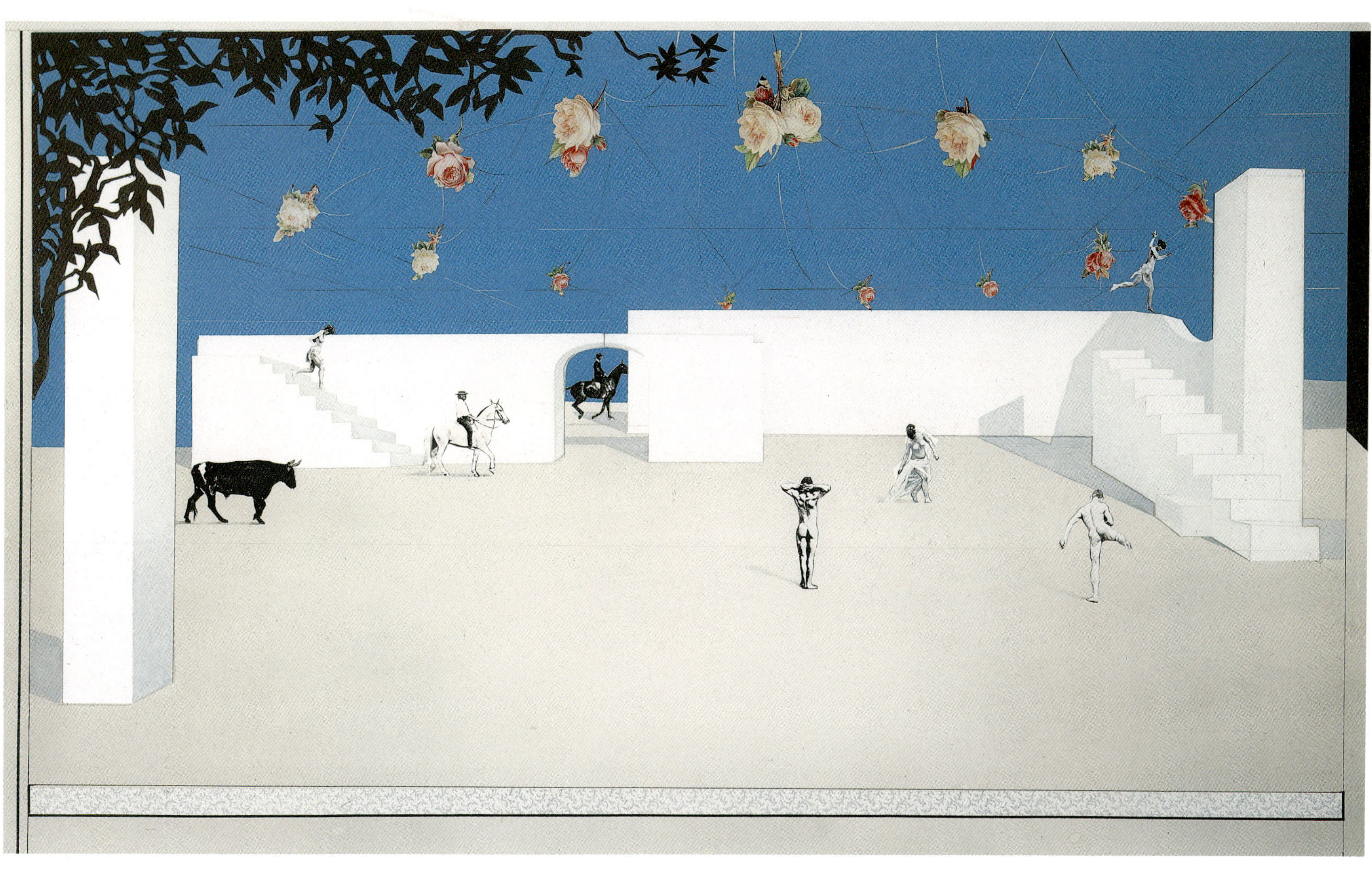

62 *Blood Wedding: Act 3, Scene 1* 1988

Mixed media on Gator board, 18 × 31½ inches
Collection of The Progressive Corporation, Cleveland

For the violent penultimate scene of the play, Lorca had envisioned a night forest full of "Great moist tree trunks. A dark atmosphere."[1] González arrives at an exciting synthesis of Lorca's moon, water, and knife imagery, brilliantly anticipating the Bride's speech at the end of the play to the Bridegroom's bitter Mother, after Leonardo and the Bridegroom have dispatched each other in the forest. The Bride explains to the Mother that, unlike the Bridegroom, Leonardo "was a dark river, choked with brush," an erotic force "like the pull of the sea," whereas her son, the Bridegroom, was "like a little boy of cold water,"[2] quite unable to assuage the Bride's burning desire.

González here creates a dark river of a stage set that is also a forest reminiscent of the drought-ruined landscape of his own *Cuatro Pilares* (Four Pillars). He elevates the allegorical figure of the Moon—Lorca's white-faced androgyne of a woodcutter (who perhaps prefigures the mystical union of male and female in *Rembrandt's Hands*)—to a high tower that looks like a diving board suspended above a waterline. The high tower/diving board may have suggested itself to the artist in connection with the poet's water symbolism, as well as enabling the audience actually to look up at the Moon, yet the placement also echoes the figures raised on columns or towers in the artist's own dreamscapes *Roma* and *New York, Year 1986*.

The waterline may be viewed as a curtain rod, from which, on the right, a rose-colored curtain beautifully trails, a symbolic river of blood, González's sensual equivalent for Lorca's spurting fountains of gore. Above the curtain, in ascension, rides the impassioned Leonardo, the night rider of previous scenes, restlessly pursuing love. In the dark forest below, his horse canters riderless, while the Bridegroom and Leonardo—metamorphosed into Muybridge wrestlers—fight to the death.

González's dread forest represents Lorca's chorus of Woodcutters, who know that the lovers must die, yet who approve of the way the lovers have surrendered to their path of blood. González's razor-sharp, stakelike tree trunks, tipped at the end with blood, recall the tethering stakes that were everywhere in the premonitory opening scene, the sacrificial knife, the "dark river, choked with brush" that is Leonardo, and the crown of thorns that the Bride in this scene feels she has already donned. In this black, still pool of a stage-set, González follows Lorca in drawing symbolic connections between water, the shifting sickle-shaped silver moon, and knives, all analogous poetic elements in the fated blood sacrifice of the young men.

The figures in the forest were all drawn, like the wedding guests, from Muybridge, whose filmic photographs of human beings and animals in motion have always fascinated González: "He has interested so many different artists, for so many different reasons. For the Minimalists, it was the structure of the pictures on the page. For me, there's a nostalgia about his pictures—but at the same time, something contemporary-looking. I suppose maybe he achieved that by having the men and women he photographed be nude, which gives them a timeless quality."

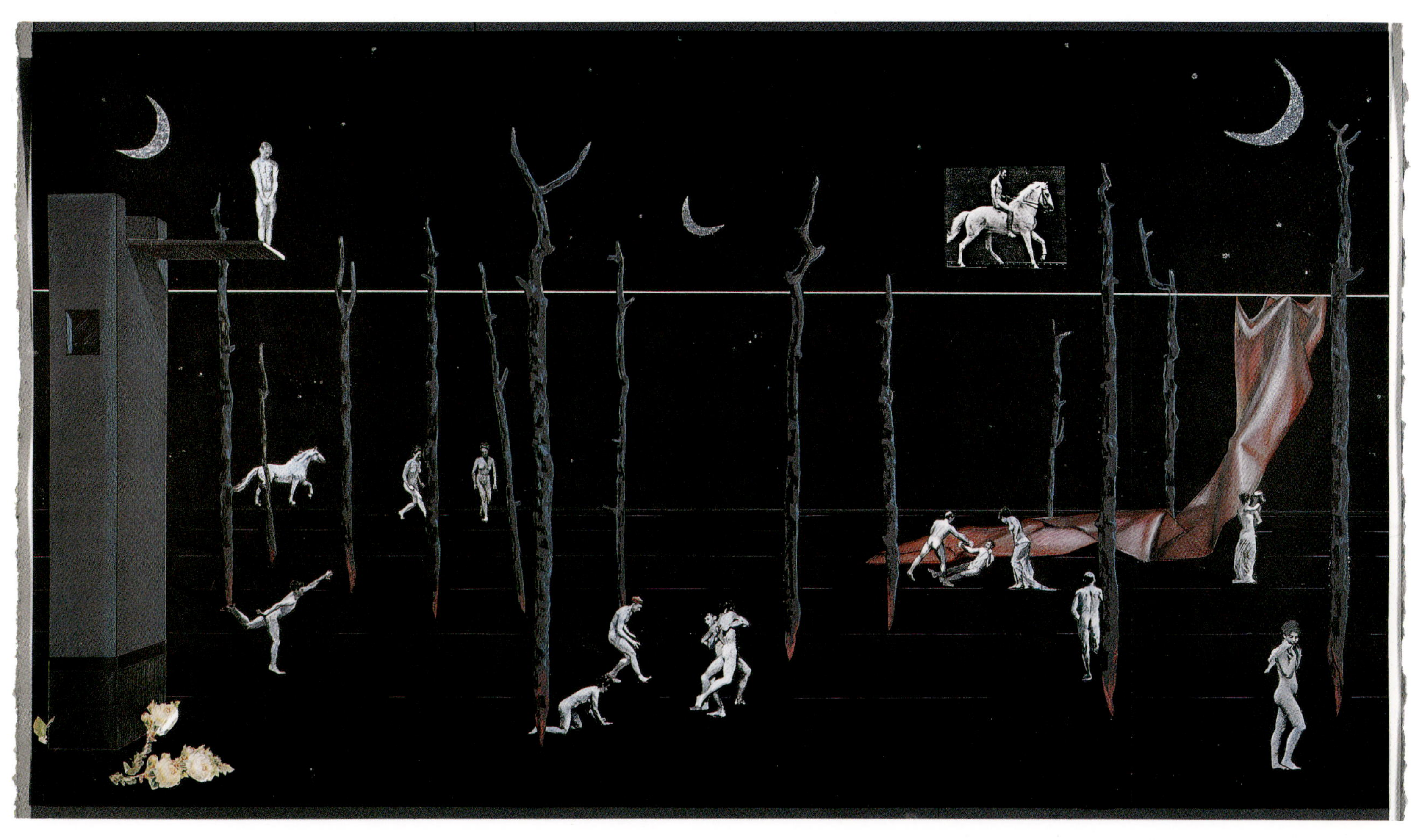

63 *The Diver's Journey* 1989

Oil and acrylic on honeycomb panel, 23½ × 29 inches
Collection of Anita and Arnold Rosenstein

This image is the third and last in a series that depicts a young male diver descending into the ocean, a series about death and its transcendence. The ancient inspiration of the *Diver* series is the roof slab of the Diver's Tomb at Paestum, Italy, allegorically depicting the journey from this life into the next.

In *The Diver's Journey* González presents the diver as completely submerged and blurrily contained within a horizontal tank below the horizon, at the conclusion of his spiritual odyssey. The trinity-leaved white roses, the striking inner and outer black borders, and the headstone-shaped central image make this a representation of a mystical final threshold crossed. The diver, the personification of González himself, is depicted as a Holy Trinity of figures, an inverted pyramid of divers—the two above in apparitional white, the one below in color. The sky is like a moving curtain above the submerged diver, opening to a transcendent void of light in the top center. This image is González's favorite in the *Diver* series, mostly because of the sky derived from Martin Johnson Heade's *Newburyport Marshes,* 1865–75 (Museum of Fine Arts, Boston). The sky is completely realistic yet at the same time resembles a theater curtain unveiling a mysterious drama.

Apparently by coincidence, the inclusion of roses in all three Paestum diver images, while a familiar symbol of love and death in González's works, is uncannily appropriate. Though the artist was apparently not aware of it, Paestum is recorded by Pliny, Horace, Ovid, and others as the most celebrated rose-growing center of the ancient world, farmers harvesting more roses there than any other crop. Virgil wrote that in Paestum, rose cultivation was so extraordinary that roses would bloom twice in one season.[1] As an instinctively chosen symbol of resurrection, the twice-blooming roses of Paestum could hardly be improved on.

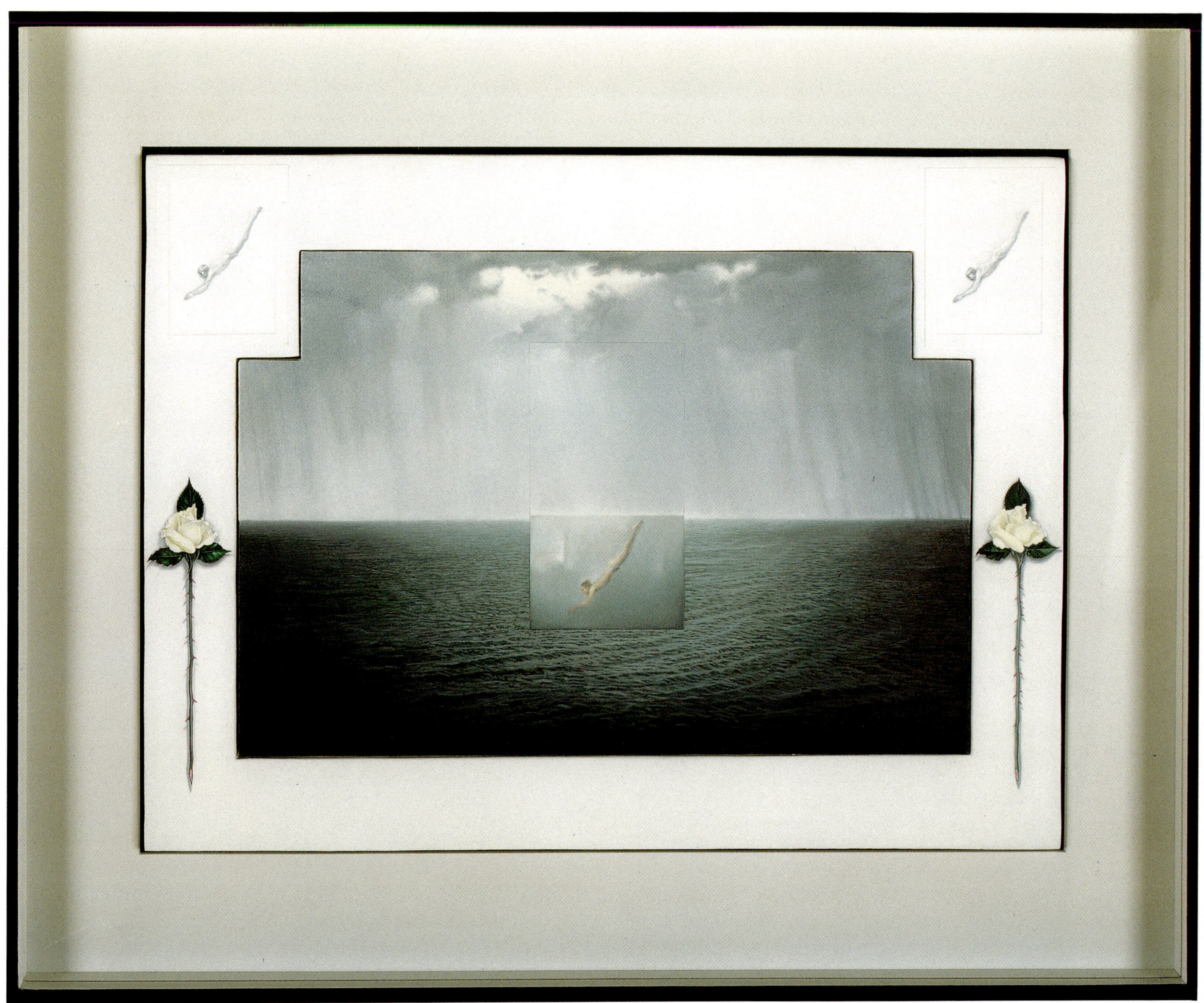

64 *Jardín Gris* 1989

Acrylic and tempera on canvas, 15¾ × 15¾ inches
M. J. H. di Giulio

González had been staying with a friend, the wife of the American ambassador in Belgium, whose home was in a lovely walled park, when he took the photographs that partially inspired this square painting. The Belgian locale and his veneration for Flemish artists such as Hugo van der Goes, Petrus Christus, and Hans Memling had much to do with this finely painted self-portrait and the artist's choice of a replica of an antique Dutch frame to surround the work. But the magical reconciliation of opposites implied in the marriage of the improbably blue evening sky to the nearly black night trees (only dimly lit by flaring lamps) owes a direct debt to René Magritte's most popular painting, *The Dominion of Light,* which exists in many versions in oil and gouache. Magritte's paradoxical blue sky and the idea of an endless reign of light form the heart of González's painting.

Jardín Gris (Gray Garden) represents the artist's exorcising dream of escape from death as he faces his own mortality. At the age of sixteen, González had experienced a fully fledged Cuban wake, following the death in his arms of a beloved grandmother. González remembers the four candles ranged at the corners of her coffin, guarding against fear in the house by binding the specter of death within the perimeter of the four flickering lights. He also remembers being spellbound by the splendor and drama of the funeral, "a beautiful, dark celebration with black carriages and black horses, in a very traditional ritual."

By contrast with his grandmother, González depicts himself surrounded by *three* candles, as if to negate the possibility of his own wake and funeral. His black sweater dissolving into the darkness, and his curiously heightened roll of hair reminiscent of the baroque quiff enlivening Juan de Mesa's severed head of John the Baptist at Seville cathedral, he appears with the black river behind his shoulder like a reborn John the Baptist. Perhaps the artist was thinking, too, of Rembrandt's mysteriously saturnine etching *Self Portrait with High, Curly Hair.* Certainly he was portraying the fact of his own advancing years, envisaging himself here as an older man.

Yet the form of the composition, with the figure posed by a river, also anticipates the transcendent child of *Memory Piece,* 1990. And the dazzling color relationships that make up the image—the variety of richly textured blacks and grays of this "gray garden," mounting circularly to the beautiful cobalt blue hole in the sky—establish a system of colors brought blazingly alive in the contrasting high-keyed blue framed within the feathered grays and blacks.

Jardín Gris is a portrait in an enclosed night garden opening onto a pocket of celestial blue, rather than veiled in a blue glaze like the night gardens of roses in *Jardín de un Sueño* (Garden of a Dream) and *Cycle.* It is a portrait like the square-formatted self-portraits with closed eyes of *El Palmar de los Locos* (The Palm Grove of the Insane) and *Pensamientos* (Thoughts), in which the artist ties himself as closely to the earth as he can, while opening up a vision of an opposite space: an ethereal, spiritual space contrasting with the rooted, foursquare material earth. It is a work of Andalusian *duende,* intended, as Lorca once put it, to "baptize in dark water all who look at it."[1] Most remarkably of all, the artist's eyes are not closed in this dark garden, nor is he made of "petrified" stone. He is restlessly awake when others would be sleeping, though he is shrouded in darkness, and the ambiguous expression on his face is a mystery impossible to decipher.

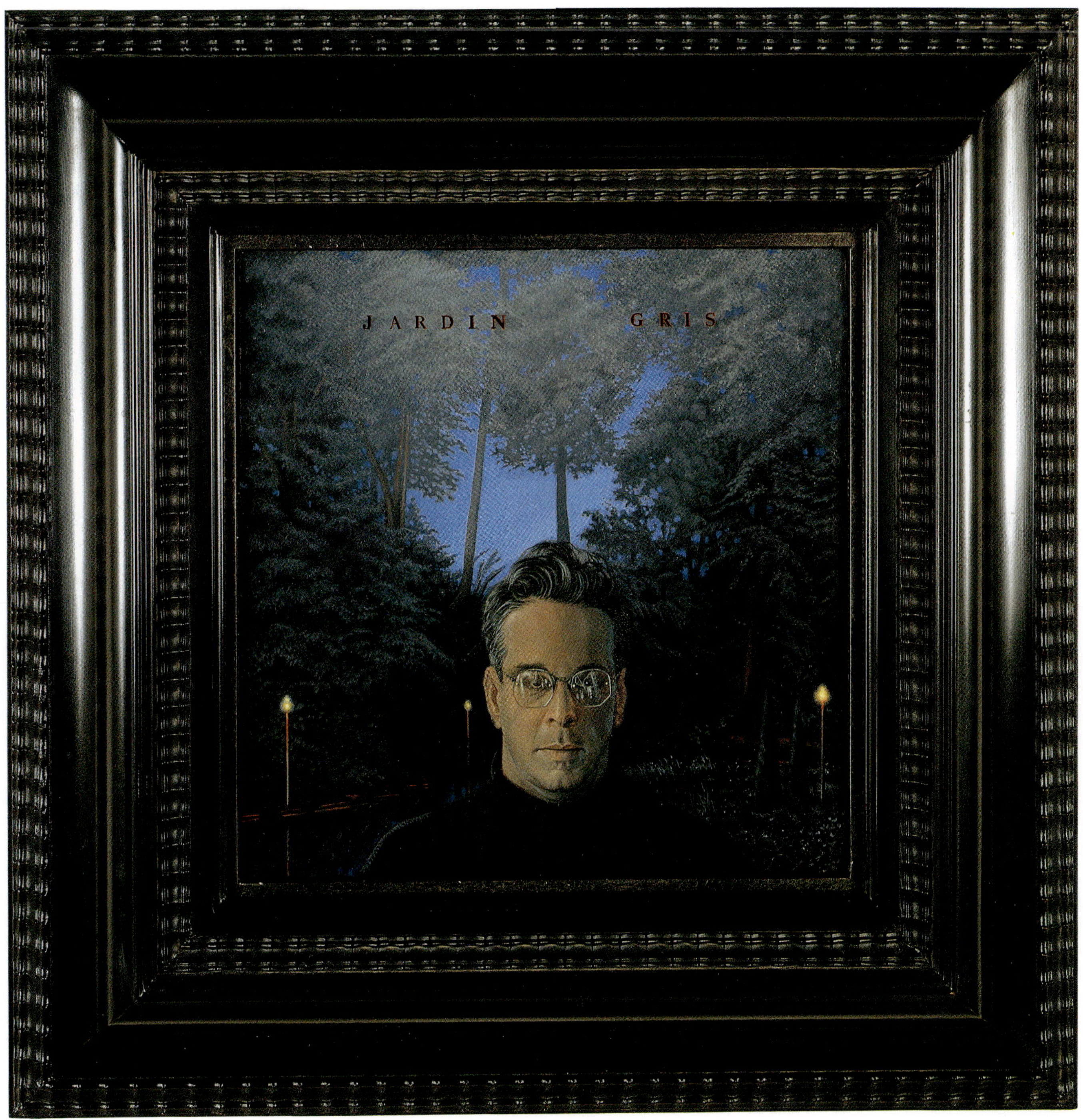
JARDIN GRIS

65 *Rebecca–Paris* 1989

Graphite and Conté crayon on paper, 11 × 14½ inches
Hoffman Greenwald Family: Nancy Hoffman, Peter Greenwald, Rebecca Hoffman Greenwald

González was in Paris and had recently visited an exhibition of drawings by Ingres when he undertook this drawing of Rebecca, the little daughter of the gallery owner Nancy Hoffman, "as a blessing upon her." The romantically antiqued mat is calculated to produce a French effect.

Rebecca's name is reverently picked out in gold. An idealized memory of Piero della Francesca's pure white dove in *The Baptism of Christ,* ca. 1440 (National Gallery, London), foreshortened into a shape like the clouds around it, gave rise to the apparitional and radiant opposition of the two doves of the Holy Spirit at the top corners of the image, framing and crowning the child.

The starry-yoked Rebecca, sensitively drawn from an image on a Christmas card, reigns over the center of the work, holding a toy cat. The artist certainly conceived of her as an image of the Immaculate Conception. The faraway look on her face, her attitude of silently "gazing into eternity," is reminiscent of the Spanish baroque sculptor Alonso Cano's small but supreme Immaculate Conception at Granada cathedral, standing only twenty inches high—the young Virgin's face that of a beautiful child, lost in wonder at the revelation of her sacred destiny. González finds in Rebecca some of the quality of spirituality and ethereality he consistently sees in his own daughter Maria. He uses Rebecca's face again in the major painting that follows this drawing, *Memory Piece,* where she metamorphoses into the Virgin's holy infant, the baby Jesus of Salamanca, intriguingly reversing Michelangelo's use of male models for female subjects to create an ideal humanity.

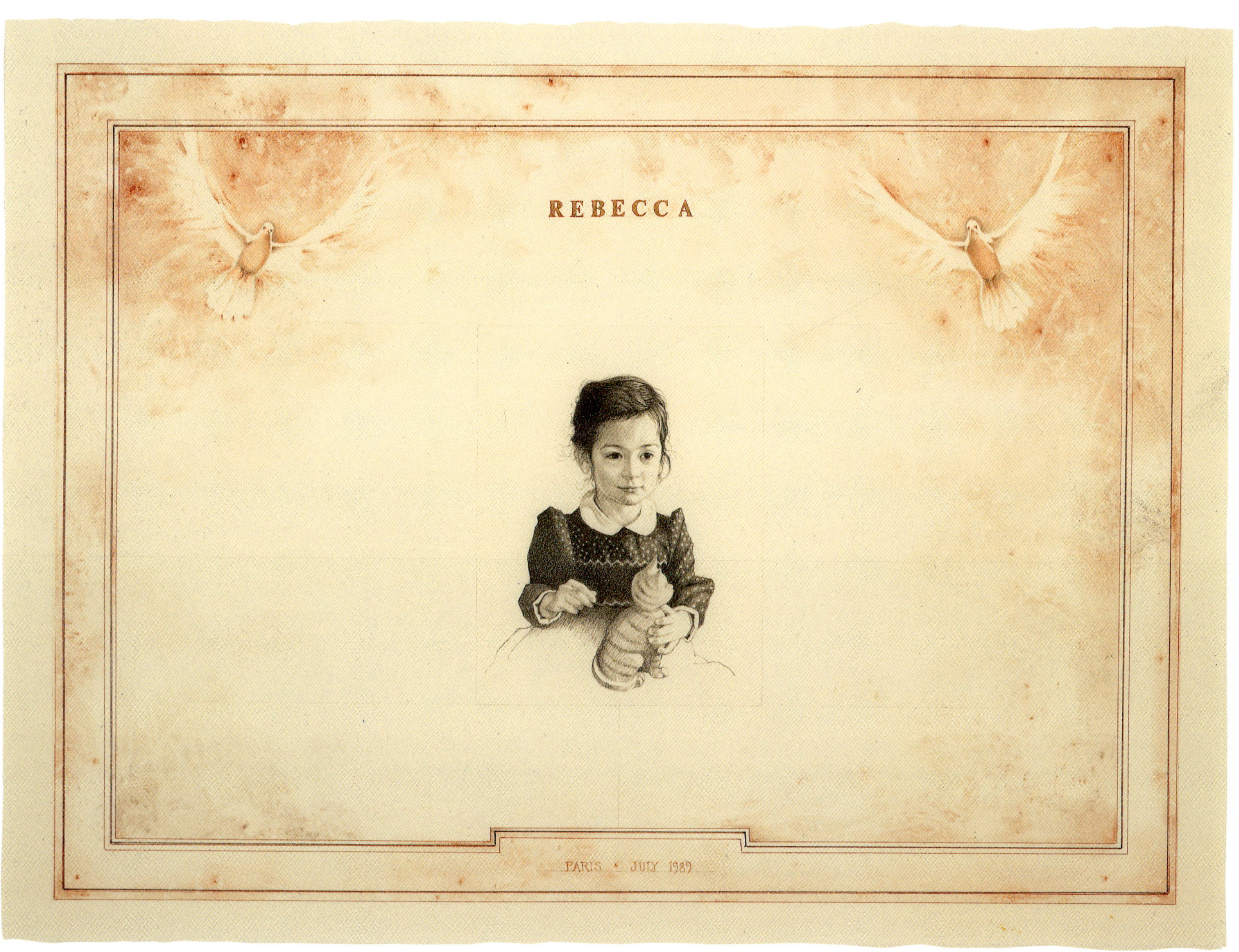
REBECCA
PARIS • JULY 1989

66 *Memory Piece* 1990

Oil on wood and silk mounted on honeycomb panel, 43¼ × 34¾ inches
Collection of Sidney and George Perutz

As both the appearance and title of this rich work suggest, *Memory Piece* is composed of reflective fragments from the artist's past life and body of work, gathered in one grand summation of the theme of the self in a magical garden.

González's sacred infant derives from both Mantegna's *Infant Redeemer* of ca. 1455–60 (National Gallery of Art, Washington, D.C.), and a polychrome Spanish baroque baby Jesus at the cathedral of Salamanca (the shrine he stands on here reproducing in faithful detail the curtained reliquary housing the Salamanca Jesus). The pyramidal grid of the glass framing the baby derives from the reflective triangled skin of a geodesic dome in Paris, visited around the time González toured the Rodin Museum. The artist welds these art and architectural references to an 1880 albumen print of a Cuban riverscape by an anonymous photographer, *A Brook in Campo Florido,*[1] and to another portrait of Rebecca Hoffman.

The multiplicity of allusions to other artists in this work is not nearly so striking, however, as the multiplicity of allusions to González's own art. The brightly colored Martin Pescador devouring a fish recalls the hummingbird shaking a frog in its beak in the 1973 *Untitled (Birds).* The stone boy with a living face of *Mar y Espejo* (Sea and Mirror) initiated the boy-and-bird symbolism arriving, through *Roma,* at a triumphant conclusion in the sacred infant of *Memory Piece.* The boy is still an ideal and immobile statue from the neck down—González again seeking to blur the boundaries between life and death, the ideal and the real. The sacred infant recalls the tiny figure of John the Baptist at the bottom center of the still life in *El Niño* (The Child), but this serene infant, his right hand raised in benediction toward the viewer, has expanded to fill the central vertical niche. Indeed, *Memory Piece* may be called the most expansive image yet made by the artist, since the pyramidal grid behind the figure (recalling the pyramidal self-portrait *Pensamientos* [Thoughts]) creates a dazzlingly rayed effect, the center flowing into the surrounding space in centrifugal motion. These cutout, meticulously pieced-together, and heavily gessoed triangles form a five-pointed star-halo behind the head of the baby, while at the same time defining the vertical glass niche that shelters the sacred infant—who is now more than ever a figure articulated and concentrated in space.

This infant Jesus in a prismatic niche is in radiant response to the caged and fragmented stone angel of *Prisma y Prisión/Prism and Prison,* to the aerially niched "mirrored" angels of *Roma,* to the mysteriously empty niche of *Jardín de un Sueño* (Garden of a Dream), and to the similarly blank niche of this image, which sets up a riddle of absence by opposing two miniaturized Rodin sculptures with the question mark of the empty third niche. "I was trying to understand how my psychology developed," comments González, "and the kind of emotional landscape that I came to act on. In the niches there are, at the top, *The Kiss*—an image of love that is obvious and stereotyped; then, on one side, this essence of a young man, *The Age of Bronze.* And on the other side I've left it open, blank, mysterious."

González had initially intended to crown *Memory Piece* with *The Three Shades* of *The Gates of Hell.* The influence of Rodin's masterpiece is still subtly visible in the central spine, which runs vertically through González's sacred infant as the axis of Rodin's great door traveled vertically through *The Thinker* and the middle Shade. The central spine and mirroring glass of the landscape recall the earlier mirrored garden of *Il Giardino delle Sorelle* (The Garden of the Sisters), its ripe yellows and palm branches evoking the flying feathers of the fighting cocks owned by the artist's father in Cuba. González combines these feathers—symbolic of the beauty and death of the birds—with a wood frame, which implied crucifixion in *In His Silence;* here the stylized palms of the frame echo in trompe-l'oeil architectural ornament the painted palms dissected everywhere in the central image.

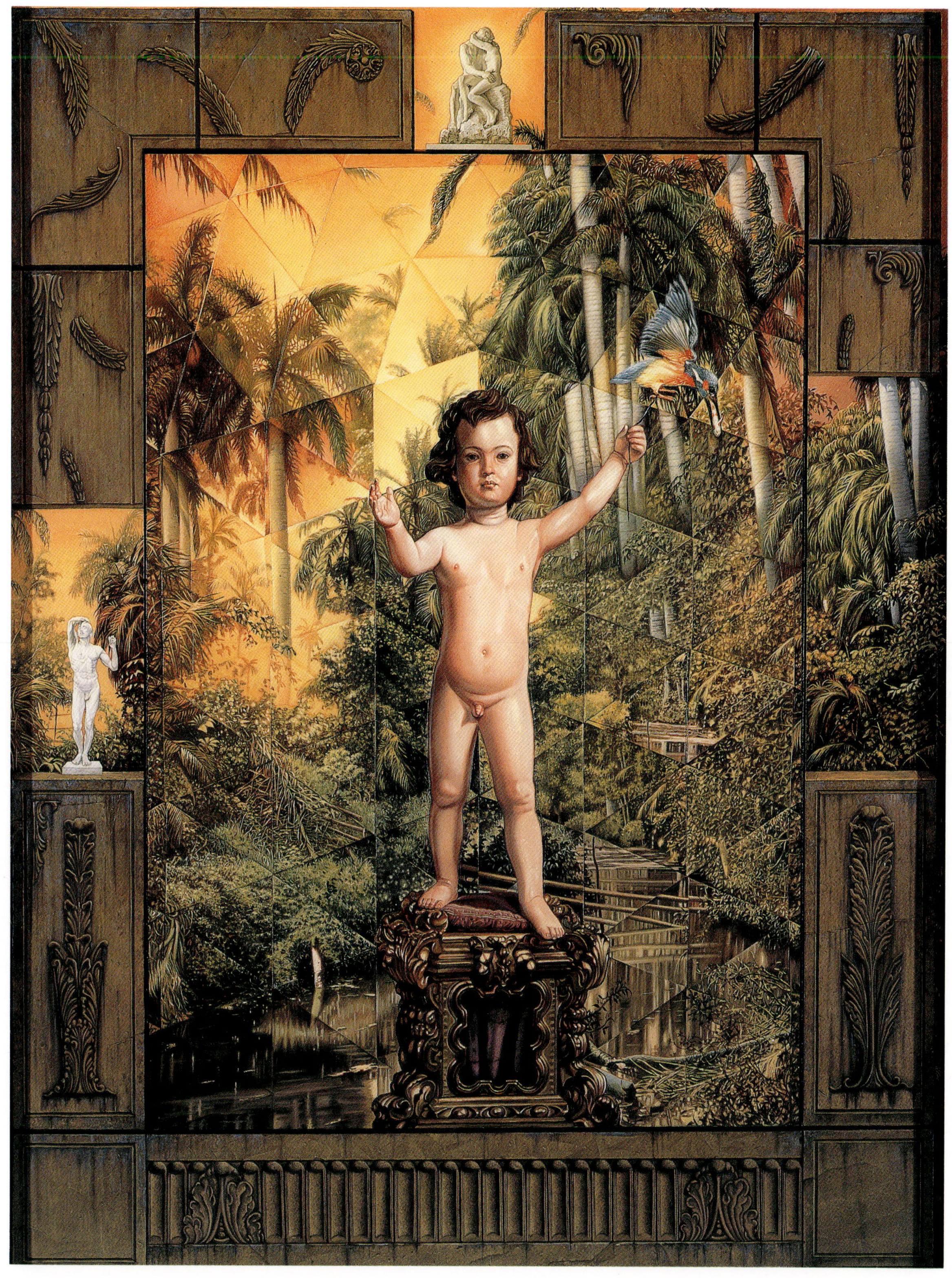

67 *Vermeer's Frame* 1990

Oil, acrylic, and Xerox copy on Gator board, 14 × 14½ inches
Collection of Rebecca and Richard Mintzer

With this image González for the first time centers himself inside a famous miniature painting-within-a-painting by another artist, converting the earlier work into a darkened stage set to accommodate the cutout character of himself. *Vermeer's Frame* takes the soft, bright little landscape from Vermeer's *Lady Standing at the Virginals,* ca. 1673–75 (National Gallery, London), and cloaks it in a veil of darkness, almost shrouding the diving-board platform from which this Friedrich- or Magritte-style isolate (González himself in his signature pose, viewed from behind) stands poised to cast himself into the abyss.

The title draws the viewer's attention to the brilliant trompe-l'oeil frame. The blazing gold of the frame, like that of the bed by the ocean in *Songs for My Father,* highlights by contrast the somber landscape, as though within the golden realism of the trompe-l'oeil frame night has magically stolen over the illusory realm of Vermeer's sunlit valley, subjecting an inanimate art work to temporal change, as the artist himself is prey to mortality. A distinct split divides the center of the frame at top and bottom—a split that runs right through González's body (his shirt luminously defines his spine), as the central spine of Rodin's Dante-inspired *Gates of Hell* runs through the body of *The Thinker* and the middle Shade. Dante called his *Divine Comedy* a "comedy" because it progressed from a gloomy opening in the hellscape of the *Inferno* to the glorious promise of redemption in the *Paradiso,* sealed by the fiery ascension of Christ and his Virgin Mother. Inside *Vermeer's Frame,* González is a Shade waiting in darkness to be taken up to paradise.

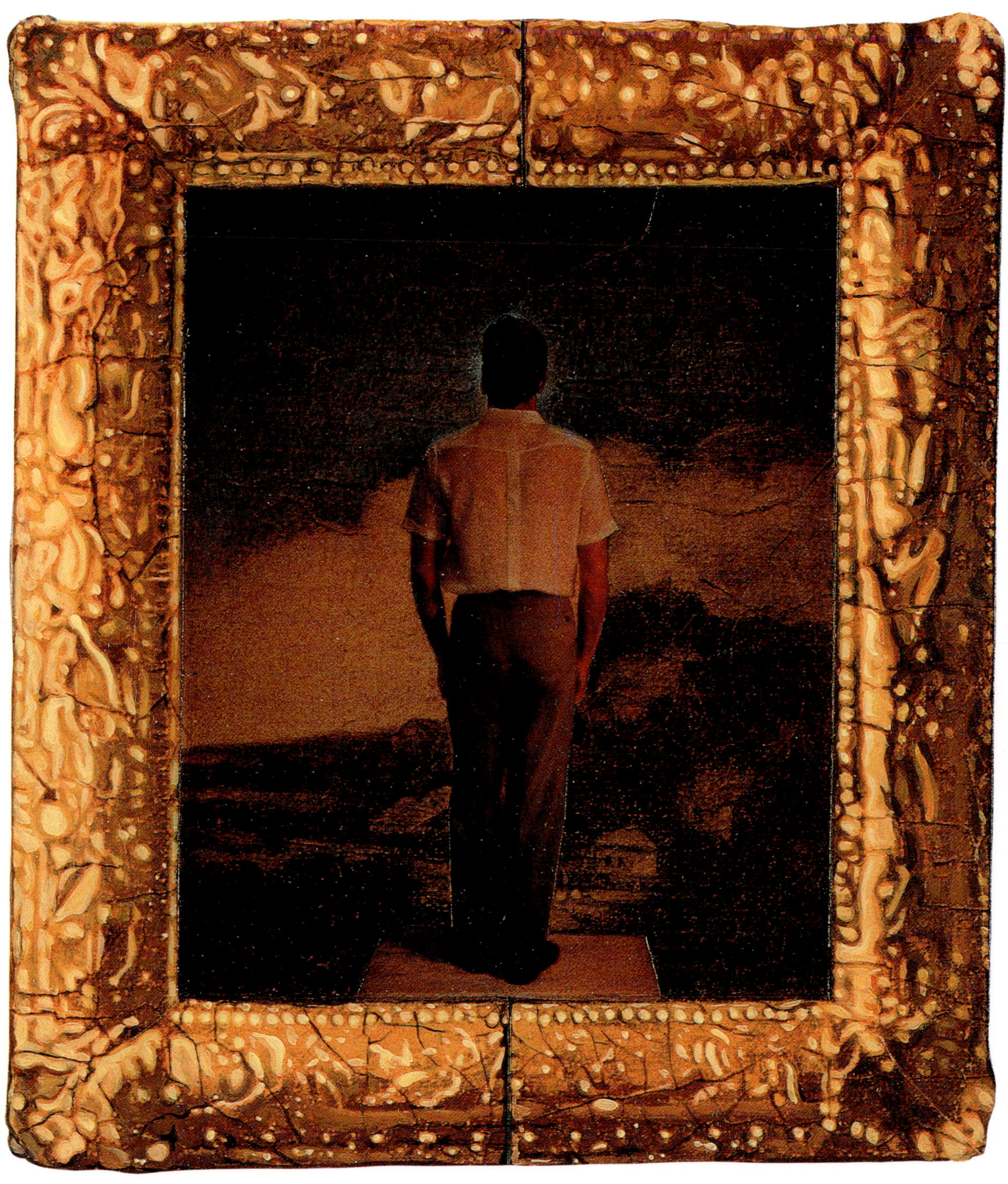

68 *Rembrandt's Hands, Vermeer's Frame and the Passing of the Moth* 1990

Oil and acrylic on honeycomb panel, 33 × 29 inches
Muriel Karasik Collection

In its startling synthesis of opposites, this extraordinary image of a conjoined male and female hand—both based on photographs of the artist's own hands—is a classic example of Jung's *mysterium coniunctionis,* an "alchemical symbol of a union of unlike substances; a marrying of the OPPOSITES in an intercourse which has as its fruition the birth of a new element, . . . symbolized by a child that manifests potential for greater wholeness by recombining attributes of both the opposing natures."[1] Rupert C. Allen, in *Psyche and Symbol in the Theater of Federico García Lorca,* identifies just this kind of "spiritual syzygy," or conjunction of masculine consciousness and feminine unconscious, sensing in the poet "the *seer* who, by retaining the androgyny of his childhood, penetrates back beyond the fragmented and incomplete world of adult monosexuality. . . . Spiritual androgyny is what Lorca most valued in himself, because it was the key to his creativity."[2] Lorca's spiritual androgyny is the source of the strangely male, rather than conventionally female, Moon of *Blood Wedding,* the white-faced androgynous young woodcutter; it is also the source of the effeminate young man of *Así que Pasen Cinco Años/When Five Years Pass,* 1991, the Lorca drama for which González went on to create a magnificent series of stage sets.

Rembrandt's Hands is an astounding work, unprecedented even for this artist: a dramatic visualization of the joining of male and female principles to yield the "spiritual gold" of the alchemists in a mystical marriage, the union of male and female giving birth to a new double being. It is interesting to note, too, that in works like *Songs for My Father* and *Memory Piece,* the artist feels the necessity to reach back to childhood to seek his "spiritual gold," even an androgynous childhood in *Memory Piece,* since the model for the face of Jesus in that painting was a young girl.

González had earlier achieved a magical conjunction in the superimposed sun and moon of *El Soñador/The Dreamer.* Here he goes further in clearly depicting himself as the redeeming offspring born of this union of opposite principles, balanced midway between the poles of death and rebirth inherent in the process of *coniunctio.* He first conceived this image after contemplating the celebrated image of a couple's hands joined tenderly over the wife's abdomen in Rembrandt's *Isaac and Rebecca (The Jewish Bride),* ca. 1666, at the Rijksmuseum, Amsterdam. González exaggerated the colors that swell up from the lower edge of the image, opposing dark with light in his field of roses, while the moth of death, which had settled on the white sheet of *La Misa Blanca* (The White Mass), is "passing" this rich cloth by, signifying changing phases in the cycle of life and death.

The clearly differentiated male and female hands of the artist speak to the presence of the androgyne, holding male and female forces in balance, as González once again takes up the theme of the radiant, apparitional, faceless bride of *The Sparrow and the Maiden* and *Mar y Espejo* (Sea and Mirror). He made the image out of inner necessity, somewhat nervous about its gathering opulence yet compelled to serve his vision, his quilt of roses a now richer-than-ever range of blazing golds, laced with gleaming pearls and sparkling gemstones. The field of densely massed roses in one way represents the ultimate blank niche within the frame in this artist's work, a theatrical golden screen that veils the more conventional image the viewer might normally expect to see inside the extravagant frame. *Rembrandt's Hands* immerses itself in everything that González ever found beautiful. It is an authentic vision, rare in a contemporary artist, of a golden paradise of roses, of love and death, entered through the dark door of *Vermeer's Frame* and predicting the artist's ascent to Dante's "Celestial Rose," the vast theater of paradise. González's florid world of golden light reinvents a pre-Renaissance vision of heaven, of mystic union with God, and of the sublime bliss of redemption.

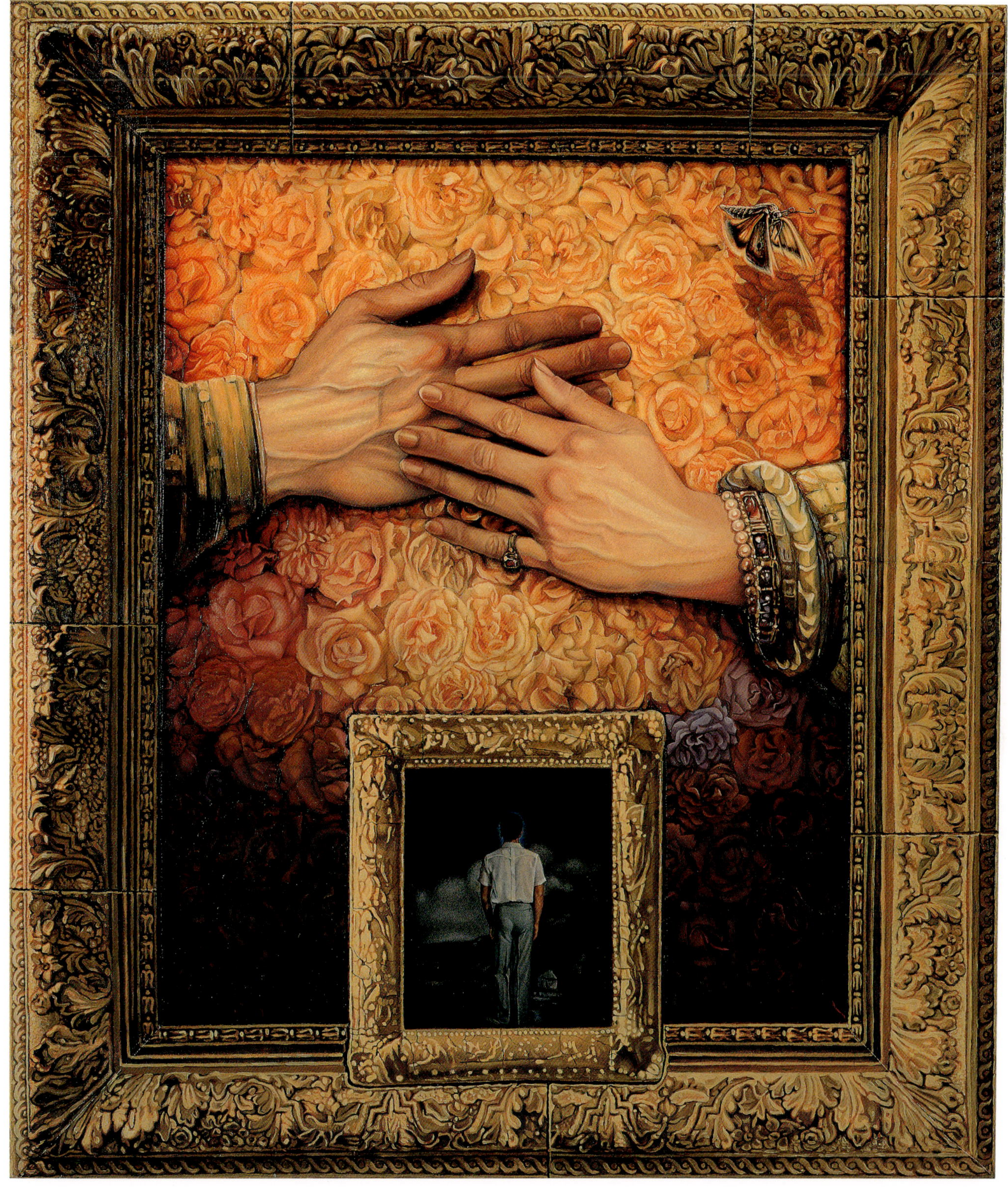

69 *To the Dream of the Apples (In Honor of Federico García Lorca)* 1990

Oil and wax on Gator board beneath antique glass, 22 × 20½ inches
Private collection, New York

The greater portion of this image derives from a collection of frescoes González saw at the Museo delle Terme in Rome. A masterpiece of classical painting, the late-first-century B.C.–early-first-century A.D. frescoes were discovered in the country villa of Livia, Augustus's wife, at Prima Porta, north of Rome. The museum exhibit encloses the visitor within four walls decorated like an abundant orchard of fruit trees, flowers, and birds. To González the intoxicating blend of theatrical scene painting and the architectural illusion of an enclosed garden—a paradisal *carmen* like the Moorish poets' gardens of inspiration in Andalusia—was irresistible. Frescoed gardens were often extensions of real gardens outside the villa, the ideal framing or contrasting with the real. Even the painted birds in these gardens reproduced and contrasted with the actual birds kept in aviaries in the gardens beyond the frescoed garden room.

González has converted this heavenly garden of beauty and inspiration into a mysterious frame that is also a womblike container for his central image, the head of a sleeping boy against a backdrop of golden roses. The head of the boy and the passing moth of *Rembrandt's Hands* in this symbolic niche present a *vanitas*—an artful meditation on the passing of time and death. The disembodied sleeping head of the boy, so familiar to the viewer after *Jardín de un Sueño* (Garden of a Dream) and *Cycle,* derives not from Carpeaux's or Rodin's dying son of Ugolino, but from a sleeping Amor at the Metropolitan Museum, a second-century Greek bronze of a winged boy, dreaming in deep calm on a cloth spread over a rock. González's dying boy has at last been transmuted into what the artist thinks of as an angel, while his blue moonlit roses have become a radiant field of thornless golden blossoms.

At the lower center of the image (usually an important point in any work by this symmetry-conscious artist), González depicts a tiny bird in a cage resting on the garden's lattice fence. The same bird is shown mirrored and released in the lower left-hand corner. These two tiny creatures are not the only pair of birds in the image: a larger white bird perched next to the cage is mirrored in the white one at the center right side of the painting, on a level with the head of the sleeping Amor. Concealed within two fruit-tree branches at the top of the painting, two miniature white doves lurk like Piero's foreshortened dove of the Holy Ghost. The overall surface of the blue wall of the fresco is riven with watery channels, evoking a cracked mirror strung with shadows.

Below the lattice fence González incorporates handwritten lines from a poem in Lorca's *Diván del Tamarit,* a collection of verse, or *divan,* composed by the poet in his garden of inspiration, the Tamarit, a relative's country farm that the poet loved to visit: "Quiero dormir al sueño de las manzanas / alejarme del tumulto de los cementarios. / Quiero dormir el sueño de aquel niño / que queria cortarse el corazon en alta mar." These opening lines of a poem—which González considered for years before responding with this image—translate as follows: "I want to sleep the dream of the apples, / to withdraw from the tumult of cemeteries, / I want to sleep the dream of that child / who wanted to cut his heart on the high seas."[1]

Lorca, while acknowledging the inevitability of his own death and burial, nevertheless proclaims his mythic identity as Orpheus, the lyric poet whose severed head continued to sing as it sailed the seas to Lesbos: "all must know that I have not died; / that there is a stable of gold in my lips." González's angelic head in a golden niche, the transcendent counterpart of the sorrowing head in *Mar de Lágrimas/Sea of Tears,* is an Orphic head, too, the timeless personification of immortality in art.

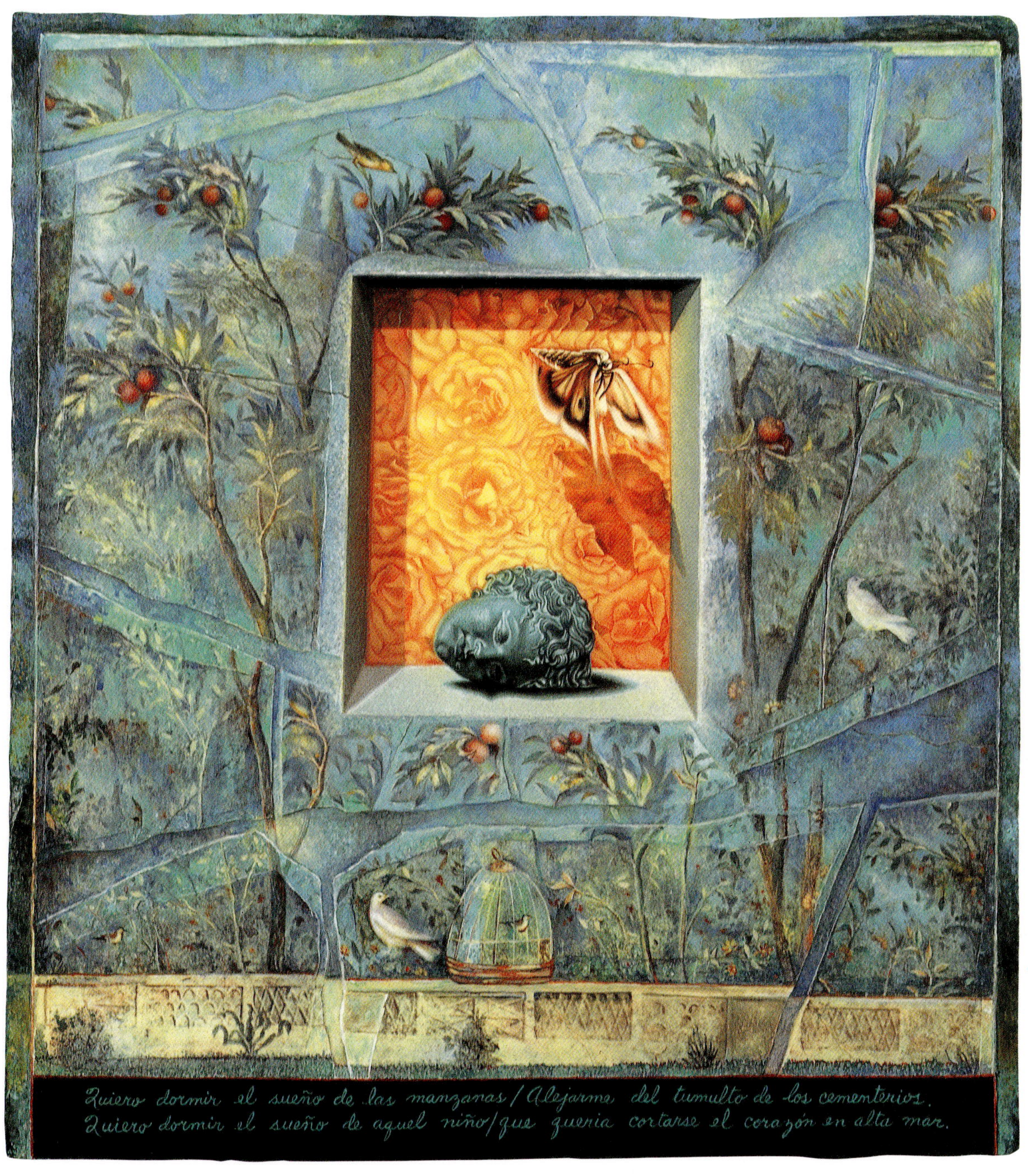
Quiero dormir el sueño de las manzanas / Alejarme del tumulto de los cementerios.
Quiero dormir el sueño de aquel niño / que queria cortarse el corazón en alta mar.

70 *Untitled* 1991–92

Watercolor on paper, 16½ × 10⅞ inches
Nancy Fried

Nancy Fried, an artist and a good friend, brought González an armful of lilies during a time when he was feeling low. In return, he made her a presentation drawing such as Michelangelo gave to his own dear friend Vittoria Colonna. An image of death and resurrection, the lily blooms are symbolic of the rebirth of Christ from the tomb after the Crucifixion.

González began the work with a drawing but, finding that the image he was after would not come forward, switched to a frescolike emerald green wash to symbolize the green of spring and the renewal of life and nature. Then he began to erase the green wash, particularly in the area of the Crucifixion, pursuing his aesthetic ideal of the hidden or apparitional art work. His drawing of Christ on the cross, miniaturized by the huge flower, was directly inspired by a pair of black chalk drawings Michelangelo executed between 1538 and 1557: *Crucifixion with the Virgin and Saint John* and the stippled and partly rubbed *Crucifixion for Vittoria Colonna* (both, British Museum, London).

Erasing the green wash creates a cloudy, amorphous surface, opening up the clean white of the raw paper within the blooms of the monumental stem of lilies, dramatically underscoring the purity of the flower. The white void of the lily blossoms against the darker ground obviously points to a connection between this work and the artist's earliest garden image, *Sara's Garden*. The big flower expansively filling the center becomes a cruciform equivalent to the Crucifixion, echoing the artist's symbolic association of the lily with the cross in *El Lirio Cuadral* (The Square and the Lily).

Most theatrical of all, the massive scale of the plant, as it towers above the low horizontal of landscape at the bottom of the image, implies ascension. Christ's Passion and his final appearance on earth before being transported into heaven are conjoined in one deceptively simple drawing. Francis Bacon, another painter of crucifixions, disclaimed any active interest in the sacred meaning of Christ's Passion, but allowed that he had a fascination with "the body raised from the ground, its more formal and abstract being elevated."[1] In the same vein, González's entire body of work may be thought of as a prolonged meditation on the mystery of the Ascension.

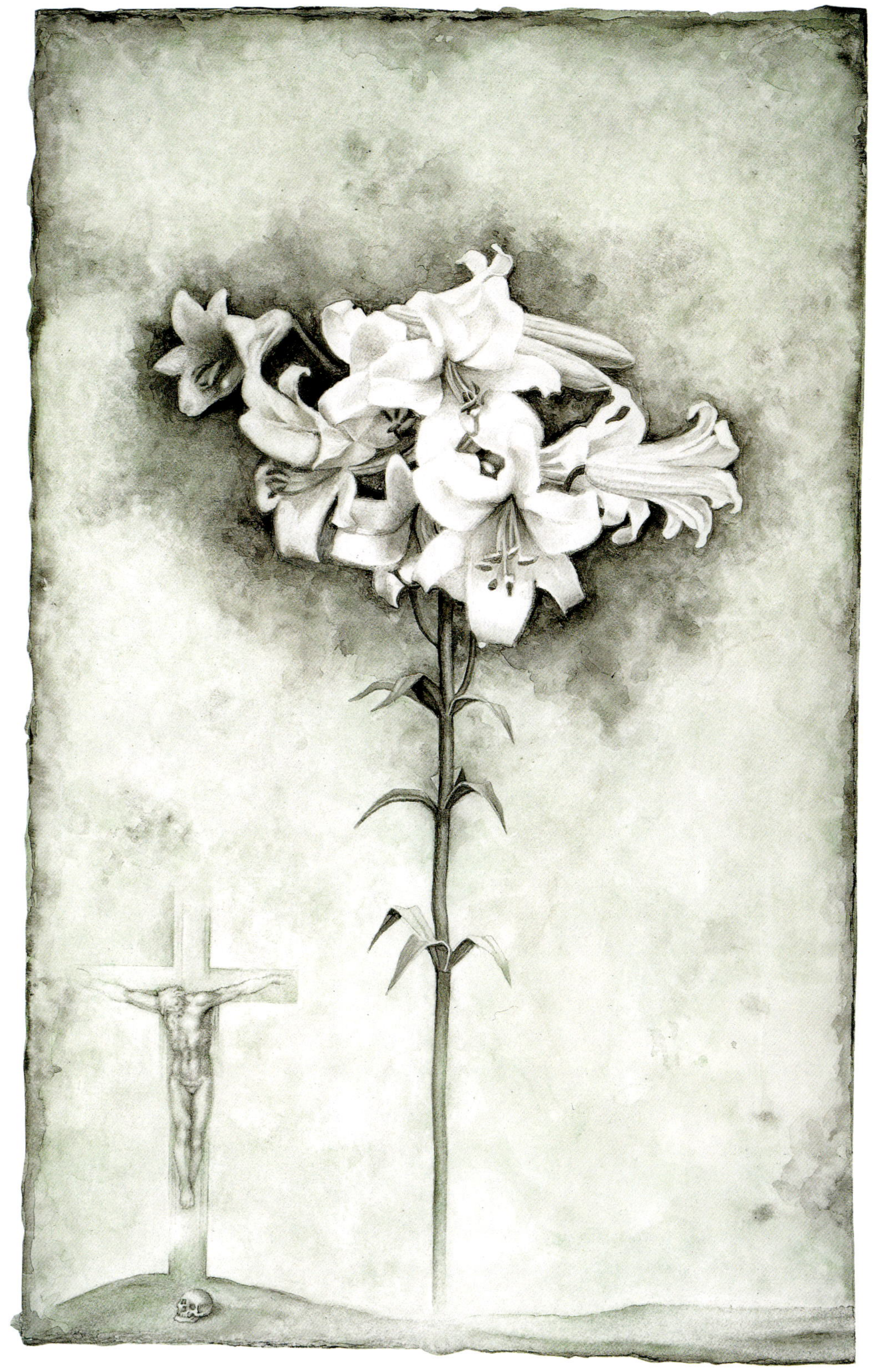

71 *Así que Pasen Cinco Años/When Five Years Pass*

Act 1, Scene 1, 1991

Mixed media on Gator board, 37 × 47 inches
Museum Acquisition Fund, Meadows Museum, Southern Methodist University, Dallas, Texas

Commissioned to design stage sets for Lorca's most original, most experimental, and uncannily prescient play (the writer died five years to the day after he finished the play), González felt liberated again to serve the vision of his favorite poet while further developing his own vocabulary. Inspired, no doubt, by the way in which he had inserted himself into the darkened stage set of *Vermeer's Frame,* he hit on the extraordinary concept of using himself, his family, and his friends as characters in Lorca's drama of interiorization.

Así que Pasen Cinco Años/When Five Years Pass externalizes the inner life of the central character, the Young Man: all the characters in the play are projections of characters existing inside the Young Man's mind, reflecting as if in a mirror himself and his innermost thoughts. At the very end of the play the Young Man's dying words are repeated by Echo, confirming that the Young Man, alone in his introspection and isolation, is a type of Narcissus, obsessed with himself and open to no one else. Nothing could be more in tune with the interiorized aesthetic of González himself, whose work always mirrors the depths of his own psyche.

It is hardly surprising, then, to see the artist refer back to the domestic space he created years before for himself in the drawing *Cuatro Pilares* (Four Pillars), which provides the pink couch round which his dog Papel still slinks and the island of carpet in a paradoxical sea of drought-ravaged earth. The bouquet of white roses in front of the Young Man are González's perennial symbol of love and death, innocence and transcendence: in this play the character known as the Dead Boy will give the Dead Cat a single white rose from his crown of white roses, lyrically comparing the rose to a shard of "broken moon." The most stunningly personal fact about this collage series, however, remains the fact that González chose to pose as the pyjama-garbed doomed Young Man himself—surrounding himself in the stage sets with the people who inhabit his own mind on a daily basis. This prevaricating character opens the drama by dreaming of the girl he is to marry "when five years pass." Right now he cannot think of marrying her, and he cannot even bear the word "bride" when he thinks of his fiancée. He prefers to call her "my little girl, my child." He prefers ideal fantasy to plain, flesh-and-blood reality. He is essentially unable to surrender to love. When his weeping Typist (played by the artist's daughter Maria) declares her deep love for him, the Young Man can only wistfully respond: "I wish I could love her with the kind of thirst we get at the sight of water."[1] The Young Man is like "the big horse who didn't like water" in *Blood Wedding.*[2]

The Old Man turning to confront the viewer represents the Young Man as he might appear in the future, advanced into cynical old age. Lorca has only one First Friend in the first scene; González transforms the First Friend into two mirror-imaged young men, both based on the same model, the artist's friend David Shapiro. These narcissistic projections anticipate the three ruthless Card Players who end the Young Man's life at the close of the play, all portrayed by Shapiro. González emphasizes the play's quality of surrealist nightmare by incorporating Goya's *Burial of the Sardine,* ca. 1800 (Royal Academy of San Fernando, Madrid), into the picture, at the back of the Young Man's library shelves on the left. The inclusion of *The Burial of the Sardine* makes a serious dramatic point, introducing the theme of death and burial and reflecting the way in which, early in the play, the death and summary burial of the Dead Boy and Dead Cat prefigure the death of the Young Man himself.

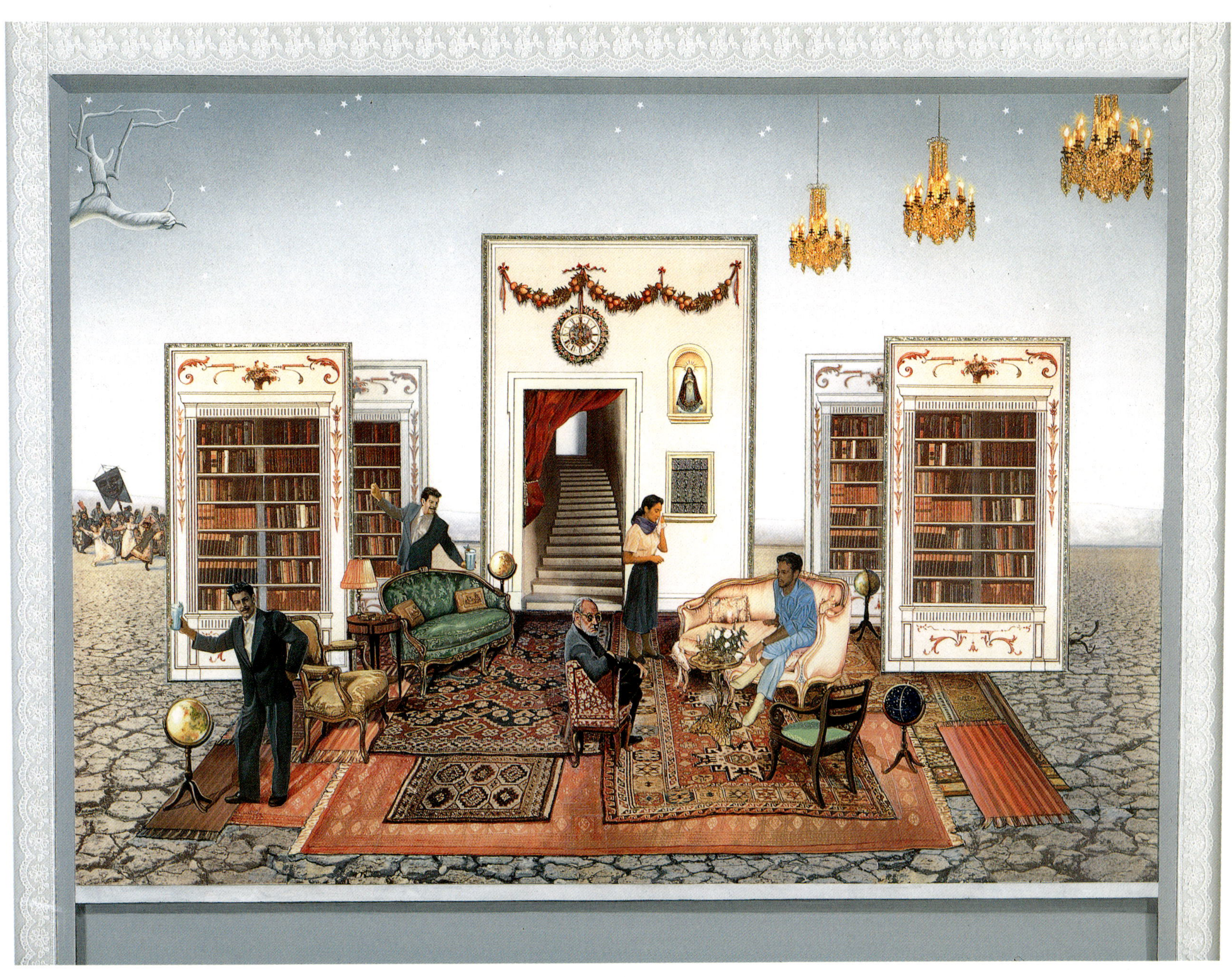

72 *Así que Pasen Cinco Años / When Five Years Pass*

Act 1, Scene 2, 1991

Mixed media on Gator board, 27¼ × 37 inches
Museum Acquisition Fund, Meadows Museum, Southern Methodist University, Dallas, Texas

In the library at night, a funeral garland and a wreath of white roses hang over the back staircase (which combines the mirror and door at the back of *Las Meninas*), in place of the matrimonial citron garland of the opening scene. The bookshelves have dissolved into starred black screens like windows open to a cosmic night. The Young Man and his First Friend hide from an approaching storm behind one of the starred screens, as the Dead Boy and Dead Cat appear to a roll of thunder and a blue storm light washes over the scene.

Lorca stipulates that the Dead Boy is dressed all in white, as though for his First Communion, with a crown of white roses on his head. The Dead Cat is blue, with two large bloodstains on its white-gray chest and head. The Dead Boy and Dead Cat engage in a fearful conversation about their mutual horror of being buried in the earth, where the lizards will devour every bit of their bodies, including their most private parts. The huge, disembodied hand of God abruptly takes them from the stage, presumably for the burial they so dread, as the hot and agitated Young Man and First Friend reappear from behind the screens, holding fans to cool themselves—only to learn from the Servant that the young son of the concierge has just died and that some children have killed a cat, reality in art and life but a step behind premonition.

In presenting the Dead Boy, González luxuriates in fond memories of his own gold-satin-ribboned First Communion costume, which he celebrates in the beauty of the silver candle, golden bows, pure white costume, and white-rose crown. His daughter Maria plays the Dead Boy, as well as the Dead Cat. Following the disappearance of the Dead Boy and Dead Cat, the androgynous Second Friend appears, a leaping apparition in the upper right contrasting with the skeletal twig "flier" in the upper left of the previous scene, dressed like the freshly departed Dead Boy, all in white. The Second Friend represents the redeeming child, born in death from the mystical conjunction of the male and female principles. The Cat has already made a point of revealing to the Dead Boy that, unlike him, she was a *girl*. The Second Friend is a character like the white-faced effeminate Moon of *Blood Wedding;* again Lorca stipulated in the stage directions that he wanted a very young actor, or even a girl, to complicate and enrich an essentially male role. The Second Friend brings to the Young Man the ghost of his own divine and irretrievable lost childhood, the Dead Boy within. His entry into the carefully sealed room is a mystery as unfathomable as the Ascension, so González has him literally "floating into the room," the artist using a photograph of Rudolf Nureyev on which to model his resplendent white androgyne.

Nor is the Second Friend the only androgynous element in the play. González finds the cross-accessorizing of the fans the men hold behind the starred screen uncommonly strange in a Spanish context: "You would *never* see, in Granada or Seville, a man carrying a fan. Only women carry fans. If you go to the cathedral, to a Mass, you hear the sound of a thousand fans, all carried by women. It's a very odd choice for Lorca to make—and must be meant to bring out the idea of femininity in the Young Man himself."

The barred window below the artist's invented, Andalusian-style Immaculate Conception underlines repeated references in the play to the Young Man's neurotic fear of life in general, and particularly of elemental imponderables over which he has no control, like the wind and the rain. The spectacular dazzle of the night library was achieved using a variety of colored glitter papers, bought in a plastics and Plexiglas shop on Canal Street in New York: "We have been so indoctrinated to think of these materials as cheap and worthless," says González, "yet they can create a truly magical effect."

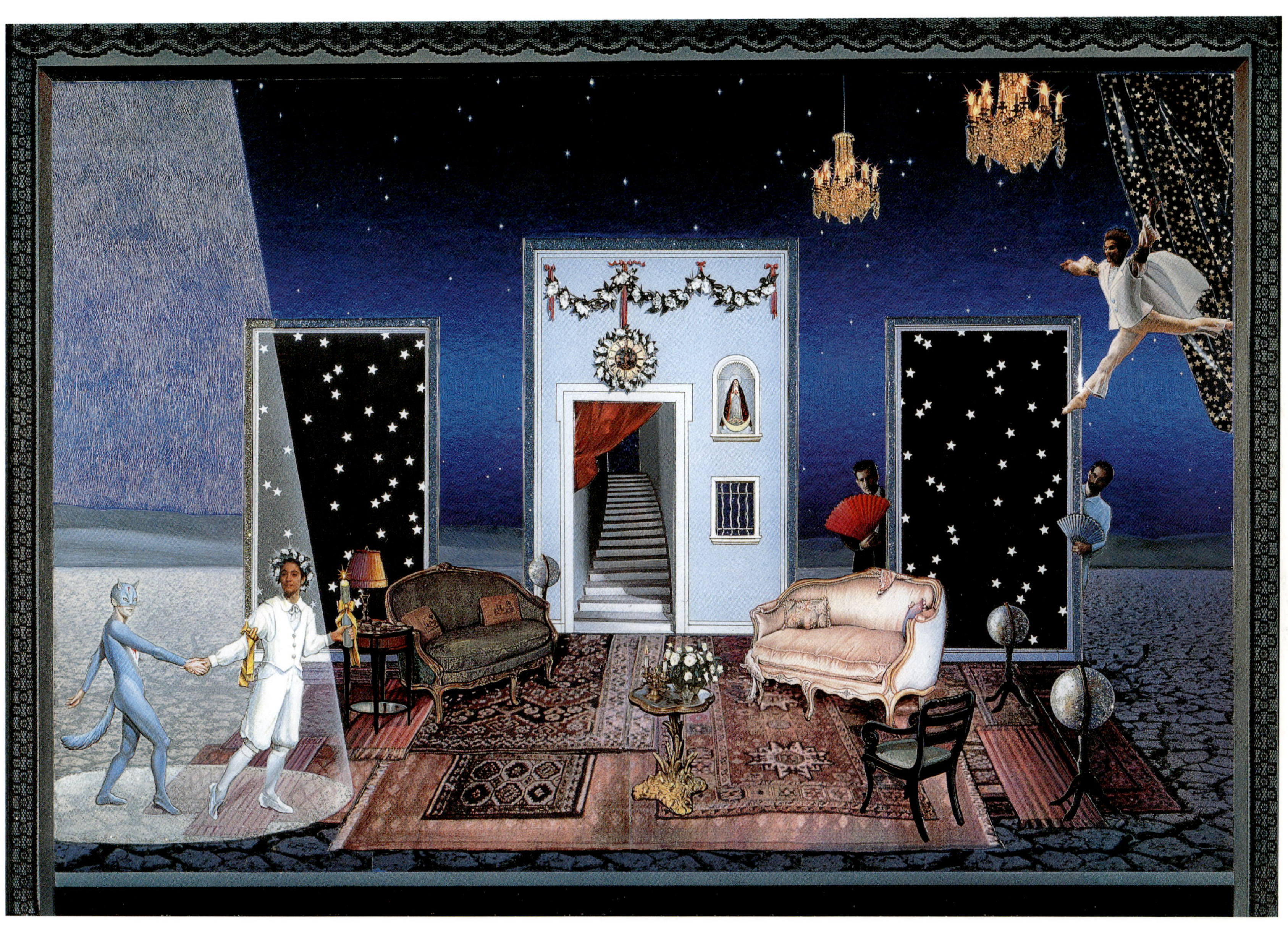

73 *Así que Pasen Cinco Años / When Five Years Pass*

Act 2, Scene 1, 1991

Mixed media on Gator board, 37 × 47 inches
Museum Acquisition Fund, Meadows Museum, Southern Methodist University, Dallas, Texas

Remaining faithful to Lorca's vision, González here turns into visual reality the second act's call for a "turn of the century bedroom with strange furniture, grand curtains covered with pleats and tassels. The walls are painted with clouds and angels. A bed center is canopied with fabric and plumes. There is a dressing table supported by angels with garlands of electric lights in their hands."[1] Yet González also seizes the opportunity to set up a dynamic opposition between the stage set for this scene, which is full of sky, and the stage set for the following scene, which he plunges to the bottom of the ocean as he countered day and night in the first two scenes.

González's angels are all based on angels in paintings by his Spanish favorite Zurbarán. The cherubs holding up the festoon over the spangled mirror, for instance, are modeled on the little angels who hold back the huge cape of mercy of *Our Lady of the Caves,* 1641–58 (Museo Provincial, Seville), so that the mirror in this collage stands in place of the absent Virgin, evoked in the festoon of her mantle, as she was previously evoked in the mantle of mercy at the side of *Songs for My Father.* The angel on the left is the glorious *Saint Gabriel,* 1631–40 (Musée Fabre, Montpelier), matched in a second Gabriel on the right, drawn from the 1637–39 *Annunciation* at the Musée des Beaux-Arts, Grenoble. The two angels at top center are based on the angels carrying the rose-crowned martyr in *Burial of Saint Catherine on Mount Sinai,* 1613–40 (private collection, Château de Courçon): taken together the four angels combine the cyclical concept of a divinely destined birth beginning with the Annunciation and the martyr's rose-crowned death and Resurrection.

The canopied bed at the center of the image, its crowning, circular sweep of fabric echoing the red festoon over the mirror, fuses the bed and festoon González himself earlier painted for *El Soñador/The Dreamer,* with Jean-Honoré Fragonard's red-canopied bed in *The Bolt,* ca. 1778 (Louvre, Paris). In the Fragonard painting a brutish man slides home a bolt on a bedroom door—prior to dragging a struggling woman onto the bed to rape her. González heightens the violence of this reference by embellishing the bedcover with a meandering trail of red embroidery like splashed drops of blood on the creamy, almost flesh-colored satin.

The Ascension backdrop of the four-paneled sky is based on sky photographs taken by the artist on a trip to the Grand Canyon. The two center panels mirror each other, subtly extending the ethereal effect of the *Soñador* drape over the red canopy. Mirroring recurs in the white portals and balcony rails of the two side panels, heightening the contrast between the virginal bride presented by the Mannequin on the right and the faithless fiancée welcoming a Football Player into her bedroom on the left; between the blind idealism of the fiancée's Father on the right and the earthy opportunism of the Athlete on the left.

At center stage, González depicts the bride-to-be, fresh from the secret embrace of her lover the Football Player, rejecting her fiancé of five long years, the timid Young Man, as she contemptuously explains, "A mirror, a table, would be closer to you than I could ever be."[2] The Young Man's gift of a sumptuous wedding dress and veil is also rejected by the fiancée. Her fragile, myopic astronomer father is bewildered, but distractedly obsessed with not missing a coming eclipse of the moon from his balcony.

The entire floor of the stage presents an impressive perspectival grid of a tesellated Andalusian floor, polished so that it gleams like a mirror, reflecting the characters of the play. In the following plate, González converts the bedroom floor into something even more overtly watery, implying that the play has reached a point where the deepest recesses of the unconscious will be delved into, that a truly oceanic state has been entered. Meanwhile, the artist himself poses as the white-haired, dimsighted old Father of the bride-to-be, standing both next to the bed at the back of the stage and in the forestage, where his binoculars project blindly toward the viewer's space.

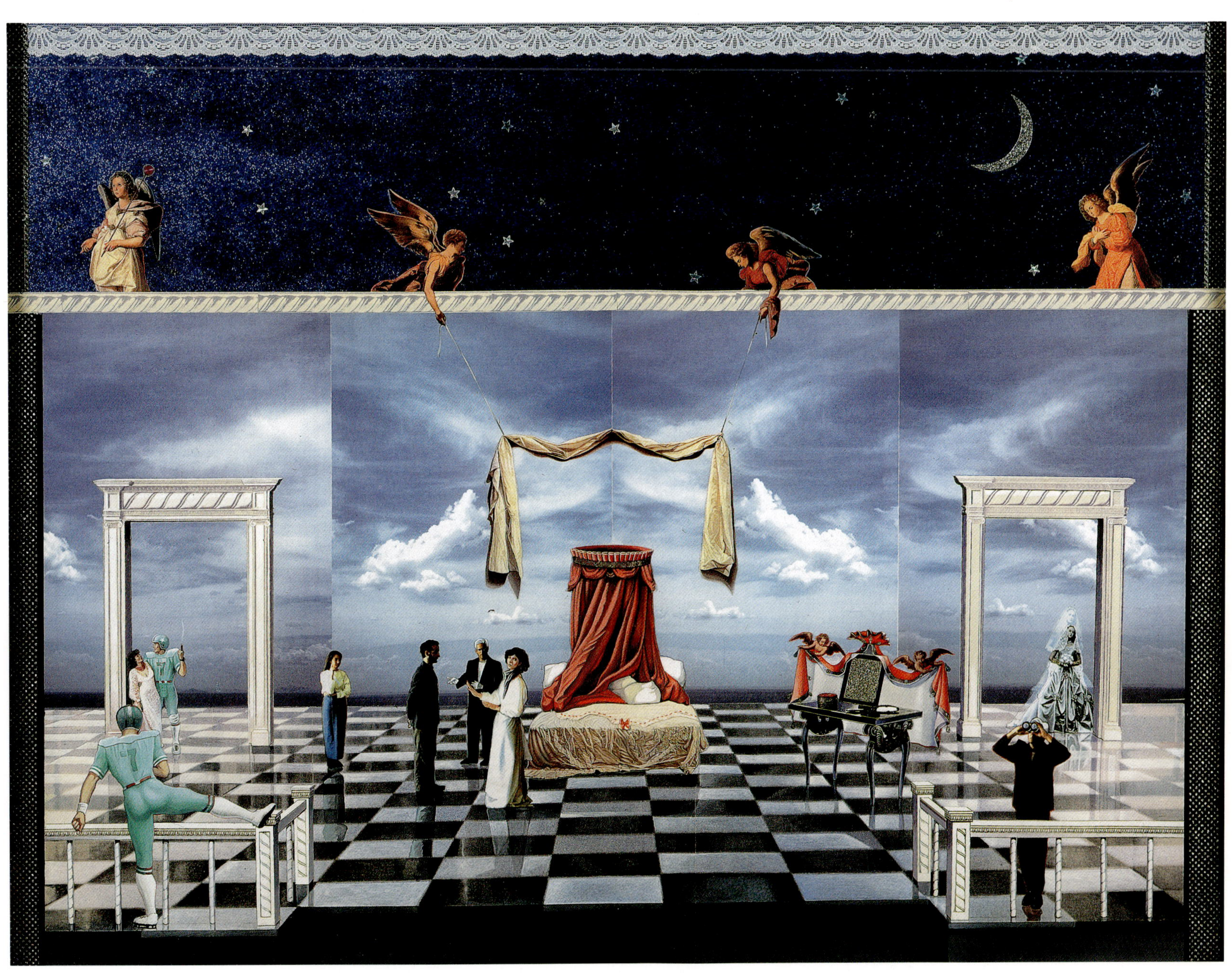

74 *Así que Pasen Cinco Años/When Five Years Pass*

Act 2, Scene 2, 1991

Mixed media on Gator board, 37 × 46½ inches
Museum Acquisition Fund, Meadows Museum, Southern Methodist University, Dallas, Texas

In this scene of a seafloor visualized within a little baroque puppet theater, the tragic Mannequin comes to the fore. González began the composition of the spectacular marine image with a panel of Metallic Silver glitter paper in the center back, flanked by side panels of Metallic Green glitter paper. The figures are combinations of colored Xerox copies, which have been painted and glazed, so that, thick with pigment, they become absolutely integrated with the image. The red baroque curtains veiling the top of the stage quote the curtains that frame Zurbarán's *Young Virgin Praying* (see page 14; the curtains earlier inspired the green fabric arch framing the artist's daughter in *La Educación de Maria* (The Education of Maria).

The Mannequin is lost in the throes of an erotic frustration common in the plays and poetry of Lorca: "I sing of death that holds no end / to the ache of an unused veil," she laments. She feels that time is running out for her, mournfully repeating throughout the scene that her golden wedding ring "is sinking in the mirror's sand."[1] Perhaps González had this refrain in mind during the making of *Mar y Espejo* (Sea and Mirror), where he places a diamond ring on the watery glass ledge at the edge of the sea, in front of the third "mirror" panel. She "yearns for the heat of the wedding night,"[2] a heat she will never know. She shows the Young Man a pink child's outfit, the outfit of the son she and the Young Man will never have (a costume uncannily recalling the pink shirt in the closet of *Ascension*). The Young Man remarks that they might have this son "If impulse goes into tortured sleep / And marries instead / the sweet smell of convention."[3] González's veiled Mannequin bride is like the *Virgen de las Angustias,* or Virgin of the Sorrows, the starry Virgin—a sculpted pinnacle of feminine pain and glory—cruelly stripped of her only son, her sacrificed child, reigning over the altar in Granada cathedral.

González has further developed Lorca's poetic hints by placing the Mannequin bride at the bottom of the ocean—making dramatic and visual capital of her bitter prediction that "the sea shall wear my bridal train," though González is also anticipating the following scene, in which a Harlequin and a Clown tease a Girl about her "bridegroom / Of the sea." In the central panel of this work, the viewer sees the "bridegroom of the sea" surrounded by swimming fish—a bridegroom deriving from a Horst portrait taken in Paris in the 1930s, a portrait the artist found irresistibly nostalgic and personal, since it reminded him of the way his own father used to look, and the way his father used to style his hair, decades ago. The ocean bridegroom, then, is a young, virile, ideally handsome portrait of the artist's father—a reconciling celebration after the unflattering realism of the aging figure in *Nacimiento/Nativity* and *Songs for My Father.*

The child drained of color at the top of this submerged fish tank of a theatrical backdrop is based on a sculpture of a child by Antonio García Lopez in Madrid, described by the artist as "a petrified child." The child is not really identifiable by clothing or anything else as male or female—though the pink dress certainly implies a feminine element. This lost, dead, or "petrified" infant, like the white-robed apparitional Second Friend in whom the male Dead Boy and female Dead Cat are mystically conjoined, is the magical child, the redemption motif arising from death, the androgyne.

Probably because González was drawn to the oceanic and bridal imagery of the scene, this collage was created before those for other scenes and before the artist had decided to have himself, his daughter, and his friends play Lorca's characters. The desolate Young Man looking out toward the viewer is played by a Muybridge figure with an invented face, rather than by the artist himself.

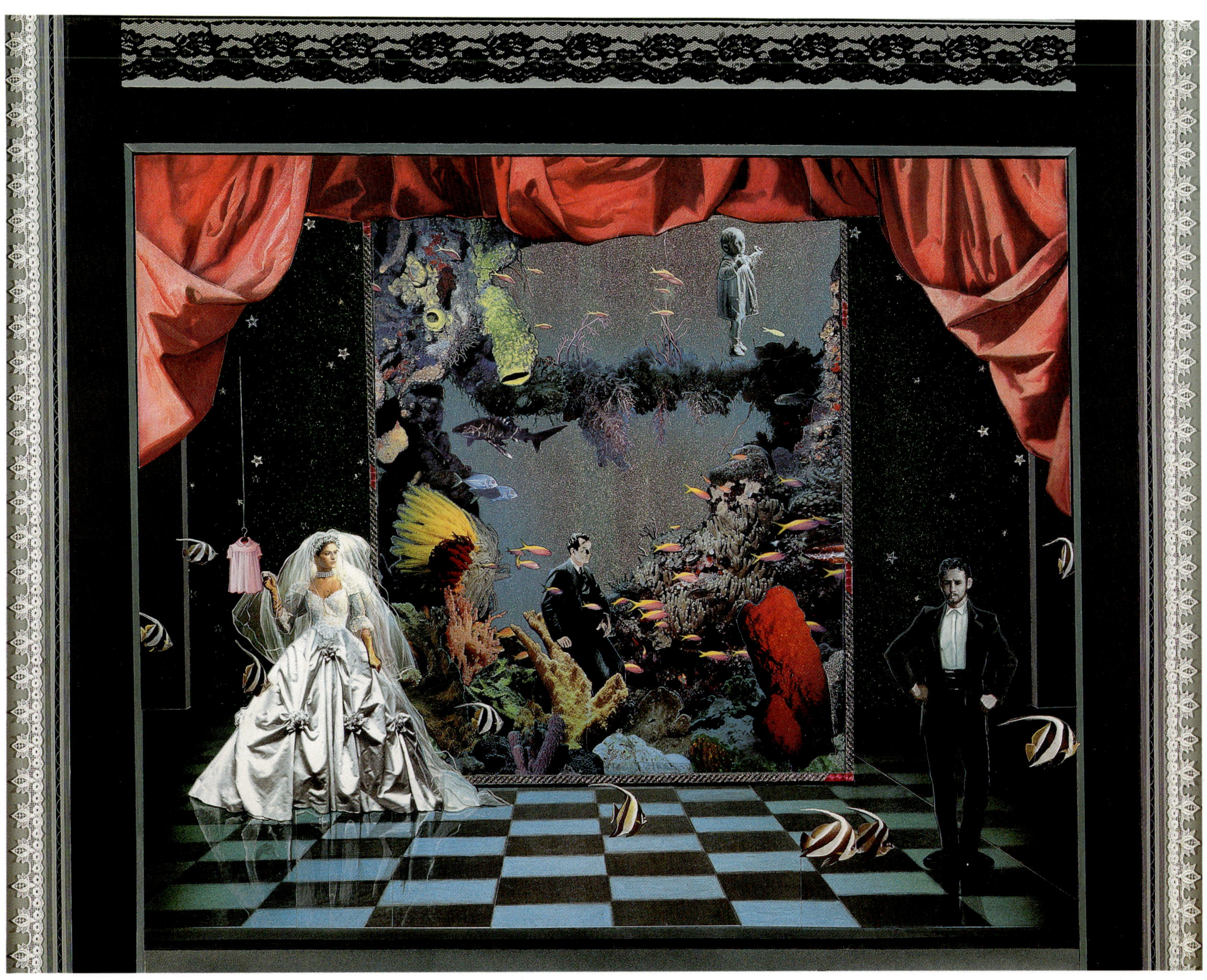

75 *Así que Pasen Cinco Años/When Five Years Pass*

Act 3, Scene 1, 1991

Mixed media on Gator board, 33 × 47 inches
Museum Acquisition Fund, Meadows Museum, Southern Methodist University, Dallas, Texas

"Forest. Huge tree trunks. In the center of the stage is another smaller proscenium stage closed off by a baroque curtain,"[1] observe the stage notes for the opening of the third act. "In Versailles, there's this little theater that's a jewel—the theater for the court," says González. "So I took a photograph of that, and transformed it into the puppet theater you see here." Lorca, who himself was fascinated by puppet theaters and plays (accorded an unusual respect in Andalusia), suggests in his notes for the play that *actual* puppets may be used in the on-stage miniature theater for part of this scene, the puppets playing miniatures of the Young Man, the Dead Boy, the Typist, and the First Mask—though González depicts only the Dead Boy in his Holy Communion outfit and crown of white roses. This metamorphosis of people into puppets is a source of wonder and enchantment for González, who plays with the concept throughout his work, most candidly in paintings like *El Niño* (The Child). Yet here he chooses not to "petrify" his human "puppets," despite the stage direction, preferring to present them as living human beings moving through sparkling layers of illusion. Also, to change them into puppets would be to lose the sense of "mirroring" that permeates this work, through the characters and scenery, through the baroque drapes of the main stage and puppet stage.

The artist's daughter Maria reappears as the Typist who had declared her hopeless love for the Young Man; here she wears tennis garb with a beret and cape, as described by Lorca. She enters the main stage with the First Mask, "who wears a bright yellow dress, the upper bodice covered with golden sequins, and with a long train, circa 1900. . . . The effect of the personage should be that of a sudden flame seen against a background of the blue moon and the tree trunks at night."[2] González revels in the rich color opportunity afforded by this creature of the night. He had one of his fellow translators of this play, Teresa ("Cuca") Gaos, pose as the First Mask, while scanning art history for a flamelike yellow personage to help fill out the role in a grand manner: he found Zurbarán's chaste Saint Elizabeth of Portugal, 1641–58 (Prado, Madrid), an amusing contrast to the louche character of the Italianate First Mask in Lorca's drama (Cuca had earlier played the faithless bride-to-be, dallying with the Football Player and scornfully rejecting the Young Man, so that her double role draws a pertinent parallel between the deceiving bride-to-be and the Mask—while also dramatizing some of the intricate mirroring and echoing that suffuses Lorca's dialogue).

González himself plays a nearly mirror-imaged pair of huntsmen blowing "ominous" horns throughout the scene, drawing the viewer's attention to the playful symmetries and dissonances between the two halves of the composition—the almost mirrored curtains of the main stage, the almost mirrored rows of tree trunks, the almost mirrored columns, couches, and bookcases of the miniature theater. González also plays the Servant bearing a candelabrum who closes the play at midnight as the Young Man dies. Translating art into life, González procured an antique mirror, inserted the cutout figure of himself playing the Servant Juan with his candelabrum into the lower center edge of the mirror, and hung it on his studio wall.

Also doubled are a Harlequin in black and green and a sequined Pierrot, whom González has dressed in luminous white, who tease the Girl, Maria, about her "bridegroom of the sea," recalling the tragic Mannequin bride of the previous scene. The Pierrot-Harlequin duo derive from Picasso's 1918 *Pierrot and Harlequin* (The Art Institute of Chicago), while the black-and-green Harlequin at the front of the stage has a head modeled on Picasso's marvelous 1923 *Seated Harlequin (Portrait of the Painter Jacinto Salvado)* at the Kunstmuseum, Basel. The backdrop of trees against a night sky comes from Velázquez's 1649–50 *Garden at the Villa Medici, Rome* (Prado, Madrid), over which González has thrown a veil of dark shadow.

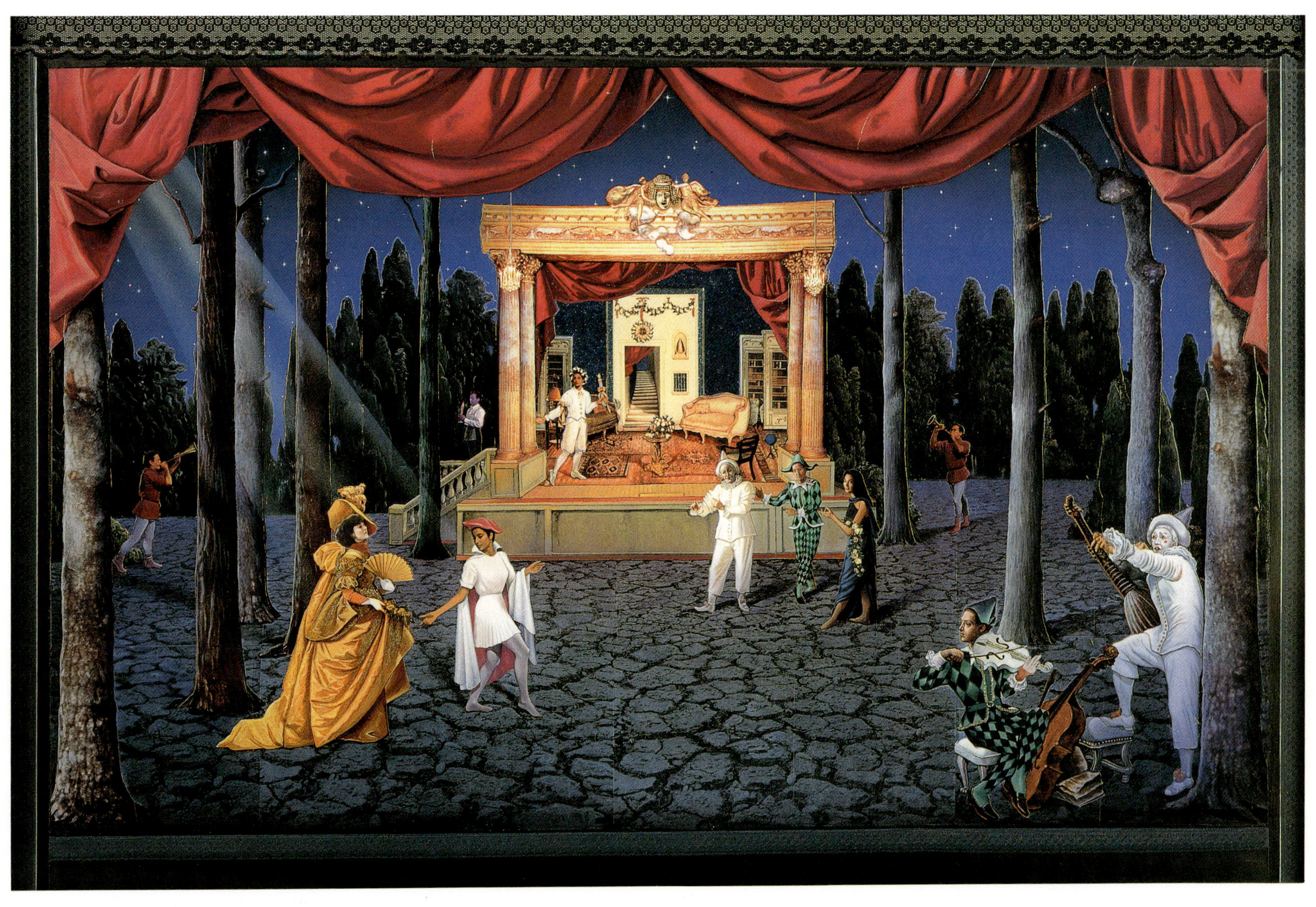

76 *Así que Pasen Cinco Años / When Five Years Pass*

Act 3, Scene 2, 1991

Mixed media on Gator board, 27¼ × 37 inches
Museum Acquisition Fund, Meadows Museum, Southern Methodist University, Dallas, Texas

In the dark closing scene of the play, Lorca's tragic bride, the Mannequin, is both headless and handless, eerily recalling the headless bride of *The Sparrow and the Maiden* and *Mar y Espejo* (Sea and Mirror), though González is simply following the stage notes that call for "a mannequin without head or arms."[1] González has cast himself as the dying Young Man, a bloody gunshot wound in his chest, as he lies slumped on his *Cuatro Pilares* (Four Pillars) couch. The model for the First Friend of the opening scene reappears in the three sinister Cardplayers wearing white capes, one of whom uses a gun to shoot an arrow (so Lorca surrealistically ordered it) into the Young Man's heart. Above and behind the Young Man, the poet called for a purely symbolic ace-of-hearts card to receive an arrow, Saint Sebastian–style, at the moment of the Young Man's death. González chose to depict a realistic-looking human heart, of a scale that would miniaturize and overwhelm the characters on the stage: with his Latin background, anything less gory and vivid would probably have seemed too tame and lackluster. The abstract effect of the oval form floating in space is not unlike that of a disembodied head by the artist.

González refutes any sense of masochism in the image:

> I grew up surrounded by that image of the open heart of Jesus. In every family house we had, there would be a reproduction of that painting of Jesus with his heart exposed, and the knife. I think the Madonna is *more* dramatic, because Jesus often has a peaceful face; that image of him with the exposed heart comes *after* the Resurrection. But the Madonna, this beautiful dark woman, is right in the middle of her agony, her heart stabbed with the seven knives of sorrow. If you don't take it literally, if you see it symbolically and poetically, it's very rich and unusual imagery—very dramatic and intense. I think Spaniards are quite blind to the reality of these sculptures, as they're blind to the reality of the bullfight. They just embrace the richness of the ritual.

But González's huge, wounded heart is not merely the Sacred Heart of Jesus beloved of the Catholic church—it is also a transparent symbol of love and death.

González loved the table he placed in front of the Cardplayers as "fantastic, because it's *mirrored*." It reminds the viewer of the bride-to-be's taunting rejection of the narcissistic Young Man: "A mirror, a table, would be closer to you than I could ever be." And, like Narcissus, the artist appears in the final scene twice: once as the pietà-like figure of the dying Young Man, and once again as the Servant, whose name happens to be Juan, tiptoeing in at the moment of death with his lighted candelabrum. The closing lines of the play (which González helped to translate) are snatches of mirrored dialogue, Echo repeating the dying Young Man's last words. "My love," utters the Young Man; "Love," repeats Echo. "Juan," whispers the Young Man; "Juan," sighs Echo. The Young Man is the artist's ultimate dreaming Narcissus, dying for love.

Comparable, too, to a pietà—perhaps specifically to the dead Christ, bleeding from his chest wound, in the lap of the Virgin of Sorrows at Granada cathedral, with a great, thickly veined, golden heart suspended within the crescent moon at the feet of the Virgin—the sacrificial figure of the dying Young Man forms, with the Servant Juan and the Mannequin bride, a Holy Trinity in opposition to the three Cardplayers at the other side of the stage. In the antique mysteries of ancient cultures (as engrossing to González as are Catholic rites and symbolism), marriage and death are identified with one another, in opposition to birth and the renewal of life. With the juxtaposition of the dying Young Man and the apparitional Mannequin bride, González integrates death and marriage in an image of *hierosgamos,* or "sacred marriage," a merging of the formerly divided sensual or material self with the spiritual self, leading to the birth of the virginal white androgyne. In the following work, González completes an unequivocal portrait of his *soror mystica*—his female inner being, the muse or anima to whom he relates at the deepest level of his psyche, the unconscious, feminine, moon- and ocean-ruled "night" level.

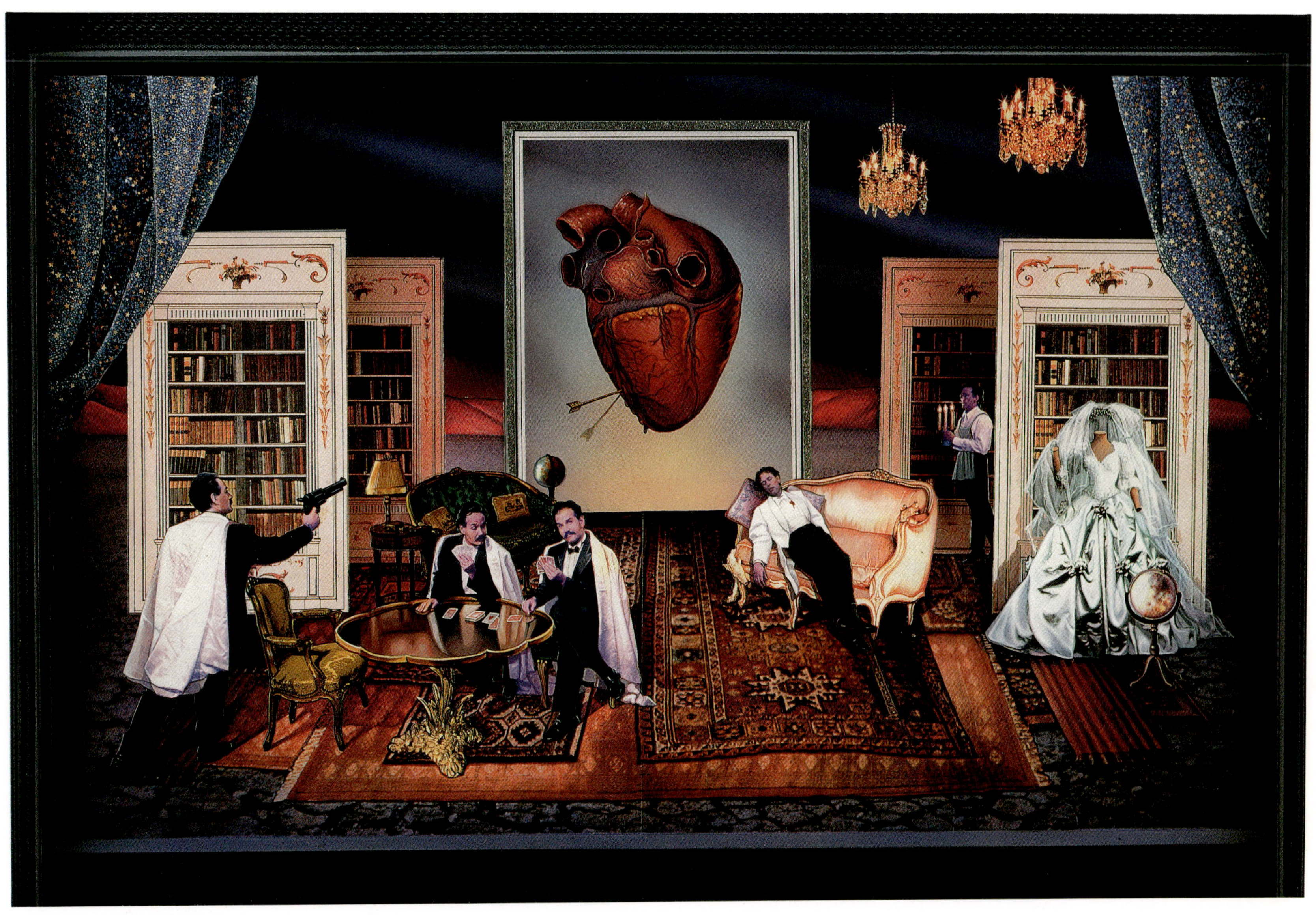

77 *A Bride for Lorca* 1992

Graphite and gouache mounted on panel, 18 × 17 inches
Maria and Daniel Schleifman

Fired with enthusiasm at the prospect of the September 6, 1992, wedding of Teresa, and the January 16, 1993, wedding of Maria, and still fascinated by the submerged Mannequin bride on the ocean floor of *Así que Pasen Cinco Años/When Five Years Pass* (to whom this bride is visibly related), González revisited a favorite theme in *A Bride for Lorca.*

González's phantom night bride, who seems to be composed of starlight, is another variant on the Virgin, niched or canopied in an enclosing dream garden, under a starred sky out of the work of Fernand Khnopff, depicted in finely hatched graphite and bordered with a mirrorlike colored edge of cobalt, Prussian blue, and purple (the only color in the whole drawing). The ground is ambiguous, perhaps metamorphosing into the rolling tide of an incoming sea. The not-quite-symmetrical trees that frame the bride are the orange trees of Andalusia, miraculously bearing fruit—like the Virgin herself—at Christmas. The bride is conceived in joyful opposition to Lorca's tragically barren brides, time slipping away from them in the plays and poems. Lorca's intense devotion to and identification with the Virgin seems to have been as significant as this artist's—both of them, on different occasions, following in the footsteps of the procession of Our Lady of the Alhambra during Holy Week in Granada (probably the pattern upon which González relied most in creating his *Bride for Lorca* was the Virgin of the Alhambra).

In 1929 the Guild of Saint Mary of the Alhambra organized its first-ever Holy Week procession, aiming "to link even more firmly Granada's two great sources of pride—the Virgin of the Sorrows and the Alhambra."[1] The costumed penitents were to leave the church with their Virgin shortly after midnight on Holy Wednesday, March 27, descending through the woods of the Alhambra, lit like a sacred grove by hundreds of colored flares, before proceeding to the town center. Just before the procession set out, Lorca showed up, begging to be permitted to walk with the Virgin and insisting that he had "promised the Virgin to accompany her on this her first outing."[2] He was thankful when a standard-bearer surrendered to him his costume and place in the procession.

In 1991 González likewise visited Granada to attend the night processions of Holy Week, marveling in particular at the beauty and drama of the procession of Our Lady of the Alhambra. He waited hours for the enthroned Virgin to emerge from her double-arched passage (a passage that may well have prompted the archway framing his *Bride for Lorca*), her float banked with white roses and orchids, a long length of white lace draped over the cross behind her shoulders. At the first appearance of the longed-for Virgin, the artist remembers, fireworks that burst into a shower of falling sparks were tossed into the double-arched passage, raining around the Virgin as stars rain around the bride in González's drawing. The rich, yet human drama of the Virgin entranced González ("It was like paradise—it was like being transported!") and undoubtedly affected this symbolist reflection of his deep identification with the poet Lorca, this ultimate vision-in-a-mirror of his veiled but eternally feminine self.

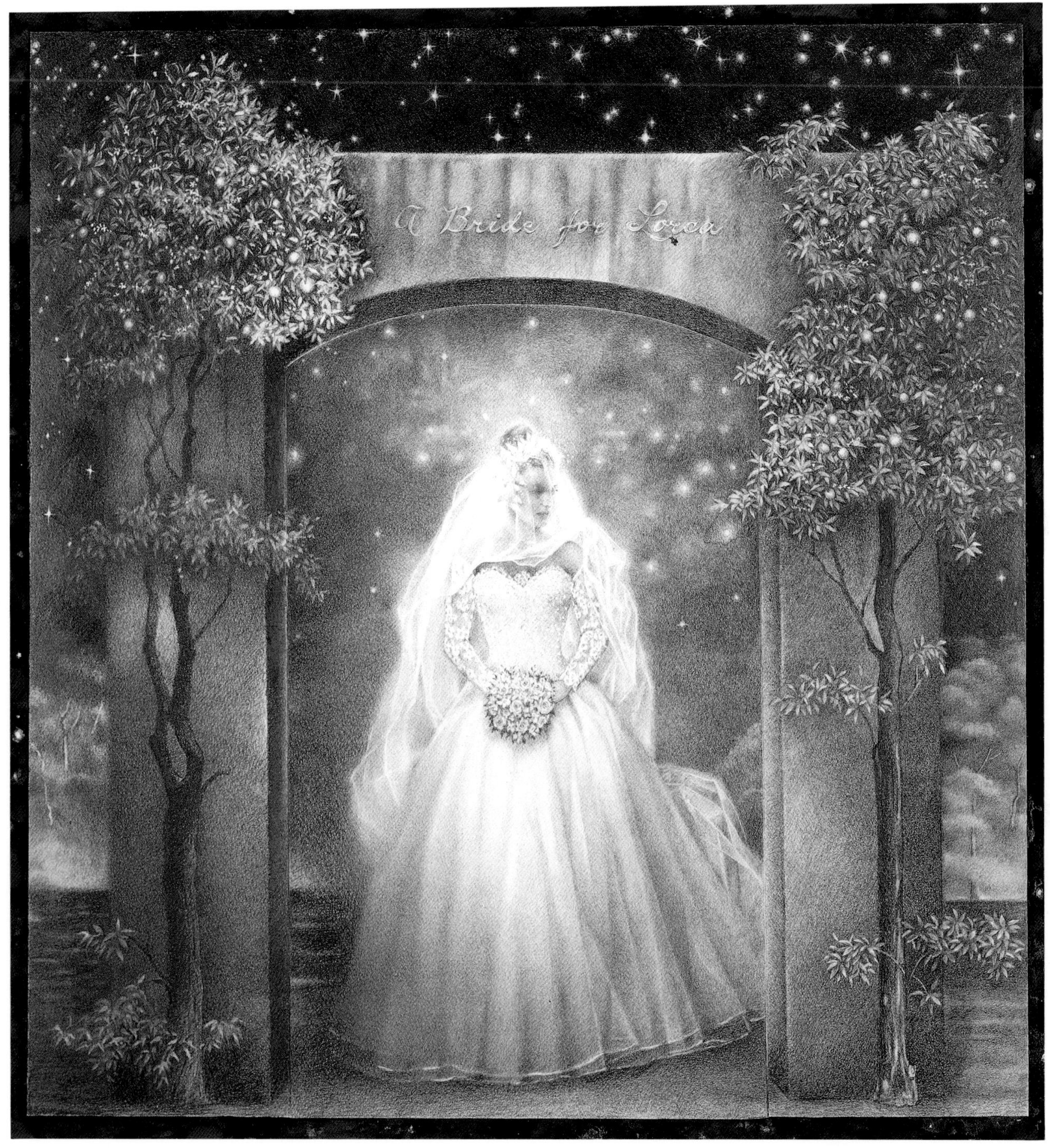
A Bride for Lorca

78 *Blue* 1993

Graphite and gouache on honeycomb panel under etched glass, 17 × 20 inches
Maria and Daniel Schleifman

Floated on a blue ground, with the title *Blue* etched in the glass pane above it, this self-portrait harks back in various ways to images such as the white-rose crown of innocence and purity on the gridded sky cloth of *New York, Year 1986,* the sleeping boy lost in the blue-rose quilts of *Jardín de un Sueño* (Garden of a Dream) and *Cycle,* and the solitary aging artist beneath the brilliant cobalt void of *Jardín Gris* (Gray Garden). González again associates the color blue with the past, memory, and loss; with the blue-glazed portraits of a Medici prince by Joseph Cornell; and perhaps with flower paintings by Mondrian, who created mystical single blue flowers—chrysanthemums, lilies, roses—in graphite and watercolor. For symbolist painters, too, the blue flower was the ultimate emblem of mystery. González may even have the "blue period" of Picasso on his mind when he makes his blue works.

But the image has a purely personal background, too: in Granada, González has an uncle who produced a painting of the delicate, clustered blue flowers of this work in a circular frame. These blue flowers are common in Cuba, where in the artist's childhood they grew so profusely that they formed hedges. After admiring his uncle's circular painting, González decided to make a self-portrait in a tondo, setting himself within a crown or wreath of the blue Cuban flowers, the crown out of scale and displaced from the head, just as it is in Redon's 1910 pastel *The Crown* at the Musée d'Orsay in Paris.

The self-portrait reflects a sad deterioration in the artist's eyesight due to AIDS: this is not literally how the artist looks when he sees himself in the mirror, but it does reflect how he feels. He had his left eye, his "good eye," photographed in focus by a friend, and his right, failing eye photographed out of focus—then joined the two eyes and the two halves of his face together, as the basis for this painting.

He fashioned *Blue* in a very physical way, as a kind of cracked golden mirror covered with thick black funereal wax, laid on with a spatula (he was influenced by some favorite black mosaic fragments from Pompeii at the Metropolitan Museum in New York). Most of the hidden lower layer of the image is gold leaf—the technique reminiscent of *estofado,* the Spanish baroque practice of laying color over a gilt ground in polychrome altarpieces, then scraping away veins of color to reveal the submerged gold. The cracks or channels in *Blue,* resembling the rivulets that mine the broad blue frame of *To the Dream of the Apples,* are real, created by the artist's drawing a sharp tool through the black wax to open up seams of gold, creating the kind of radiant dissolution prefigured years before in the visionarily veined wall of *Untitled (Birds).* And, like the prismatic raying outward of *Memory Piece,* the golden seams in the black night space and baroque frame of the blue-flowered wreath framing the artist in *Blue* have the tendency to divert the image out of the center, toward infinity.

A stray lock of hair and a furrow on the artist's brow hint at his sense of duality and fragmentation, like the lines that split the artist's face in *Letter to Veronica* and his body in *Vermeer's Frame.* The cracking of the black "mirror" heightens the splintered effect of the overall image, while the conjunction of man and flowered wreath is mythic, creating a parallel between the artist and the boy flower gods of ancient times: the beautiful youth Narcissus and Apollo's favorite, Hyacinth. Like the eternal loop playing "in his silence" over and over for the lost Angel of Saint Sebastian in the work *In His Silence,* González mourns his diminishing sight with the continuous line "ay, mis ojos / oh, my eyes," precisely etched into the glass pane that covers the image. This etched line casts blurred reflective shadows at the sides of the portrait, dramatizing for the viewer the artist's difficulty in seeing clearly. At the center top the title *Blue* fuses with the etched line "ay, mis ojos" to form a subtle crest of sovereignty or coronet of divinity, the artist in this fractured mirror proclaiming his sainthood (his life has been, like the life of Genet's Divine, an expression of God's purpose) and his sense of himself as the sacrificed child, the instrument of redemption entering, through death, an immortal life.

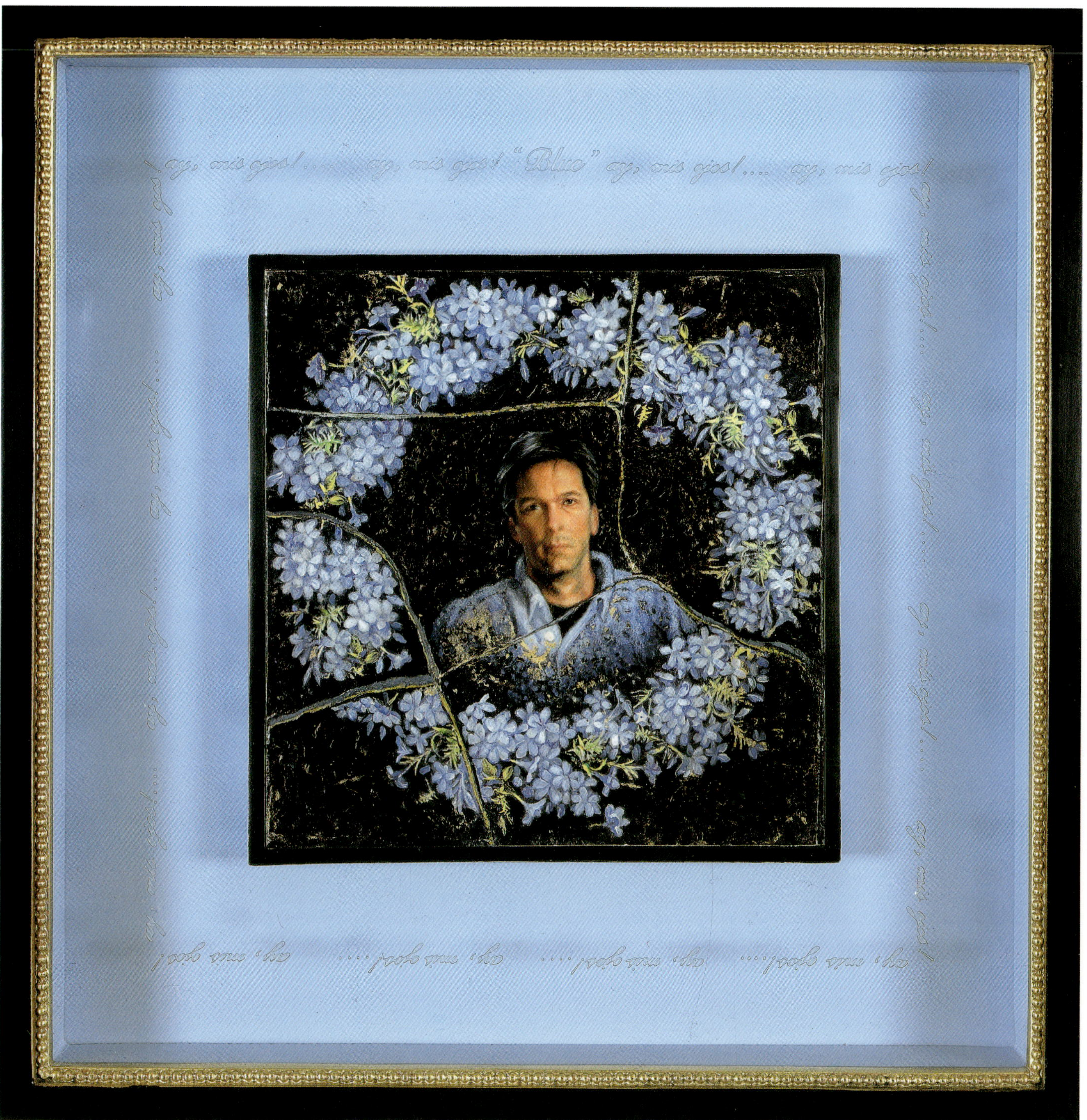
ay, mis ojos!.... ay, mis ojos! "Blue" ay, mis ojos!.... ay, mis ojos!

Notes

Introduction

1. Holliday T. Day and Hollister Sturges, *Art of the Fantastic: Latin America, 1920–1987* (Indianapolis: Indianapolis Museum of Art, 1987), p. 11.

2. All quotes from the artist come from the author's series of taped interviews with him, recorded during visits to his New York studio on December 6–7, 1991, and in telephone-taped interviews, January and February 1992.

3. Glenn Hughes, *Imagism and the Imagists* (New York: Biblo & Tannen, 1972), p. 28. González often speaks of himself as an "imagist" or an "image maker." In common with the imagist poets he has a passion for combining ancient and modern sources, together with an eye for the particular, the minutiae of life, T. E. Hulme's beauty sought "in small, dry things" (Hughes, *Imagism,* p. 17). Like that of the perfect imagist poet "H.D." (Hilda Doolittle), González's work is a kind of "accurate mystery," precise as goldsmith's work yet mysterious and evocative (Hughes, *Imagism,* pp. 119–20), to paraphrase a fellow imagist poet, F. S. Flint.

4. Hughes, *Imagism,* p. 29.

5. Jean Genet, *Our Lady of the Flowers* (New York: Grove Press, 1963), p. 215.

6. Gaston Bachelard, *Water and Dreams,* trans. Edith R. Farrell (Dallas: The Pegasus Foundation, 1983), p. 23.

7. "Song of the Barren Orange Tree," in *The Selected Poems of Federico García Lorca,* ed. Francisco García Lorca and Donald M. Allen (New York: New Directions Publishing, 1955), p. 63. This paperback edition of Lorca's poems was "a Bible" for González throughout the seventies, and will hereafter be referred to as *Selected Poems.*

Plate 2

1. Tennessee Williams, *Collected Stories* (New York: Ballantine Books, 1986), p. 316: "Trade ceased to have much distinction. One piece was fundamentally the same as another, and the nights were like waves rolling in and breaking and retreating again and leaving you washed up on the wet sands of morning."

2. Quoted in Edward Lucie-Smith, *Symbolist Art* (London: Thames & Hudson, 1972), p. 49.

Plate 3

1. Bachelard, *Water and Dreams,* p. 6.

2. Odilon Redon, quoted in Robert Delevoy, *Symbolists and Symbolism* (Geneva: Editions d'Art Albert Skira, 1982), p. 62.

Plate 4

1. Genet, *Our Lady of the Flowers,* p. 61.

Plate 5

1. Genet, *Our Lady of the Flowers,* p. 306.

2. Ibid., p. 144.

3. Ibid., p. 295. Genet actually wrote of his character Louis Culafroy, the child who in later life became Divine: "Exceptionally strange circumstances had chosen him as their place of election, without informing him, had adorned him with a mysterious text. He served a poem in accordance with the whims of a rhyme without rhyme or reason. It was later, at the hour of his death, that, in a single wonder-struck glance, he was able to reread, with his eyes closed, the life he had written upon his flesh."

Plate 9

1. Mary Matthews Gédo, "The Pigeon Who This Evening Seemed the Holy Ghost," *Picasso: Art as Autobiography* (Chicago: University of Chicago Press, 1980), p. 12. On the same page, Gedo interestingly recalls the tale of Picasso's exaggerated memory of a favorite canvas by his father, a supposedly enormous painting of a pigeon coop depicting "millions of birds." The painting was found to contain a total of nine birds, when Jaime Sabartés located it in Málaga Museum.

Plate 11

1. Ovid, *Metamorphoses,* trans. Rolfe Humphries (Bloomington: Indiana University Press, 1955), p. 73. The boy-into-flower transformation holds a lasting appeal for González, though he uses it in subtle, indirect ways.

2. Herbert Marcuse, *Eros and Civilization* (Boston: Beacon Press, 1966), p. 171. Marcuse interprets both Narcissus and Eros as archetypes of human existence, expressing a nonrepressive erotic attitude toward reality, reconciling man and nature in a liberated sensuousness.

Plate 14

1. Charles Rycroft, *The Innocence of Dreams* (New York: Pantheon Books, 1979), p. 123: "In view of the fact that visions of pure light and moments of positively perceived nothingness occur in the *via negativa* of the mystics, and that Freud interpreted mystical states and oceanic feelings as phantasies of fusion with the breast, it seems likely that there is some connection between screen dreams and mystical experiences."

Plate 17

1. Leon Battista Alberti, *On Painting,* trans. John R. Spencer (New Haven and London: Yale University Press, 1966). González seems to have taken some of the points in Alberti's 1435–36 treatise to heart—the insistence that Narcissus invented painting, for example: "Narcissus who was changed into a flower, according to the poets, was the inventor of painting. Since painting is already the flower of every art, the story of Narcissus is most to the point. What else can you call painting but a similar embracing with art of what is presented on the surface of the water in the fountain?" (p. 64). Alberti advised artists: "A good judge for you to know is the mirror" (p. 83). Alberti invented the *velo,* a veil or reticulated net widely used by other artists and still in evidence in popular drawing books today, according to Spencer. Alberti's veil was very thin, "finely woven, dyed whatever color pleases you and with larger threads (marking out) as many parallels as you prefer. This veil I place between the eye and the thing seen, so the visual pyramid penetrates through the thinness of the veil. This veil can be of great use to you. Firstly, it always presents to you the same unchanged plane. Secondly, you will easily be able to constitute the limits of the outline and of the planes. Here in this parallel you will see the forehead, in that the nose, in another the cheeks, in this lower one the chin and all outstanding features in their place. On panels or on walls, divided into similar parallels, you will be able to put everything in its place" (pp. 68–69). González, fascinated by Narcissus, mirrors, and veils, not to mention Renaissance art techniques, begins all his self-portraits in front of a grid-marked mirror, acknowledging this grid in works like *Letter to Veronica.*

Plate 19a

1. Lorca, *Collected Poems,* ed. Christopher Maurer (New York: Farrar Straus Giroux, 1991), p. 101, hereafter referred to as *Collected Poems.*

2. *Collected Poems,* p. 275.

Plate 19b

1. Gwynne Edwards, *Lorca Plays: Two* (London: Methuen Drama, 1990), p. 157.

2. Satia Bernen and Robert Bernen, *Myth and Religion in European Painting, 1270–1700* (New York: George Braziller, 1973), p. 263.

Plate 19c

1. The quote comes on p. 36 of the artist's personal copy of a 1991 translation, never published, of *Así que Pasen Cinco Años,* the result of a collaborative effort among the artist, Frank Louis Salerni, and Teresa Gaos (the "Cuca" Gaos who puts in an appearance as the flamelike First Mask in González's stage set for act 3, scene 1 of the drama).

Plate 20

1. Barbara G. Walker, *The Woman's Dictionary of Symbols and Sacred Objects* (New York: Harper & Row, 1988), p. 123: "The lighting of a candle was a highly symbolic gesture, often linked with a theoretical preservation of the soul, which was viewed as a small light in the darkness of death (or, of the womb)."

2. Joseph Campbell, *The Masks of God: Occidental Mythology* (New York: Penguin Books, 1976), pp. 73–74. Campbell compares the exposure on the waters of the Greek Erichthonius, the Hindu Vyasa, and the Hebrew Moses.

3. Andrew Samuels, Bani Shorter, and Fred Plaut, *A Critical Dictionary of Jungian Analysis* (London: Routledge & Kegan Paul, 1986), p. 35: "*coniunctio* An alchemical symbol of a union of unlike substances; a marrying of the OPPOSITES in an intercourse which has as its fruition the birth of a new element. This is symbolized by a child that manifests potential for greater wholeness by recombining attributes of both the opposing natures.

"Because the *coniunctio* symbolizes psychic processes, the REBIRTH and TRANSFORMATION that follow take place within the psyche. Like all archetypes *coniunctio* represents two poles of possibility, one positive, the other negative. Hence, when it occurs, death and loss as well as rebirth are inherent in the experience. Bringing it to consciousness means the redemption of a previously unconscious part of the personality."

Plate 27

1. *Selected Poems,* p. 165. The poem opens with the line, "I want to sleep the dream of the apples," a line that would haunt González for the next twelve years, until in 1990 he made the image called *To the Dream of the Apples.*

2. Written for the catalogue accompanying Cornell's 1948 exhibition at Copley Galleries, New York, quoted in Dore Ashton, *A Joseph Cornell Album* (New York: Viking Press, 1974), pp. 64–65.

Plate 30

1. The parrot is an oblique reference to a favorite poem by Lorca, *Canción del Mariquita/Song of the Fairy* (*Collected Poems,* pp. 465–66), incorporating the detail, "In patios shriek parrots." This short poem vividly celebrates the touching flamboyance of the *mariquita* or "fairy"—the effeminate homosexual in his silk dressing gown, curls, and jasmine perfume—at a period when to be gay in any Hispanic culture was to be perceived as subhuman.

Plate 31

1. *Selected Poems,* p. 33.

2. *Collected Poems,* p. 169.

Plate 33

1. J. C. Cooper, *An Illustrated Encyclopaedia of Traditional Symbols* (London: Thames & Hudson, 1978), p. 128.

Plate 34

1. *Federico García Lorca: Selected Letters,* ed. and trans. David Gershator (New York: New Directions, 1983), p. 2. This is often understood to be a delicate reference to Lorca's mostly covert homosexuality.

Plate 35

1. Delevoy, *Symbolists and Symbolism,* p. 63.

2. Manuel Moreno and Maria Elena Gómez Moreno, *The Golden Age of Spanish Sculpture* (New York: New York Graphic Society, 1964), p. 54.

Plate 37

1. Truman Capote, *Other Voices, Other Rooms,* first published in the U.S.A. in 1948 (London: Penguin Books, 1964), p. 157.

Plate 39

1. The "dreamer" is Ronald McKenna, a lifelong friend of the artist's who appears as the strolling man in the *Untitled* landscape with lizard and as the bare-chested man adjacent to the artist's father in *Nacimiento/Nativity,* as a kind of alternative father.

2. *Selected Poems,* p. 129.

Plate 42

1. Julián Gállego, *Zurbarán* (New York: Rizzoli Publications, 1977), p. 51.

Plate 43

1. *Aunt Anais Haumonté-Faivre on Her Deathbed,* illustrated in a book that influenced González's drawing at this period, Erich Franz and Bernd Growe, *Georges Seurat Drawings* (Boston: Little, Brown and Company, 1984), p. 86.

2. Ibid., p. 42.

Plate 44

1. Gállego, *Zurbarán,* p. 52.

Plate 45

1. Jimmy Burger lived for two years with AIDS before committing suicide in 1993.

Plate 47

1. The pyramid is a classical symbol of ascension and spiritual attainment. As Barbara G. Walker points out (*Woman's Dictionary,* p. 340), the Greek word "pyramid" actually meant "a spirit, thought, symbol, or idea of fire," suggesting spiritual aspiration. González's conjunction of the thought/pyramid with inner, upward vision seems strikingly reminiscent of the *Mysteriosa* portrait of Mrs. Stuart Merrill by the symbolist poet-painter Jean Delville from 1892 (Collection of Edwin Janss, Thousand Oaks, Calif.), clutching to her chest a dark tome inscribed with a large triangle, as her eyes roll sightlessly back into her head. González and Delville share a need to communicate mystery through their art and a conviction that, as Delville wrote in 1899, "Beauty is one of the manifestations of the Absolute Being" (Delevoy, *Symbolists and Symbolism,* p. 196).

Plate 48

1. *Collected Poems,* pp. 825–26.

Plate 52

1. *Collected Poems,* p. 57. In view of the "yellow environment" created in this image it is worth nothing that the poem continues: "Look at that bird! Just look / at that yellow bird!"—particularly since the palm trees evoke for González the feathers of fighting cocks. The yellow-gold garden recalls the yellow-gold curtain of *Nacimiento/ Nativity* and the golden bed of *Songs for My Father.* The Royal Plaza Park is a meeting place for gay men, the "sisters" of the title.

2. Marcuse, *Eros and Civilization,* p. 169.

Plate 53

1. *Three Tragedies by Federico García Lorca,* trans. James Graham-Luján and Richard L. O'Connell (New York: New Directions, 1955), p. 60.

2. *Three Tragedies,* p. 48.

Plate 54

1. *Selected Poems,* pp. 165–66.

Plate 55

1. The rose is "a highly complex symbol; it is ambivalent as both heavenly perfection and earthly passion. In the symbolism of the heart the rose occupies the central point of the cross, the point of unity. As the flower of the feminine deities it is love, life, creation, fertility, beauty and also virginity. The evanescence of the rose represents death, mortality and sorrow; its thorns signify pain, blood and martyrdom. As funerary, it portrays eternal life, eternal Spring, resurrection."

The red rose symbolizes passion and consummation, the white rose innocence and spiritual unfolding, the blue rose, "the unattainable, the impossible" (Cooper, *Encyclopedia of Symbols,* p. 141).

2. *Three Tragedies,* pp. 42–43.

Plate 56

1. The red ball is reminiscent, too, of the red tennis ball Mr. Sansom, the paralyzed father of Joel Knox in Capote's *Other Voices, Other Rooms,* drops with his one partially functioning arm to draw his son's attention, which might suggest that for González the red ball is associated with actual or surrogate father-son relationships.

Plate 59

1. Ian Gibson, *Federico García Lorca: A Life* (New York: Pantheon Books, 1989), p. 339.

Plate 60

1. *Three Tragedies,* p. 55.

2. *Selected Poems,* p. 147.

3. *Three Tragedies,* p. 95.

Plate 61

1. *Three Tragedies,* p. 67.

2. Gerd Krüssmann, *The Complete Book of Roses* (Portland, Oreg.: Timber Press, 1981), p. 38.

Plate 62

1. *Three Tragedies,* p. 79.

2. Ibid., p. 96.

Plate 63

1. Krüssman, *Book of Roses,* p. 35 ("The Rose of Paestum").

Plate 64

1. *Collected Poems,* p. lix. In his introduction to Lorca's *Collected Poems,* Maurer examines the poet's 1933 lecture, "Play and Theory of the *Duende,*" noting that Lorca "sees poetry as a dialectical struggle between the forces of irrationality (personified in the *duende,* the impish earth spirit of Spanish folklore), and the forces of reason (personified in the classical Muse). His sympathy clearly lies with the *duende.* It is striking that in formulating his own aesthetic of the irrational Lorca turns not to the language of Freud and Breton (much discussed in literary journals of the day) but to an expression drawn from colloquial Andalusian Spanish. To 'have duende,' to produce great art, to write the poem that will 'baptize in dark water all who look at it,' one must—Lorca argues—draw close to the earth, i.e., acknowledge one's own death and the mortality of all things, and the limitations of reason" (p. lix).

Plate 66

1. González found the albumen print in *Salon and Picturesque Photography in Cuba, 1860–1920* (Daytona Beach, Fla.: Museum of Arts and Sciences, 1988), p. 9.

Plate 68

1. Samuels, Shorter, and Plaut, *Critical Dictionary of Jungian Analysis,* p. 35.

2. Rupert C. Allen, *Psyche and Symbol in the Theater of Federico García Lorca* (Austin and London: University of Texas Press, 1974), p. 202.

Plate 69

1. *Selected Poems,* p. 165.

Plate 70

1. Hugh Davies and Sally Yard, *Francis Bacon* (New York: Abbeville Press, 1986), p. 12.

Plate 71

1. *Lorca, Plays: Two,* trans. Gwynne Edwards (London: Methuen Drama, 1990), p. 130.

2. The Young Man's equation of heterosexual love (the type of love he suspects he will always be incapable of) with something as natural as drinking water provides a fascinating gloss on "the big horse who didn't like water" (*Three Tragedies,* p. 42) in *Blood Wedding,* both images reflecting the "lily impossible to water" that was Lorca's reference to his masked homosexuality.

Plate 73

1. Salerni, p. 22.

2. Salerni, p. 33.

Plate 74

1. Salerni, p. 36.

2. Salerni, p. 37.

3. Salerni, p. 38.

Plate 75

1. Salerni, p. 42.

2. Salerni, p. 48.

Plate 76

1. Salerni, p. 59.

Plate 77

1. Gibson, *Lorca,* p. 232.

2. Ibid., p. 233.

Select Chronology

1942
Juan Jesus Modesto González born on January 12 to Enelia Ramirez de González and Juan Demetrio González (both of Spanish descent) in Camagüey, Cuba, one of the oldest and grandest large towns on the island, relatively untouched by modern times, the "Boston of Cuba." The artist lived a sheltered and affluent early life at Lugaraño 120, Camagüey, part of an extensive family block, and at rural retreats, until Fidel Castro's revolution against the Batista government in 1959, after which family properties were expropriated.

1945
Younger sister Sonia born on August 2.

1948
González began twelve years of schooling at the Marist Brothers' School, Camagüey, from which he graduated in 1960. A shy and solitary child, he found support among several teachers. In particular, Brother Leandro was a favorite mentor and protector.

1961
Fresh out of high school, a passionately Catholic adolescent contemplating a career in the priesthood (though secretly drawing since early childhood, having been forbidden to draw by his mother, who disapproved of his obsession with the faces of female film stars), González was arrested by Castro's military during the Bay of Pigs invasion and imprisoned for several months in a colonial jail. Through friends, his family located and finally released him.

Married Josefina Camacho in June, and on October 12 went alone into exile, making his way to Knoxville, Tennessee, where he stayed with relatives of his wife's mother. Josefina later followed him to Knoxville. In November he started working at Knoxville's Eastern State Hospital, where he oversaw a ward of forty mentally ill patients, though he was barely able to speak a word of English. He stayed in this job for about eight months, also finding time to work unpaid for six or seven months at the Knoxville Scenery Studio, helping to create a mural of the twelve apostles for a local church and staging effects for the *Holiday on Ice* extravaganza, his earliest apprenticeship in art.

1962
On September 6, the artist's first child, Maria, was born at the Catholic Hospital of St. Mary's, where he had begun working nights. In December, González moved on to Miami alone, later to be followed by his family, to take up a job at Miami Airport, secured for him by Josefina's family. He worked in the airport offices during the week, unloading Venezuelan cargo flights on weekends to make extra money.

1963
Began making idealized pastel portraits of tourists on Collins Avenue, Miami Beach, having been inspired by another portrait artist doing similar work.

1965
On January 1, the artist's second child, Teresa, was born in Miami.

González entered the University of Miami with a Kennedy Scholarship, majoring in architecture for his first year to appease his parents, who were by now also living in Miami after fleeing Cuba.

1966
Transferred to the Art Department. His real contact with art history and contemporary art began at this point. Reluctant to submit to Abstract Expressionism, struggling to make figurative art (the human figure and face being his abiding fascinations), González found his first niche in Pop Art, identifying with artists like David Hockney and James Rosenquist, and pursuing the idea of art as illusionist magic.

1969
B.F.A., University of Miami. Summered in New York after one of his teachers made a collection on his behalf. During this first trip to New York met Allan Stone and Nancy Hoffman; he later showed at both their galleries.

That Christmas, left his wife and children, divorcing Josefina Camacho the following summer.

1970–72
M.F.A., University of Miami. Reading Jean Genet's *Our Lady of the Flowers* and Federico García Lorca's plays and poetry at this time. May 1972: first solo show at the Allan Stone Gallery and was included in the "Annual Exhibition of Contemporary American Paintings" at the Whitney Museum of American Art, New York.

1972–73
Abandoned large acrylic wall paintings, working up a set of nine drawings for a solo show at the Corcoran and Corcoran Gallery, Miami, finding his true métier in this radically new departure.

1973
Summer: moved to Weehawken, New Jersey.

1974
First show with Nancy Hoffman, a group of drawings.

Cintas Fellowship Award.

First vacation on Fire Island, during which González almost lost his life when his plastic raft was swept out to sea, an event memorialized in the pastel *July 11, 1974*.

1975
First solo exhibition at Nancy Hoffman Gallery.

1976
Begins to teach drawing and painting at the School of Visual Arts, New York.

Cintas Fellowship Award.

1977
Makes home and studio in New York City.

CAPS (Creative Artists Program Services) Award.

1978
First trip abroad to study art in museum collections: a month in Italy, followed by several weeks in France, Spain, Morocco, Belgium, and Holland.

1979–80
NEA (National Endowment for the Arts) Award.

In 1980 worked in Morocco as a painting instructor for the School of Visual Arts. Visited Claudio Bravo after first encountering him in New York. Spent many afternoons at Paul Bowles's open house for visitors in Tangiers. Began a portrait of Bowles, never finished. Traveled to Andalusia, home of a grandparent and the part of Spain González feels closest to. Also visited France and Germany. Focused in particular on Hamburg, in search of paintings by a favorite artist, Caspar David Friedrich—by chance discovering the mystical German romantic painter, a contemporary and friend of Friedrich, Philipp Otto Runge. The subjective and emotional landscapes of these painters exerted a great influence over González.

1981
Feeling he had rediscovered painting and color in Europe, González, after years of drawing, returned to painting with his Venetian Madonna–inspired *Portrait of Mari,* his self-portrait *Whistler,* and Narcissus-like portrait of a friend *El Soñador/The Dreamer.*

1979–82
Served as a panelist on the New York State Council on the Arts.

1984
González learns that he is HIV-positive.

1984–87
Served on Board of Governors, New York Foundation for the Arts.

1985–86
NEA Award.

1986
Patrick McDonough dies of AIDS complications.

1988
Worked in collaboration with Graciela Danieli and Jerry Freedman on a production of Lorca's *Blood Wedding,* González designing the stage sets, for a production of the play at the Great Lakes Theater Festival, Cleveland, Ohio.

1990–91
Designed stage sets for a production of Lorca's *Así que Pasen Cinco Años/When Five Years Pass,* incorporating self, daughter Maria, and friends as players in the drama.

Visited Granada for the Holy Week processions; impressed by the beauty of the late-night, taper-lit procession through the woods of Our Lady of the Alhambra and by the cathedral's sumptuous Virgin of the Sorrows, *Virgen de las Angustias,* patroness of the city.

1991–92
NEA Award.

1993
Died around 5:30 P.M., Christmas Eve, in his New York apartment, having lucidly received Last Rites a few days earlier at a mass attended by friends and family.

Bibliography

Books

Arthur, John. *Contemporary American Works on Paper: Realist Drawings and Watercolors.* Boston: New York Graphic Society, 1980.

———. *Spirit of Place: Contemporary Landscape Paintings and the American Tradition.* Boston: Bulfinch Press, 1989.

d'Otrange Mastai, Marie-Louise. *Illusion in Art.* New York: Abaris Beck Publisher, 1975.

Catalogues

The American Experience: Contemporary Immigrant Artists. Philadelphia: The Balch Institute of Ethnic Studies; New York: Independent Curators Incorporated, 1985 (illus.).

American Realism and Figurative Art, 1952–1990. Miyagi, Japan: The Miyagi Museum of Art, et al., 1991 (illus.).

Arthur, John. *American Realism: The Precise Image.* Tokyo: Asahi Shimbun for The Isetan Museum of Art; Osaka: The Daimaru Museum; Yokohama: Yokohama Takashimaya, 1985.

Art on Paper. Greensboro, N.C.: Weatherspoon Art Gallery, The University of North Carolina, 1990.

Barnitz, Jacqueline. *Latin American Artists in New York since 1970.* Austin: Archer M. Huntington Art Gallery, University of Texas, 1987.

Baro, Gene. *Juan González.* Miami: Frances Wolfson Art Gallery, Miami-Dade Community College; Charleston, S.C.: Gibbes Art Gallery, 1980 (illus.).

Baur, John I. H. *1972 Contemporary American Painting, Annual Exhibition.* New York: Whitney Museum of American Art, 1972.

Belz, Carl, et al. *A Private Vision: Contemporary Art from the Graham Gund Collection.* Boston: Museum of Fine Arts, 1982.

Blanc, Giulio V. *The Miami Generation: Nine Cuban American Artists.* Miami: Cuban Museum of Arts and Culture, 1983 (illus.).

Brandt, Frederick R. *Works on Paper.* Richmond: Virginia Museum of Fine Arts, 1974 (illus.).

Brewer, Donald J. *Reality of Illusion.* Denver: Denver Art Museum, 1979 (illus.).

Callner, Richard. *Faculty Choice.* Albany: Art Gallery, State University of New York, 1979 (illus.).

The Chase Manhattan Bank Art Collection, 1981 Acquisitions. New York: 1981.

Cobarrubias, Juan. *Looking Inside: Latin American Presence in New York.* New York: Latin American Museum of Arts Project at New York Botanical Garden, 1976.

Collins, Bradford. *Watercolor: An American Idiom.* Tallahassee: Florida State University Gallery and Museum, 1989.

Cuba–USA: The First Generation. Fondo del Sol Visual Arts Center, 1991.

Cummings, Paul. *Twentieth-Century American Drawing: The Figure in Context.* New York: National Academy of Design, 1984.

Divergent Styles: Contemporary American Drawing. Gainesville: University Gallery, University of Florida, 1990 (illus.).

Duncan, Barbara, and Damian Bayon. *Recent Latin American Drawings, 1969–1976/Line of Vision.* Washington, D.C.: International Exhibitions Foundation, 1977–78 (illus.).

Gamwell, Lynn, and Victoria Kogan. *Inside/Out: Self beyond Likeness.* Newport Beach, Calif.: Newport Harbor Art Museum, 1981 (illus.).

Goodyear, Frank. *Perspectives on Contemporary American Realism: Works of Art on Paper from the Collection of Jalane and Richard Davidson.* Philadelphia: Pennsylvania Academy of the Fine Arts, 1982.

Haime, Nohra. *Dibujantes Latinoamericanos en N.Y.* Bogotá: Galería Garces Velásquez, 1981 (illus.).

Hamilton, Patricia, and Check Boterf. *Drawing Today in New York.* Houston: Sewall Art Gallery, Rice University, 1976.

Henry, Gerrit. *Exquisite Paintings.* Orlando, Fla.: Orlando Museum of Art, 1991.

Hoffman, Nancy. *Drawings.* New York: Nancy Hoffman Gallery, 1974 (illus.).

———. *Drawings.* New York: Nancy Hoffman Gallery, 1976 (illus.).

International Painting Biennial. Cuenca, Ecuador: United States Information Agency, 1991.

Joachim, Harold. *Drawings of the '70s*. Chicago: The Art Institute of Chicago, 1977.

Knaub, Donald. *Juan González: A Twentieth-Century Baroque Painter.* Dallas: Meadows Museum, Southern Methodist University, 1991.

Landes, Renee. *Juan González/Baruj Salinas.* Miami: Frances Wolfson Art Gallery, Miami-Dade Community College, 1982 (illus.).

Lugo-Saavedra, Denise. *Aquí: Twenty-seven Latin American Artists Living and Working in the United States.* Los Angeles: Fisher Gallery, University of Southern California, 1984 (illus.).

Martin, Alvin. *American Realism: Twentieth-Century Drawings and Watercolors from the Glenn C. Janss Collection*. San Francisco: San Francisco Museum of Modern Art, in association with Harry N. Abrams, Inc., New York, 1986.

Outside Cuba/Fuera de Cuba. New Brunswick: The State University of New Jersey, Rutgers; Miami: University of Miami, 1989.

Poras, E. Linda. *SELF-aMUSEd: The Contemporary Artist as Observer and Observed*. Fitchburg, Mass.: Fitchburg Art Museum, 1993.

Schiff, Gert. *Images of Horror and Fantasy.* Bronx, N.Y.: The Bronx Museum of the Arts, 1977.

Schmid, Frederick. *The Chosen Object: European and American Still Life*. Omaha, Nebr.: Josyln Art Museum, 1977.

Signs of the Self: Changing Perceptions. Woodstock, N.Y.: Woodstock Artists Association, 1990 (illus.).

Speyer, A. James. *Seventy-first American Exhibition*. Chicago: The Art Institute of Chicago, 1974 (illus.).

Tight and Loose. Albany: University Art Gallery, State University of New York, 1974 (illus.).

Visual Art/Graphic Artists Painters Photographers Sculptors, 1976–1977. New York: Creative Artists Public Service Program.

Warrum, Richard. *Painting and Sculpture Today, 1974*. Indianapolis: Indianapolis Museum of Art; Cincinnati: Taft Museum, 1974.

Wolfe, James B. *Six Cuban Painters Working in New York*. New York: Center for Inter-American Relations, 1975 (illus.).

Young, Christopher R. *The Purloined Image*. Michigan: The Flint Institute of Arts, 1993 (illus.).

Zuver, Mark. *Ancient Roots/New Visions.* Washington, D.C.: Fondo del Sol Visual Arts Center, 1978.

Articles and Reviews

Alvarez Bravo, Armando. "La fantasia barroca de Juan González." *El Nuevo Herald* (Miami), January 29, 1992, 2–5 (illus.).

Art Calendar, 1991–1992 Annual (Sterling, Virginia), 5, no. 12 (cover illus.).

Arthur, John. "Juan González." *Arts Magazine* (Summer 1985): 6 (illus.).

"Artists of the Americas Showcased: Upcoming Season Focuses on Latin America." *Artline* (West Nyack, N.Y.), no. 1 (Fall–Winter 1989): 1 (illus.).

Blanc, Giulio. "Juan González." *Arts Magazine* (December 1991): 68 (illus.).

———. "The Miami Generation: Nine Cuban American Artists." *Unveiling Cuba* (October 1983): 11, 12 (illus.).

Bobrow, Robert. "The Choice to Die." *Psychology Today* (June 1983): 70–72 (illus. only).

Cabrera Leiva, Guillermo. "Juan González: Reconocido pintor cubano de Nueva York exhibirá en Bellas Artes." *Diario Las Americas* (Miami), January 24, 1992, 2B (illus.).

Casalins, Rafael. "Y al final nos ha quedado un buen saldo." *El Miami Herald,* October 12, 1980, 13 (illus.).

Cohen, Ronny H. "Drawing the Meticulous Realist Way." *Drawing* 3, no. 6 (March–April 1982): 121–25 (illus.).

———. "The Art of Juan González." *Arts Magazine* (May 1983): 118–21 (illus.).

Crossley, Mimi. "Art: Drawing Today in New York." *The Houston Post,* October 18, 1976, 15-A.

Cullinan, Helen. "A New Marriage of the Arts." *The Plain Dealer* (Cleveland), July 9, 1988, 2-C.

Dobbs, Lillian. "Exquisite Realism Core of Cuban Artist's Work." *The Miami News,* October 10, 1980, 3D (illus.).

"Exposición de dibujantes latinoamericanos." *El Tiempo* (Bogotá), April 8, 1981.

ffrench-Frazier, Nina. "Juan González." *Arts Magazine* (September 1978): 4 (illus.).

Freligh, Rebecca. "Fantastico! Let the Celebration Begin." *The Plain Dealer* (Cleveland), July 9, 1988, 2-C.

Gamwell, Lynn. "The Reality of Illusion." *Artweek,* November 3, 1979, 6, 7 (illus.).

Henry, Gerrit. "Juan González at Nancy Hoffman." *Art in America* (February 1992): 112–13.

Hoelterhoff, Manuela. "Four Artists Who Draw." *Arts Magazine* (November 1976): 78–80.

Kaplan, Morton A. "Juan González: A Dialogue of Symbols." *The World and I* (April 1992): 208–17 (illus.).

Kohen, Helen L. "Bright Days for Art in South Florida." *Art News* 79, no. 10 (December 1980): 96–99 (illus.).

———. "Juan González: Artist Searches for Tradition." *The Miami Herald,* January 1, 1989, 3K–4K (illus.).

———. "'Miami Generation': Cuban Artists in Transition." *The Miami Herald,* October 14, 1983, 2C–3C (illus.).

———. "A Passion for Painting." *The Miami Herald,* January 26, 1992, 11, 41 (illus.).

———. "Something for Every Taste at Miami-Dade College Shows." *The Miami Herald,* October 10, 1980, 1D, 14D (illus.).

Langer, Sandra L. "The Art of Juan González: Gibbes Art Gallery (Charleston, South Carolina)." *Art Express* (September–October 1981): 64 (illus.).

"A Latin Perspective on Art." *The Journal-News* (West Nyack, N.Y.), January 11, 1990, 3 (illus.).

Lewis, JoAnn. "Portfolio: The Immigrant's Vision and Twentieth-Century Painting." *Dialogue,* no. 57 (1982), cover, 7–19 (illus.). (Also in Spanish issue *Facetas.*)

Martinez, Maria Eugenia. "Guía cultural de Bogotá." *Avianca,* no. 53 (April–May 1981): 55.

McManus, Irene. "Juan González." *Latin American Art* 4, no. 2 (1992): 56–59 (illus.).

Morsella, Astur. "Las imágenes congeladas de Juan González." *Miami Mensual* 1 (c. 1980): 58–63 (illus.).

Newsweek, May 24, 1993, 6.

New York Magazine, September 23, 1991, 62.

"El pintor cubano Juan González exhibe en NY." *Excelsior* (Mexico City), June 25, 1982.

Russell, Gloria. "Realistic and Abstract Works Seen at Museum of Fine Arts." *Springfield Republican-Union News* (Massachusetts), September 13, 1992, D-1 (illus.).

Tolomea, Ben. "A Look at the Arts." *Moultrie News* (South Carolina), February 18, 1981, 19.

Twardy, Chuck. "OMA Presents the Real Thing in Realism." *The Orlando Sentinel* (Florida), March 17, 1991, F1, F11.

Wright, Patricia. "Artistic Illusions Make Historical, Religious Allusions." *Daily Hampshire Gazette* (Northampton, Mass.), September 24, 1992, 25 (illus.).

Public Collections

The Art Institute of Chicago

The Carnegie Museum of Art, Pittsburgh

Cleveland Center for Contemporary Art, Ohio

Danforth Museum of Art, Framingham, Massachusetts

Hirshhorn Museum and Sculpture Garden, Smithsonian Institution, Washington, D.C.

Indianapolis Museum of Art

Meadows Museum, Southern Methodist University, Dallas

The Metropolitan Museum of Art, New York

The University of Oklahoma at Norman

Vassar College Art Gallery, Poughkeepsie, New York

Solo Exhibitions

1993

International Bird Museum, Boca Raton, Florida

1991–92

The Meadows Museum, Dallas. Traveled to: Center for the Fine Arts, Miami; City Gallery of Contemporary Art, Raleigh, North Carolina; Museum of Fine Arts, Springfield, Massachusetts

1991

Nancy Hoffman Gallery, New York

1988

Cleveland Center for Contemporary Art

Nancy Hoffman Gallery, New York

1985

Nancy Hoffman Gallery, New York

1982

Nancy Hoffman Gallery, New York

1981

Center for Inter-American Relations, New York

1980–81

Frances Wolfson Art Gallery, Miami-Dade Community College, Florida. Traveled to: Gibbes Art Gallery, Charleston, South Carolina

1978

Nancy Hoffman Gallery, New York

Tomasulo Gallery, Union College, Cranford, New Jersey

1975

Nancy Hoffman Gallery, New York

1973

Corcoran and Corcoran Gallery, Miami

1972

Allan Stone Gallery, New York

Group Exhibitions

1993–94

"The Purloined Image," The Flint Institute of Arts, Michigan. Traveled to: Columbus Museum of Art, Ohio; Louisiana State University School of Art Gallery, Baton Rouge; Oklahoma City Art Museum; Wichita Art Museum, Kansas; Bergstrom-Mahler Museum, Neenah, Wisconsin

1993

"A Moment Becomes Eternity," Bergen Museum of Art and Science, Paramus, New Jersey

Museo Statale d'Arte Medioevale e Moderna, Arezzo, Italy

"Representing Representation," Arnot Art Museum, Elmira, New York

"SELF-aMUSEd: The Contemporary Artist as Observer and Observed," Fitchburg Art Museum, Massachusetts

"Twenty Years," Nancy Hoffman Gallery, New York

1992

"Drawing Exhibition," University of Florida, Gainesville

"The Figure in the Twentieth Century," National Academy of Design, New York

"An Ode to Gardens and Flowers," Nassau County Museum of Art, Roslyn Harbor, New York

"Preview," Nancy Hoffman Gallery, New York

1991–1992

"American Realism and Figurative Art, 1952–1990," The Miyagi Museum of Art, Miyagi, Japan. Traveled to: Sogo Museum of Art, Yokohama; Tokushima Modern Art Museum, Tokushima; Museum of Modern Art, Shiba, Otsu; Kochi Prefectural Museum of Folk Art, Kochi, Japan.

"Cuba–USA: The First Generation," The Fondo del Sol Visual Arts Center, Washington, D.C. Traveled to: Museum of Contemporary Art, Chicago; the Minnesota Museum of Art, St. Paul; The Art Museum at Florida International University, Miami

1991

"Black and White," Nancy Hoffman Gallery, New York

"International Painting Biennial," United States Information Agency, Cuenca, Ecuador. Traveled to: Museo del Banco Central del Ecuador, Guayaquil and Quito

"Exquisite Paintings," Orlando Museum of Art, Florida

1990–91

"Art on Paper," Weatherspoon Art Gallery, University of North Carolina at Greensboro

"Winter Gold," Nancy Hoffman Gallery, New York

1990

"Divergent Styles: Contemporary American Drawing," University Gallery, College of Fine Arts, University of Florida, Gainesville

"Enigma," Phyllis Rothman Gallery at Fairleigh Dickinson University, Madison, New Jersey

"Figurative Perspectives: Six Artists of Latin American Background," The Emerson Gallery, Rockland Center for the Arts, West Nyack, New York

"Signs of the Self: Changing Perceptions," Woodstock Artists Association, Woodstock, New York

1989

"Summer Pleasures: Water," Nancy Hoffman Gallery, New York

"Watercolor: An American Idiom," Florida State University Gallery and Museum, Tallahassee

1988–89

"Fantasists' Realities," Pratt Institute, Manhattan Center, New York; The Rubelle and Norman Schaffler Gallery, Pratt Institute, Brooklyn, New York

1988

"Convergences/Convergencias: Caribbean—Latin American—North American," Lehman College Art Gallery, City University of New York

1987–89

"Outside Cuba/Fuera de Cuba," Jan Voorhees Zimmerli Art Museum, The State University of New Jersey, Rutgers, New Brunswick; traveled to Museum of Contemporary Hispanic Arts, New York; Miami University Art Museum, Oxford, Ohio; Museo de Arte de Ponce, Puerto Rico; Center for the Fine Arts, Miami; Atlanta College of Art and New Visions Gallery of Contemporary Art, Atlanta, Georgia

1987

"Latin American Artists in New York since 1970," Huntington M. Archer Gallery, University of Texas at Austin

"New Works: Drawings," Danforth Museum of Art, Framingham, Massachusetts

1986

"Into the Mainstream: A Selection of Latin American Artists Working in New York," Jersey City Museum, New Jersey

"N.Y.C. New York," Delaware Art Museum, Wilmington

"Works on Paper," Nancy Hoffman Gallery, New York

"Summer Group Show," Nancy Hoffman Gallery, New York

1985–86

"The American Experience: Contemporary Immigrant Artists," The Balch Institute for Ethnic Studies, Philadelphia, and Independent Curators Incorporated, New York. Curated by Cynthia McCabe. Exhibited at Bass Museum of Art, Miami Beach; The Balch Institute for Ethnic Studies, Philadelphia; Lakeview Museum of Arts and Sciences, Peoria, Illinois

1985

"American Artists of Cuban Origin," Miami-Dade Community College, Florida

"American Realism: Twentieth-Century Drawings and Watercolors from the Glenn C. Janss Collection," San Francisco Museum of Modern Art. Traveled to: DeCordova and Dana Museum and Park, Lincoln, Massachusetts; Archer M. Huntington Art Gallery, University of Texas at Austin; Mary and Leigh Block Gallery, Northwestern University, Evanston, Illinois; Museum of Art, Williams College, Williamstown, Massachusetts; Akron Art Museum; Madison Art Center, Wisconsin

"Focus on Realism: Selections from the Glenn C. Janss Collection," Boise Art Gallery, Idaho

"Major New Works," Nancy Hoffman Gallery, New York

"Representations from the Nancy Hoffman Gallery," Calkins Gallery, Hofstra University, Hempstead, New York

"Summer Pleasures," Nancy Hoffman Gallery, New York

"Winter Solstice," Nancy Hoffman Gallery, New York

1984–85

"The Miami Generation (Phase II)," Meridian House International, Latin American Institute, Washington, D.C.; Balch Institute for Ethnic Studies, Philadelphia

1984

"Aquí: Twenty-seven Latin American Artists Living and Working in the United States," Fisher Gallery, University of Southern California, Los Angeles. Traveled to: Mary Porter Sesnan Gallery, Porter College, University of California, Santa Cruz

"Major New Works and Old," Nancy Hoffman Gallery, New York

"Past and Present, Part I," Nancy Hoffman Gallery, New York

"Summer Group Show," Nancy Hoffman Gallery, New York

"Twentieth-Century American Drawings: The Figure in Context," National Academy of Design, New York

1983

"American Realism: The Precise Image," Isetan Museum of Art, Tokyo. Traveled to: The Daiumaru Museum, Osaka; Yokohama Takashimaya, Yokohama

"The Miami Generation: Nine Cuban American Artists," Cuban Museum of Arts and Culture, Miami, Florida

"Summer Group Show," Nancy Hoffman Gallery, New York

1982–83

"Perspectives on Contemporary American Realism: Works of Art on Paper from the Collection of Jalane and Richard Davidson," Pennsylvania Academy of the Fine Arts, Philadelphia; traveled to The Art Institute of Chicago

1982

"Juan González/Baruj Salinas," Miami-Dade Community College, Florida

"Major New Works," Nancy Hoffman Gallery, New York

"A Private Vision: Contemporary Art from the Graham Gund Collection," Museum of Fine Arts, Boston

"Works on Paper," Nancy Hoffman Gallery, New York

1981

"Dibujantes Latinoamericanos en N.Y.," Galería Garces Velásquez, Bogotá, Colombia

"Drapery in Contemporary Art," Sewall Art Gallery, Rice University, Houston

"Exhibition of CAPS Grant Recipients," Albany Museum of Art, New York

"Inside/Out: Self beyond Likeness," Newport Harbor Art Museum, Newport Beach, California. Traveled to: Portland Art Museum, Oregon; Joslyn Art Museum, Omaha, Nebraska

"Major New Works," Nancy Hoffman Gallery, New York

1980

"First Person Singular," Pratt Manhattan Center, New York

"The Flower Motif in American Art: Second Half of the Twentieth Century," Heritage Plantation of Sandwich, Massachusetts

"Group Show," Newhouse Gallery, Staten Island, New York

"Religious Art: Contemporary Directions," Thorpe Intermedia Center, Thornhill, New York

1979

"Faculty Choice," Art Gallery, State University of New York, Albany

"Pastel in America," Odyssia Gallery, New York. Traveled to: Grand Rapids Art Museum, Michigan

"Photo-Realism," Virginia PolyTechnic Institute and State University, Blacksburg

"Reality of Illusion," Denver Art Museum, Colorado. Traveled to: University of Southern California Art Galleries, Los Angeles; Honolulu Academy of Art; The Oakland Museum; University Art Museum, University of Texas, Austin; Herbert F. Johnson Museum of Art, Cornell University, Ithaca, New York

1978

"Drawing the Line," Montclair Art Museum, New Jersey

"Variations on Latin Themes in New York," Center for Inter-American Relations, New York

1977–78

"Line of Vision: Latin American Drawings, 1960–1976," International Exhibitions Foundation, Washington, D.C. Traveled to: Arkansas Arts Center, Little Rock; Center for Inter-American Relations, New York; Florida International University, Miami; The Indianapolis Museum of Art; Oklahoma Art Center, Oklahoma City; College of Fine Arts, University of Texas at Austin; Vassar College Art Gallery, Poughkeepsie, New York

1977

"Ancient Roots/New Vision," Fondo del Sol Visual Arts Center, Washington, D.C. Traveled to: National Collection of Fine Arts, Washington, D.C.; Albuquerque Museum, New Mexico; El Paso Museum of Art, Texas; Colorado Springs Fine Arts Center; Los Angeles Municipal Art Gallery; Sarah Campbell Blaffer Gallery, University of Texas, Houston; Everson Museum of Art, Syracuse, New York; Witte Museum, San Antonio, Texas; Museum of Contemporary Art, Chicago; Palacio de Mineria, Mexico City

"The Chosen Object: European and American Still Life," Joslyn Art Museum, Omaha, Nebraska

"Contemporary Latin-American Art," Melon Art Gallery, Northeastern University, Boston

"Drawings of the '70s," The Art Institute of Chicago

"Images of Horror and Fantasy," The Bronx Museum of the Arts

"Still Life," Boston University Art Gallery

"Drawings Today in New York," Sewall Art Gallery, Rice University, Houston. Traveled to: Dayton Art Institute, Ohio; Oklahoma Arts Center, Oklahoma City; Southern Methodist University, Dallas; University of Texas at Austin; Tulane University, New Orleans.

1976

"Drawing Show," DM Gallery, London, England

"Drawings," Nancy Hoffman Gallery, New York. Traveled to: Delaware Art Museum, Wilmington

"Looking Inside: Latin American Presence in New York," Latin American Museum of Arts Project at New York Botanical Garden

"Nine Cuban Artists," St. Peter's College, Jersey City, New Jersey

"The Presence and Absence of Realism," The Art Gallery, State University of New York at Potsdam

"Six Cuban Painters Working in New York," Center for Inter-American Relations, New York

1975–77

"Aspects of Realism from Nancy Hoffman Gallery," The Art Gallery, University of Notre Dame, Indiana

1974

"Drawings," Nancy Hoffman Gallery, New York

"Painting and Sculpture Today, 1974," Contemporary Art Center and Indianapolis Museum of Art; traveled to the Taft Museum, Cincinnati

"Seventy-first American Exhibition," The Art Institute of Chicago

"Tight and Loose," University Art Gallery, State University of New York at Albany

"Works on Paper," Virginia Museum of Fine Arts, Richmond

1973

"Group Show," Sacramento State College, California

1972

"Annual Exhibition of Contemporary American Paintings," Whitney Museum of American Art, New York

"Exposición de Pinturas Cubanas," Galería Internacional, Caracas, Venezuela

"Master of Fine Arts Thesis Exhibition," Lowe Art Museum, University of Miami, Coral Gables, Florida

"Pintura Cubana," Miami Art Center

"Phase of New Realism," Lowe Art Museum, University of Miami, Coral Gables, Florida; traveled to Museum of the Four Arts, Palm Beach, Florida

1971

Museum of Art, Fort Lauderdale, Florida

"Thirty-three Miami Artists," Miami Art Center

Index

Page numbers in *italics* refer to illustrations.

Photo Credits

Except as otherwise indicated, numbers refer to *plate* numbers.

J.P. Augerot, 9

Fred Boyle, 25–27, 30–32, 35, 37

Michael Cordell, 23

Mark Francis, 29

Greg Heins, 24

Stephen Kovacik, 10

Bob Mates/Paul Katz, 6, 7, 13, 18

Photograph Services, The Metropolitan Museum of Art, All rights reserved, page 14 Zurbarán

© Photo Réunion des Musées Nationaux, page 14 Ingres and Redon

Maria Schleifman, frontispiece

Schopplein Studio, 12

David Stansbury, 16, 54

Thompson Lab, Miami, Florida, 5, 17

Michael Tropea, 21, 34, 38

Christopher Watson, page 15, 1, 2, 8, 11, 15, 20, 28, 33, 41, 44, 48, 51, 55–57, 59, 64, 65, 68–78

David Wynne, 36, 39, 40, 42, 45, 47, 49, 50, 52, 53, 58, 60, 61, 63, 66, 67

Michael Zirkle, 14, 46, 62